Buddhism in Russia

THE STORY OF AGVAN DORZHIEV
LHASA'S EMISSARY TO THE TSAR

John Snelling, world-renowned Buddhist scholar, died in 1991. He was General Secretary of the Buddhist Society and Editor of *The Middle Way.* He is the author of *The Sacred Mountain, The Buddhist Handbook* and *The Elements of Buddhism.*

IN MEMORIAM
KHAMBO LAMA AGVAN DORZHIEV
AND FOR
THE BUDDHISTS OF RUSSIA,
BURYAT, KALMYK AND EUROPEAN,
ESPECIALLY
ALEKSANDER BRESLAVETZ
AND
VEN TENZIN-KHETSUN SAMAYEV
OF KUNTSECHOINEI DATSAN, ST PETERSBURG

BUDDHISM IN RUSSIA

THE STORY OF
AGVAN DORZHIEV
LHASA'S EMISSARY TO
THE TSAR

John Snelling

ELEMENT
Shaftesbury, Dorset ● Rockport, Massachusetts
Brisbane, Queensland

Published in Great Britain in 1993 by
Element Books Limited
Longmead, Shaftesbury, Dorset

Published in the USA in 1993 by
Element, Inc.
42 Broadway, Rockport, MA 01966

Published in Australia in 1993 by
Element Books Limited for
Jacaranda Wiley Limited
33 Park Road, Milton, Brisbane, 4064

Cover design by Max Fairbrother
Design by Roger Lightfoot
Maps by Countryside Illustrations
Typeset by Electronic Book Factory Ltd, Fife, Scotland
Printed and bound in Great Britain by
Redwood Books, Trowbridge, Wiltshire

British Library Cataloguing in Publication
data available

Library of Congress Cataloging in Publication
data available

ISBN 1–85230–332–8

Contents

Foreword

It would be neither an understatement nor a cliché to say that John Snelling gave his life to this book. He was still tinkering with the final form of the text only days before he died on 28 February 1992. John's struggle to make sense of the life of Agvan Dorzhiev, enigmatic Buddhist monk from Buryatia, was poignantly mirrored in his own final battle to overcome leukaemia. Periods of intense writing would be followed by bouts of intensive care in the Royal Free Hospital in London, where, in his last months, he would be found seated cross-legged on his bed working furiously on his newly acquired lap-top to complete one more chapter.

Like many writers absorbed in the creation of a book, John was convinced that this would be his magnum opus. Perhaps this was just a necessary conceit for the completion of a project of this magnitude: the distilling and ordering of a bewildering array of information that emerged in a stuttering flow from archives and long-forgotten texts. The 'Dorzhiev Book', as he called it, was the most ambitious project he had ever undertaken. It demanded from his failing body the stamina required to bring to life the first portrait of a man who had died in the obscurity of a Stalinist military prison seven years before John was born, written in languages John did not read.

The high point of John's research was the two-week visit he and I made to Leningrad in May 1991. The thrill of exploring the Buddhist temple Dorzhiev had built there in 1915, of tramping around the elegantly crumbling city in search of addresses where Dorzhiev and others had stayed, of visiting the gilded palaces where Dorzhiev had been received by the Tzar, of interviewing contemporary Russian Buddhists – all granted John the last joyous abundance of energy he would know.

While in Leningrad John was able to meet an ancient Buryat-Mongol lama who had attended an initiation Dorzhiev had given in 1928. Although this was the first person he had met who had known his subject in the flesh, the result of the interview – meticulously translated from Mongolian via Russian to English – was disappointing. The most

John could extract from his informant was the unremarkable comment that Dorzhiev 'was a great lama'.

This difficulty of gaining insight into Dorzhiev's personality was a contant irritant and puzzle, which compelled John to burrow in increasingly obscure sources. At the end of the day he had to confess that he was still unsure of the kind of person Dorzhiev was. Yet, as an unexpected product of his research, the most extraordinary story was revealed. Dorzhiev emerges as a vital thread that unites Tibet, Mongolia, Russia and British India at a tumultuous and critical period in their history. He pops up everywhere: as a wily player of the Great Game; as tutor, confidant and emissary of the 13th Dalai Lama; as witness to the fall of the House of Romanov and an ambiguous convert to Bolshevism. More than anything else, though, he is the key to unlocking the fascinating but obscure account of Buddhism's two hundred and fifty year history in Russia and its fate at the hands of Lenin and Stalin.

Perhaps because of its ever-enlarging canvas the Dorzhiev Book turned out to be almost twice as long as that for which John had been contracted, leaving his daughter Sarah and I with the unenviable prospect of having to cut large sections of John's final work. Fortunately, however, Michael Mann of Element Books agreed to publish the text in its entirety and entrusted it to the sensitive editorial hands of John Baldock. Apart from the correction of some minor technical details and the rewording of a couple of ambiguous passages, *Buddhism in Russia: The Story of Agvan Dorzhiev – Lhasa's Emissary to the Tsar* is exactly as John Snelling left it.

Stephen Batchelor
Sharpham, 1993

Preface

I first encountered Agvan Dorzhiev's name when I was writing *The Sacred Mountain* (London, 1983), a book about Mount Kailas in Western Tibet. It was at the point where I was dealing with the travels of the Japanese Buddhist monk Ekai Kawaguchi, who heard about Dorzhiev's alleged machinations when he was in Lhasa around the turn of the century. At about the same time I was also editing *The Middle Way*, the quarterly journal of the Buddhist Society, and often brief press releases would arrive on my desk from TASS giving details of Buddhist activities in the USSR. They were usually very propagandistic – Bandido Khambo Lama Gomboyev, the Head of the Buddhists of the USSR, calling for 'peace' at some obscure Buddhist conference in Asia – but fascinating for all that.

Some years later, when working on *The Buddhist Handbook* (London, 1986), I wanted to investigate these matters more fully and put them into some kind of coherent shape, for it was by then clear that there was – or at least had been – a lot more Buddhism in Russia and the USSR than most Western Buddhists supposed, yet for some obscure reason nothing very substantial had been written about it. After some research, I not only had more than enough material to write my piece for the *Handbook* but had also come to know a lot more about the less well publicized aspects of Dorzhiev's life. This was a highly remarkable but untold story in its own right. I therefore drew up a proposal for a BBC radio feature, which was accepted, recorded and finally broadcast in 1989 under the title 'The Lama of St Petersburg'.

Altogether, my researches to date had resulted in the accumulation of a great heap of books, articles and other materials, many in foreign languages. Most notably they included a copy of Dorzhiev's own Tibetan-language autobiography. Of course the whole thing could have died at some point and all that research become the usual clutch of superfluous paper in an old box-file; but somehow it did not. The Dorzhiev Project had a power of its own and it maintained a quickening momentum. Unexpected but marvellous things would happen, like the arrival of strange packages from the USSR containing documents typed in Cyrillic, handwritten transcripts, archival photographs and other materials. Without contriving it, news of my interest had mysteriously filtered through to there.

*

Inevitably the notion of writing a book proposed itself. Having had Dorzhiev's autobiography translated from the Tibetan, I fancied I could use this as the backbone for a brief work in which I would give the general reader a glimpse of the full expanse of Dorzhiev's remarkable career, showing that he was more than he is often superficially taken to be: that is, not just a politically meddlesome monk, Lord Curzon's bogey-man, in part at least responsible for triggering the British invasion of Tibet in 1904, but someone of high energy and wide-ranging interests in whom deep spiritual learning and commitment were to be found in rare combination with worldly skills and talents of an equally high if not higher order, notably as a diplomatist and organizer.

As usual, these were sanguine projections. As I got down actually to write the book, I found I had embarked on a vastly more complex undertaking.

Though I am dealing here with the story of a great Buddhist lama, I must emphasize that I am not writing Buddhist hagiography. Conventionally, biographies of great lamas are inspirational rather than investigatory and consequently tend to extol the virtues of their subjects and overlook or deny their flaws and peccadillos. My approach follows the classic Western one of a concern for the truth – with what is or was the case. This means that I am very interested in what actually happened rather than what might have happened, and also in character and personality – that is, in psychology – which again are not concerns of the traditional hagiographers.

My task has been made more absorbing but less easy by the amount of folklore that has come to surround the Dorzhiev phenomenon. This ranges from absurd suggestions that he and the Armenian mystic G. I. Gurdjieff were one and the same person,[1] to a whole gamut of writings that mix truth and untruth together, that exaggerate, mystify and at worst may have been intended to spread disinformation for politically mischievous reasons. I have chosen not to ignore these materials, but I have treated them with caution and made this clear in the text and notes.

I also gathered a great deal of oral information, much of it at first hand from Russian friends and contacts. The accuracy of such information is always hard to gauge, so I have again used it with caution and made it clear in my text or notes where I have done so.

This work is the first biography of Agvan Dorzhiev and no doubt more material will emerge concerning his remarkable life as archives in the former Soviet Union, and especially in Buryatia, are opened up. Perhaps certain enigmas will then be clarified, such as whether he did in fact train at one of the great monasteries on Wu T'ai Shan after his first brief visit to Tibet, and what precisely caused him in 1918 to throw in his lot with the Bolsheviks and to begin working for Narkomindel, the Peoples' Commissariat for Foreign Affairs.

As regards linguistic matters, my task was made difficult by the fact that not only were my source materials in a variety of languages – English, French, German, Russian, Tibetan – but these often used Sanskrit, Tibetan, and/or Mongolian names and terms, as well as Kalmyk and Buryat variations of Mongolian ones. A variety of transcription methods had been adopted, so I was obliged to attempt to achieve some measure of consistency and coherence in my text. Accordingly:

- Tibetan names and terms are rendered in forms meaningful in terms of English phonetic usage, though in some places and in the glossary I also give the academic form. Where Tibetan names and terms occur in Mongolian, Buryat or Kalmyk contexts, I usually give local forms, or the forms that appear in sources, which often follow Russian transcriptional procedures, for example, 'dorzhi' for 'dorji'.
- Mongolian names and terms and their Buryat and Kalmyk variants are usually rendered as they occur in source materials; again these often follow Russian transcriptional procedures.
- Russian names and terms are also rendered as they occur in source materials, though where possible I have looked at the Cyrillic originals. Again, I have tried to provide forms that accord with English phonetics, for example, the Russian 'e' is usually rendered 'ie' or 'ye' as it is pronounced, though I have not been rigorously constant here and, in the case of established spellings – like Lenin, Nevsky, Neva, etc., – have left things as they are usually found.
- Russian Christian names have not been rendered in Anglicized forms, such as 'Theodore' for 'Fyodor', 'Nicholas' for 'Nikolai', 'Sergius' for 'Sergey'. The exception is the case of Emperors and Empresses. Just about every English-language historian speaks of 'Peter the Great' rather than 'Piotr the Great' and so forth, so it seemed senseless to go against such a strongly established convention.

I have generally sought expert guidance in these matters where possible, but any egregious inconsistencies or errors are due entirely to my own lack of linguistic expertise.

Furthermore, because this book is intended primarily for the general reader, accents and diacriticals have been kept to the minimum; and while many foreign language terms have been introduced into the text, the prim convention of italicization, which stigmatizes them as oddities, has been avoided. We now live in a global culture where English is fast becoming the lingua franca: a flexible and cosmopolitan new form of English that readily absorbs foreign words. Such words in any case have their own singularity, local colour and music – surely one of Gogol's down-trodden clerks is better called a 'chinovnik' than a 'bureaucrat', for example, and the great spiritual insights transmitted by the Buddha collectively constitute his 'dharma' rather than his 'teachings' or 'Law'.

As regards dating, the Russians adhered to the old Julian Calendar until February 1918; this placed dates some ten days earlier than in the Gregorian Calendar long current in the West. Where my research material has been of Russian origin and predates February 1918, the dates are usually given in Old Style; New Style after February 1918. Some writers have amended their dates, however, sometimes without saying so. In cases where ambiguity might arise, I have therefore inserted (OS) or (NS) after a particular date.

*

I mention above that the Dorzhiev Project at some point seemed to acquire its own power and momentum. This in fact followed right through to the completion of the book, and gave me the feeling that I was not merely rearranging the dry bones of moribund history but working with material that was still marvellously alive – and becoming more so as the months went by. Russia is, its recent Soviet history notwithstanding, a deeply spiritual country, and Buddhism is a part, albeit a small part, of the Russian spiritual heritage. Now, because of the momentous events that are occurring over there just as I write these lines – the amazing overnight demise of the Communist Party and its vast agencies of repression, the break-up of the Soviet Union – there is every indication that those powerful but long-suppressed spiritual energies will re-emerge and flower. The great danger of course is that the Russians will fall prey to the tawdry materialist consumer and entertainment culture of the West; one only hopes they will have more sense.

Buddhism may well have something special to offer European Russians in the spiritual and ideological vacuum that has emerged since Marxism-Leninism became discredited. It is, after all, attracting an ever increasing following in the contemporary West, but ironically the Orthodox Church may have prepared especially fertile ground for its spread in Russia because there are distinct similarities between the two religious traditions. Not only are Buddhism and Orthodoxy mystically inclined and endowed with strong monastic and eremetical traditions, but some of their practices are similar. For instance, the repetitious Jesus Prayer of the mystical Hesychasts could be said to be a kind of mantra;[2] both the icon image and the Tibetan thangka religious painting image are used as aids to visualization; and the Tibetan view of a graduated path to liberation has affinities with Ioann Lestnitsvich's vision of the spiritual life as a kind of ladder or staircase.

Political and cultural links have also long existed between Russia and the great Buddhist heartland of Central Asia, an area where Dorzhiev himself discerned millennarian possibilities. If similar changes begin to take place there, particularly if the modern Chinese Communist Empire soon crumbles – and if the changes in Russia confirm anything with special force it is that the era of empires is now certainly past – this could also liberate suppressed but equally powerful spiritual energies lying dormant in Tibet, Mongolia and parts of China as well. Who knows then but what I call Dorzhiev's Shambhala Project for a great Buddhist confederation stretching from Tibet to Siberia, but now with connections across to Western Europe and even internationally, may well become a very real possibility.

Looked at from these positive perspectives, the spirit of Agvan Dorzhiev is not at all dead. For the past fifty years or so it has merely been asleep.

John Snelling
Sharpham,
September 1991

Acknowledgements

This book could not have been written without the generous help of friends and institutions in the USSR, who provided information, documents, translations, photographs, maps, advice, feedback and hospitality. My kind benefactors include: Aleksandr Breslavetz and Elena Kharkova of the Kunsechoinei Datsan, Leningrad; Aleksandr Andreyev of the Soviet Cultural Foundation, Leningrad; USSR Peoples' Deputy Dr S. Shapkayev of Ulan-Udé; the Library of the Buryat Scientific Centre of the Siberian Department of the USSR Academy of Sciences, Ulan-Udé; Dr Bata Bayartuev, Scientific Collaborator of the Institute of Humanities, Buryat Scientific Centre, Siberian Division, USSR Academy of Sciences, Ulan-Udé; Dr Yaroslav Vasil'kov of the Oriental Institute of the USSR Academy of Sciences, Leningrad; Gennady Leonov, Keeper of Tibetan and Mongolian Antiquities at the State Hermitage Museum, Leningrad; Elena Nikolaievna of Leningrad University; Oleg and Svetlana Borisov; Aleksandr Gavrilov; Bandido Khambo Lama Erdineyev; Doramba Lama Tenzin Gyatso; Aleksandr Pobents; Mikhail Momot and Dennis Dobrunin; Inessa Lomakina; Vladimir Montlevich; and Lama Samayev, Abbot of Kunsechoinei Datsan, Leningrad.

Otherwise, kind help was also provided by Alexander Piatigorsky of the School of African and Oriental Studies, London University; Caroline Humphrey of King's College, Cambridge; Jeffrey Somers of Fine Books Oriental; Jeremy Russell of the Library of Tibetan Works and Archives, Dharamsala; and Francis Macouin of the Musée Guimet, Paris. Also by lan Heron (who gave invaluable advice on the life and career of Nikolai Roerich); also Thomas Nivinson Haining, Nicholas Rhodes, Angela Paynter, Nick Ribush, Anthony Aris, Alastair Lamb, Peter Lewis of Samyé-Ling Tibetan Centre, and Amar Kaur Jasbir Singh of the India Office Records and Library.

Special thanks are due to those who translated Russian language materials, notably Ann Armitage, Richard Bancroft, Eva Hookway and John Aske, and to my Russian friends, Aleksandr Breslavetz and Aleksandr Andreyev, who not only located obscure Dorzhiev material in Russian archives but sent me translations of documents. Ann Armitage kindly checked Russian transcriptions and provided much indispensable help in other ways.

Eva Hookway also went to enormous trouble to translate German language materials, and throughout demonstrated enthusiasm and generous support for the project in innumerable ways. My debt to her kindness cannot be over-stated.

Stephen Batchelor translated Dorzhiev's Tibetan autobiography as well as providing invaluable advice on matters relating to Tibetan Buddhism and to the transcription of Tibetan words and names; he was also a sterling companion on a research visit to Leningrad.

Finally, my thanks to Revd Yoshiaki Toeda of the Japan Mission Conference, who took a serious and practical interest in this project, and arranged a grant of US $500 to help defray the costs of research in the USSR.

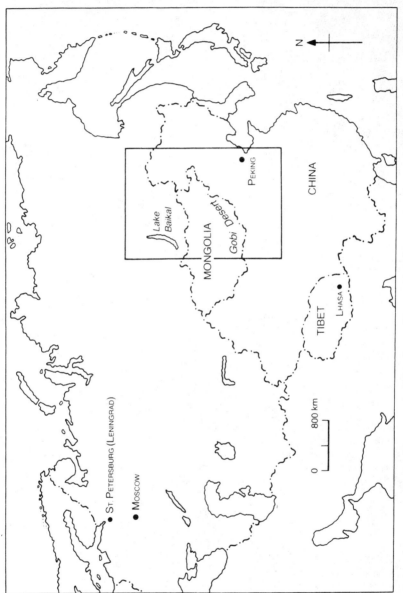

Northern Europe and Asia

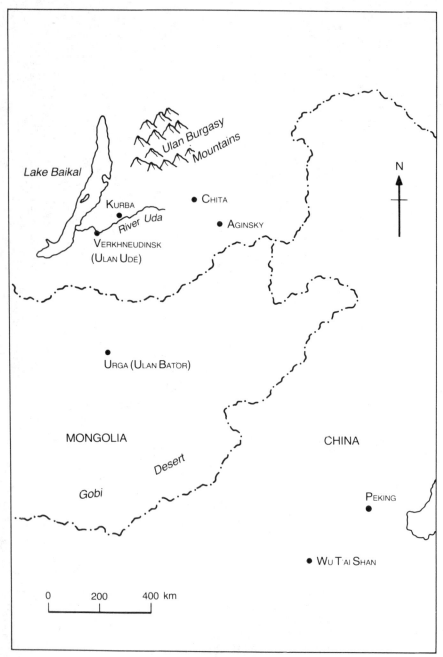

The Buryat region of Trans-Baikalia

CHAPTER ONE

The Buryats

Any one living at Kiachta may learn that the Russians of Siberia hold Lake Baikal in great veneration and ascribe to it something of a sacred character, speaking of it as the Holy Sea![1]

So wrote James Gilmour (died 1891) of the London Missionary Society, who spent some twenty years working among the Mongols in the latter part of the nineteenth century. His first winter view of the lake, which is about two hundred and fifty miles long by twenty to forty-five miles wide, was certainly dramatic. The southern shore was 'a confused mass of ice heaped up in ridges', some of it looking 'exactly like the tops of walls that are defended by having pieces of glass set in lime'.[2] Later he came to smooth, snow-covered ice, and then to transparent ice through which ran huge cracks by which it was possible to gauge the depth of the ice at ten to twelve feet. In the centre of the lake was a makeshift stall at which the good missionary paused for refreshment. Below the wafer of support on which he stood as he drank his 'hasty tea' the water plummeted to prodigious depths – perhaps well over five and a half thousand feet, for Baikal is the deepest body of fresh water in the world. In more clement seasons, however, its grandeur fully comes into its own, and it is then truly the 'Blue Miracle', the 'Pearl of Siberia'.

*

Legend has it that three water babies once emerged from the waters of Lake Baikal to play on the shore. Their names were Ekhirit, Bulagat and Khoridai, and from them sprang the three eponymous Buryat tribes of Ekhirit, Bulagat and Khori.

One day Khoridai went to Ol'khon, the sacred shaman island in Baikal, where he spied three swans washing themselves. They were really heavenly princesses, Khoridai realized, so he took one of them to be his wife, hiding her wings so that she could not fly away. Years

later, having borne him thirteen children and lost her looks, the heavenly
princess persuaded her husband to give her back her wings. She promptly
departed, leaving behind a prophecy that one of their sons would become
a shaman and one of the daughters a witch . . .[3]

More factual sources maintain that the various Buryat tribes probably
originated in the Mongol lands to the south and, having gravitated to
Trans-Baikalia by a circular route at some indefinite period, coalesced
into a distinctive ethnic entity in the early eighteenth century, around
the time that the border separating Siberia from Mongolia was defined.
They are classified as a Mongolian people on linguistic and cultural
grounds; also on the basis of physical type, having 'flat Mongolian
features, high thin noses, yellow-brown skins, and big squat bodies'.[4] A
number of ethnic groups, including Uighurs, Altaians, Dzungarians and
Tungus (or Evenki, who spoke a language that had strong affinities with
court Manchu) also attached themselves to the main clans and called
themselves Buryat. Moreover, those Buryats living to the west and north
of Lake Baikal – that is the putative descendants of the mythical Bulagat
and Ekhirit – possess more European characteristics, probably through
interbreeding with Turkic peoples.

Some Buryats are still to be found living in the Mongolian People's
Republic and the Barga region of Manchuria, but nowadays most live
in Buryatia, an autonomous region within the Russian Federation,
though even here they have long been a minority. Besides other
ethnic peoples, there was a great influx of Russian colonists from
the seventeenth century onwards. Political and criminal exiles from
European Russia were also posted there; also Old Believers, those
long-haired and bearded stalwarts who clung defiantly to the old
religious forms that Peter the Great, in his obsession to Westernize
Russia, wished to sweep ruthlessly away. As most of the new arrivals
were straight Orthodox believers, Orthodox proselytizing and other
forms of Russian influence exerted an increasing pressure upon the
Buryats, but though the Cis-Baikalian ones succumbed to it to a
considerable extent, those in Trans-Baikalia resisted and clung to their
Mongolian traditions.

In Trans-Baikalia the principal Buryat tribes are the Khori and
the Selenga. The former, the putative descendants of the eponymous
Khoridai, gravitated to an area to the east of the regional capital,
Verkhneudinsk, now Ulan-Udé, on a tributary of the River Uda, one
of the numerous feeders of Lake Baikal. The Selenga Buryats, on the
other hand, a more recent grouping, established themselves to the south
in the environs of the River Selenga, another of the lake's feeders. The
minor tribes include the Kudarin Buryats, who found their way to the

area around the mouth of the Selenga, and, to the north of them, the Barguzin Buryats.

The Buryats have a reputation of being more peaceable than many other Mongol nations – the Kalmyks, for instance, gained Cossack status on account of their martial talents – and they became loyal subjects of the Russian empire. Their traditional organization was based on individual households, a number of which constituted a basic grouping known as an ulus. Several ulus constituted a clan and several clans a tribe. At the apex of the tribal hierarchy stood the taisha or zaisan, the tribal boss, each of whom had his own kontora or official headquarters.

At first the Russians treated the Buryats remarkably well, for their grip on this far-flung outpost of their empire was tenuous and to antagonize or alienate the indigenous peoples might have touched off troublesome resistance. This enlightened policy was enshrined in the Speransky Statute of 1822 which classed the Buryats as inorodsky (outsiders) and established a policy of minimal interference in their internal affairs. Though Russian governors were appointed, they were encouraged not to tamper with tribal organization or interfere in its workings. The Buryats were also granted certain special privileges, including exemption from taxation and military service. They were in addition left remarkably free to pursue their own non-Orthodox religious persuasions – far more so than the Old Believers, for instance.

Towards the end of the nineteenth century, however, moves were made to scrap this policy. Assimilation into the Russian Empire then became the order of the day, privileges were rescinded and Orthodox missionary activity was stepped up. This displeased many Buryats and led to the development of nationalism.

Traditionally the Buryats pursued the classic Mongol lifestyle of nomadic pastoralism, keeping herds of cattle, sheep and horses (and sometimes a camel or two). A century or more ago they were economically probably better off than the general run of Russian peasants, for the meat they produced – and produced very efficiently, certainly more efficiently than after Soviet collectivization – fetched a good price. They were also to some extent involved in trade with Mongolia and China through Kyakhta, and with such pursuits as fishing and farming. Their nomadic pastoral way of life was seriously undermined by the Russian government policy changes at the end of the nineteenth century, however, especially when the authorities began to carve up Buryat lands and allot them to Russian and Ukrainian settlers. Tribal solidarity was thereby threatened – but then that was among the government's objectives.

Traditional to the Buryats too was the circular yurt or felt tent (locally known as ger), though latterly the felt was exchanged for wood and finally there was a trend towards settled living in wooden buildings. Inside the yurt would be found revered items such as ongon (spirit-dolls) for, like the other Mongols, their original religious traditions included shamanism as well as folk beliefs and practices.

Buddhism did not begin to interest the Buryats until the latter part of the seventeenth century, about the time that they were being subjugated by the Russians, and then perhaps only moderately. It was first brought to them by refugees from Mongolia, who carried buddha-rupas (Buddhist images) in their baggage, and by a small number of monks, though these initially had difficulty in dealing with the local spirits of mountains and rivers and the various shamanistic cults.[5]

Among the first lamas to work among the Buryat was a Mongol named Sanjaya, who in 1701 set up a yurt-temple on the banks of the river Khimni (or Temnik), which joins the Selenga just south of Gusinoye Ozero (Goose Lake). Then in 1720 a group of a hundred and fifty lamas arrived, about fifty of them renegade Tibetan lamas who had been thrown out for fomenting some kind of hocus-pocus at Gomang College at Drepung, the great monastic university just outside Lhasa; the rest were Mongols who had thrown in their lot with them. On hearing that their arrival had been of benefit to the local people, the government allowed them to stay; it also exempted them from taxation.

Two local characters who figure prominently in the early history of Buryat Buddhism are Damba Darzha Zayayev (1710/11–1777) and Lubsan Zhimba Akhaldayev (died 1797), who were Tsongol and Selenga Buryats respectively. Both went abroad to study Buddhism but later returned and worked among their own people.[6]

Damba Darzha Zayayev was the son of a nobleman named Zaya Sakhulakov. In 1724, when he was hardly fourteen, he set off for Urga with two companions, but ill omens prompted the superstitious Jebtsundamba Khutukhtu to forbid them to stay, so they went their various ways. Zayayev eventually reached Lhasa and remained there for about seven years, studying at monastic centres like Gomang College and Ratö monastery.[7] He received his getsül (novice) ordination from the Second Panchen Lama, and his gelong (full monk) ordination from the Seventh Dalai Lama. When he broached the subject of founding a monastery in Buryatia with these illustrious preceptors, the Panchen Lama gave him the conical cap of a pandit (teacher), and the Dalai Lama handed him a 'black drawing', saying: 'If you have to construct a monastery, then it should have the form of Samyé monastery, modelling Mount Sumeru and the four continents . . .'[8]

Returning to his homeland in the early 1740s laden with sacred texts and images, Zayayev found that during his absence a yurt-temple had been established in the domains of the Tsongol and Tabungut Buryat clans by a lama named Agvan Puntsog. One source maintains that, having bested Puntsog in religious debate, Zayayev was accorded the accolade of Master of the Dharma and 'invited . . . to the high seat';[9] another suggests that he worked in partnership with Puntsog (who may actually have been his root guru) in establishing and running a yurt-temple in the Khilgantai region on the Chikoi river, to the south-east of Selenginsk and that after Puntsog's death he 'moved over to Khilgantai'.[10] This simple foundation, which was later replaced by a grand set of buildings in the Tibeto-Mongolian style, would seem to be the beginnings of the Tsongol monastery, which Zayayev is certainly credited with founding. When Piotr Simon Pallas of the Imperial Russian Academy of Sciences visited it in 1772, he found that the seven constituent temples of the Tsongol had been built of wood by Russian carpenters according to the specifications of the senior lamas; ordinary lamas coming from outlying regions to attend religious rites meanwhile pitched their yurts in a fenced area.[11]

The Buryats usually use the term 'datsan' to describe their monasteries. This is a variant of the Tibetan 'dratsang', the term for a college that is a component part of a larger monastic foundation, such as Gomang at Drepung or Mé at Sera. However, in Trans-Baikalia the word came to mean an actual monastery with accommodation for lamas and other facilities in addition to areas for philosophical study. We also sometimes come across the term 'dugan'. This is the local variant of the Tibetan 'dukhang', signifying a hall in which monks assemble for meetings, to chant the sutras and so forth.

Lubsan Zhimba Akhaldayev went in 1721 to study the dharma in Mongolia – some chronicles say at Da Khüree, the great monastery of the Jebtsundamba Khutukhtu. On returning to his native Selenga region, he too had ambitions of setting up a monastery; he was also hoping to make Damba Darzha Zayayev his disciple. Though he favoured a beautiful location on the western shores of Gusinoye Ozero (Goose Lake) as the site for his new monastery, he was for some reason reluctant to go ahead alone, so he visited Zayayev and Batur-un, an astrologer who had also studied in Tibet, with a view to having the site tested. No doubt sensing the seeds of future rivalry, Zayayev was reluctant to cooperate; Batur-un, however, having made his astrological calculations, was sure that he had found a perfect place, so he forced the issue by plunging an arrow into the ground.[12]

Rivalry between the Tsongol and Gusinoye Ozero datsans did develop

just as Zayayev had foreseen, for the erection of the Gusinoye Ozero
Datsan effectively terminated the Tsongol diocese at the Selenga river.
There was also competition as to who was the top man of Buryat
Buddhism: the lord abbot of the Tsongol Datsan or that of Gusinoye
Ozero. This was complicated by the fact that the government, recognizing
that Buddhism was becoming a potent force in Trans-Baikalia, began
attempting to assert some measure of control over the new church and
to designate its leader from the 1740s onwards – that is, during the
reign of the Empress Elizabeth. In some early official edicts, Zayayev
was declared to be preeminent, much to the chagrin of Akhaldayev's
followers. He also later went to Moscow with other Buddhist delegates,
and presented the emperor with letters from the Panchen and Dalai
Lamas, communicated news of Tibet, China and Amdo, and offered
gifts from Tibet;[13] in return he was 'made Khambo'.[14] Finally, in 1764,
during the reign of Catherine the Great, the imposing title of 'Chief
Bandido Khambo Lama of all Buddhists dwelling on the southern
shore of Lake Baikal' was conferred upon him.[15] The term 'khambo'
is a Mongolization of the Tibetan 'khenpo', meaning a Buddhist abbot
or one who has attained high scholastic honours. 'Lama', on the other
hand, is the Tibetan equivalent of the Indian term 'guru', that is a
teacher, who may be but is not necessarily a monk (Tib. gelong), as is
often thought. Finally, 'Bandido' is a local form of the Sanskrit 'pandit':
a wise teacher.

After Zayayev's death in 1777, his successor Sodnompil Kheturkheyev
applied for confirmation of his title, which he held for three years.
However, Akhaldayev also applied to be confirmed as Bandido Khambo
Lama of the five datsans falling within the purview of the Gusinoye
Ozero Datsan. After government officials in Irkutsk had been bribed,
the titles were duly confirmed, though technically there could only be
one Bandido Khambo Lama. The contention between the two monastic
factions continued for some time, but eventually Akhaldayev gained the
title and passed it on at his death in 1796/7 to his successor, Danzan
Demchik Ishizhamso (died 1808).

In this way the official seat of Khambo Lama was finally located at
Gusinoye Ozero Datsan, though at first this was, in terms of splendour,
a poor rival to the establishment on the Chikoi river. By the early
nineteenth century, however, it had burgeoned into 'an exotic tourist
attraction, affording a unique opportunity to inspect a lamasery and
attend its services, and few of those who were privileged to see it failed
to comment on its peculiarities, its Sino-Tibetan style of architecture, its
noisy lama orchestra, its altars crowded with images and sacred vessels,
its incense burners, and, most picturesque of all, the curious carriage

on which the image of the Maitreya Buddha was paraded around the lamasery once a year, as it was in lamaseries in Mongolia itself.'[16]

Once Buddhism had established itself on a solid footing in Trans-Baikalia, datsans increased in number. The Ana Datsan was established around 1775, the Aga, which in time became a leading centre of learning and book production, around 1811, and the Tsugol around 1826.[17] Figures for 1822 specify some nineteen monasteries and 2,500 lamas, and by 1846 this had gone up to thirty-four monasteries and 4,509 lamas, about half of them in the districts of Khorinsk and Aga. Professor N. Poppe has reckoned on the basis of census statistics that this indicates a proportion of one lama to every fourteen or fifteen persons.[18]

Clearly, the support of such a high proportion of 'non-productive' religious would bear heavily upon the lay population. This concerned the Russian authorities and in 1853 a Law on the Lama Clergy of Siberia was approved which allowed for thirty-four datsans accommodating one Bandido Khambo Lama, two hundred and sixteen lamas and thirty-four bandi or novices. In practice, the law was not strictly enforced beyond placing a tax on unofficial and self-appointed lamas, and the numbers of lamas increased steadily in some thirty-seven datsans – three over the legal limit. By 1916, the official lama population of Buryatia had risen to around 16,000.

The Buryat datsans were once fine architectural monuments in their own right, as well as repositories of rare artistic and literary treasures. In addition they were great centres of culture and education. The monks were usually conversant with Mongolian and also Tibetan, the lingua franca of the Lamaist world, so had access to the wealth of learning of that sphere. At their disposal were good libraries of Tibetan and Mongolian texts on philosophy, medicine, religion, history and other subjects. Some datsans had tsenyi[19] schools – that is, schools of advanced Buddhist dialectics. The first tsenyi school was opened at the Tsugol Datsan in 1845, and subsequently others at the Atsagat, Ana and Enghetu datsans, and at Khambaliin Kuriye, the residence of the Khambo Lama. The datsans were also lay educational centres, providing good general education to Buryat boys and to some extent to girls.

Manba, schools and clinics of Tibetan medicine, also existed in some Buryat datsans. There was a manba at the Tsugol Datsan, for instance, where courses lasted about four years and the title manramba, doctor of medicine, was conferred upon those who successfully completed them.[20] Tibetan medicine is still practised today. It can provide very precise diagnoses using a complex system of reading the pulses, examining urine and so forth; for remedies, it extensively depends on herbal remedies, dietary therapy, special pills and often spiritual practices, for many physical ailments are thought to result directly from spiritual dysfunctions. Two Buryat practitioners of this kind of medicine, the brothers Badmayev, ran a thriving practice in St Petersburg at the turn of the century, and one of them, Piotr, attended Emperor Nicholas II himself.

Such a deep concern for culture and education led to the emergence of a Buryat intelligentsia. The first Buryat scholars are reckoned to have been Dorzhi Banzarov (1822–55) and Galsan Gomboyev (1822–63). Banzarov was educated at the Russo-Mongolian Military School at Troitskosavsk and at the University of Kazan, where, besides Russian, he studied Latin, French, English and Turkish. For his doctorate he submitted a thesis on the shamanism of the Mongols, a pioneering work that was later published. Gomboyev, on the other hand, also lectured at Kazan and taught Mongolian at St Petersburg University.

In the late nineteenth/early twentieth centuries, however, there was a remarkable new wave of intellectuals, some of whom will feature in the forthcoming narrative. Besides Agvan Dorzhiev, they include B. B. Baradin, G. Ts. Tsybikov, Ts. Zh. Zhamtsarano, M. Bogdanov, B.D. Ochirov and E. D. Rinchino – men of an extremely high intellectual order who became both cultural and political leaders not only in Buryatia itself but in Kalmykia and Mongolia too. In spirit they were liberal rather than revolutionary nationalists, their primary concern being to protect the culture and traditions of their people. Robert Rupen has written:

> Some facts are common to the lives of all these men: their early years were spent in a typical Mongolian setting; the folklore and superstitions of their people were known to them, and even shared by them; they had excellent educations, most of them at the University of St Petersburg, where they co-operated closely with Russian Orientalists; they wrote scholarly (historical and philological) works in the Russian language; they all spoke and wrote Russian fluently. They travelled widely in Siberia, Central Asia, and European Russia, and some of them even in Western Europe. They always remained Mongols, with close ties to their native land.[21]

The presence of ethnic Buddhists within the Russian Empire stimulated scholarly interest in Buddhism in European Russia – or rather it added stimulus to an interest that had already arisen when those valiant pioneers who spear-headed Russian expansion in central Asia first encountered Mongolians and Tibetans. It was recognized in official circles that it would be useful to know more about the languages, cultures and religious traditions of these peoples.

An interesting development took place in the eighteenth century as an indirect result of a gold-seeking expedition that Peter the Great dispatched under Ivan Mikhailovich Licharov in the direction of Yarkand. This discovered the remains of an abandoned yurt-monastery, Ablai Khid, in the Altai region near modern Ust-Kaminagorsk, that had once been occupied by Dzungarian Kalmyks; it had reputedly been consecrated in 1657 by Zaya Pandita, the leading Kalmyk lama of the day. Among Licharov's finds at the site were a few pages of Tibetan manuscript, which he took back to St Petersburg, where they aroused considerable interest. Schumacher, Peter's librarian, dispatched one page to Leipzig, where it was published and described by Menke in his *Acta Editorum*; further pages were dispatched to France, where a rough attempt at translation using Fano's Latin-Tibetan dictionary was attempted by Michel and Étienne Fourmon. Peter the Great was shown this translation and expressed himself well pleased with it; he also ordered that more manuscripts be gathered in order to further understanding. Subsequently, Russian investigators succeeded in obtaining from one Agvan Puntsok Dorzhi a Mongolian translation of the text and from this a Russian one was eventually prepared by Piotr Surivanov, who knew Mongolian. This showed that the pages were in fact fragments of the *Maha Sudari Sutra* ('The Sutra for Recollecting the Great Sutra'), which purports to record discussions between the cosmic buddhas Vairocana, Samantabhadra and Maitreya on techniques for using mantras to gain bodhi or wisdom.[22]

From such somewhat bizarre origins, a powerful tradition of academic studies blossomed in Russia in the late nineteenth and early twentieth centuries under the auspices of the Oriental Institute of the Imperial Russian (later the USSR) Academy of Sciences. During that period, Russian scholars (or 'scientists' as they prefer to call them) like I. P. Minayev (1840–90), S. F. Ol'denburg (1863–1934), F. I. Stcherbatsky (1866–1942), O. O. Rosenburg (1888–1919), Y. Y. Obermiller (1901–35) and A. I. Vostrikov (1904–37) became pioneers in the translation and study of Mahayana Buddhist scriptures and commentaries from Sanskrit, Tibetan and Mongolian sources, much as their British counterparts were pioneers in those from Pali sources.

A more committed, less academic interest in Buddhist philosophy and practice also arose among European Russian intellectuals and sophisticates, particularly in St Petersburg, where a Buddhist community emerged around the turn of the century. This was a time of great ferment in Russian culture and many people, growing dissatisfied with the conventionalities of Orthodox Christianity, were casting around for new spiritual directions. Important new movements emerged at this time, two of which, the Theosophical movement of Madame Helena Petrovna Blavatsky (1831–91) and the mystical system of the Armenian mystic Giorgy Ivanovich Gurdjieff (1877–1949), were successfully transmitted to the West, where their influence has been wide-ranging and long-lasting.

Theosophy rests on the notion that there once existed a great wisdom religion which atrophied and fragmented into the various more or less superficial religious traditions that survive in the world today. Madame Blavatsky and her colleagues had a particular feeling for Buddhism because they believed that this contained more of the lost esoteric wisdom than the other religions. The formidable lady herself first encountered Buddhism among the Kalmyk Mongols of Astrakhan province where her grandfather had once been civil governor. In her writings she claims to have 'lived in their kibitkas'[23] and partaken of the lavish hospitality of the Prince Tumene, their late chief, and his princess'.[24] She also claims to have visited Tibet, where she stayed in Tibetan Buddhist convents, visited the great monastery of Tashilhunpo and generally ventured where no other European had been or could hope to go.[25]

Gurdjieff's system also purports to be based on lost esoteric teachings, in his case rediscovered during a series of adventurous spiritual quests in remote parts of the Middle East and Central Asia. Although these are mostly Sufi in origin, some Buddhist elements are included, for, like Madame Blavatsky, Gurdjieff too claims to have ventured to Tibet around the turn of the century and to have studied under tantric lamas. Ironically, both Dorzhiev and his amanuensis Ovshe Norzunov have been wrongly identified with Gurdjieff, who quite possibly was a Russian secret agent.

The initial tolerance with which the Imperial Russian government treated Buddhism spawned a reciprocal attitude in the Buryat Buddhist church.[26] Harking back to Mongol precedents, the lamas fully and gratefully believed that in the Great White Emperor they had found a benign patron. What else was the Emperor but a Russian Khubilai Khan and the Bandido Khambo Lama a Buryat Sakya Pandita or Pagpa? Some even believed that Catherine the Great was an incarnation of White Tara, a Buddhist deity – and that the compassionate spirit of Tara reincarnated in each succeeding monarch, whether male or female.

It was into this Trans-Baikalian Buryat milieu that a child was born to a pious Buddhist couple named Dorzhi (or Yeshé) and Drölkar[27] in mid-January of what was reckoned locally as the Wood Tiger year of the fourteenth sixty-year cycle. This would be 1853 in the Tibetan style of annuation, 1854 in the European, though some sources argue for 1853 or 1852 as the true date. Bearing afterwards his patronymic, he was known to the world as Dorzhiev.

CHAPTER TWO

Early Life
1854 – 1873

Agvan Dorzhiev's parents, Dorzhi and Drölkar, were registered with the Galzut clan of the Khori Buryat. Their ancestor, Ukhin Akhaldayev, however, who was probably on Drölkar's side of the family, had migrated to alien territory west of Lake Baikal in the 1770s, 'wishing to find faith and education'.[1] He had settled for a time in the Verkholensk district of Irkutsk province, where the old shamanistic traditions persisted even in Dorzhiev's maturity, a fact which prompted him to found datsans and to attempt to convert the local people to the Buddha-dharma. Around 1810, however, Ukhin had returned to the Khori heartland, and resettled in the vicinity of the village of Kurba, which can be reached by following the Uda river upstream from Ulan-Udé, then known as Verkhneudinsk. It was near there that his remarkable descendant was born in a small village of wooden houses called Khara-Shibir. This was in the Zaigrayevsky rayon (district), and for administrative purposes fell within the purview of the Khorinsk steppe duma. Today, a mill-stone marks the exact spot.

In his memoirs,[2] written in Tibetan around 1924, Dorzhiev recalls that at Khara-Shibir a river flowed from the 'left armpit' of a mountain called Dhab-kar-tsa-gen. The village is in fact situated in the broad valley of the Uda river, which a little upstream, at the village of Kurba, receives the waters of the Kurba river. To the south there is open steppe. To the north there are the mountains of the Ulan-Burgasy range, which runs for about two hundred kilometres between the Turka and Kurba rivers, its peaks between fourteen and about twenty thousand feet high. Nearby, in its forested foothills, once nestled the Chulutai Datsan – a magical place.[3]

As the Uda flows south-west towards Ulan-Udé, it passes near the remains of the old Atsagat Datsan, where a wooden dukhang or monastic assembly hall of two storeys was first erected in 1825. It was at this datsan that Dorzhiev, who records in his memoir that he started to learn to read at the age of seven, laid the foundations of what the sympathetic German Mongolist, W. A. Unkrig (1883–1956), calls 'a quite unusual general education'. In particular, he possessed a remarkable flair for languages, as indeed did many Asiatics of the period. In time he not only acquired 'a solid knowledge of Asiatic languages but of French and Russian as well'. Unkrig goes on:

> It might sound strange that we are emphasising this, because after all he was a Russian citizen, but in fact it was rare to come across a fluent Russian speaker or writer among the lamas of that country, despite their linguistic talents: one has only to think of their mastery of the obligatory and much more difficult Tibetan language.[4]

In fact Unkrig may be gilding the lily. Tibetan lamas who have examined Dorzhiev's Tibetan writings, including his memoirs and autograph, have found their literary and calligraphic qualities somewhat homespun; his Russian may also initially have been somewhat rudimentary, for pre-1901 sources mention that he needed the assistance of an interpreter. Other accounts speak of Dorzhiev as being proud, ambitious and ready to prosecute his aims to their conclusion; also extremely charming as well as genuinely good-hearted and compassionate.

*

By all accounts Dorzhiev's parents were among the first Buryats in their locality to become partially settled. In winter they would have lived in fixed wooden dwellings, but when summer came around they would have followed their cattle, sheep and horses to their pastures, which before the communists began decimating the forests were well-watered. They may also have grown crops of wheat, a portion of which they would have been obliged to turn over as tithe to the government. Measured against contemporary standards in provincial Russia and even more so in Mongol lands, such a life was relatively stable and materially well-provided. Some Buryats were even prosperous: a traveller in Urga some thirty-five years later records that those who went on pilgrimage there made their Khalkha cousins envious with their rifles, their talk of sewing machines, warm houses, stacks of hay and garnered harvests: 'Rich, smooth Buryats! Great lords!' the Mongols would shout. 'Give candle, give sugar, give tobacco, give vodka.'[5]

A serious interest in religion arose in Dorzhiev at an early age. In his memoirs he simply records that at thirteen a 'pandit and abbot' named Chögyel gave him an Amitayus long-life empowerment in the tradition of Machig Drubpa'i Gyelmo (Skt Siddharajni), a female siddha who had lived in ancient India and transmitted the practice to Rechungpa (1083–1161), the great yogi Milarepa's foremost disciple, who had thereby derived the blessing of long life.[6] Dorzhiev afterwards recited the dharani connected with that practice, which would have been a verbal formula, longer than a mantra, thought to be imbued with magical potency.[7]

On the scant evidence available, it is difficult to say precisely who this Chögyel was, for the name could simply be a Buddhist honorific meaning 'dharma raja' or 'king of the Buddhist doctrine', indicating a man well-versed in both Buddhist scholarship and practice. In his memoirs Dorzhiev mentions two other teachers who were of important influence upon him in his youth: Sonam and Chöpel Pelzangpo. Again, these are just combinations of conventional Buddhist names and honorifics and so do not give much solid indication as to whom he is referring. Other sources, however, cite a Buryat lama, Namnanai-Gegen, as his root guru.[8] According to the notes supplied to Dorzhiev's memoirs by Khensur Ngawang Nyima, this lama was 'a great Permission Master for the major preliminary retreats of Vajrabhairava for twenty-two years',[9] though where he does not say. As this is the first tantric initiation that Gelugpa monks receive and is basically a protector practice, Namnanai-Gegen may actually have given the neophytes the necessary teachings. An oral report maintains that after he became his disciple, Dorzhiev spent time in retreat at a holy place in Alkhanai, about two hundred kilometres to the south of Chita.[10]

As R.E. Pubayev maintains that it was Namnanai-Gegen who encouraged Dorzhiev to go to Tibet and who also ordained him as a monk[11] and Dorzhiev himself records that it was Chöpel Pelzangpo who was responsible for these, we might venture to deduce that these names in fact refer to one and the same person. The only problem with this neat little piece of speculation, however, is that in his Tibetan memoir Dorzhiev does specifically refer to one 'Namnang Pakshi'. 'Namnang'[12] is the Tibetan name of the dhyani-buddha Vairocana, so it would seem quite probable that 'Namnanai' was its Mongolian variation. Unfortunately, Dorzhiev makes only passing reference to this lama, which leaves us still in the dark as to whom Chögyel, Sonam and Chöpel Pelzangpo were. Perhaps one of them was Iroltuev Lama, at the time just a monk (gelong) but later to win fame as an expert in Buddhist philosophy and dogmatics, to travel extensively in Asia and eventually be exalted to the rank of Bandido Khambo Lama – Dorzhiev would quite likely have come under his spiritual tutelage at the Atsagat Datsan. Hearsay evidence cites one other important early spiritual influence: Galschiyev Erdenyo Khyabsun, a Buryat who graduated from Drepung monastic university near Lhasa with a Doramba geshé degree.

When he was fourteen, Dorzhiev went to the holy city of Urga to continue his education. This may have been shortly after his father's death. Urga lay in Outer Mongolia, then under Manchu Chinese suzerainty. To go there would not have been a long journey by Central Asian standards. Dorzhiev would probably have crossed the Russo-Mongolian frontier near Kyakhta, where the white tower of the Russian church could be seen for miles, a beacon of Orthodoxy on the edge of an ocean of Lamaism, and from there Urga itself was about a hundred and seventy miles due south across rolling grass-covered hills, many of which were crowned with pine forests.

Urga was in fact what the Russians called the place; it was their corruption of the Mongol word 'Örgöö' meaning the palace of an important person. To the Mongols themselves, however, it was Yekhe Khüree or Da Khüree, literally 'Great Monastery'. Mention of it first appears in Mongol records in 1649, where it is stated that Öndör Gegen, the first Jebtsundamba Khutukhtu, returned from Tibet to found seven dratsang or monastic colleges. Thereafter, this nomadic monastery moved from place to place until finally coming to more or less permanent settlement on the north bank of the Selbi river, a tributary of the Tula, in 1779. As by then it had become the permanent seat of the Khutukhtu (locally known as Bogdo-Gegen or Bogdo-Khan) and of the Chinese and Mongol Ambans or Imperial Residents, it assumed the status of capital of Outer Mongolia. Subsequently it grew rapidly in importance as a religious, administrative and trading centre, but though permanent buildings were erected on the site, late nineteenth century Urga still retained much of its traditional character as a tent city, for the local citizens were loath to forsake the cosy amenities of their felt yurts, especially in winter, and large numbers of these continued to be pitched in courtyards behind wooden palisades in and around the city. Nowadays the modern secular city of Ulan Bator stands on the site: the prosaic concrete capital of the until recently Communist Mongolian Peoples' Republic.

The vanished Buddhist city of Urga was not a single settlement but an agglomeration of separate enclaves spread over a wide area in the valley of the River Tula. The Russian ethnologist A. M. Pozdneyev,[13] who first stayed there in 1877, identified three principal enclaves: the original Khüree or Monastery, where the Jebtsundamba Khutukhtu had his residence; Gandan, a separate monastic enclave dedicated to higher Buddhist studies; and Mai-mai-ch'eng, the commercial centre.

By the time that Dorzhiev arrived in Urga in 1868, the Khüree itself incorporated twenty-eight dratsang, known locally as aimaks, to which were attached a total of around thirteen thousand monks. The temple facilities for each dratsang fell into two parts: a felt yurt in which monks foregathered for religious ceremonies, and a wooden sanctuary housing massive buddhas (locally called burkhans), votive objects and other Lamaist paraphernalia. These facilities, which Pozdneyev remarks were 'extremely wretched and dirty', were surrounded by wooden palisades, while the monks lived in adjacent yurts and hutments, also surrounded by palisades. Dominating the Khüree, however, and lending it a touch of magnificence, were its great temples. These were situated at the centre of the enclave, in a wide square where two broad streets crossed, and were permanent wooden structures in fine Sino-Mongolian or Tibeto-Mongolian style, with gilded decorations known as ganjira and gyaltsen on their wide-gabled roofs. They included the Tsokchin, the assembly hall containing the throne of the Jebtsundamba Khutukhtu, where the monastic congregation gathered four times a year at major festivals. Yuri (George) Roerich, who was in Urga in 1926/7 with his illustrious father's Central Asian Expedition, witnessed one of these great assemblies:

> First one sees purple and yellow-clad lamas in high hats and flowing monastic robes, ascending the *bura-yin shata* or 'platform of the trumpet' and summoning the monks with the deep drawling sounds of their long trumpets or *dung-chen*. The narrow lanes and streets of the monastic city suddenly fill with purple-clad lamas; imposing gray-haired *geshé* and *gabju* (Tib. *bka-bcu*) or fully-pledged priests who observe the ten commandments, move in procession to the assembly hall. Young *getsul* or novices and probationers throng the entrance to the hall. The presiding lamas take up their seats to the left and right, in front of the throne of Bodgo Gegen, which is usually covered with the red mantle and the ceremonial hat of the Pontiff. The *Tsok-chin Gebkö* or the Provost Marshal of the assembly hall takes his seat at the entrance of the hall. The rest of the clergy sit down on the low mattresses spread in rows parallel to the northern wall. At the ends of the rows, close to the entrance of the hall, sit the lama musicians with long trumpets, hautboys, and tambours. The service starts, and the low voices intone a chant, occasionally interrupted by the deep sounds of the trumpets and the sharp ringing tones of the hautboys. Tambours, rhythmically sounded, join in the service, and sometimes the harrowing sounds of the cymbals rise in the semidarkness of the hall. The deep low voices of the elder monks are accompanied by the shrill high voices of the boy novices, who rhythmically shake their heads and bodies while chanting their prayers. It is quite unlike the chants in Tibetan monasteries, but is similar to that of the Tsaidam Mongols. This temple music, a remnant of the ancient past, going back to shamanistic antiquity, is not without a peculiar charm of its own, and never fails to make a deep impression on the visitor.[14]

Other temples in the Khüree were the Da-ching Galba-yin Sümä (founded 1739), beside which in Dorzhiev's time the Khutukhtu's residential yurt was pitched in an enclosure surrounded by a yellow fence; the Emchi-yin-sümä or Temple of Medicine; the Barun Örgö, which was consecrated to Abatai Khan; the Manla-yin-sümä or Temple of the

Medicine Buddha; the Jude-yin-sümä, which was dedicated to Tantra; and the Tsurkha-yin-sümä or Temple of the Astrology, where students applied themselves to astrology and astronomy before going on to be initiated into the mysteries of Kalachakra. Finally, and considered by some to be the most striking, was the domed temple built to contain a colossal statue of Maidari (Maitreya, the Coming Buddha), the handiwork of the Chinese craftsmen of Dolo-Nor, which contained relics of Tsongkhapa.

Situated about a mile and a quarter from the Khüree and built on a similar quadrangular central plan was Gandan, the monastic enclave dedicated to tsenyi or Buddhist dialectics.[15] Here Dorzhiev would have found the most learned geshés (doctors of divinity) and lama students. Founded in 1756, Gandan was originally part of the Khüree until the latter's rise as an administrative and trading centre, whereupon its studious incumbents began to demand a separate location, which was granted them in 1809. In Dorzhiev's time, it included the palace and tombs of some of the Jebtsundamba Khutukhtus, four monastic colleges and two temples of tsenyi, including the Janraisig Temple, founded in 1838 and dedicated to the Bodhisattva of Compassion (Tib., Chenrezig, Skt, Avalokiteshvara). In greatly diminished form Gandan survives today, separated from the main city of Ulan Bator by the River Suvag, which flows from Green Lake into the Tula, now partly underground. It is the seat of the Khambo Lama, the head of the Buddhists of Outer Mongolia and President of the Asian Buddhists' Conference for Peace. His Holiness the Dalai Lama visited it in 1982 and gave a Yamantaka Initiation to about a hundred and forty lamas while a crowd of twenty thousand reportedly gathered outside.

About six miles to the east of the Khüree, in what is now the modern suburb of Amgalan, lay the trading centre of Mai-mai-ch'eng, which consisted of a Chinese centre surrounded by a ring of Mongolian suburbs. The best class of shops, which stocked such goods as cloth, haberdashery, toys, confectionery, sugar, toiletries and tobacco, were to be found in the former and were elaborate establishments built within mud-walled compounds. The more modest shops lay in the Mongolian peripheries, and they opened directly onto the streets and specialized in cord, saddles, bridles, harness and suchlike. There were also street traders and, to the south, many timber yards. Besides a substantial Mongol population, several thousand Han Chinese lived in Mai-mai-ch'eng in a state of voluntary exile under the Edicts of the Li Fan Yuan (Board of Dependencies), which was also responsible for the control of Tibet. These edicts, which saved Mongols and Mongolian culture from being overwhelmed by the Han Chinese, forbade the Chinese from bringing their families to Urga, so some naturally sought the consolations of Mongol concubines.

In addition to these three principal enclaves, there were other satellite quarters, including various markets, a suburb that had grown up around the yamens of the Ambans and a 'townhouse section' in which the Mongol dzasaks or princes had built dwellings where they very occasionally resided. There was also a Russian consulate, known as the Green House, which still stands on elevated ground once known as Konsuliin Denzh (Consular Embankment), now Marshall Zhukov Avenue, overlooking the site where formerly the Chinese fortress was situated. Unfortunately, its impressive view of the river is nowadays blocked by the Soviet trade delegation building, which once housed the Soviet embassy. The Green House was built between 1863 and 1865, and replaced an older building on a separate site dating from 1786. A fine view of Urga was to be had from the stony hill that rose immediately behind it. Mai-mai-ch'eng lay some distance to the left or east and the temple city to the right or west. The whole prospect was encircled by a tangle of mountains, out of which stood one dominant peak, Bogdo-Ula, which was heavily wooded. From the mountains to the east appeared the Tula river, whose gleaming waters enlivened the sombre monotony of the valley as they flowed past the city and wound away into the broad plain that was partially visible through a wide gap in the hills to the west.[16]

The British missionary James Gilmour was in Urga for a couple of days in the late nineteenth century. Unfortunately, though clearly a warm-hearted man with a lively curiosity, his Christian prejudices rather jaundiced his responses to the city, which appeared to him as nothing less than a 'stronghold of unblushing sin'. He was prepared to concede that from afar its temples looked 'lofty and grand', but close up they lost 'much of their imposing effect'. Rather more impressive were the many prayer-wheels that he encountered at street corners and other busy places: 'These praying-cylinders seem to be seldom left long at rest . . .', he says. In front of the temples, meanwhile, he saw 'long sloping wooden platforms', at which men and women were busy making rapid prostrations; and 'all about the stony environs of this great stronghold of Buddhist faith' he encountered other more ardent devotees making circuits of the holy places by measuring the full length of their bodies on the ground over the whole route – an arduous and painful practice known as 'falling worship'. Arguably the deepest impression that he carried away, however, was of the pitiful legion of ragged beggars that thronged the market-place, which was also frequented by opportunistic eagles that swooped out of the sky to scavenge any titbit left accessible to their talons.[17] Other writers also mention Urga's packs of wild dogs, which not only rapidly disposed of the dead bodies that were left exposed outside the city but were also known on occasion to attack and consume living ones.

Such was the remarkable monastic city to which the young Dorzhiev came as a bright-eyed young aspirant in 1868. From his later accomplishments in the field of tsenyi, one might have expected him to have gravitated to Gandan, but he seems in fact to have gone to the Khüree, for according to his own account, Sonam, who gave him basic instruction, was the second abbot of the Great Monastery. From this lama, one 'oceanically endowed with the virtues of scriptural knowledge and direct insight', he also received the precepts of an upasaka or Buddhist layman, by which he undertook to restrain himself from killing, stealing, indulging in irresponsible sexuality, lying, and blunting his awareness with intoxicants. Sonam seems to have laid particular emphasis on the last: 'Alcohol is the root of all evil,' he declared unequivocally. 'Never touch it!'

Dorzhiev took his preceptor's injunction to heart and on his own admission curtailed his drinking. Later, when no doubt well established in temperance himself, he vigorously exhorted others to do likewise, and the evils of the demon drink became one of the principal themes of his Buddhist sermons, though it is unlikely that his worthy efforts bore any more success than those of his earnest Christian counterparts in Victorian England.

Two people who certainly did not exemplify the admirable virtue of sobriety were the last two incarnations of the Jebtsundamba Khutukhtu. Both were 'oceanically endowed', not with commendable Buddhist restraint, wisdom and meditative proficiency, but with colourful vices.

The seventh khubilgan in the line that stemmed from Öndür Gegen, some of whom were regarded as incarnations of the spirit of Taranatha (one of the leading pandits of the allegedly heretical Jonangpa school of Tibet,[18] which was suppressed by the victorious Fifth Dalai Lama in the seventeenth century), died in 1868, the year in which Dorzhiev arrived in Urga. He had been born near Lhasa in Tibet in 1850, the son of a layman, and declared a khubilgan in 1851. He was brought to Urga in 1855 and his general education and Buddhist training began in his seventh year. Early on, he showed great talent as a sculptor, turning out commendable buddha-rupas. However, around the age of twelve or thirteen, he began to be systematically corrupted by Tsetsen Khan Artased, the Mongol Amban in Urga, who had designs on his treasuries.

The Khutukhtu seems, however, to have been fertile ground for corruption. He gave himself up with enthusiasm to drinking, tobacco-smoking, whoring and homosexuality. While standards in Mongolia at this time generally fell far below the pristine norms established by the Buddha, some senior lamas were seriously concerned and appealed to the Manchu Amban for help. As a result, an order was issued at the end of 1866 making it a criminal offence for religious to behave improperly. However, the Khutukhtu merely removed himself to the Amurbayasalant monastery and continued his excesses there. He did display a little temporary restraint, at least in public, when he returned to his capital in 1867, but soon returned to his old ways when Tsetsen Khan's sons presented him with their sister, with whom he is said to have 'let himself down . . . to the life of an ordinary layman'. The ensuing scandal resulted in the banishment of some of the Khutukhtu's profligate cronies, including a son of Tsetsen Khan. In 1868, he fell ill: rumour had it that separation from his cronies had undermined his health and induced severe nose-bleeding. He died in December that year having been bed-ridden for the last two months. The grief-stricken old tutor who had schooled him in the art of making buddha-rupas promptly offered up prayers and took his own life.

As usual upon such an occasion, there followed an uncertain interregnum during which the appearance of the next khubilgan was awaited. In the interim, possible causes for the late khubilgan's untimely death were hotly debated and scapegoats sought by the grieving population of Urga, for his rakish life had not impaired the reverence in which they held him. Naturally the blackest suspicions fell upon Tsetsen Khan and there were hopes that a special inquest would be ordered by Peking which would bring him to book. Disappointingly, no coroner appeared, but two of the Khutukhtu's personal attendants who were thought to have been in Tsetsen Khan's pay were clapped in wooden cells and taken out of Urga to be punished. It was also rumoured that the sinister Amban had bribed a certain lama named Diba-samba to bring about the Khutukhtu's death by sorcery. The fact that this lama was stricken with quinsy and conveniently died was deemed proof of his guilt.

At the same time, omens and portents bearing upon the nature and place of the new birth were also eagerly examined and interpreted. The Mongolians were not the ultimate arbiters in these occult matters, however: that privilege was retained in Tibet. A special expedition was therefore dispatched to the Land of Snows in 1869, and it was there that the new khubilgan was found, having been born early in 1870 into the family of one of the Dalai Lama's closest officials. He was brought to Urga along with his family in 1874, and although in his early years the positive influence of his strong-minded mother kept him in line, he too gradually began to grow restive with his cloistered life and the company of old lamas. At the age of fifteen he finally kicked over the traces and enthusiastically followed his predecessor into the realms of debauchery, both homosexual and heterosexual, particularly offending monastic proprieties by taking at least two consorts. He lived on until 1924, still held in high awe by his people, having enjoyed for a brief period the distinction of being the first and only ruler of an autonomous Outer Mongolia.

It must have been against the backdrop of the dramatic events following the death of the Seventh Jebtsundamba Khutukhtu, and the discovery and installation of the Eighth, that Dorzhiev's first visit to Urga took place. However, it is unlikely that he was there continuously for any great length of time. For, though he does not mention it in his memoirs, which stress the religious aspects of his life, he was during this period briefly married to a girl named Kholintsog and held down a job as a minor official (some say a clerk) of the local stepped duma (council).[19] One oral source has even reported that he fathered a child, though what became of this offspring is not known.

Gradually, however, he describes himself as becoming convinced by his studies that 'the household life, both in this and future births, is like sinking in a swamp of misery' and increasingly to appreciate the 'inconceivable benefits of ordination'.

Dorzhiev says that he was influenced in this direction by the spiritual biographies that his 'kind and fatherly teacher' encouraged him to study, along with edifying works like the *Uliger-un Dalai* or *Ocean of Narratives*, known in Tibet as the *Do Zang Lun* ('Sutra of the Wise Man and the Fool').[20] This is a collection of about fifty-one jatakas or birth stories, the purpose each of which is to show how the karma created by actions in past lives ripens to condition present ones. Many of the stories in the *Ocean of Narratives* exist in early Buddhist sources, but the collection in its present form was apparently put together by Chinese monks, who heard the stories retold at the great oasis centre of Khotan on the Silk Route in Chinese Turkestan many centuries ago; it was subsequently translated from the Chinese into Mongolian, Oirat and Tibetan.

Young Dorzhiev must also have been mightily impressed by the lamas that he met in Urga, the best of whom must have provided a young man of his intellectual and spiritual qualities with more stimulating company than he had hitherto encountered. There must, however, have been an element of self-interest in his wish to join their number by seeking ordination, for, though he naturally does not say as much himself, the inconceivable benefits to be derived from it would certainly have included access to increased educational opportunities and the possibility of preferment.

But when his kindly teacher heard of his young devotee's intention to ordain, he adopted a somewhat cautious stance. 'First consider the respective virtues of the monastic and the lay lifestyles,' he suggested with a benign smile, perhaps thinking of Kholintsog. 'If you fail to live up to the proper standards of monastic life, your lot will be an unhappy one. You will undoubtedly be reborn as a poor lay person in your next life. If, however, you remain a lay person but pay due respect to the Buddha's teachings, then you will acquire merit and enjoy a fortunate rebirth.'[21] But in spite of the warnings, Dorzhiev was not deterred. Accordingly, in the presence of 'the great abbot Chöpel Pelzangpo', he received the vows of a celibate layman and, he adds wryly, 'made a pretence of keeping them'.

But where should an able and ambitious young man with a religious vocation look next to deepen his Buddhist education? There was really only one place.

CHAPTER THREE

Tibet and Wu T'ai Shan
1873 – 1888

In the winter of 1873, his nineteenth year, Dorzhiev left his homeland and travelled to Tibet under the compassionate care of the great abbot Chöpel Pelzangpo. It would have been a long and difficult journey, taking about four months if he travelled directly and suffered no undue delays.

We are not sure precisely which caravan route he took, but the most direct one ran south-westwards from Urga across the grasslands of northern Mongolia to the monastic settlement of Yum-beise khüree or Yungdrung-beise khüree,[1] and from there south-south-west across the arid and stony expanses of the Gobi, plying from one nomadic encampment of black yurts to the next to the Chinese city of An-hsi (Anxi) in Kansu province. The route then ran across the desolate Tsaidam region at the foot of the Tibetan plateau. Yuri Nikolaiveich Roerich, who passed that way in 1927 with his father's expedition, wrote of Tsaidam:

> This dreaded salt marsh stretches for more than 200 miles from west to east, with an average elevation of 8,000 feet, forsaken of animal life, a land of unapproachable salt lakes and bottomless salt pits, engirdled by quicksands and ridges of sand dunes ... Towards the north and south barren and wind-eroded mountain ridges form its natural boundaries. To the north is a succession of mighty mountain ranges belonging to the Nan Shan system, to the south a mountain country gradually rising towards the great highlands of northern Tibet. Scanty vegetation exists in the river valleys ...[2]

Here lived various 'banners' or clans of Qoshot Mongols, a branch of Oirat or West Mongolians who, like their kinsmen the Kalmyks, had migrated from Dzungaria in the seventeenth century. Administratively, Tsaidam proper was divided into five principalities, notably Kurluk-beise, so named because the dzasak or prince of the Kurluks had been invested with the Chinese rank of pei-tzu or beise. To the south lay the domains of the Teijiner Mongols.

Beyond Tsaidam, the route rose to the Tibetan plateau and crossed the Chang-Tang or great northern plain of Tibet, which Roerich describes as 'a country of climatic extremes', of burning sun, bitter cold and great wind storms, all of which had together conspired to make it what it had topographically become: 'a series of weathered mountain chains which have been considerably levelled, and broad intermontane plains, the home of herds of wild yaks'.[3] Here, on either side of the Tangla range, lived the Horpas: the inhabitants of the Tibetan province of Hor. The first Tibetan settlement of any consequence on this route was Nagchukha (Nagqu), a customs and militia post and trading centre through which many caravan routes passed. Dorzhiev would have been just one of a profusion of exotic Central Asian types rubbing shoulders with each other in the squalid streets and bazaars of Nagchukha where, besides the obligatory monastery, Shabden Gompa, he would also have found a dzong in which lived lay officials. It is quite likely that his caravan changed their tired pack animals for fresh ones here.

Many travellers from Urga opted for a slightly less direct route that brought them to Nagchukha by way of the great monastic centre of Khum-Bum in the north-eastern Tibetan province of Amdo, near the turquoise lake of Koko-Nor. This was the country from which Tsongkhapa, the founder-father of the Gelug school, originally came. Here the caravans from the north joined up with those plying the major Sining – Koko-Nor – Nagchukha – Lhasa route. What the journey from Koko-Nor entailed is described by Sir Charles Bell, one-time British Political Officer in Sikkim and friend of the Thirteenth Dalai Lama:

> The caravan from Mongolia assembles at Küm-bum, near the Koko Nor Lake. With it come men from Am-do and the Koko Nor, and even Buriats from distant Siberia. All march together, finding in their large number their protection against brigands of the Go-lok country. At Nag-chu-ka, some ten days' march from Lhasa, the danger from robbers being now past, the large company breaks up; and the formal permission of the Dalai Lama having been obtained, proceeds in driblets to Lhasa. Twice yearly the caravan, merchants and pilgrims together, crosses the 'Northern Plains' of Tibet, once in the floods of summer, and once when this desolate expanse, several hundreds of miles across, seventeen thousand feet above sea-level, and swept by hurricanes of wind, is in the grip of an Arctic winter. Camels, yaks, and ponies are used both for riding and carrying loads.[4]

Lhasa lay about a hundred and fifty miles south-south-west of Nagchukha, beyond the Nyenchen Tangla range, which was crossed by way of the Shang-shung Pass. In 1846 the French Lazarist padres, Huc and Gabet, made that journey:

The road which leads from Na-Ptchu [Nagchukha] to Lha-Ssa [sic] is, in general, rocky and very laborious, and when it attains the chain of the Koéran mountains it becomes fatiguing in the highest degree. Yet, as you advance, your heart grows lighter and lighter, at finding yourself in a more and more populous country. The black tents that speckle the background of the landscape, the numerous parties of pilgrims repairing to Lha-Ssa, the infinite inscriptions engraved on the stones erected on each side of the way, the small caravans of long-tailed oxen [yak] that you meet at intervals – all this serves to alleviate the fatigue of the journey.[5]

Within a few days' march of Lhasa, Huc and Gabet found the black tents of the nomadic pastoralists giving way to the houses and fields of settled agricultural people. Here, in a well-watered plain that Huc calls 'Pampou' (he probably means the valley of the Pempo-Chu) and which he describes as 'the vestibule of the holy city', they rediscovered the amenities of civilized life. Before resuming their journey, they took advantage of this to tidy themselves up and to exchange their yak for robust donkeys. They had then to negotiate only one more mountain to reach Lhasa, but this was 'the most rugged and toilsome that we had as yet encountered' – so much so, in fact, that Tibetans and Mongols believed that all who reached its summit gained remission of all their sins. Finally –

The sun was nearly setting when, issuing from the last of the infinite sinuosities of the mountain [probably the Go-La pass], we found ourselves in a vast plain and saw on our right Lha-Ssa, the most famous metropolis of the Buddhic world. The multitude of aged trees which surround the city with a verdant wall; the tall white houses with their flat roofs and their towers; the numerous temples with their gilt roofs, the Buddha-La [Potala], above which rises the palace of the Talé [Dalai] Lama – all these features communicate to Lha-Ssa a majestic and imposing aspect.[6]

If the first glimpse of Lhasa impressed those Lazarist padres, how much more so would it have moved the young Dorzhiev, for whom it was not just another city but the most sacred site on earth. At the Go-La, devotional joy would have overflowed from his heart and he would have fallen to his knees to offer thanks that, after so many weary and perilous months in the wastes of Central Asia, he had at last arrived at the spiritual centre of his universe. He would also have added a stone to the cairn on the pass before passing on.

*

Lhasa lies in the wide valley of the Kyi-Chu, surrounded by a curtain wall of bare mountains. It is dominated by the Potala (commenced c. 1645), a 'majestic mountain of a building' painted gleaming white and dark red, which seems an organic extension of the rocky outcrop known as the Red Hill on which it is built. Nearby is the crag known as Chakpori, literally Iron Hill, where the old traditional medical college has since been replaced by a high broadcasting aerial. The old city itself lies to the south-east, a warren of low Tibetan-style houses clustering around the Jokhang (established seventh century), the great temple inside which, in a legion of chapels, hundreds of butter-lamps fill the air with light and rancid fumes. Here pious pilgrims pay reverence to the ancient statue of Shakyamuni Buddha known as the Jowo Rinpoché. This, the most venerated image in the land, is said to have been brought from China as part of the dowry of the Chinese wife of the seventh century king, Songtsen Gampo, who is credited with unifying the Tibetan state and establishing the Buddhist religion. Around the Jokhang and its ancillary buildings runs the circumambulation route known as the Barkhor, where in Dorzhiev's day strange and colourful pilgrims from every region of Tibet and Central Asia would be seen twirling their prayer-wheels, tolling their beads or measuring the length of their bodies on the ground. Shaven-headed lamas in red and golden robes would be much in evidence everywhere in the city, and those exalted in the religious-political hierarchy would wear splendid silks and brocades. More pilgrims might be seen circumambulating the Lingkhor, the outer route running around the old city, the Potala and Chakpori.

Being a great religious centre, Lhasa was of course replete with religious buildings of all kinds, including Gyu-tö and Gyumé, the Upper and Lower Tantric Colleges (the former housed in the Ramoché Temple), and three of the so-called 'Four Lings', Tengyé Ling, Tsomo Ling and Tsechob Ling. The three great monastic universities of Ganden, Drepung and Sera, which housed tens of thousands of Gelugpa monks, were, however, situated outside the city proper. Surrounding Lhasa's temples were narrow, insanitary streets, along some of which traders plied their business, selling goods from the outlying provinces, from faraway China and Russia, and even cheap manufactured goods of European origin. There was also — it still survives — a Moslem area to the south-east of the Barkhor, complete with its own mosque, where Ladakhis and Kashmiris lived and plied their own traditional trades, which, as the killing of animals (though not the eating of meat) was proscribed for practising Buddhists, included butchery. Unfortunately, when Dorzhiev first came to Lhasa in 1873 there was a grave impediment to his monastic ambitions. The Dalai Lama's permission for him to live and study there had neither been obtained nor, if applied for, would have been forthcoming — and for a substantial reason. The fierce xenophobia that had caused the Tibetans to debar Europeans from crossing their frontiers applied equally to citizens of the Russian Empire – and Dorzhiev was most certainly a Russian citizen. Furthermore, the penalties for flouting this law were draconian. A Tibetan who assisted a prohibited alien to trespass on the sacred soil of the Forbidden Land was liable to have his property confiscated and afterwards be sewn up in a hide sack and tossed into a river to drown. Such was the grisly fate said to have befallen Kyabying Sengchen Lama, who assisted the Bengali scholar and agent Sarat Chandra Das during his illicit foray into Tibet between 1881 and 1883.

Moreover, such was Tibetan ignorance of the outside world and its inhabitants at this time that they are unlikely to have been able to distinguish Buryat Buddhists from other outsiders. Chöpel Pelzangpo therefore became very anxious for his protégé's safety. Dorzhiev might perhaps have been able to stay illegally with some Mongol lamas had he possessed the funds for greasing the necessary palms, but he was not sufficiently affluent, so his teacher eventually decided that it would be best if he returned to Urga. Before going, however, he was enrolled at Gomang College at Drepung monastic university.

Founded in 1416 by Jamyang Chöjé, a disciple of Tsongkhapa, Drepung was at the time the largest monastic establishment in the world: a vast and crowded complex of whitewashed stone buildings, the most important graced with gilded roofs. It sprawled across the lower slopes of a stony defile some five miles west of the holy city of Lhasa. In its heyday, it housed upwards of seven thousand monks divided between four constituent dratsang or colleges: Loseling, Ngag-pa, Deyang and Gomang. All had courtyards, sutra halls and chapels, which were connected by narrow cobbled alleyways. Dominating the whole was the Tsokchen, the great assembly hall, which still houses an image of Jhampa Tongdrol, the Lord of Drepung. Sadly, there are only about four hundred monks at Drepung today, though of all the great monasteries of the Lhasa region it suffered least at the hands of the Red Guards who, between 1966 and 1976, conducted an enthusiastic orgy of destruction in Tibet with a view to inaugurating a brave new Marxist world.

Gomang College, which possesses impressive murals depicting scenes from the life of Shakyamuni Buddha in its main sutra hall, was the establishment in the Lhasa region to which Mongol lamas gravitated. This tradition could be traced back to the Fifth Dalai Lama, Losang Gyatso (1617–82), who had been established in political dominance in Tibet by Gushri Khan and with whom the Mongols therefore felt a special connection. Charles Bell makes the point that it was the

Mongols and the men from northern and eastern Tibet who enjoyed the reputation of 'numbering in their ranks the keenest students and the most learned professors', for only the most highly motivated would have been prepared to make the long and hazardous journey to Lhasa. Moreover, cut off from all family ties, they were able to apply themselves to study and practice without distractions. That Dorzhiev would have been of this breed we can have no doubt.

Back in Urga and now twenty-one years of age, Dorzhiev was given full ordination as a bhikshu or Buddhist monk by Chöpel Pelzangpo. He also continued his spiritual training under the direction of a number of notable lamas. From Jabtru Losang Jinpa, a lama attached to the temple known as Tagten Puntsok Ling who was entrusted with offering jabtru, a purification ritual, to the Jebtsundamba Khutukhtu, he received the four initiations of the single form of the Higher Yoga Tantra yidam (deity), Vajrabhairava, who is closely related to Mañjushri. This yidam enjoys special importance in the Gelug school as Tsongkhapa himself was initiated into Vajrabhairva's sadhana by Dongrub Rinchen and it thereafter became his central lifelong practice. Meanwhile, from Ngari-pa,[7] a lama born in the Trä-khang below the Potala in Lhasa, who eventually became tutor to the dissolute Eighth Jebtsundamba Khutukhtu, Dorzhiev received initiation into the thirteen deity form of Vajrabhairava.

These initiations empowered him to begin the preliminary practices of the sadhana or specialized yogas associated with each particular yidam. These would have involved practices designed to develop devotion to the guru, who, as the specialist guide to the occult world of powerful deities and dreadful forces, occupies a very special role in Tantra; also practices like a hundred thousand mantra recitations and a hundred thousand prostrations, which develop mental calm, concentration and humility. More precisely, Tantric practices would come into play later, like detailed visualizations of the yidam and either worship of these as external forms, or actual personal identification with them with a view to actualizing the yidam's enlightened qualities. Dorzhiev also continued to study the sutras or Buddhist scriptures and their commentaries, the shastras.

But Dorzhiev was not exclusively in Urga. He records in his memoirs that he also studied at what he calls 'the Five Peaked Mountain'. When Tibetan Buddhists use this term they invariably mean Wu T'ai Shan, the great Buddhist holy mountain situated south of the Great Wall in Shansi (Shanxi) province, not far from Peking. Here, from a great terraced plateau about eight thousand feet high, rise five cloud-girt peaks replete with shrines, stupas, batteries of prayer-wheels, auspicious sites, rock-cut inscriptions and images, temples and monasteries. Many of the latter had walls of faded crimson or yellow-ochre surmounted by roofs of golden-yellow tiles. The mountain is dedicated to Mañjushri, the celestial bodhisattva who wields the Sword of Wisdom.[8]

Besides temples of modest proportions, there were at Wu T'ai Shan monasteries that were truly vast. P'usa Ting, for instance, housed hundreds of monks and was said to be larger than the famous Lama Temple in Peking. It was built on a ridge running from the surrounding mountains and was approached by a steep flight of over a hundred steps. When James Gilmour visited it with two missionary friends during this period, he found inside the walls a street lined on both sides with houses built in the Tibetan style. P'usa Ting was the seat of a grand lama, the Dzasak Lama, sometimes alternatively called the Kusho Lama,[9] appointed from Lhasa to exercise authority over the thousands of Tibetans and Mongols of the area; for although situated in China, Wu T'ai Shan was a great centre of Lamaism, which of course would have been why Dorzhiev went there.

'As Jerusalem is to the Jews, Mecca to the Mohammedans, so is Wu T'ai Shan to the Mongols', wrote James Gilmour. Mongol pilgrims of all types came here in large numbers all year round, travelling either alone or in groups, mounted or on foot, for to their thinking this was the Supreme Pure Land: a kind of heaven on earth that will be spared devastation when all else perishes in the apocalyptic destruction that will come at the end of the present world-cycle. One pilgrimage would not only secure benefits for health but would ensure happiness in a future life; two visits would double the benefits, three triple them – and so on.[10] On a more immediate, mundane level, however, they had to take care not be fleeced by the Chinese inn-keepers and other opportunists from whom they would have to buy goods and services. One inn along the pilgrim route to Wu T'ai Shan that Gilmour noticed bore an enticing advertisement to the effect that its management was honest, its prices low and its service prompt. Gilmour and his friends found to their chagrin that they 'had to wait a long time for a poor dinner, and when it came it was not cheap'.[11]

Though Dorzhiev does not tell us at which monastery he stayed during his sojourn here (if it in fact took place), P'usa Ting would be the most likely. As for his spiritual life, however, he is quite precise: as well as studying the sutras further, he received more initiations and doctrinal instruction from learned lamas like Jangchub Tsultrim Pelzangpo, Yeshé Lhundrup Pelzangpo (who was a Lharampa Geshé – a Gelug Doctor of Divinity of the highest degree) and from a Buryat tulku whom Dorzhiev calls Dzasak Rinpoché. Could this be the Dzasak Lama, the Lord High Abbot of P'usa Ting?

The young Buryat must have shown great promise and generally

pleased his teachers with his considerable charm, for steps were taken
to find a way for him to continue his studies in Tibet. The plan that was
devised was basically that his way should be smoothed by the liberal
distribution of offerings in pertinent places around Lhasa. While he was
engaged in preliminary practises like the first of four sets of a hundred
thousand prostrations in order to become qualified to attend one of the
preliminary retreats of Vajrabhairava, Dzasak Rinpoché provided him
with a fund-raiser,[12] Jadrel Rinpoché, and also gave animals and other
necessities. Dorzhiev does not seem to have known precisely who urged
Dzazak Rinpoché to favour him in this way: perhaps it was a lama
named Drubwang Jangchub, or it may have been Namnang Bakshi, his
own root guru.

James Gilmour was highly critical of such 'collecting expeditions' as
he witnessed. These usually consisted of several lamas, he records, who
set off from Wu T'ai Shan each spring with carts and tents to spend
the summer soliciting alms all over Mongolia and even up into Buryat
territory, where the people were richer and the pickings accordingly
better. They would return before winter laden with food, tea, skins,
money, and driving herds of cattle and flocks of sheep – 'all eagerly
received'. In return, they would reward their benefactors by placing their
names on a 'subscription list' that gave the good people the pleasure of
thinking that they were patrons of the temple and therefore had special
connections with Wu T'ai.[13]

Dorzhiev was therefore following a well-established tradition when
he returned to his Buryat homeland with Jadrel Rinpoché and raised a
very considerable collection. Not only did comparatively affluent Buryat
Buddhists show generosity out of gratitude for the initiations, blessings
and advice they had received from great lamas like Dzasak Rinpoché,
to whom they were particularly devoted, but the less well-off gave
generously too. When Dorzhiev and Jadrel Rinpoché returned to Wu
T'ai Shan and offered their collections to Dzasak Rinpoché, he was
understandably delighted. 'Normally we only receive such kindness
from our parents', the good lama declared; and then went on to lavish
particular praise on Dorzhiev's efforts.

Rinpoché now personally took over all the arrangements for Dorzhiev's
return to Tibet. He obtained various necessities, including clothing, from
Peking, arranged that Dorzhiev would again travel with Jadrel Rinpoché
and even fixed the precise time when he would leave. Jadrel Rinpoché
was impatient, however, for although an old man he had a strong spirit
and was eager to be on the trail. So they set off on foot a little early,
bearing the offerings which Dzasak Rinpoché had entrusted to them.

There was one important meeting en route: with a Tibetan zaisan

who had been employed in the government of the Jebtsundamba
Khutukhtu and was now on his way to Lhasa to become the Dalai
Lama's Mongolian translator. Significantly, he and Dorzhiev talked
high politics: 'The British and the Russians are two different nations:
the Tibetans should understand this', Dorzhiev explained, pointing out
something that was not generally understood in Tibet. 'Moreover, the
British fear the Russians, who belong to the mightiest nation on earth.
Therefore if the Tibetans wish to avoid falling into the hands of the
British they should make friends with the Russians. Moreover, the
Manchu Emperor of China respects the Russian Tsar. He sends him
gifts and in return has received rifles and cannon. Please convey this
to the Tibetans.'[14]

Dorzhiev was twenty-six when in 1880 he at last reached the holy city
for the second time. He and Jadrel Rinpoché then made generous offerings at the three great Lhasa monasteries, Ganden, Sera and Drepung,
as well as at Tashilhunpo near Shigatsé in southern Tibet, where the
Panchen Lama, second only in the Tibetan hierarchy to the Dalai Lama,
had his seat. Furthermore, during Monlam Chenmo, the Great Prayer
Festival held straight after the Losar or New Year celebrations, when
annually Lhasa used to be taken over by thousands of monks for three
weeks of intense and exotic ceremonies designed to protect Tibet during
the coming year, more lavish distributions of offerings were made.
Finally, offerings were made at Gomang College, and these must have
been extremely munificent for they qualified Dorzhiev for the title of
chomzé: one who makes offerings to the entire assembly of monks in
a monastic institution.

By this means, which may not exactly have been bribery but something
very much like it, the earnest and energetic young Buryat was able to
'create favourable conditions for my studies'. He apparently suffered
no more problems.

At Gomang, Dorzhiev would undoubtedly have been attached to a
Mongol tutor who would have superintended his continuing geshé
studies – the term 'geshé' is roughly the Lamaist equivalent of a doctorate
in divinity – which can be broken down into five constituent parts.
Firstly, he would have studied the Collected Topics of Valid Cognition
(i.e., logic); secondly, Buddhist dogmatics based on the Prajñaparamita
or Perfection of Wisdom literature; thirdly, Nagarjuna's Madhyamaka
or Central Way philosophy; fourthly, the Vinaya or Monastic Discipline;
and lastly, Abhidharmakosha, Vasubandhu's treasury of early Buddhist
realism, which includes the exposition of the theory of dharmas
(elements). The overall aim of the course would have been to establish
clearly in Dorzhiev's mind, through reasoning, the nature and goal of

the Buddhist path. In practice he would have studied and memorized texts. He would also have tested his knowledge and understanding in actual debate in the special debating courtyard at Gomang, perhaps continuing until far into the night. But mere intellectual understanding does not transform a mere mortal into a buddha. That can only be brought about by special practices, notably meditation. By this system, therefore, theory plus practice equals realization.

During the following years, Dorzhiev was fortunate to receive dharma teachings and initiations from 'the Great Protector and his sons, holy beings and actual buddhas.'[15] These included among others Trichen Dorji Chang; also Purchok Ngawang Jampa, a distinguished lama of Mé College at Sera monastic university, generally regarded as a manifestation of the Indian pandit Atisha. In order to penetrate deeply into the meaning of the teachings as well as to practise in accordance with the instructions he had received from 'the famous Rabjam Peldrup', he would also periodically go on retreat at Gonsar, a secluded hermitage in the mountains outside Lhasa, where he also received guidance from the 'incomparably kind' Geshé Khetsun Zangpo.

All did not go completely smoothly according to Dorzhiev's own testimony, however. 'My stupid mind was greatly distracted and so my studies did not progress very well', he maintains; 'I accordingly turned my efforts towards various lesser sciences'.[16]

This must be a rhetorical piece of conventional self-deprecation, for when in 1888 he finally came to take his geshé examinations, which were traditionally held publicly in the presence of many distinguished scholars as part of the Monlam Chenmo cycle of events in Lhasa, Dorzhiev passed with the highest honours and was awarded the Lharampa degree. It is, however, a little puzzling that he managed to complete the course so quickly, for there is usually a waiting list and ample funds are necessary to pass the final hurdles. Everything points to Dorzhiev having an influential patron and sponsor. Perhaps money was reaching him from Russia – and perhaps from high places in Russia. Naturally he is reticent about anything of this kind.

Dorzhiev was known in Tibet as Ngawang Losang, and among his fellow Buryats after graduating, as Tsenyi Khenpo: a learned instructor in Buddhist logic and debate – something broadly along the lines of professor of Buddhist dialectics. He did in fact instruct Mongol and Buryat students in tsenyi at Drepung.[17] It was a position commanding great respect, and meant he had become a recognized member of the monastic elite of Lhasa.

Then almost at once – and as if he had been prepared and groomed for it – an extremely auspicious door opened for him.

CHAPTER FOUR

The Thirteenth Dalai Lama
1888 – 1898

Even towards the end of his life, Tubten Gyatso, the Thirteenth Dalai
Lama of Tibet (1876–1933), still possessed powerful presence. He was
then old by contemporary Tibetan standards and two periods of exile
as well as many stressful years of political struggle had taken their
toll. Consequently, the jaunty gay hussar moustache that he had once
sported was gone, the fiery, impetuous temperament of his youth had
mellowed, his teeth were rotten, his enormous ears stuck out from his
shaven head like those of a monstrous elf, and his skin was puffy.
His eyes were still compelling, though, and left the few Westerners
that met him in no doubt that here was a very remarkable man, both
spiritually and politically.[1] History has confirmed these impressions.
Tubten Gyatso is now generally recognized as one of the great Dalai
Lamas, the line of whose incarnations stretches back through fourteen
physical vehicles to Gendun Drup (1391–1474), the nephew of Jé
Tsongkhapa.

It was Tubten Gyatso's fate to grapple with the momentous changes
that beset Tibet towards the end of the nineteenth century. Until then,
the Land of Snows, her borders sealed against foreign intrusions,
had successfully enjoyed seclusion for almost a century. Beyond the
traditional priest-patron ties with China, no channels of communication
existed with the outside world, and any outsider, especially any European
who crossed her frontiers, was turned back. Virtually no outside
influences, therefore, and no modern innovations had penetrated that
hermetic world in which the ancient Mahayana and Tantric Buddhist
traditions of ancient India were preserved by devoted guardian monks.
But the outside world could not be kept at bay forever, and if Tibet
would not yield to friendly overtures then more vigorous, even violent
methods would sooner or later be used to force her to open her doors.

During Tubten Gyatso's reign there was constant pressure on Tibet from her powerful neighbours, British India and China, as well as from less powerful ones like Nepal. She was invaded several times and her precarious independence was in almost constant jeopardy. But in the Thirteenth Dalai Lama, Tibet was fortunate to have a leader capable of responding to the challenge of the times. At the height of his powers, his capacity for work was prodigious. He would rise at four a.m., earlier if necessary, and labour on through the day, alternating spiritual with worldly duties until past midnight.[2] To complicate matters, his efforts were often frustrated by reactionary political factions within the country itself, notably the ultra-conservative caucuses in the great monasteries of the Lhasa area. Yet for over twenty years, between 1912 and 1933, he secured the de facto independence of Tibet while at the same time maintaining inviolate her ancient Buddhist traditions.

When in 1875 the Twelfth Dalai Lama died, a regent, Tatsak Rinpoché, was appointed to rule Tibet until the next Dalai Lama was found and brought to maturity. He was a monk of Kundé Ling,[3] one of the four royal colleges of the Lhasa area from which, with three other monasteries, the Fifth Dalai Lama had decreed that regents should be drawn. At once efforts began to locate the new body in which the compassionate spirit of the Buddhist deity Chenrezi (Skt Avalokiteshvara), thought to inhabit each Dalai Lama, would reappear in the world. Tradition had set up elaborate occult methods for doing this. An official group would, for instance, visit the Oracle Lake, Lhamoi Latso, situated near the Chokhorgyal monastery some ninety miles east-south-east of Lhasa, in whose mystic waters mysterious signs and portents would appear. Afterwards search parties would be dispatched to follow them up.

The wily Chinese, always with a keen eye for their own political advantage, had attempted to gain some influence over proceedings by pressing upon the Tibetans a golden urn in which the names of candidates could be put and a 'winner' drawn as in a lottery. Fortunately, in this case the urn was not needed, for all the indications, including the pronouncements of the State Oracle who lived in a small temple at Nechung, were particularly powerful and clear that the new incarnation would be found in the village of Langdun in the Dakpo region of south-east Tibet. A likely child, born amidst marvellous portents to a worthy couple named Kunga Rinchen and Losang Drölma on 27 May 1876, was duly found and tested along with two other candidates. When shown a selection of articles, he unerringly chose those items that had belonged to the previous incarnation. The Regent and other high officials were convinced, the appropriate declarations were made and the child was brought to his capital, Lhasa, and initially installed at the Gunthang monastery near the holy city in 1878, then moved to Samtenling, a monastery just to the north of Lhasa.

After his formal enthronement at the Potala in Lhasa in July 1879, the infant Dalai Lama lived a cloistered life mainly in the company of adults. In anticipation of his future spiritual role and 'in accordance with the procedures set by my predecessors', he took various monastic vows, received major and minor Tantric initiations, and was given a thorough Buddhist education. He had numerous gurus drawn from different schools of Tibetan Buddhism, his Senior Tutor being the Regent, Tatsak Rinpoché, but the main brunt of his day-to-day teaching fell on the Junior Tutor, Purchok Ngawang Jampa of Sera Mé College, with whom he forged a special bond of affection. It was Purchok who taught him how to read and write, who steered him through the complex Gelug programme of study and who gave him various Tantric initiations as well as a host of oral transmissions. He also presided over his full monastic ordination in 1895 and guided him in meditation. After his tutor's death, the Lama wrote:

> [Purchok Rinpoché] never allowed my training to become one-sided, always watching to see that my practice of contemplation and meditation kept a proper balance with my efforts in study. He revealed the entire path of enlightenment to me, like teaching a child how to walk and talk. His kindness to me was inconceivable, and there is no way I could ever hope to repay it.[4]

The Dalai Lama was also instructed in logic and exercised in formal debate – he was dazzlingly good at it, according to Purchok Rinpoché – and for this, suitable tsenzab[5] or assistant tutors were chosen from each of the major monasteries. These were lamas of the finest intellectual and spiritual calibre. One was the well-respected khenpo of Drepung Gomang College, Ngawang Losang.

The connection between Dorzhiev and the Dalai Lama began about 1888, the year in which Dorzhiev took his geshé examinations and the Dalai Lama was twelve or thirteen. As the two events followed so closely upon each other, the likelihood would be that Dorzhiev had been picked out already as a suitable tutor and hastened through the notoriously slow, cumbersome and expensive geshé examination process. His spiritual and scholarly qualities must have attracted attention, and he was also appreciated for his personal charm and practical acumen. But he was not without opponents. There were some Tibetans who muttered that it was insupportable that a Russian subject should hold so high a position, and they repeatedly called upon the Regent and his ministers to dismiss Dorzhiev and send him back to his homeland. At one point they nearly had their way, but the Dalai Lama and Purchok Rinpoché interceded on his behalf.[6]

For the next ten years, Dorzhiev, by his own account, served as the young Dalai Lama's 'inseparable attendant', and His Holiness came to look upon him as his 'true guardian and protector'.[7] During this time a close and lasting relationship was formed with the result that down to 1913 Dorzhiev was the Lama's closest political advisor. It may well have been, furthermore, that it was Dorzhiev who, either alone or with political allies, encouraged his young protégé to avoid the fate of his predecessors – the last four Dalai Lamas had all been bumped off before attaining maturity by power-hungry regents – by taking temporal power into his hands as soon as he was able to do so. 'There was never previously a man who had risen so high in Tibet', wrote the Kalmyk Baza Bakshi of Agvan Dorzhiev.[8]

Being an assistant tutor to the Dalai Lama also had distinct spiritual advantages for Dorzhiev. He was able to be present when Purchok Rinpoché gave His Holiness blessings, teachings and initiations into the sadhana of such yidam as Vajramala, Chakrasamvara, Guhyasamaja and Vajrabhairava; also Kalachakra, literally the 'Wheel of Time', thought by many to be the apogee of the Tantric path and especially relevant in the present Kali Yuga or spiritual dark age. To develop the spiritual skills required by these practices, the Lama would retire into short retreats[9] for periods of a week or two twice or three times each year, and at least once during his teens for three months. Dorzhiev was able to accompany him on some of these. Meanwhile, the special duties entrusted to him included the performance of occult rituals to ensure that the Dalai Lama enjoyed a long life, and either organizing or himself offering special 'life substances'.[10] He moreover oversaw the carving and printing of the wood blocks whenever the Dalai Lama ordered new impressions of sacred texts.

*

As Dorzhiev's relationship with his young protégé developed, he gradually began to broach political matters. Always deeply devoted to the interests of his fellow Buryats – and to the Kalmyks as well – he certainly wished to ease their lot in Lhasa. So he informed the Dalai Lama and also the Panchen Lama that these devout students of the Buddha Dharma had to come illicitly to the holy city to pursue their higher spiritual studies. Such men could do enormous good in their native lands when at last they returned there, fully-trained, and he cited the case of Damba Darzha Zayayev. Both the Dalai and

Panchen Lamas were impressed by Dorzhiev's vigorous championship of his fellow-countrymen's case and the position of Russian Buddhists in Lhasa was improved.

More importantly, as history was eventually to show, Dorzhiev now also began to urge upon the Dalai and Panchen Lamas the wisdom of looking to Russia for support against the British, since the Manchu Empire of China, then in a state of decay, lacked the necessary strength to be a viable patron-protector of Tibet and might even be prepared, for money, to give Tibet into the hands of some other foreign nation. The British sahibs, lording it away below the Himalayas in India, had for some time been exerting pressure on Tibet's southern frontiers. On the face of it this did not amount to much more than a series of vexing border squabbles and unwanted overtures, but to the Tibetans it was sinister – evidence that Britain wished to engulf Tibet as she had engulfed India and was engulfing various Himalayan enclaves, notably the kingdom of Sikkim, with which Tibet traditionally had very close ties.[11] Engulfment, the Tibetans believed, would mean that their spiritual traditions, the jewel they valued over all others, would be destroyed.

'Because she herself is an enemy of Great Britain, Russia will come to the assistance of the Land of Snows to prevent her being devoured by the British,' Dorzhiev explained to the Dalai and Panchen Lamas, 'Also the stainless teachings of the Buddha still flourish in Russian-controlled Torgut[12] and in Buryat[ia].'

*

During the Thirteenth Dalai Lama's minority, two particular but unrelated events took place which gave the young prelate a foretaste of political things to come.

The first was the penetration of Tibet by the Bengali babu Sarat Chandra Das (1849–1917)[13] who successfully combined scholarship – he compiled a pioneering Tibetan-English dictionary – with work as a British agent. Kipling modelled Hurree Chunder Mookerjee of *Kim* upon him – 'Do you know what Hurree Babu really wants? He wants to be made a member of the Royal Society by taking ethnological notes'. Das lived undercover in Tibet from 1881 to 1883 and, among other things, visited Lhasa and mapped the sacred Yamdrok lake near Gyantsé. He escaped arrest but his helper, Losang Palden, Sengchen Lama of Shigatsé, was arrested and punitively drowned. The largest estate of the aristocratic Phala family was also seized, since one of Sengchen Lama's accomplices had been of that family.

The other crucial event was the invasion of parts of Western Tibet in

1888 by the Gurkhas of Nepal demanding compensation for the looting of Nepalese shops in Lhasa following a quarrel between two Tibetan women and a Nepalese shopkeeper.

*

In 1886, after twelve years of service, Tatsak Rinpoché died and his office passed according to time-hallowed tradition to a senior lama of one of the other six special monasteries. Thus Demo Trinley Rapgay, the incarnate lama of Tengyé Ling, became the new Regent. Tengyé Ling was not large and populous but it was exclusive and very well-endowed. It was also very conservative and traditionally pro-Chinese, so Demo Khutukhtu would have been a partisan of the Manchus and in consequence, both anti-Russian and anti-British. On assuming power he ill-advisedly appointed his brothers as aides, and their corrupt and oppressive behaviour won them many enemies; this was later to cause severe problems.

*

The policy of exclusion maintained by the Tibetans was an open challenge to a certain adventurous type of European. Almost for the sport of it, a number of intrepid travellers and explorers were tempted to make a dash through the Forbidden Land to the holy city of Lhasa, which, veiled so long from Western eyes, had acquired an almost irresistible mystique. One of these was the Frenchman Gabriel Bonvalot, who decided to try to reach the holy city from the North, crossing the Altyn Tagh and traversing the vast northern plain of Tibet. Bonvalot relied not merely on courage and determination but on close secrecy: such secrecy in fact that his two European companions, the Belgian missionary Father Dedeken and the young French aristocrat and sportsman Prince Henri of Orléans, were kept in the dark about their true objective until the expedition was well advanced.

In February 1890, after surviving the bitter Arctic conditions of the Chang-Tang in winter, Bonvalot and his party were eventually stopped by a large force of armed Tibetans just south of Tengri-Nor, a lake about ninety-five miles north of Lhasa. A number of Tibetan officials went out to meet them and several days of parleying and political discussion ensued. It is interesting to speculate whether Dorzhiev was present. Certainly Bonvalot does not mention him specifically in his published narrative, nor can he be picked out in Prince Henri's photographs; but it is interesting to note that Bonvalot records that the negotiations were carried on through a Mongolian and that at least two other interpreters were sent out from Lhasa, one of whom he describes as a native of Urga who had come to Tibet some time ago and been obliged to stay because he lacked the funds to return home.

The Tibetans initially believed that Bonvalot's group were either British or Russians, enemies in either case, but Prince Henri advised them that they were neither; they were French – and he spoke of ways in which the French, working in conjunction with their allies the Russians might 'prevent Tibet from being devoured by Britain'. Tibetan officials were adamant that Bonvalot and his companions should not under any circumstances proceed to Lhasa and eventually it was agreed that they should leave for China via Batang;[14] nevertheless, Prince Henri's advice was noted in Lhasa, where it served to confirm what Dorzhiev himself had been telling the Tibetans.

At about the same time, the Nechung Oracle went into ritual trance and afterwards made two pronouncements that could also be interpreted as supportive. Firstly, he announced that a great spirit, a manifestation of a supremely compassionate being, a bodhisattva no less, had appeared in the north and east, which might be construed as a reference to the Russian Emperor, who of course was regarded as an incarnation of White Tara by Russian Buddhists. He also talked in the cryptic way that oracles do of 'treating an open wound with the fat of a dog', which could be interpreted as meaning, if an improbable remedy works then don't hesitate to use it, or more precisely: if Russia can help Tibet then she should be approached.

*

As inside Tibet a fear of external encroachment began to mount, secret high level political meetings were also now convened to discuss the possibility of seeking protection from an outside power. Dorzhiev, asked to attend one of these, argued his case that Russia could offer the best protection. Subsequently, the Tibetans began to keep a close watch on the activities of the Russians, and when the Heir Apparent, the future Emperor Nicholas II, visited Buryatia during his grand tour of the Far East in 1890/1, they were favourably impressed:

> Word of the reverent reception by the Buryat people of their deified monarch and of the favours loaded [upon them] after the passage of His Imperial Majesty penetrated deep into distant Tibet, and in the eyes of everyone, from the Dalai Lama and high officials down to the most humble commoner, the prestige of Russia was increased considerably, and this naturally suggested the notion that such a bodhisattva of a Tsar could be of great benefit to Tibet as well.[15]

The young and impressionable Dalai Lama was certainly among those persuaded by Dorzhiev's arguments. He had virtually no knowledge of the outside world and absolutely no knowledge of the workings of international politics – which was true of just about everyone else in Tibet at the time. His tsenzab, however, was very much a man of the world: comparatively well-educated, well-travelled in Central Asia, and moreover a person of intelligence, acumen, charm and character. One witness who personally met him testifies that his 'science, energy and, above all, the vivacity of his mind ... predestined him to become a great statesman or a great adventurer.'[16] He may also have lent a certain urgency to his arguments by invoking a prophecy then current in Lhasa that some nemesis was about to overtake Tibet that would mean there would only be thirteen Dalai Lamas. But perhaps Charles Bell sums up the situation most succinctly: 'The professor of theology was clever and pushful, and the god-king was cut off from contact with the outside world'.[17]

*

Because of the air of mystery that has always surrounded him and the central part he played in Central Asian politics during this period, it has been suggested more than once that Dorzhiev was a sinister Russian agent. For instance, in *Sturm Über Asien*, a ripping yarn (Central Asian style) published in Berlin in 1926 by the German Oriental traveller and geo-physicist Wilhelm Filchner,[18] it is alleged that Dorzhiev was recruited by the Russian Foreign Office and Intelligence Service in 1885, and that he was the master of many lama-agents, including a Mongolian named Zerempil (born 1870), whose memoirs form the basis of Filchner's book. This would seem improbable since at the time Dorzhiev was immersed in the study of higher Buddhist dialectics; and moreover, it might be argued that no mere mole would have possessed the motivation to pursue these notoriously difficult intellectual disciplines for years on end and to the highest academic levels.

On the other hand, Dorzhiev was a highly political animal and there exists solid evidence that he was by no means hermetically cut off from contact with the Russian empire while he was in Lhasa. Indeed, W. A. Unkrig talks of him being liberally rewarded with medals and decorations by the highest authorities in St Petersburg for his promotion of Russia in Tibet. Also Russian records report that when in 1896 three Buryats were decorated by Nicholas II, a certain 'Lama Agvan' received a monogrammed watch, while one of the others, who both received gold medals, was a Buryat named Ocir Dzhigmitov, whom Dorzhiev himself reports had got through to Lhasa with a message from Dr Piotr Badmayev, a Buryat healer influential in high policy circles in St Petersburg who at the time was in Peking, having obtained Russian government finance to the tune of five million rubles for a far-fetched scheme to use Buryats to incite the Mongols and Tibetans to rebel against their Chinese suzerains. To conceal Ocir's true purpose, Dorzhiev passed him off as an ordinary pilgrim, 'and so he went back, after performing religious observances with some Mongols.'[19]

When the Dalai Lama assumed full temporal responsibilities in September 1895 at the age of nineteen, Dorzhiev continued to be a member of his spiritual staff. He also attended His Holiness in a personal capacity. According to Charles Bell, he was appointed 'Work Washing Abbot . . . part of his duties being to sprinkle water, scented with saffron flowers, a little on the person of the Dalai Lama, but more on the walls of his room, on the altar, and on the books, as a symbol of cleansing.'[20] Bell also reports that for his various duties Dorzhiev received a combined salary amounting to no more that £140 per annum. A Russian source, on the other hand, maintains that Dorzhiev held the exalted office of 'Keeper of the Golden Teapot'.[21]

With the Dalai Lama's political coming-of-age, the Regent, Demo Trinley Rapgay, resigned. He and his brothers did not, however, depart the spiritual arena with good grace for, like many of their predecessors, they had become attached to the delights of power. A power struggle – and in all likelihood a sinister one – seems to have taken place, and one, moreover, because of the political loyalties of Demo Khutukhtu and his monastery, which would also at root have been about Chinese power in Tibet. The upshot was that Demo Khutukhtu and his brothers were accused of using black magic to secure reinstatement. Thus arose the notorious Case of the Cursed Pair of Boots, which began in suitably melodramatic fashion when, during the Monlam Chenmo or Great Prayer Festival of 1899, the Nechung Oracle predicted danger to the life of the Dalai Lama and suggested the thorough investigation of a pair of Tibetan boots given to the Dalai Lama's friend and tutor Terton Sögyal by Chöjor, the steward of Tengyé Ling. Whenever Sögyal wore these boots his nose started bleeding. The cause was soon rooted out: when torn apart, the soles of the boots were found to contain slips of paper on which were scrawled the Dalai Lama's name and horrible curses invoking his sudden death. The ex-Regent, his brothers and their accomplices were arrested and put on trial. Found guilty, their lives would probably have been forfeit had not the Dalai Lama been compassionately opposed to capital punishment. Instead, Demo Trinley Rapgay was stripped of his estates and imprisoned for life along with his accomplices.[22]

Such indeed was the murky political world in which the new ruler of Tibet had to try to assert his own political will. It recalls as much as anything Italy under the Borgias – with sinister occult nuances. A picture of what was going on politically in Lhasa towards the end of the nineteenth century was outlined in a pamphlet that Dr Badmayev passed on to the St Petersburg newspaper *Novoye Vremya*. It was presented as a report by a 'Buriate of Chorinskaia' – obviously Dorzhiev. British officials sent home the following resumé:

> In this report, the customs of Lhasa and the intrigues surrounding the Dalai Lama are described. His Court consists of a number of Lamas divided into parties and quarrelling among each other. The party in power holds the seals and acts in the Dalai Lama's name. The latter is indifferent to party strife, and is concerned only that his authority should not be diminished, so that the people should continue to revere him. As a diminution of his authority is contrary to the interests of the parties, he remains outside their disputes.[23]

*

Dorzhiev could hardly have enjoyed his close relationship with the Dalai Lama without becoming involved in these intrigues. Indeed, there was a moment when he debated whether it might be wise to retreat to his native Trans-Baikalia,[24] but he maintains that he was concerned for the Dalai Lama, who was disturbed by the prevailing contention. Communication between the two of them seems to have been broken at some point. Perhaps the young god-king was in retreat; or perhaps – which seems more likely – Dorzhiev's political opponents managed to isolate him from His Holiness. The position had clearly become very tense and delicate.

The next news that Dorzhiev received was that it was His Holiness's personal wish that he leave Tibet for three years and while away he should visit China, Russia and France in order to find out more about the 'order of life' in those countries and whether political support might be forthcoming, as Prince Henri of Orléans had suggested.[25]

Dorzhiev therefore began to make arrangements for leaving. He dutifully visited Purchok Rinpoché, who offered him the fatherly advice that he should spread the Buddha Dharma by whatever means were open to him for the spiritual welfare of all sentient beings and also bestowed on him protective blessings in the sadhana of Mahakala and the 'Poisonous Black Dharmaraja', as well as giving him three symbolic gifts that would give him support of body, speech and mind. These were a statue of the goddess Tara (body), a copy of a liturgical rite containing guidance on the Pratimoksha or Code of Monastic Discipline (speech), and a Kadampa stupa (mind). From the Nechung Oracle, meanwhile, Dorzhiev received further advice on the worthy Buddhist enterprises that he could undertake as well as more auspicious presents, including a gold thumb-ring and a red knotted khada[26] or offering scarf.

So in 1899, Dorzhiev, then in his forty-fifth year, set off from Lhasa 'bearing both worldly and spiritual riches'.[27] It was a beginning of a great journey that was to take him far beyond his Central Asian stamping grounds, far beyond Asia . . . far beyond even his own most extravagant projections . . .

CHAPTER FIVE

Ukhtomsky's Summons
1898

When Dorzhiev left Lhasa in 1898 – with who knows what simple or mixed feelings – he was not, as might have been expected, a member of a caravan heading for Koko-Nor. Ever a man of surprises, he headed in exactly the opposite direction: south towards British India – according to contemporary Tibetan perceptions the pit of all evil and menace.

Certainly this would have given him access to modern means of transportation that could carry him to Trans-Baikalia far more quickly than if he had gone by the more direct but arduous overland routes. But there is also this to bear in mind. The sinister British presence notwithstanding, India was – and still is – for Tibetans the supreme holy land. There, in the sultry heartland of the Gangetic plain, lie the sacred sites associated with Shakyamuni Buddha. To make a pilgrimage to one or more of these was the earnest aspiration of every pious Tibetan Buddhist, for the blessings and spiritual merit that would thereby accrue to him would be immeasurable and at least ensure a fortunate rebirth in his next life.

Having left Lhasa and been ferried across the River Tsangpo, Dorzhiev and his unnamed companions reached Nedong, near the modern administrative centre of Tsetang, one of the five gates on the road to India noted for bureaucratic complications and corruption, where they were stopped on the orders of the military commander. Dorzhiev's fame must have preceded him, however, for when he realized who he was, the officer in charge prostrated himself three times, offered him a lot of money and 'happily sent us on our way'.

The view a few days later of the crisply snowcapped Himalayan peaks rising from the barren Tibetan tableland to touch the ultramarine sky must have lifted Dorzhiev's heart. It would have been lifted for a second time soon afterwards when, having crossed the high passes into the state of Sikkim, he caught his first glimpse of the plains of India. In the distance they looked like a vast and mysterious map spread out at his feet. He could descry great rivers, roads, jungles, towns, villages and cities. 'Is this not like a deva loka', he asked himself; 'a land of the gods?'

Then the steep descent from the snowline to the treeline, and, like so many adapted to life at high altitude, he found the heat overpowering and began to experience difficulty in breathing. Just to walk a short distance was too enervating, and sleep when it came was fitful. He quickly acclimatized however, and afterwards experienced no more difficulties in that direction, though others were in store. At the Indian frontier he was stopped and interrogated by British officials. Coolly, he explained that he was a Chinese subject, a Mongolian; in fact, 'I am the first Mongolian who has decided to return to his homeland by the easier sea route', he announced, showing them a Mongolian passport he had purchased for twenty-five yüan from the Chinese representative in Lhasa. 'Many more of my fellow countrymen will shortly follow.'[1]

The commercially-minded British, no doubt pleased at the prospect of a fresh influx of travellers with cash to spend, allowed him to pass. They had in any case nothing really to be suspicious about. India, as Kipling noted, was a land of pilgrims, and it was not unusual to see Tibetans plying their way along the hot and dusty roads – Kim's Lama was just such a one, though probably few others wandered as far as Lahore. Many Tibetan and a few Mongolian traders also came regularly to do business in Darjeeling and Calcutta: Alexander Ular talks of a thousand Tibetans a year at Calcutta at about this time.

In due course Dorzhiev reached Siliguri, the railhead that served the hill station of Darjeeling, where he caught a train for the bustling city of Calcutta, then capital of the Indian Empire. The architecture of the great buildings of the city fully reflected the arrogant self-esteem of the proud people that had built them. There were government offices, museums and libraries with Corinthian columns; a cathedral reminiscent of St Paul's; triumphal monuments and Wren-style churches; imposing banks and houses of the great trading companies . . . Certain sections of the city might have been transported intact from the City of London itself, except that just a stone's throw away there were overcrowded native quarters that were totally Oriental. Government House on the edge of the great open park known as the Maidan was the official residence of Her Majesty's Viceroy. Next year, 1899, that 'most superior person', George Nathaniel Curzon, would be appointed to that plummy position. Had he already been installed and caught the slightest whiff of a suspicion that a Russian citizen high in the councils of the Dalai Lama was in his capital he would have been extremely dismayed. As it was, the British intelligence agencies allowed Dorzhiev to slip through their net without even noticing.

Though Calcutta was the first great modern city Dorzhiev had clapped eyes on, he did not linger there but instead caught another train, this time to the 'greatest of Pure Lands', Bodh-Gaya. In that Bihar town he duly made pious prostrations at the Bodhi Tree beneath which Shakyamuni Buddha had achieved full spiritual enlightenment, and paid his respects to various other 'objects of reverence'. He also made offerings, including gold.

In those days Bodh-Gaya had been in the hands of Shaivite Hindus for about three hundred years. They regarded the Buddha as a manifestation of their god Vishnu, and had set up their own temple. Accordingly, they were somewhat contemptuous of Buddhist claims to the place, which had just begun to be advanced by Western sympathizers like Colonel Henry Steel Olcott (who with Madame H. P. Blavatsky (1831–91) and others founded the Theosophical Society in New York City in 1875) and Sir Edwin Arnold, author of *The Light of Asia*, a best-selling poetic life of the Buddha. Arnold wrote in the *Daily Telegraph*:

> If you walked on that spot which [400,000,000] Buddhists love so well, you would observe with grief and shame . . . ancient statues plastered to the walls of an irrigating well . . . Stones carved with Buddha's images . . . used as weights in levers for drawing water . . . I have seen three feet high statues in an excellent state of preservation buried under rubbish . . . and the Ashokan pillars, the most ancient relics on the site – indeed, 'the most antique memorials in all India' – which graced the temple pavement, are now used as posts of the Mahant's [i.e., the Hindu priest's] kitchen.[2]

Returning to Calcutta, Dorzhiev took passage in a ship sailing for China. During the voyage a mighty storm erupted, perhaps one of those terrible typhoons of the South China Sea whose furies Joseph Conrad has evoked so compellingly. Completely out of his element, the Buryat lama began to fear that he was about to be precipitated into his next rebirth. He was spared, however, and in due course reached Peking, from where he travelled on to Urga. There he was reunited with his old mentor, Chöpel Pelzangpo, and received further blessings and initiations from him as well as from the Jebtsundamba Khutukhtu.

News that Dorzhiev was in Urga quickly filtered through to Trans-Baikalia, and soon two representatives appeared who had been sent by the Buryat monks and laity to request him to return to his own people. Naturally he agreed to do so. It was probably not the first time that he had been back in Buryatia since settling in Lhasa in 1880. There are records that maintain that he had returned there in 1889 on a

fund-raising mission for his monastic college, and as late as 1896, on the
orders of the Dalai Lama, he is said to have spent a year at the Gusinoye
Ozero Datsan near Selenginsk, seat of the Khambo Bandido Lama, 'not
as a political agent but as a scholar'.[3] There may have been other occasions too. This time he certainly visited the Atsagat Datsan near Khara-
Shiber, where, with great pleasure, he collected the inscribed gold watch
which the Emperor had presented to him for services rendered to Dr
Badmayev's agents in Lhasa. He also proposed to his fellow Buryats that
a great religious meeting-place be established where monks of the main
monasteries could foregather for great assemblies at which teachings
might be given and ceremonies conducted. The suggestion was unani-
mously accepted, and Tehor Kangyur Lama was invited to take charge of
the meeting-place; Dorzhiev himself was also given a responsible post.

Then events began to take a decidedly momentous turn. Some time
before, when he had passed through the Chinese city of Tientsin en route
for Peking, Dorzhiev had met the Russian consul, Aleksey Dimitrievich
Startsev, a man of complex family background. His natural father was
the Decembrist, Nikolai Aleksandrovich Bestuzhev (1791–1855), who had
been exiled to Siberia along with his brother for their part in the palace revolution attempted in December 1822 by some liberal officers of the Guard,
the élite corps of the Russian army staffed by members of the new gentry.
During his exile, which he had put to good use investigating Buryat customs,
economic conditions and so forth,[4] Bestuzhev had found consolation in the
arms of a Buryat lady, who bore him two sons. Later this lady contracted
a more permanent liaison with a merchant, D.D. Startsev, who magnanimously accepted both boys into his family and gave them his name.[5]

Dorzhiev had told Startsev about his mission but the consul had
refused to accept him on an official basis because he was travelling
without retinue or formal substantiation of status. He did, however,
wire the news of Dorzhiev's progress to a very prominent figure in
the highest court circles in St Petersburg: Prince Esper Esperovich
Ukhtomsky (1861–1921).

*

The old Imperial Russian eagle faced in two directions and foreign
policy was subject to a similar dualism. There were those who urged a
westward orientation, notably concentration on the Balkans, maritime
access to the Mediterranean through the Black Sea and the Dardenelles,
and Pan-Slavism in Eastern Europe. But there were also those who felt
that Russian destiny lay in the East, even at the risk of conflict with
Great Britain, China and the rising power of Japan. Reverses in the

West caused Russia to turn increasingly to the East during the latter part of the nineteenth century, which perfectly suited certain other great powers, notably Germany. Within the Eastern lobby at least two factions were active. One was concerned with economic concessions in Korea: the so-called Yalu Timber Concession. The other faction, of which Ukhtomsky was a leading member along with Count Sergey Yulevich Witte, the highly capable Finance Minister, and Dr Piotr Aleksandrovich Badmayev, had more grandiose notions of Russia's role in Asia.

Scholar, collector, traveller, political thinker, poet, entrepreneur, publisher and editor, Prince Ukhtomsky was a remarkable man by any token – but a man too of contrasts if not of contradictions. A deep interest in mysticism, for instance, was combined with great commercial acumen, and political manoeuvring with a lifelong devotion to disinterested scholarly research.

Princes were not rare in Imperial Russia; they were certainly not scions of the Imperial House of Romanov but landowning aristocrats of a lesser kind, inferior to the likes of grand dukes and counts. Ukhtomsky could therefore only boast of relatively blue blood, though on his mother's side his ancestors included Sir Samuel Greig (1735–88) and his son Aleksey Samuilovich (1775–1845), who, though of Scottish origin, saw distinguished service as admirals in the Russian Navy during the wars against the Turks. Ukhtomsky's father, Esper Alekseyevich, was a naval man too and founded a steamship company to link the Baltic with India and China via the Black Sea.[6]

While still a student of Philosophy and Slavonic Studies at St Petersburg University, Ukhtomsky developed a keen interest in Buddhism. It was therefore quite appropriate for him on graduating in 1884 to enter the service of the Department of Foreign Creeds of the Ministry of the Interior, which put him at once in direct touch with the Buddhists of Russia and enabled him both to study their religion and culture closely and to start assembling his great scholarly collection of Lamaist art. Upon this collection, the first of its kind in the world, the German orientalist Albert Grünwedel based a pioneering study to which the prince himself contributed a spirited and self-revealing preface.[7] Ukhtomsky wrote that he loved the noble spiritual ideals of Buddhism, as he did all the high mystical endeavours of humanity. He loved too its humanitarian tolerance, and he admired the valour of the missionaries who had borne Shakyamuni Buddha's teachings across lofty mountain ranges and inhospitable deserts to the far-flung corners of Asia. But above all he believed that a revitalized Buddhism, perhaps based at a restored Bodh-Gaya and under the spiritual leadership of the Dalai Lama of Tibet, could reawaken and unify the disparate Buddhist groups of

Asia and initiate a regeneration, the basic aim of which would be to 'set again the great mass of people on the road of adoration of "the master"'.[8]

Between 1886 and 1890 Ukhtomsky made several journeys to the East, visiting the Buddhist temples of Trans-Baikalia and Peking as well as travelling extensively in Mongolia and as far afield as Ceylon (Sri Lanka).

This and his burgeoning reputation as an Orientalist secured him, at the very last minute, an invitation to be the chronicler of a grand tour of the East that Crown Prince Nicholas, the future Emperor Nicholas II, was to make in 1890 and 1891. Designed to further Nicholas's diplomatic education, this was also a cunning ploy to take the prince's errant mind off the bright young things that were over occupying his attention in St Petersburg.

The tour started with a train journey to Trieste, where a Russian naval squadron including the frigate *Pamyat Azova* was waiting to sail the Imperial party via Greece, Egypt, the Suez Canal and Aden to India, where the obligatory tiger hunt took place as well as visits to Delhi, Jaipur and some of the Buddhist holy places. Later, when the frigate docked at Colombo, some of Nicholas's entourage took the opportunity of inviting Colonel Henry Steel Olcott aboard. One of them, undoubtedly Ukhtomsky, had earlier tried to contact the American Theosophist at Adyar near Madras, where the Theosophical Society had established its international headquarters, but unfortunately he was away in Burma at the time. This unidentified Russian visitor had expressed interest in Theosophy and bought some books. Olcott later recalled:

> I went aboard the frigate and spent an hour in delightful conversation with Prince Hespère Oukhtomsky [sic], Chief of the Département des Cultes in the Ministère de l'Intérieure, who was acting as the [Crown Prince's] Private Secretary on this tour, and Lieutenant N. Crown of the Navy Department at St Petersburg, both charming men. I found myself particularly drawn to Oukhtomsky because of his intense interest in Buddhism, which for many years he has made a special study among the Mongolian lamaseries. He has also given much time to the study of other religions. He was good enough to invite me to make the tour of the Buddhist monasteries of Siberia. He asked me for a copy of my Fourteen Propositions,[9] so that he might translate them and circulate them among the Chief Priests of Buddhism throughout the empire. This has since been done.[10]

After Ceylon, the tour proceeded to Siam, Indo-China, Japan (where an attempt was made on Nicholas' life) and China, then the Imperial party returned to St Petersburg via Vladivostok and Siberia. In Buryatia, where, as we have noted, he was reverently received by the local people, the Heir Apparent camped for a night or so in the vicinity of the Atsagat Datsan. The lamas took advantage of this opportunity to obtain permission to build a new dukhang of some two storeys on the very spot where Nicholas' tent had been pitched. Aptly, it was dedicated to White Tara and served as a choira (a school for the study of higher Buddhist dialectics).

The book of the tour that Ukhtomsky subsequently wrote, published in six parts between 1893 and 1897 by the Leipzig firm of Brockhaus, won him instant acclaim and fame. Lavishly produced with many fine engravings, it was the first popular ethnographic work in the Russian language, and soon afterwards English, French and German editions appeared.[11] Such was the level to which it lifted Ukhtomsky's standing that for several years he was consulted by the Emperor on Far Eastern policy as well as giving advice on the government of the eastern regions of Russia.

*

The prince naturally possessed very evolved political views of his own and he was not reticent about them. Through his newspaper, *St Peterburgskiye Viedomosti* (St Petersburg News), of which he was editor as well as publisher, he could, moreover, shape public opinion.[12] He argued forcefully that Russia possessed deep spiritual affinities with the peoples of Asia and so was their natural leader: the one world power that could benevolently introduce science and progress into that unawakened continent and guide it towards spiritual renaissance. Russia should therefore pursue an expansionistic policy for 'essentially there are not, and there cannot be, any frontiers for us in Asia'.[13] What he had in mind, however, was not a crude, bludgeoning imperialism of the kind practised by the British, who had paltry understanding of the spiritual traditions of their subject peoples and were mainly interested in commercial exploitation. Russia, Ukhtomsky felt, being on a higher spiritual plane altogether, would not need to use forceful means as it could depend mainly on benevolence to fulfil its manifest destiny. Indeed, he at times talked as though the whole matter were so divinely ordained that it must happen of its own accord: organically, as it were, by some 'process of natural fusion'. This might explain why he also made what seem on the surface to be very contradictory statements, such as: 'No one has any int·ntion of attacking England in Asia',[14] while he clearly regarded India as a natural part of the future Russian hegemony in Asia that he foresaw.

*

Despite his disparagement of Anglo-Saxon huckstering, Ukhtomsky built up considerable commercial interests of his own. Besides his newspaper interests, he was Director of the Russo-Chinese Bank, which was formed in 1895. The bank benefitted enormously from the defence treaty he helped negotiate the following year in St Petersburg with Li Hung-chang (1823–1901), a statesman who at the time was virtual ruler of China. In the treaty, China granted Russia permission to build a railway across Manchuria with the bank's finance; as the railway zone was leased to and policed by Russians, it became in effect a strip of Russian territory within Manchuria, and hence the major spearhead of Russian penetration in the area. Ukhtomsky was a member of the Board of the Manchurian Railway too, as well as being involved in Mongolor, a gold-mining concession in Mongolia operated by a Franco-Belgian company partly owned by the Russo-Chinese Bank. Mongolor was managed from Urga by a certain Russian of German origin named von Groth, who had previously worked for the Chinese Customs Service – he had reputedly been assistant to Sir Robert Hart – a connection he exploited when first starting out gold-mining on his own account in Mongolia before the turn of the century. It was in fact his own concession to mine in the Tushetu and Setsen Khan aimaks that was later transferred to Mongolor, but it was never very profitable.[15] Von Groth was also believed by the British – who imputed many sinister things to this shadowy figure – to be interested in extending Mongolor's activities into Tibet, where there were known to be rich gold deposits, and in 1902 it was reported that he had applied to the Chinese for permission to extend the Trans-Siberian railway into the Land of Snows.[16]

*

Tibet itself had for a long time been a focus of Russian interest. During the late nineteenth century Russian explorers tried to force their way to Lhasa in much the same way as their British and French counterparts. Some of the earliest attempts were those of Colonel (later Major-General) N. M. Przhevalsky (1849–85). His first expedition took him only as far as the northern parts of Tibet and the headwaters of the Yangtse, but that of 1879–80 was a more determined affair personally backed by the Emperor. Accompanied by an escort of picked Cossacks, Przhevalsky got within a hundred and fifty miles of Lhasa before being turned back by a large Tibetan force. Then in 1899 the Imperial Russian Geographical Society, of which Ukhtomsky was a prominent member, sent an expedition to Central Asia and Tibet under the leadership of Captain Petr Kuzmich Kozlov (1863–1935). This too was financed by the Emperor and had an escort of soldiers. Kozlov got as far as the eastern Tibetan town of Chamdo but was also refused permission to proceed to Lhasa. Again, Tibetan soldiers were dispatched to prevent him from advancing, and his party skirmished with them. The first Russian explorer to reach the holy city did so in August 1900 and was able to stay there until September 1901. This was Gombozhav Tsebekovich Tsybikov (1873–1930), who as a Buryat was able to pass himself off as a pilgrim in Tibet.

Ukhtomsky was a member both of the Imperial Russian Geographical Society and of the Russian Committee for the Study of Central and Eastern Asia, which was set up by Professors S.F. Ol'denburg and V. V. Radlov. At these learned institutions and elsewhere he rubbed shoulders with the cream of Russian orientalists and explorers during what is often called the Golden Age of Russian Orientalism. He himself was throughout his life a keen advocate of what the Russians call scientific and we in the West call scholarly research, and when in a position to do so was also a staunch protector of ethnic minorities, notably the Buryats. His championship of their cause in St Petersburg brought him many heart-felt letters of gratitude, often accompanied by presents. He called for better health care for them, for instance, and defended them against both forcible conversion to Christianity and the arbitrary excesses of local officials.

In religious matters Ukhtomsky was on the side of tolerance, for though a Christian himself, he was conscious of the spiritual authenticity of other religions, notably of course Buddhism, and may well have sympathized with the universalist view that in their highest forms all the religions of the world point to the same ultimate reality. This is not to say that he had reservations about Christian missionaries proselytizing in Asia, however. Far from it; he wanted to see the Gospel disseminated there:

[The study of the Buddhist cult] is, without mentioning its scientific importance, the basis from which our missionaries, whose success is still so limited, can, if they want to lead our country towards a spiritual renaissance and if they propose making themselves pioneers for the Christian faith, obtain the wherewithal to make themselves educational workers and scouts in order to carry into unexplored deserts of High Asia the light of a superior faith.[17]

Ukhtomsky was also an advocate of reform and greater social freedom. He used *St Peterburgskiye Viedomosti* as a medium through which to express his liberal views – but at a cost. The wrath of the reactionary authorities, who maintained a draconian censorship of the press, fell upon him and *St Peterburgskiye Viedomosti* was subjected to a series of

warnings and punitive bans. Eventually Ukhtomsky was even forbidden
to sign his editorials. For this and other reasons, his political star
gradually waned and by 1900 he could write 'I have not the influence
which I formerly enjoyed'[18], and he had completely lost the Emperor's
ear by the time Rasputin appeared on the scene, though he still retained
his senior court rank as a Gentleman of the Bedchamber. Thereafter he
turned more and more to his scientific interests.

*

It is clear, then, why in 1898, when his star was still very much
in the ascendant, Ukhtomsky should have shown a close interest in
the movements of Agvan Dorzhiev. For a start, Buryat lamas like
Dorzhiev, who regularly and freely commuted from Russia across the
Lamaist heartland of Central Asia to Urga and Lhasa, were the natural
harbingers of his grand vision of Russian leadership in Asia.

'Trans-Baikalia is the key to the heart of Asia', Ukhtomsky wrote;
'the forward post of Russian civilization on the frontiers of the "Yellow
Orient."'[19] But more than that: with his entrée to the Dalai Lama,
Dorzhiev was in a unique position to be able to help Ukhtomsky and
his associates further their plans and projects – if Dorzhiev was not
already engaged in doing so.

So in 1898 Dorzhiev received a letter from Ukhtomsky summoning
him to St Petersburg. It took the good lama by surprise and threw
him into something of a dilemma. He was an influential person in
Trans-Baikalia, he reflected, but if he were to depart, would his plans
for the advancement of his fellow Buryats be accomplished? But the call
was not one to be lightly dismissed, so in company with Taizan Tseten,
a high Buryat official, he set off for the Russian capital, travelling on the
still uncompleted Trans-Siberian Railway. Once across the Urals he was
in country that was entirely new and foreign to him: Europe, the dynamic
cradle of contemporary civilization and culture. Here secular values held
sway as opposed to the ancient spiritual ones to which he was so deeply
devoted. How would Ngawang Lobsang (Dorzhiev), the master Buddhist
dialectician of the debating courtyards of Drepung monastic university,
fare in such a Babylonian milieu? It was an interesting question.

CHAPTER SIX

Mission to Europe
1898 – 1899

In his visions of grandeur, Peter the Great conceived of building himself a palace to match the splendours of Versailles. The autocrat's dreams became reality twenty-nine kilometres west of his capital, on an incline overlooking the steel waters of the Gulf of Finland. Here arose his summer residence of Peterhof (now Petrodvorets): a place of magnificent palaces and pavilions set in a manicured parkland of arbours, gilded statues, fountains and waterways. Somewhere in this magnificent complex, Prince Ukhtomsky presented Agvan Dorzhiev to Nicholas II, Emperor of all the Russias, early in 1898.

History has heaped ignominy upon Nicholas II. Certainly he had fine feelings, high ideals, perfect manners, a deep love of his family and a streak of genuine religious devotion – some even say a dash of mysticism – but he conspicuously lacked the robust qualities essential in anyone wishing to continue to play the Great Autocrat in the tradition of his domineering father, Alexander III. So this 'frail, bearded figure with the strange, wistful eyes ... whose feeble shoulders seemed incapable of supporting the mantle of authority which, like a shroud, hung over them',[1] misjudged and vacillated when he should have been clear and decisive, and time and again during periods of crisis in his anguished reign he steered the ship of state onto the rocks of disaster.

Two very brief accounts survive of the meeting at Peterhof: that of Dorzhiev himself, and that of the Narkomindel official L.E. Berlin, which disagree quite fundamentally on which party took the initiative.

According to Dorzhiev, the Emperor, speaking through Ukhtomsky, mentioned 'ways in which Russia could benefit Tibet' while the 'hand of the enemy [i.e. Britain] was not withdrawn', and suggested that a Russian representative be sent to Tibet. To this Dorzhiev could only explain that both the Dalai Lama and his government, as well as lay and monastic opinion in Tibet, were all firmly resolved that no foreigner should enter their land, so for the time being the notion of a Russian representative in Lhasa or even of Russo-Tibetan rapprochement was not feasible. With diplomatic handling, however, and two or three meetings of the present kind, there might be a possibility of disposing the Tibetans more favourably towards the Russians. The Emperor, Ukhtomsky and other Russians present were not pleased with this.

Berlin, however, suggests that Dorzhiev transmitted a verbal request from the Dalai Lama to the Emperor that Russia give assistance to Tibet. To this the Emperor apparently replied that before any answer could be given the request would have to be submitted in proper written form. Altogether, Dorzhiev's reception in St Petersburg was 'restrained and mistrustful', except in Imperial 'great power' circles, where the idea of Russo-Tibetan rapprochement found favour. Here Dorzhiev was promised support.[2]

Putting both accounts together and weighing them against subsequent events, it would seem that Dorzhiev probably did ask the Emperor if Russia was prepared to help Tibet if she needed assistance. Nicholas was not prepared to commit himself, but he and Ukhtomsky did raise the question of Russian representation in Lhasa. Dorzhiev could in his turn give no positive response, so neither party derived much satisfaction from the meeting, but it was nevertheless important in opening communications between Lhasa and St Petersburg.

Dorzhiev also presented petitions from the Dalai Lama at the Russian Foreign Ministry. Among these was a request for the establishment of a Buddhist meeting place in St Petersburg: not necessarily a purpose-built temple but some kind of shrine, perhaps in one of the foreign embassies. As the journal *Stoitel* announced:

> In view of the great number of people professing the Buddhist faith living permanently in Petersburg it has been reported to us that there has arisen a petition for the opening of a small Buddhist oratory for one hundred to two hundred people. The oratory will be situated in one of the central parts of the capital.[3]

Census figures certainly bear out that the numbers of St Petersburg Buddhists were rising at this time. That of 1869 had recorded only one, an intellectual, but in 1897 there were seventy-five and by 1910 a hundred and eighty-four. Most were Buryats and Kalmyks, some of them students and army personnel stationed in the capital; there were also some Buddhists attached to foreign embassies (Chinese, Japanese, Thai); and there was an élite coterie of European sophisticates and intellectuals, most of them from the upper echelons of society, who 'saw in the mystic cults of India and Tibet a kind of universal religion of the future'. These people, if not exactly card-carrying Buddhists, were certainly highly sympathetic. Ukhtomsky is the best known of them.[4]

We can be sure that Ukhtomsky introduced Dorzhiev to all segments of this growing community, as well as to members of the thriving school of St Petersburg orientalism: men like P.K. Kozlov, D. A. Klements, S.F. Ol'denburg and F.I. Stcherbatsky. We have no concrete record of it, but it must have been immensely stimulating for them, far removed as they were from the vital centres of the Buddhist world, to have a learned lama from the court of the Dalai Lama among them; and for his part, Dorzhiev may have begun to appreciate that European Russia could be relatively fertile ground for the dissemination of Buddhism.

*

Characteristically, Dorzhiev has left us no record of his impressions of St Petersburg, but it must have impressed him deeply, for it is a city in the grand style: intended by its founding genius, Peter the Great, to be a full expression of the glory of his Russian empire. Impressive classical and baroque palaces designed by architects from France and Italy, soaring churches with gilded domes, cupolas and spires, triumphal columns and statues, and elegant stucco apartment blocks flank its expansive boulevards and streets, while down its main thoroughfare, Nevsky Prospekt, trams and carriages and even a few motor cars would have bowled along beside the fashionable theatres and shops and coffee houses frequented by the beau monde.

But St Petersburg always had its dark side too: those Dostoyevskian quarters where the poor lived the blighted and brutal lives that sometimes ended in madness or murder; and it was here too that Gogol's down-trodden chinoviks were engulfed by mountains of superfluous paper. It is also a city of water: built on a swamp, sliced in two by the broad Neva and laced with glassy black canals. According to the writer, Vladimir Nabokov, who before his exile was one of the occupants of St Petersburg's palaces, the shadow aspect of the city derived precisely from its watery origins. What, for instance, was the periodic flooding of the Neva if not a 'dim mythological vengeance' (as Pushkin described it) of the primordial swamp gods, 'trying to take back what belonged to them'?[5]

*

From St Petersburg Dorzhiev travelled south to visit the Kalmyks.[6] These people were the remnant of a loose confederation of West

Mongolian clans that had, from around 1632, migrated in successive waves from Dzungaria in Central Asia to the lower Volga region, then a wild Cossack frontier zone. Subduing the local Tatars, they had pursued their traditional Mongolian nomadic lifestyle, augmented with a little occasional banditry, on the steppe between Astrakhan and Stavropol. However, as the expanding Russian empire began to assert its power over the region, particularly during the reign of Catherine II, friction arose for the Kalmyks feared that they might be forced to abandon their old ways for some kind of settled mode of life. As a result, on 5 January 1771 – a propitious day selected by the Dalai Lama's oracle – their leader, Ubashi Khan, inaugurated a grand migration back to their old Dzungarian homelands. However, those living on the far side of the Volga, including members of the Torgut, Lesser Dörbet and Greater Dörbet clans, were unable to cross the river because it did not freeze that year, so could not join the exodus and were therefore obliged to continue to live on European soil. Though many resisted it – some Kalmyks joined the revolt of Emelian Pugachev, the Peasants' Tsar (1773–75) – the price of this was further russification; but even so, they stuck spiritedly to their nomadic ways.

Marvellous horsemen, they contributed crack Cossack cavalry to the Russian Army, some of whom distinguished themselves in the fight against Napoleon in 1812. For this, Emperor Alexander I royally rewarded them with a vast tract of land, the income from which was to be used for the benefit of their people in perpetuity. With these funds a hospital and a number of dispensaries and schools were established. The schools further exposed the Kalmyks to Russian culture, but attempts were made to preserve their own culture too. First the Kalmyk nobility, and later the ordinary people, had been converted to Tibetan Buddhism before the migration from Asia. This was maintained in the lower Volga region, and during the early days connections with Lhasa were maintained. Young Kalmyks made the arduous journey to the holy city to pursue their higher religious studies. The outstanding Kalmyk lama of this period was Zaya Pandita (1599–1662), who devised a Kalmyk alphabet (the so-called 'clear writing,' 1648) and translated many Tibetan texts.

From the accounts of people like Benjamin Bergmann, who travelled among the Kalmyks in the early nineteenth century, it is clear that Kalmyk spirituality very closely followed its Mongol-Tibetan prototypes, even to the extent of retaining vestiges of pre-Buddhist ecstatic shamanism and folk religion. Their Buddhist pecking order included high lamas, bakshis or teachers, and ordinary monks (gelong); below these there were novices and lay followers (khuvarak[7]). All religious people were held in high esteem. Their khurul or temples, meanwhile, like their homes, were tents of the classic Mongolian sort – lattice-work frames covered with thick felt – or else wooden structures that could be dismantled and carted from place to place. From about the eighteenth century onwards, brick and stone khurul were also constructed:

> The monasteries contained temples, chapels, cells and workshops. The main temple usually had a high central space crowned by a tower; it was richly ornamented with carving, painting, bronze sculpture, and religious figures.[8]

Obos or cairns, primitive sorts of Buddhist stupas, were also erected for ritual purposes.

Dorzhiev's decision to visit the Kalmyks may have been in part at least inspired by a Kalmyk lama named Baza Bakshi (Baza Menkedzhuyev) whom he had met some years previously in Lhasa. Baza had set out for the holy city in the summer of 1891 with the aspiration 'to make known and renew a path that could be taken by the many spiritual beings in our country'. On the way he heard of a 'Gegen Soibun, a Mongol, a Buryat, and according to the tales of his people there was no man more elevated in Tibet than he'. Certainly Dorzhiev gave great assistance to the Kalmyks in Lhasa – 'He managed everything for us in every way', Baza reported. While among the Kalmyks, Dorzhiev stayed at Baza Bakshi's monastery, Dundul Khurul, in the Maloderbet ulus.[9]

As the link with Lhasa had been discontinued during the time of the Seventh Dalai Lama, Kelsang Gyatso (1708–1757), and a hiatus of a hundred and forty years elapsed, the Kalmyks were honoured and delighted to greet Agvan Dorzhiev, a Tsenyi Khenpo at the right hand of the Dalai Lama, when he arrived among them in March 1898. He performed religious rites in their nomadic encampments and, with good command of the Kalmyk dialect, gave wise discourses in which he spoke particularly of the evils of alcohol abuse, to which many of the less pious were prone. The Kalmyk faithful reciprocated by giving him gifts for the Dalai Lama.

This was the first of a number of visits Dorzhiev made to the Kalmyks, and for many years he took them under his wing:

> ... the welfare of the Kalmyks, both as co-religionists and fellow Mongolians, was close to Agvan Dorzhiev's heart. As they were separated by hundreds of miles from the important centres of the 'Yellow Faith' – the word 'lamaism' was not known to them – and entirely left to their own devices spiritually, his main objective was the training of an indigenous clergy endowed with inward steadfastness.[10]

He helped establish religious schools among them as well as higher educational establishments (choira). He also attempted to unify the Kalmyk and Buryat dialects, and to Latinize Kalmyk spelling. His efforts to draw the Kalmyks more closely into the Lamaist fold were not entirely successful, however: they were simply too far out on a limb ever to liaise closely with the other Mongolian and the Tibetan peoples.

It would seem that Dorzhiev visited Kalmykia twice in 1898. On the first occasion he was approached by a young zaisan (nobleman) of the Greater Derbet clan named Ovshe Norzunov (born 1874?), who had faithfully attended his religious meetings. Though educated, Norzunov had elected to adhere to the traditional nomadic lifestyle rather than take up an official post. He was also seriously devoted to Buddhism, influenced in this direction after the death of his father by his pious mother. He now asked Dorzhiev how he could strengthen his religious practice. Dorzhiev urged him to make a pilgrimage to Lhasa.

*

A month or so later, in June 1898, Joseph Deniker (1852–1918) had an unusual visitor at his Paris home. The caller, a Buryat, presented letters of introduction from one of Deniker's Russian friends, and asked whether he would like to make the acquaintance of a Tibetan priest attached to the court of the Dalai Lama. Deniker said he would. An hour later Agvan Dorzhiev was at his door.

Though of French origin, this worthy scholar had in fact been born Iosif Egorovich Deniker in Astrakhan, and had gone to school with Kalmyk and Cossack children. After studying Chemistry in Moscow and St Petersburg, he became interested in anthropology and moved to Paris, where he obtained his doctorate and in 1888 was appointed Librarian of the National Museum of Natural History. Today he is best remembered for a classification system of human races based purely on physical characteristics, but he was also a keen student of Buddhism and, with a native command of Russian, served as a channel of communication between Russian orientalists and the Western world, translating the learned articles that appeared in the Russian scholarly press into French. He was in constant correspondence with V.V. Grigoriev, the Secretary General of the Imperial Russian Geographical Society, and he certainly knew Prince Ukhtomsky.[11]

Deniker wrote that on their first meeting Dorzhiev was in European dress. He was 'short and stocky' and

His bronzed face was of the keen Mongolian type, and he appeared intelligent and kindly. In the course of conversation, I questioned him about Buddhism; and then, in his turn, he began to question me, wishing to know if there were many Buddhists in Paris. I told him that the number of his co-religionists in my country was very small, but that many French scholars were interested in the doctrine of the Buddha, and that in the Musée Guimet there was a collection of many objects of the Buddhist cult. A few days later I took him to see the museum. He was very pleased with his reception . . .[12]

On 27 June 1898, Khambo Lama Agvan Dorzhiev celebrated a Buddhist ceremony at the Musée Guimet: an 'Invocation at Shamyamuni Buddha and All the Buddhas to Inspire all Beings with Love and Compassion'. Dorzhiev himself says that a very large audience of some four hundred people was present. According to the published programme, his translator was Buddha Rabdanov (1853–1923), an educated Buryat from the Aga steppe who in his time visited both Tibet and several Western European countries, including France, where he lectured on Mongolia and Tibet at the Musée Guimet, Italy and Belgium. [13] Two other sources mention that Deniker acted as translator, so perhaps more than one person served in this capacity.

If he adhered faithfully to the official programme, Dorzhiev first prostrated himself before the altar, on which were disposed various sacred objects and offerings, then sat down in the seat prepared for him and went on to summarize, through his translators, the history of the propagation of Buddhism in Tibet. After that he recited a Tibetan prayer requesting all buddhas, bodhisattvas and enlightened beings to descend among the assembly.

He then recited *Puntsok*, a prayer of five shlokas (verses) 'denoting love and respect for Shakyamuni Buddha, the Future Buddha Maitreya, Nagarjuna, Aryadeva, Asita [Atisha], and the other sages who have propagated Buddhism in Tibet'. Next followed a prayer of a single shloka asking the Buddhas to accept the offerings which had been prepared, after which his assistants repeated three times, 'either out loud or mentally', the Sanskrit formula *Namo Buddhâya, Namo Dharmâya, Namo Sanghâya* ('Homage to the Buddha, his Teaching, and the Community of his Followers'). This done, Dorzhiev flung flowers on the altar, his assistants following suit. After another short prayer, he finished by reciting a prayer in three shlokas entitled *Kyabné*, asking the holy buddhas to protect all beings for all time and deliver them from evil, misfortune and unhappiness; also to spread happiness both in religious and secular society.[14] 'Just through this it was possible that some aspirations [arose] which left good karmic interests', the good lama later wrote.

Seeing some of these proceedings recorded on old-fashioned wax cylinders, Dorzhiev was greatly impressed and, fired with enthusiasm, he bought a phonograph and some wax cylinders for his own use. He seems to have acquired a camera too. Obviously he had a propensity for modern Western gadgetry.

Dorzhiev was also impressed with Paris. 'It is a very beautiful city to behold', he wrote, 'and has an extremely large population'. Nothing very much seems to have come out of his visit from the political point of view, however. He was unable to meet Prince Henri of Orléans as he had hoped because he was out of the country, but he was introduced to someone he calls 'Khlemintso' (Clemenceau?): an aristocrat who had great respect for Buddhism.

He also met a woman whom he simply calls 'Alexandra'. This may have been the remarkable French traveller, mystic and writer Alexandra David-Néel (1868–1969), who was herself to go to the East in 1911 and spent some twenty years there studying Tibetan language and Buddhist philosophy. We know that Madame David-Néel frequented the Musée Guimet, for it was there when she was just twenty-three years old that she first developed a liking for things oriental. She may well, then, have attended Dorzhiev's ceremony, and if so, it was probably an important formative influence on her remarkable life of spiritual adventure. This was to culminate in 1924, when she became the first European woman to enter Lhasa. Dorzhiev for his part was impressed with this 'Alexandra', saying that 'even though she was born as a female she had trained herself to be wise' – high praise from someone who was no feminist. Less gallantly, he also calls her old, though at the time she would only have been about thirty-one.[15]

*

Joseph Deniker also makes the remarkable assertion that after Paris Dorzhiev went to London, though whether as a matter of transit or for some specific purpose is not stated. This is of course feasible, for in England too there were scholars who were connected with the international Buddhist network, so Dorzhiev would have had contacts. No records of such a visit have been discovered, however, though it is difficult to rule out the possibility that Dorzhiev did visit Britain at some stage, for other sources assert as much. The Buryat explorer A. I. Termen, for instance, quotes a fellow Buryat called Aginsky as saying that Dorzhiev 'hopes to spread it [Buddhism] in the Russian capital as effectively as in London and Paris', and Joseph Deniker's son, George, says quite explicitly in a letter of 1981 that Dorzhiev visited London in 1913.[16] Finally, there is in the Russian archives an undated letter from Dorzhiev to the explorer Piotr Kuz'mich Kozlov which says:

Greetings. Please let me know as soon as possible, so that I can set out via London for Darjeeling. I would humbly suggest that it you are coming to Peter[sburg] in the near future that we discuss things, if that is not inconvenient to you.[17]

A couple of months after Paris, Dorzhiev was back among the Kalmyks, where he found Ovshe Norzunov determined, even though married and the father of a baby child, to make a pilgrimage to Lhasa. This was in its way very useful for Dorzhiev. He promptly suggested they travel together, and in August 1898 they left the lower Volga region, taking the Trans-Siberian as far as Verkhneudinsk and then proceeding in a tarantass[18] to Urga, where they were put up for a month by Euzon Bakshi, the Tutor of the Jebtsundamba Khutukhtu. Then, on 5 October, Norzunov set out for Lhasa bearing a sealed letter for someone Dorzhiev calls 'the Kalön'; that is, one of the members of the Dalai Lama's Kashag or Cabinet, the chief executive body of the Tibetan government. He also bore gifts for the Dalai Lama himself. Dorzhiev, who for some obscure reason remained in Urga, was in effect reporting on what had happened in St Petersburg and asking for further orders.

Norzunov and his two companions, a Mongol lama and a Kalmyk bakshi of the Lesser Derbet clan named Ochir Dzungruev, followed the official postal route for several days, then veered off to visit the monastery of Yungdrung-beise (probably Roerich's Yum-beise Khüre) before exchanging their horses for camels to cross the Gobi. After travelling for twenty-two days they reached An-hsi, where, taking advantage of his Oriental features to pass himself off as a Mongol pilgrim, Norzunov joined the caravan of a group of Kurluk Mongols, who agreed to guide him across their uninviting domains in the Tsaidam region.

Unfortunately, as the caravan approached its destination, Norzunov's cover was blown. So far he had attempted to conceal the fact that he was a Russian subject by writing his travel journal in Kalmyk script, and though this differed only slightly from Eastern Mongolian script, the differences were spotted. Then, as he undressed during a halt, it was also noticed that he was wearing a cloth jacket of European cut under his fur outer garments. It looked for a moment as though he would end up being ignominiously dragged before the beise, the hereditary prince of the Kurluks whose headquarters were at Kurluk-Nor, but a bribe of ten lan[19] secured his guides' silence; he also burned the offending jacket in front of them for good measure. Duly appeased, the Kurluks then led him on to the domains of the Teijiner Mongols on the southern edge of Tsaidam, where he hired horses to carry him up onto the Tibetan plateau and on across the Chang-Tang to Nagchukha.

Having evaded the guards posted at Nagchukha to prevent foreigners
gate-crashing the Forbidden Land, he crossed several passes across 'the
high mountain ranges of Gandan' without experiencing any of the
adverse effects against which he had been warned in Urga. In due
course, safe and sound, he came to the Go-La, where he caught his
first glimpse of the gilded roofs of Lhasa. The sight filled him with
overwhelming joy. He jumped down from his horse, prostrated three
times upon the ground and recited several prayers.

A few days after his arrival in March 1899, Norzunov went to the
Potala to present the Dalai Lama with the letter and the gifts with which
he had been entrusted by Agvan Dorzhiev. He was conducted to the
Red Palace, an angular building rising out of the massive main white
structure, which is where the Dalai Lama lived and worked when in
residence. On the roof, which is where the main entrance to the building
is situated — to get to the lower storeys you actually have to work your
way down from the top — were the Dalai Lama's private quarters
and Namgyal Dratsang, the 'magnificent palace' that accommodated
his private staff. Norzunov was immediately reminded of his teacher,
Agvan Dorzhiev, for it was here that the Buryat lama formerly lived.

Marvellous as these sights were, they did not compare with the
'astonishment and joy' that overtook Norzunov when he at last gazed
on the 'luminous face' of the Dalai Lama, who was seated on his
throne dressed in sumptuous yellow robes and surrounded by acolytes.
Respectfully, Norzunov knelt down and touched his head to the ground
three times, then handed the great lama Dorzhiev's presents. The Dalai
Lama reciprocated by laying his hands on the Kalmyk's head in blessing,
after which he was given some rice and tea thought to possess special
mystic qualities because the Dalai Lama had already tasted it. 'The tea
was very good', Norzunov later wrote, 'with a delicious bouquet'.[20]

Finally, as Norzunov was leaving the audience, he was given two
hundred lan (one lan = 10 units of gold) on the orders of the Dalai
Lama for faithfully carrying out Dorzhiev's commission.

Norzunov left Lhasa reluctantly in April 1899 with what Dorzhiev
calls 'a genuine answer from the Dalai Lama'. Following in the footsteps
of his master, he travelled south to Darjeeling and Calcutta, where he
retained the services of a Mongolian called 'Lup-San' (Lobsang?), who
spoke Chinese and Hindi, before catching a boat for China.

During the voyage 'Lup-san' noticed that Norzunov was carrying
a lot of money. 'You're lucky you've an honest man like me to deal
with', the Mongol said; 'anyone else would have quickly snatched all
you've got.'

'How would they have done that?' Norzunov asked.

'Oh, it would have been easy – just a matter of slipping a little poison into your food and running off with the loot.'

Norzunov smelt a rat. From that moment onward he was on his guard: if, for instance, he found that a cup of tea had been poured out for him, he would offer it politely to his man and pour another for himself.

They were quarantined in Penang for six days in May, then went on to Hong Kong, by which time things had gone from bad to worse. Knowing no Chinese himself, Norzunov was at Lup-san's mercy – and the wily Mongolian knew it. It finally became a case of the servant becoming the master – and if not actually stealing his funds, then spending them as though there were no tomorrow. The parting of the ways came at Tientsin, and from there Norzunov went on alone to Peking, where he arrived on 17 June. On 25 June, he hired camels and guides at Kalgan to take him to Urga, where he was reunited with Agvan Dorzhiev on 25 July.

*

Lev Berlin says that in the letter that Norzonov brought, Dorzhiev was requested to 'return immediately to Lhasa to help with a number of state problems'. Dorzhiev himself says that the Dalai Lama thanked him for his own letter and presents, and described the political situation in Lhasa, saying that opinion was split between three factions and asking him to come quickly to discuss matters on a personal basis.[21] He needed no further bidding but at once got ready to leave, and in September was once more on the caravan trails of Central Asia heading for Peking and the Chinese ports. It was then on by sea to Calcutta and so via Darjeeling back to Lhasa.

Dorzhiev arrived back in the holy city in December 1898. He must have been heavily laden with treasures, for at the Monlam Chenmo festivities of the following February, when 'the supreme leader of men and gods' was invited to take his place in a vast gathering of thousands of learned lamas, he presented him with 'diamonds and many other kinds of gems, various silks, and one hundred and eight silver ingots':

And to each of the noble assembly I offered five zho. At the row of golden butter lamps offered by Longdol Ngawang Lobsang [1719–1795, tutor of the Seventh Dalai Lama] before Lhasa's great Jowo, I placed new golden lamps made from about forty sang of gold. I also made gifts of gold and donated thousands of the five kinds of offerings to all the supreme supports, the greatest of which are the two Jowo [the statues in the Jokhang and Ramoché temples]. In each of the great monasteries of Sera, Drepung and Ganden I offered or requested an abundant distribution of provisions. Without wasting the faith-substances [given by] many benefactors, this was the best I could do to produce the good fortune capable of fulfilling all their wishes.[22]

Despite this, which one would have expected to heighten his popularity, Joseph Deniker maintains that he 'found that his standing was very much compromised'.[23] His liberalism greatly offended the traditionally ultra conservative monastic establishment, who were particularly scandalized by a photograph he brought back showing him sitting with . . . a Russian woman! Dorzhiev pointed out in his own defence that the revered and compassionate White and Green Taras were of female form; moreover,

> 'In the West, if you wish to have friends, you must have the influence of women. For this reason I would not have wished to displease the Russian lady, who is already a fervent admirer of our religion.'[24]

He was denounced too for having taken photographs of Tibet to exhibit in the West and was forced to destroy his camera in front of the whole court of the Dalai Lama. Nevertheless, Deniker maintains that 'with a tact characteristically Asiatic' he managed to redeem his position.

Dorzhiev himself understandably says nothing of all this, merely recording that in reward for his services, the Dalai Lama, 'mistaking a clod of earth for a nugget of gold,' conferred on him the rank of Great Abbot, which was a political rather than a religious accolade. He also gave him presents and offered up prayers for the success of the Buddha-dharma. Purchok Rinpoché moreover bestowed on him the authority to perform monastic ordinations. 'Make sure you create a lot of fully ordained monks', the great tulku told his former student.

Politically, Dorzhiev did indeed find opinion split three ways on his return to Lhasa. Firstly, there was a pro-Chinese faction which maintained that 'since the kindness of the Manchu Emperor is so great, even now his compassion will not fail us; so we must not separate ourselves from China'. The second faction disagreed, arguing that the best way to stave off the British threat was to make friends with the Government of India. The third, pro-Russian faction meanwhile maintained that, as Russia was powerful enough to defend Tibet against the British, yet far enough away not to seek to 'devour us', close relations should be established with that nation.

These factions were more or less evenly matched but the pro-Russian one seems to have had the ear of the Dalai Lama and ultimately triumphed, for Dorzhiev was entrusted with another official letter bearing the Dalai Lama's own seal as well as the obligatory presents and told to take them to the Russian Emperor. The exact nature of his brief for this second mission is not clear, but it seems that while the Tibetans in general wished to maintain their policy of isolation, they were now more positively interested in obtaining Russian protection. Berlin merely says that 'Dorzhiev was sent to Russia by the Dalai Lama to obtain a more definite answer from the Russian Emperor'.[25]

There is also in British official records an interesting report by the Deputy Commissioner for Darjeeling, dated 7 October 1901, to the effect that Dorzhiev had been giving out in Lhasa that 'China has been conquered by the English, who have driven the Imperial Court out of Peking, and that within a short time they would invade Tibet'; the Dalai Lama should therefore secure the protection of the Emperor of Russia. His Holiness, 'attaching much weight to his representations', spoke to his advisers (probably the members of his Kashag or Cabinet), upon whose advice he three times consulted the Tsongdu (National Assembly), but this body was 'not unanimous . . . considering that the Russians, like the English, were not Buddhists, and it was moreover uncertain whether China had collapsed altogether as a great power'. After deliberating again with his Kashag (Cabinet), however, His Holiness decided to send Dorzhiev to Russia again with valuable presents, including the one hundred and eight volumes of the Tibetan scriptural canon (Kangyur) written in gold; also 'the consecrated cushion-seat on which the Grand Lama sat on the occasion of his ordination', which was being sent, it was thought, as a prelude to the Lama's visiting St Petersburg himself.[26]

It is not precisely clear to which year this report specifically refers or whether it is in fact a conflation of various reports culled over a period of time. Whatever the case, in March 1900 Dorzhiev did set out for Russia once more, again taking the route through British India. When he arrived at Darjeeling, however, he received some rather disturbing news. Norzunov was in deep trouble.

CHAPTER SEVEN

The Affair of the Steel Bowls
1899 – 1901

After parting from Agvan Dorzhiev in Urga, Ovshe Norzunov had arrived back on his native steppe in August 1899. But he was not to stay there long, for 'On 10 January 1900 I was sent by Agvan Dorzhiev to Paris, on Tibetan business, notably to take delivery of sacred bowls that had been manufactured in that city for Tibetan lamas, because they were unable to make them as well themselves. At the same time the Imperial Russian Georgraphic Society commissioned me to take photographs of Tibet and lent me an excellent camera [for that purpose].'[1]

As regards the bowls, Khensur Ngawang Nima in his notes to Dorzhiev's autobiography records that a Dzungarian named Tsering Dondrup had made an offering of five hundred begging bowls to the Lower Tantric College in Lhasa. Shortly afterwards some were lost when a coracle carrying a group of lamas to a religious ceremony at the college capsized. Tsenzab Rinpoché sent Norzunov to Paris to have replacements made.[2]

On his way to Paris Norzunov may have passed through St Petersburg and had an audience with the Emperor, for a note from Prince Ukhtomsky to Nicholas II begs the Emperor to receive two members of the Kalmyk nobility: one Arlyuev, who 'on his own account has recently equipped and led the expedition known to Your Highness to the Kalmyks of western Mongolia', and Norzunov, who had given the Imperial Russian Geographical Society the notes on the journey to Lhasa for publication. Ukhtomsky adds characteristically:

> You know how I love Buryats, but Kalmyks are closer and more akin to us on account of their martial character and other virtues. We have not yet had the last word on the awakening of Central Asia.[3]

And so to Paris, where Norzunov arrived on 13 (NS 25) January. There, everything to do with the collection and shipment of the bowls was arranged by Joseph Deniker, who no doubt, like everyone else, was fascinated by the Kalmyk's descriptions of Tibet. Some sort of deal must have been struck between them, for Deniker subsequently began publishing Norzunov's accounts of his travels, along with photographs, in the Western press. The two were to remain in contact for many years. Deniker also introduced his guest to Baron Hulot, the Secretary of the Paris Geographical Society, and he attended one of the society's meetings. He inspected the Buddhist collection at the Musée Guimet too.

*

On 28 January (NS 9 February), Norzunov left Paris for Marseilles, where he boarded a steamer, the S S *Dupleix*. A small portion of the steel bowls plus some other articles packed in three crates went along with him; the rest, packed in twenty-eight crates, were to follow a month later on the S S *Annam*. Norzunov reached Calcutta on 22 February (NS 6 March), where he booked into the Continental Hotel, signing the register in the name of 'Myanoheid Hopityant', specifying 'Russian Asiatic' as his nationality and describing himself as belonging to the 'Post and Telegraph Department, Saugata, Stavoopol [sic] Government'. He also had a letter of introduction to the French Consul.

Almost at once things began to turn sour. According to Norzunov's own account, a rifle that he was carrying was found by customs officials and confiscated. Then he learnt from a British citizen of Jewish origin who happened to speak Russian that he would be arrested on his journey to Tibet. This was probably Branson, the Accountant-General of Bengal, who understood Russian and to whom Norzunov was sent by the French Consul. The arrest story was at most only slightly true; so far the Government of India had merely noted him as a suspicious character; but the whiff of trouble was enough to throw Norzunov into paranoia and on 10 March he changed into Chinese dress, booked out of the Continental and caught the train for Darjeeling, where he planned to make a dash for the Tibetan frontier, and from there send some trustworthy person back for his crates.

The train journey north was a nightmare. Not only was his carriage packed, but the heat was suffocating. To make matters worse, opium was being smoked, which gave the good Kalmyk such a headache that he almost passed out. A drink of water might have helped, but he dared not go to station buffets lest the British detect him, and the Indians in his compartment refused to share their water with him for reasons of caste propriety. He did, however, at some unknown station before the railhead at Siliguri, persuade a kindly porter to pour some water into his cupped hands; that was the only refreshment he got.

Worse things were in store at Darjeeling. According to Norzunov himself, when he got there on 11 March, he was stopped and questioned by a police officer. Frightened, he tried to bluff his way out of the situation, pretending he did not understand what he was being asked, but the observant officer spotted a label on his luggage on which his name was written.

Norzunov then went to stay at Ghoom monastery, about five kilometres from Darjeeling, where he was the guest of a Buryat lama named Sherab Gyatso. This man had been sölpön (an attendant who elicits offerings) to the Sengchen Lama of Shigatse: the man who had been executed for assisting the Bengali scholar, Sarat Chandra Das, during his illicit travels in Tibet. Sherab Gyatso also helped Das compile his Tibetan-English Dictionary and, like Das, was a British agent, receiving a stipend of Rs 55/- a month for supplying information on the Tibetans who frequented the Darjeeling markets.[4] As A. Earle, the Deputy Commissioner for Darjeeling, had been detailed to watch Norzunov and see that he did not escape over the border to Tibet, he interviewed Sherab Gyatso about his guest. The lama gave the truth, though economically.

By Norzunov's account, he was on 13 March summoned to the District Commissioner's Office in Darjeeling for further interrogation and then allowed to go free in the charge of Sherab Gyatso until further orders arrived. For the next few months he had to walk every two or three days from Ghoom to present himself at Darjeeling, where the Deputy Commissioner would make a few token notes, after which he would walk back to Ghoom.

Official British records differ somewhat. They maintain that Norzunov was first interrogated by the Darjeeling Police at Ghoom on 12 March. He then declared that he was a trader coming from Peking and proposed to go to Yatung in the Chumbi Valley to await remittances from his agents in Tibet and Mongolia. He disowned the names Hopityant and Norzunov – the Darjeeling Police around this time reported that his real name was Obishak, and that he claimed to be a Khalkha Mongolian. He revised his earlier stories when interrogated again on 26 March, admitting that he had come directly from Paris and concocting a cock-and-bull story to explain his previous fictions.[5] He was also interviewed on 3 April, and then gave confusing information about the ships on which he had sailed to Calcutta.

While at Ghoom, Norzunov got word of his arrest through to Lhasa and at the end of May three men arrived from Tibet with a document certifying that he was a Buddhist and had already made a pilgrimage to Lhasa. Though for some reason he chooses to remain reticent about it – perhaps, to plagiarize Kipling, he was 'muddying the wells of inquiry with the stick of precaution' – one of these travellers was Agvan Dorzhiev, as British intelligence later deduced.

Unfortunately, the letter from Lhasa cut no ice with the Deputy Commissioner, to whom it was delivered by a servant, so, beyond commiserating with his hapless amanuensis, there was little Dorzhiev could do to help the situation. He therefore proceeded on his own way to Calcutta, where he heard that the British had issued a writ offering a reward of Rs 10,000/- to anyone 'who kills and then brings the head of that evil man Dorzhiev'. This must be an instance of poetic licence: the British did not offer rewards for people dead or alive, and in any case Rs 10,000/- was a sum beyond the dreams of Croesus.

The high degree of pressure under which Norzunov was kept eventually eased, and he began to take photographs of the district. Another man also arrived from Tibet in July, to whom he entrusted the three crates that he had personally brought from Paris. Unfortunately, this man died shortly afterwards and his wife refused to return the crates. This upset poor Norzunov so much that he sent several appeals to Joseph Deniker, though for some sinister reason some of Deniker's replies did not reach him: marked 'UNKNOWN', they were returned to sender. Growing ever more desperate, Norzunov again contemplated fleeing to Tibet but his confinement ruled this out, so instead he sent his translator down to Calcutta to find out about his other crates, which had also been subject to various misadventures.

On 24 August the hapless Norzunov was escorted down to Calcutta by three armed policemen. On arrival he was put into a car and whisked to the police station, where, through an interpreter, he was again interrogated about his journey by a stern English officer with white hair. At the end of the interview he was told that he could consider himself under arrest.

While in detention, where by his own account he was fed on Indian food and generally treated well, he heard that his twenty-eight crates had been collected by a powerful person named 'Koukanson'. The ensuing days were an ordeal. Not only was Norzunov suffering from fatigue (probably stress induced) but he was plagued by the enigma of who the mysterious Koukanson could be. Finally, a desperate man, he reported the matter to the police, who made inquiries that subsequently revealed that Koukanson was in fact an employee of the esteemed shipping agents Thomas Cook & Son. Apparently the crates had been impounded in Calcutta because their owner was deemed suspicious by the Government of India. When a day later a man from Cooks came to find out what he wanted done with the crates, Norzunov told him to deliver them to a named person in Tibet. This was done. Cooks were also able to reclaim the three lost crates from the dead man's widow, threatening her with the wrath of the Dalai Lama and possible excommunication if she refused to co-operate. For all these admirable services they billed Norzunov a modest Rs 497/-.

The British had now thoroughly examined Norzunov's luggage. It was found to consist of five cases of personal baggage containing inter alia, one telescope, two phonographs, photographic apparatus, and of course the aforementioned rifle: total value, Rs 295/-. In addition, there were thirty-one boxes of trade goods containing 590 metal bowls, a quantity of strong metal beads and hooks 'for suspending the bowls', three small spirit lamps, five specimen coral branches, three coral necklaces, camera film and silk curtains: total value, Rs 3,300/-. All was cleared through customs apart from the rifle, though due to the various delays that they had undergone the telescope, phonograph and various eletrical gadgets were ruined – or so Norzunov maintained.

As for the man himself, the British authorities had decided that he should be deported 'on the ground that it was undesirable that a Mongolian or quasi-Russian adventurer with several aliases should trade with Tibet through British India, and that though Norzunoff's goods seemed to be harmless, his intentions might be the reverse'. Before the deportation order was carried out, however, he was again interviewed by the Calcutta Police and it was then discovered that he was carrying a passport in the name of 'Ovshe Moutchkindoff Norzunoff' issued in Stavropol Gubernia in September 1899. He had also, it was ascertained, signed his name as 'Ovisha Muchkanoff Norsunoff' on the back of a photograph he had given to a Mongolian in Darjeeling on 26 July, at the same time specifying his age as twenty-six. In addition, he had in his possession a letter of recommendation on Imperial Russian Geographical Society notepaper signed by Prince Ukhtomsky, in which he was described as a member of the society 'undertaking a journey to Tibet on a pilgrimage and in the interests of commerce and science'; also a similar document signed by the General Secretary of the Paris Geographical Society – his friend Baron Hulot, no doubt. He now admitted, too, that he was travelling at the expense of a rich Chinese Mongolian lama living in Urga, by name 'Akchwan Darjilicoff', who had studied in Lhasa for fourteen years and also visited Paris and . . . London. Though only slightly scrambled, Dorzhiev's name seems to have rung no bells in Calcutta.

When this thoroughly undesirable alien was asked by the British authorities whether he wished to be sent home by way of Peking or Paris, he replied, 'Send me via Odessa'. So on 30 August, at the expense of the Government of India, he became a second class passenger on the same ship on which he had made his outward voyage, the S S *Dupleix*. On disembarking at Odessa on 3 October, he lamented that, apart from a few photos of Darjeeling and environs, his journey had been largely unprofitable.

After leaving Norzunov in Ghoom, Dorzhiev had spirited himself out of India and made his way by sea to China. However, in the summer of 1900 the Chinese finally struck back against the innumerable humiliations that the European powers had been inflicting upon the terminal Manchu empire. Since in Peking itself the foreign legations were besieged by the Boxer rebels, Dorzhiev was obliged to travel to Japan. Landing at Nagasaki, he was a keen observer of Japan and its way of life, noting, for instance, that there were 'many people but little land' and 'many Buddhist temples but few people to support them'. He also sensed Japanese xenophobia and nationalism, as well as detecting what he calls the 'mental uniformity' of the people: a characteristic to which he perceptively attributed Japan's rise in the modern world.

From Japan he went to Vladivostok, where he boarded a train for Khabarovsk, proceeding thence by steamer up the Amur River, along which marched the frontiers of Manchuria and Russia. At this time the Russians regarded Manchuria as one of their spheres of influence and the Boxer Uprising was gleefully welcomed in some powerful circles as a golden opportunity for fresh aggressions against the Chinese. In the Chinese town of Aigun, for instance, Dorzhiev saw that 'all had been burned and killed without trace' in reprisal; he also saw women and children drowned in the Amur River. 'Thus even human beings can be more vicious than tigers and leopards', he reflected sadly.

Arriving at last at Sretenka, he boarded the train for St Petersburg, where he arrived probably in August 1900 to find that Prince Ukhtomsky was away in Peking. We do not know whether he was actually there during the siege, but if so, he would certainly, as a scholar and antiquarian of great sensitivity, have deplored the disgraceful looting perpetrated by Russian troops after their entry into the city in August.

In Ukhtomsky's absence, Dorzhiev applied to the Foreign Minister, Count Lamsdorff, for a second audience with the Emperor. While this was being arranged he again took himself off to Paris, where he arrived in September and was reunited with his friend Joseph Deniker. This time Dorzhiev recounted his life history to Deniker – they always spoke together in Russian – but the main purpose of the visit was again to order the manufacture of Buddhist votive objects. Deniker talks of 'some metal vases [bowls] for the use of the Buddhist monks, and other objects'.[6] Whether these were the original bowls – in which case he had his dates mixed up – or a new set is not clear, nor of what the 'other objects' consisted.

His business completed, Dorzhiev left Paris in September 1900, and on the 30 September was received for a second time by Emperor Nicholas. The setting on this occasion was the Imperial summer residence of Livadia near Yalta on the Black Sea, the scene years later of the famous meeting of Allied heads of state towards the end of World War II. As usual, we have only the sketchiest details of what took place. Berlin is most forthcoming:

> The Tsar received Dorzhiev, who arrived with gifts and an official letter from the Dalai Lama. Nicholas II gave a gold watch decorated with diamonds to Dorzhiev for the Dalai Lama, declared to Dorzhiev the necessity of establishing links with Tibet and the exchange of information, and promised help in extremely vague terms.[7]

Dorzhiev himself merely says that he handed over the letters and gifts he was carrying, that the Tsar reciprocated with valuable gifts and told him to carry them quickly back to Tibet.

In wider discussions that he held with Count Lamsdorff, Count Witte and General Kuropatkin, however, it was made clear to Dorzhiev that Russian protection could only be promised if the Tibetans would agree to a Russian consulate being set up on their soil. Dorzhiev again explained that the Tibetan authorities could not countenance this as it would only pave the way for a general influx of Europeans, which would in the long term prove deterimental to Russia. A compromise was finally reached whereby the Russian consulate would be set up, for the purpose of 'establishing direct and constant relations between the Imperial Rusian Government and the highest Buddhist authorities of Tibet', not in Tibet itself but in Tatsienlu[8], which while populated by ethnic Tibetans, was technically in the Chinese province of Sichuan, near the city of Chengdu. Though it seems unlikely that such a consulate was ever set up, Dorzhiev's peripatetic Buryat friend, Budda Rabdanov, was at some stage considered for the post of political agent.

*

When this audience was reported in the official *Journal de Sainte-Pétersbourg* on the 2 (N S 15) October 1900, an extract of the item was at once forwarded to London by Charles Hardinge, the British Chargé d'Affaires in St Petersburg, who added to his communiqué, 'I have not been able, so far, to procure any precise information with regard to this person [i.e. Dorzhiev] or to the mission on which he is supposed to come to Russia'.[9] Subsequently, having quizzed the enigmatic Dr Badmayev, who assured him that Dorzhiev's mission 'was merely of a complimentary nature', Hardinge surmised that its purpose might be to settle some pastoral matter relating to the Buryat and Kalmyk Buddhists of Russia. Whatever the truth, he was sure that the Russian Government would try to make political capital out of the visit: another representative of an oppressed people seeking protection from the fount of all magnanimity, the Emperor of Russia. This was somewhat ominous; the extension of 'protection' was a contemporary Russian euphemism for annexation.[10]

Though news of the Livadia audience was also reported in the Indian press, it caused no great stir in official circles. Sarat Chandra Das was consulted but claimed to know nothing of it, which is puzzling as he was well aware that Dorzhiev had visited Norzunov at Ghoom (Das lived in Darjeeling himself); indeed it was he who provided the British with the proper name of the mysterious 'Tsanite Khamba' who had come from Lhasa to Ghoom. The sleek Bengali babu merely surmised that if such a mission did visit Russia it had probably been dispatched by the Jebtsundamba Khutukhtu of Urga; he also suggested to his masters that they make discreet inquiries at the annual Kalimpong fair at the end of November, which many Tibetans would attend. As for the russophobic Lord Curzon, he was not perturbed either; in fact he was inclined to think 'the Tibetan Mission to the Tsar is a fraud', and that the notion that 'the Tibetan Lamas have so far overcome their incurable suspicion of Europeans to send a Mission to Europe seems to me most unlikely'.[11] He was sufficiently dissatisfied with the inadequate information that he had received, however, to note in a communiqué to Lord George Hamilton, the Secretary of State for India, that there needed to be 'some better arrangement at Darjeeling for the acquisition of political intelligence'.[12]

As for Agvan Dorzhiev, he was by this time back in his native Trans-Baikalia, from where he sent a letter to Norzunov, asking him to join him in Urga. The Kalmyk needed no special inducements; to return again to Lhasa was his dearest wish, his previous misadventures notwithstanding. He therefore travelled with all possible haste by train and horse to Urga, from where with six other companions he and Dorzhiev set off on 5 December 1900. Despite the fact that caravans did not usually ply during that season, they travelled day and night to cross the Gobi in record-breaking time and arrived in Lhasa in February 1901. Berlin maintains that during this journey, which Dorzhiev says took him in all seventy-two days, the Buryat lama became convinced of the imminent fall of the Manchu dynasty having witnessed for himself the 'widespread corruption of the Chinese authorities'.

At the Monlam Chenmo of 1901, Dorzhiev again distributed munificent hand-outs and also witnessed the Dalai Lama make precious offerings before the Jowo Rinpoché. Norzunov, meanwhile, was interviewed by the Dalai Lama and, through an interpreter, asked how he had been treated during his captivity at the hands of the British. After the Kalmyk recounted all – in minute detail – he was given a 'gift of the third class: a kind of carpet made from tiger skin', traditionally the covering of the seat of honour at lamaist rites, a gift so important that its donation was entered in a register. He was also able, during the short time that he and Dorzhiev were in the holy city, to take photographs with a camera given him by the Secretary of the St Petersburg Geographical Society, V.V. Grigoriev. Norzunov's photographs, which were subsequently published by Deniker, were some of the first of the Tibetan capital seen in the West.

The Dalai Lama and his ministers gave Dorzhiev an enthusiastic welcome and were very pleased with the result of his mission. Old doubts about Russia dissolved and the general feeling was 'that Tibet had finally found its patron, more [strong] and more reliable than China'. However, inside Tibet popular prejudice against Europeans had, as a result of the trouble in China, built up to such a degree that it was thought impolitic for the time being to invite Russian representatives, even though the higher authorities apparently now fully wished to do so. It was therefore decided to dispatch Dorzhiev to Russia for a third time 'to explain these circumstances and conclude a treaty on a firmer foundation'. On this occasion, however, it was not to be a modest one-man show but a full-scale official mission: Dorzhiev would be accompanied by three high Tibetan dignitaries – consular representative Losang Khechok, his assistant Gyaltsen Puntsok, and Ngawang Chö-dzin, a consular secretary. Two men whom Dorzhiev simply calls Jigjé and Tsultrim, who may have been Jigjé Gazonov (probably a Mongolian) and Dorzhiev's sometime Mongolian lama-secretary, Tsultrim Gyatso, went along too, as did Ovshe Norzunov.[13]

*

The Buryat scholar, Gombozhab Tsebekovich Tsybikov, also happened to be in Lhasa at this time and he records in his diary[14] that Agvan Dorzhiev invited him to his house on 22 March (OS), along with the other Buryats who were in town.

Tsybikov, who is generally regarded as the first Russian scholar to have carried out scholarly research in central Tibet, had studied at Tomsk and St Peterburg universities. He had left his native Urdo-Aga for Urga, and from there set out for the Land of Snows in the autumn of 1899 with another Aga Buryat named Markhaem Sanchzhiev. Travelling by way of Alashan and Kum-Bum, he made a detour to the great monastery of Labrang (Labrang Tashi Kyil, founded in 1709 by Jamyang Zhepa, an abbot of Drepung), afterwards returning to Kum-Bum to join a caravan bound for Lhasa by way of Nagchukha. During this long journey he had begun translating Tsongkhapa's *Lam Rim Chenmo*.

On arrival in the holy city on 3 August 1900 (OS), one of the first people Tsybikov met in the streets was a fellow Aga Buryat named Gonchok Sanzhiev, who conducted him to the Eastern House (its name could also be translated as House of Arts) in the city centre, where lived yet another Aga Buryat, Dampel Sukhodoyev (died c 1937), a plump and benign old man who had spent some twenty years in Tibet and had become both 'a master of Tibetan sciences' and 'close to the Dalai Lama'.[15] Sukhodoyev arranged for Tsybikov to stay in his own house and helped him set up business connections; he also carried Tsybikov's first mail home when he left for Russia in September 1900 — letters to Tsybikov's father and to orientalists like Veselovsky and Grigoriev. Tsybikov also made contact with Dagdan Badmayev, the husband of an elder sister, who had come to Lhasa to 'defend a dissertation for the degree of gabzhi [geshe]'. Badmayev was to act as his guide and interpreter on all his subsequent expeditions in Tibet.

Tsybikov spent over a year in Lhasa and central Tibet, gathering information, taking photographs and amassing a useful collection of books and artifacts. He of course visited many important sites in the holy city and environs, including the three great monasteries, the Potala palace, where His Holiness touched him on the head with his rosary, the medical college at Chakpori, and the old Lhasa mint at Dodpal below the Potala, where he observed a man wearing European dress and a white turban who, he was told, had something to do with building operations. He was also several times at the Norbulingka, the Dalai Lama's summer palace, where he organized theatrical performances, competitions and races, and where he again saw His Holiness, who was sitting in a palanquin. 'No one hindered Tsybikov', writes Sergey Markov, 'and he conversed with Buddhist monks and carried on his great scholarly work'.

Tsybikov was also able to travel outside Lhasa to the southern cities of Shigatsé and Gyantsé as well to places like Tsetang on the Brahmaputra, about 170 kilometres south-west of the capital, where the local bed-bugs inflicted three sleepless nights on him. He also visited Samyé, the first monastic foundation of Tibet, the great monastic university of Tashilhunpo, and Samding monastery near Yamdrok-Tso, where he photographed Dorje Pamo, a holy lady who enjoyed the rare distinctions of being both a female tulku – she was considered an incarnation of Vajravarahi,[16] the consort of the yidam Chakrasamvara – and the abbess of a community of monks.

On 1 January 1901 (OS), Tsybikov finished his translation of Tsongkhapa, and on the same day Dagdan Badmayev gained his degree at Gomang College, an event which Tsybikov also photographed. Thereafter, Badmayev was preoccupied with the onerous duty of treating the thousands of monks at Drepung with the obligatory food offerings.

About eight months later, on 10 September 1901 (OS), after further expeditions and a period of illness from which he recuperated at a monastery, Tsybikov finally left the holy city. He returned to Russia with some of the earliest photographs of Lhasa and later wrote a pioneering book, *A Buddhist Pilgrim in the Holy Places of Tibet* (1919). In 1902, he was appointed a professor at the Oriental Institute in Vladivostok.

On a high pass somewhere outside Lhasa, Tsybikov met a party of six Buryats. They had delayed their arrival because of a rumour they had picked up to the effect that Agvan Dorzhiev had been executed. In fact, Tsybikov notes, the great man was by then in his native land, working on a report for the Russian Government.

*

Shortly before receiving Tsybikov at his house – that is, at the end of March 1901 (OS), Dorzhiev had taken his leave of Purchok Rinpoché, who gave him three pieces of advice: 'You will need blessings for the success of your teaching activities . . . Your intentions will be realised by dint of great merit . . . You should travel through Nepal.'[17]

According to intelligence gleaned much later by the British, he then left Lhasa suddenly because the Chinese Amban,[18] angered no doubt by his conducting diplomatic activities without authorization from Peking, had issued a warrant for his arrest. He was, however, carrying lamyiks, or special permits, issued by the Dalai Lama entitling him to transport and anything else he might require, so he was able to get away expeditiously on this, his most important mission to date.

Nevertheless, to get to a boat sailing for Russia, he and his companions still had to negotiate the vast expanses of India, so they were by no means out of danger yet.

CHAPTER EIGHT

The Tibetan Mission of 1901

The Tibetan Mission (as we shall call it) broke its journey at Tashilhunpo, the great monastic university near Shigatsé founded in 1447 by Gendun Drup, the nephew of Tsongkhapa. Accommodating around three thousand Gelugpa monks, this was the seat of the Panchen Lama, second only in the Lamaist hierarchy to the Dalai Lama. Unfortunately, the Chinese had since the eighteenth century conspired to build up the power of the Panchen Lamas as a foil to the growing power of the Dalai Lamas in Lhasa. Thus rivalry existed between the two patriarchs – or at least between the political cabals surrounding them.

During the two days they were at Tashilhunpo, Dorzhiev received from the Ninth Panchen Lama, Chökyi Nyima (1883–1937), gifts (including some golden statues), secret teachings and, most significantly, oral readings of the *Prayer of Shambhala*, a popular text composed by Losang Palden Yeshé, the Third Panchen Lama (1737–80), concerning the millennial Buddhist kingdom of Shambhala, which was of central importance to the visions of Agvan Dorzhiev.

According to Buddhist mythology, the Buddha himself propagated the teachings known as Kalachakra (lit. 'The Wheel of Time'), thought by many to be the apogee of the Tantric system and, with its portrayal of the destruction and renewal of the Buddha-dharma, of special relevance in our own spiritual dark age. These teachings were heard by King Suchandra and taken to his kingdom of Shambhala, where they were preserved for a millennium until Indian masters arrived to recover them. They were later transmitted from India to Tibet between the eleventh and fourteenth centuries CE. Kalachakra is still a very highly venerated tantric teaching within the repertoire of the Gelug school, and in modern times high lamas, notably His Holiness the Dalai Lama, have given initiations at huge gatherings both in Asia and in the West.

The kingdom of Shambhala is a pure land where fortunate though still slightly imperfect beings lead charmed lives, with enlightenment assured them in either this or their next life. Shaped like a lotus, it is surrounded by an outer curtain wall of snow mountains, with radial ranges separating eight internal regions from each other. A smaller circle of mountains at the heart of the kingdom defines the central pericarp of the lotus, and in this raised sanctum is situated the jewelled city of Kalapa, a place so lustrous that night and day are indistinguishable there and the moon fades to a pale disc. To the south of Kalapa, in a sandalwood pleasure garden, is a great three-dimensional representation of the Kalachakra Mandala.

The gloriously outfitted and radiant kings of Shambhala are called kalkis, which connects the Kalachakra myths with those relating to the great Hindu god Vishnu, whose avatars (incarnations) are thought to appear in the world at times of extreme crisis. Such a time will be reached about four hundred years from now, Kalachakra devotees believe, when the world will have become such a sink of corruption that the Twenty-fifth Shambhala Kalki, Raudra Chakri, will ride out of his kingdom on a 'stone horse with the power of wind' to lead his warriors with all their war elephants, stone horses and chariots in a great battle against the barbarians and demons who have come to dominate the world. In this Armageddon, the forces of darkness will be completely defeated by the forces of light and a new Krita Yuga or Age of Perfection inaugurated.

In his *Prayer of Shambhala*, the Third Panchen Lama expressed the wish to be reborn in Shambhala during the reign of Raudra Chakri and to rank foremost among his disciples. He also wrote a guide-book to Shambhala, the so-called *Shambhala Lamyig*: based on pre-existing texts, this describes the route to the mythical kingdom. This devotion was not restricted to Losang Palden Yeshé, however: a special connection was thought to exist between the whole line of Panchen Lamas and Shambhala, and indeed some of them were thought to be incarnations of particular Shambhala kalkis. At Tashilhunpo there was moreover a Kalachakra college, Dukhor Dratsang, where selected students studied and practised these abstruse teachings.

Of course the Kalachakra myths, particularly that of the final Armageddon, could be esoterically interpreted as a metaphor for the internal struggle that each Buddhist must join with the defilements that hinder enlightenment; but there were – and continue to be – literal interpretations that look forward to a real Armageddon, a kind of future Third World War waged with the most technologically advanced weapons. Shambhala too could be regarded as a metaphor for a state of consciousness; but many Kalachakra devotees, including the present Dalai Lama, believe that it is an actual place, though admittedly not to be found on any map and visible only to the eyes of the spiritually enlightened.

But if it does actually exist, where is Shambhala to be found? This question has long exercised Central Asian Buddhists and numerous possible locations have been suggested. Usually it is said to be vaguely to the north of India, but one writer, the Japanese Buddhist monk, Ekai Kawaguchi, who was in Tibet between 1900 and 1902, reports rumours that he heard in Lhasa to the effect that Dorzhiev had written a pamphlet to prove that 'Chang [ie. North] Shambhala' *was* Russia. The Emperor, moreover, was an incarnation of Je Tsongkhapa, and would 'sooner or later subdue the whole world and found a gigantic Buddhist empire'.[1]

No solid evidence exists that Dorzhiev wrote a pamphlet of this sort and even Kawaguchi himself admits that he himself could not get hold of a copy,[2] though a book with that general drift of argument was published in St Petersburg much later by the Kalmyk lama Dambo Ulyanov. It would be wrong to dismiss Kawaguchi's remarks out of hand, however, for we do certainly know that Dorzhiev, having received an abhisheka or initiation from Purchok Rinpoché, was a practitioner of Kalachakra and that he took the Shambhala myths very seriously. In fact, he linked them with the potential he saw in the great heartland of Central Asia for a glorious Buddhist regeneration, as W. A. Unkrig recalls:

> In my opinion, the religiously-based purpose of Agvan Dorzhiev was the foundation of a Lamaist-oriented kingdom of the Tibetans and Mongols (and all other small Lamaist peoples) as a theocracy under the Dalai Lama . . . [and] under the protection of Tsarist Russia . . . In addition, among the Lamaists there existed the religiously grounded hope for help from a 'Messianic Kingdom' in the North . . . called 'Northern Shambhala . . .' Agvan Dorzhiev had on occasion identified this Shambhala with Russia.[3]

Admittedly, history has taken a very different course and the whole area has long since been devoured by the great empires of China and Russia, which, coming under the domination of Marxist regimes, have decimated the local Buddhist traditions. But less than a century ago the possibilities were very different: the Buryat lands in the north, Mongolia, parts of eastern China and the whole of Tibet could well have become the zone of a great Lamaist Buddhist confederation of the kind envisaged by Dorzhiev. Perhaps, despite everything that has happened, dormant vestiges of that potential remain.

*

After the Shambhala teachings at Tashilhunpo, Dorzhiev and his party, plus the fifteen Tibetans who were carrying their baggage, crossed the Great Himalaya into Nepal. Unable to use horses in the mountains, they were all obliged to go on foot, except for Dorzhiev, who Norzunov maintains was carried over on a porter's back. After paying off their porters, they then proceeded to the Nepalese capital – Norzunov calls it 'Yamb' and Dorzhiev 'Yambo': one presumes they mean Kathmandu – and stayed there for five days while permission was being obtained from the King of Nepal to cross into India. They were at this stage masquerading as a group of pilgrims wishing to visit the Buddhist holy places in northern India.

Dorzhiev had political business in Nepal. Following the news of his reception at Livadia, he says that the British newspapers had begun to declare that before Russia could seize Tibet by using the Buryats, Britain would do so using the Nepalese. He then mentions three letters which he claims were sent to the Dalai Lama by the British via the Kings of Nepal and Sikkim and the Governor-General of Ladakh – actually this is very garbled, as we shall see in the next chapter – inviting His Holiness to conclude a joint treaty for mutual benefit. The Nepalese were not apparently ready to be inveigled into the British game, however, and, as a token of their good will towards Tibet, their king had recently presented the Dalai Lama with a horse worth Rs 15,000/-, a 'brilliant carriage' and had promised shortly to send an elephant with a lavish caparison adorned with silver and gold. Dorzhiev's brief in Nepal was to make sure that these tokens of friendship were sincere.

Dorzhiev records that dark deeds had recently been perpetrated in Nepal:

> In January 1901 the king was murdered by his minister, who took his place, and I witnessed him inspecting [his] troops and [also] when he was present at a sports game together with an English official, who delivered a letter of congratulation from London. The king comes from the Gurkha tribe . . .[4]

He was not much impressed with religious life in the Kathmandu valley. 'In general, monasteries and khuvarak are not many in number', he records. But he was moved by the height and antiquity of two great suburgans (stupas), notably 'the great Jarung Khashor', by which he probably means the great stupa at Bodh-Nath, where, after he had made offerings of several ounces of powdered gold, saffron and so forth, a sudden shower broke and washed the stupa clean. 'I took this as a sign that my objectives would be realized,' he says.[5] He was also indiscreet enough to show the stupa's presiding lama his 'curious' watch, boasting that it was worth Rs 300/- and had been bought in Russia. This information was subsequently picked up by British intelligence.

*

Written permission to proceed eventually came through from the King of Nepal, but to obtain it Dorzhiev's party had to deposit three trunk-fulls of clothing and other property with the landlord of the place where they stayed. Free passage was then granted them, but an additional clause stipulated that the papers they carried were to be thoroughly examined. This made them very anxious, for they anticipated three customs checks at the Indian frontier. Dorzhiev was especially worried in case the official letters he was carrying should be found, while Norzunov took the precaution of hiding some of his photographic film in a small box sewn inside some fabric which he suspended by strings beneath his trousers; the rest he hid in a box of tsampa while his Russian passport was concealed in the sole of one of his boots. It says a great deal for their sang froid that they should contemplate traversing British territory after Norzunov's misadventures of the previous year, let alone doing so in such a large party.

They were, however, only cursorily searched by the border guards, for their masquerade as pilgrims was accepted. This is a little surprising as the British were now alert to Dorzhiev's comings and goings, and indeed at one railway station where his party spent a day waiting for a connection he claims to have caught sight of another wanted poster, this one bearing his rough likeness and again offering a reward of the unlikely sum of Rs 10,000/- for his head. Later, at another station, perhaps Ragpur, where on 10 May his party tried to buy through tickets for Bombay, the unsuspecting station master told Norzunov about a sinister Russian of Mongolian stock who had the year before tried to slip into Tibet from Darjeeling but had been caught and deported. 'The Russians do not have good intentions,' the station master said. 'They should not be allowed to reach Lhasa.' Norzunov, looking suitably concerned, agreed wholeheartedly and swore to keep a keen look out for any sinister foreigners; at the same time he was silently praying to all the buddhas for help. His prayer worked: they got their tickets.

*

Though no Kim or Hurree Babu foiled the Mission's transit through India, Dorzhiev himself claims that the police watched them the whole time, and indeed on this occasion British intelligence was able to piece together some information about their movements, though only after the birds had flown. One British report talks of the party going by train from Raxaul to Bombay, where the youngest of four Mongolian lamas who were travelling with them — the British strongly suspected them of being Russians – shaved, donned European dress and went on board a ship for Singapore. This man apparently knew English, for he had been 'always able to read their railway tickets and detect when they were overcharged'. These 'Mongolian' lamas were also, the British ascertained, great meat-eaters, and they could not understand Tibetan – further evidence that they were probably Russians.[6]

Then, on 21 June 1901, the British Military Attaché in Peking, Colonel G. F. Browne, reported in a memorandum that Dorzhiev had arrived in the Chinese capital in May and left the city for Chita and Trans-Baikalia about two weeks later. 'During his stay in Peking Dorjief [sic] lived with M. Gomboieff, the Russian postmaster,' Browne added. 'This official is by birth a Buryat, and his brother, who died a few years since, was a Hutukhtu [Khutukhtu], or re-embodied saint, commonly called "a living Buddha"'.[7]

The first report is very strange, unless there were Mongolians travelling with the party who separated from the rest and travelled on to their homeland via Singapore and Peking. The second is probably a clumsy conflation of garbled rumours arising from Dorzhiev's other journeys, though the information about N. Gomboyev is interesting. This man, who was head of the post office through which the whole official mail of the Russian Mission in Peking was sent, put together two collections of Lamaist and Chinese Buddhist art, the first of which was stolen during the Boxer Uprising. He also supplied Prince Ukhtomsky with such items, a connection which would make it seem quite likely that Dorzhiev did lodge with him during some of his transits through Peking.[8]

What in fact happened was that when the members of Dorzhiev's party reached Bombay they found that their ship had already sailed. They were therefore obliged to continue their travels through south India, where some kind of epidemic was raging, so they voluntarily quarantined themselves at the railway junction of Tuticorin for five days before travelling on to Ceylon. There they visited a number of Buddhist sites, including the Temple of the Tooth in Kandy, before finally, with the aid of the Russian consul and an agent named Malygin, boarding a Russian steamer of the Dobrovolnyi Flot, the *Tambov*, at Colombo on June 12 1901.

*

A fortnight later the world knew that something politically important was afoot. 'Odessa will welcome today an Extraordinary Mission from the Dalai Lama of Tibet which is proceeding to St Petersburg with diplomatic instructions of importance', the newspaper, *Oddeskia*

Novosty, proclaimed in the columns of its edition of 25 June. It went on:

> The personnel of the Mission consists of eight prominent statesmen with the Lama Dorzhiev at its head. The chief object of the Extraordinary Mission is a rapprochement and a strengthening of good relations with Russia . . .
>
> The Extraordinary Mission will among other things raise the question of the establishment in St Petersburg of a permanent Tibetan Mission for the maintenance of good relations with Russia . . .[9]

Smith, the British Consul General in Odessa, wired a copy of the item to the Foreign Office in London on the same day. The British could no more regard Dorzhiev as a small fish or a figment of the imagination; from now on virtually his every move was watched, reported, pondered and debated.

The Mayor of Odessa welcomed the Tibetan Mission in the traditional manner with bread and salt; Dorzhiev later wrote to thank him for the warmness of his reception. The Mission then proceeded by rail to St Petersburg. Norzunov in his own writings says that he went his own way at Odessa and returned to his Kalmyk steppe, but he has been identified in a photograph published in *The Graphic* on 17 August 1901, where he sits in an open carriage beside a Tibetan aristocrat in European dress. Opposite, grim, bemedalled and finely hatted, sit two other men with heavy moustaches, one of whom may be Dr Badmayev. In the background rears the famous Bronze Horseman: the equestrian statue of Peter the Great by Falconet which stands in the former Senate Square, now Decembrists' Square, in St Petersburg.

On 25 June (NS 8 July), the *Méssager Officiel* reported that on 23 June (NS 6 July) the Emperor had received the 'Extraordinary Envoys of the Dalai Lama of Tibet' at Peterhof. Afterwards they were received by the Dowager Empress, Maria Fyodorovna. Also presented was a 'Second Captain Ulanov', a Kalmyk officer of the 1st Don Cossack Regiment, who was attached to the Tibetan Mission as interpreter. This is almost certainly Dambo Ulyanov, a gelong (Buddhist monk) attached to the Guards Regiment, who travelled to Tibet several times and wrote the book, *Predictions of the Buddha about the House of Romanov and a Brief Account of my Travels to Tibet in 1904–5* (St Petersburg 1913), in which he linked the destiny of the House of Romanov with the Shambhala myths.[10] That Dorzhiev needed his services as translator indicates that at this point he was none too proficient in Russian.

Again we have vague and contradictory reports of what went on at Peterhof. Dorzhiev merely says, 'We met the Great Tsar together and offered him letters and gifts from Tibet. We received in return abundant gifts and letters in gold [discussing] relations with the Land of Snows.'[11] He also adds elsewhere that he discussed a problem that had arisen among the Kalmyks with the Emperor and his ministers, and also received the Emperor's permission to build a Buddhist temple in the Russian capital. L. E. Berlin, on the other hand, records that the Emperor 'promised Tibet assistance and expressed the desire that closer friendly relations be established between Tibet and Russia'. When the two Tibetan envoys returned to Lhasa bearing the usual 'letters and gifts', the Tibetan Government was encouraged by what they were told and took a tougher stand against the British, who, then embroiled in the Boer War, were in no mood for embarking on new contentions.

C. Nabokov, at the time Second Secretary at the Russian Foreign Office, was present at interviews between Dorzhiev and Count Lamsdorff. He maintains that these were 'a painful ordeal' for the Foreign Minister because he was 'utterly ignorant of the history and geography of Tibet'. However, 'not a single reference to political matters was made', proceedings never progressing beyond 'the flattest banalities'. Any suspicions that the British might have harboured that deeper machinations were in progress were therefore based 'not on facts but on fancies'.[12]

A rather different and more multi-faceted account is that of the highly able Russian diplomat, Ivan Yakobevich Korostovets, who met Dorzhiev, whom he maintains

> had orders to put out feelers and try to direct the attention of the Russian government to Tibet, and particularly to gain diplomatic support against China and Britain. Dorzhiev was presented to the Tsar, who benevolently accepted his reports on the present situation and on the personality of the Dalai Lama. The Tibetans, Dorzhiev said, were looking with great hopes on Russia, the protector of all the religions of the East, and they hoped for the White Tsar's assistance against their enemies. Tsar Nicholas II, as was well-known, was especially interested in the Far East, where he had travelled when he was Tsarevitch, and he had a weakness for all sorts of Eastern and exotic adventures, which were often not worth attention. Dorzhiev spoke with marked authority and expertise, and mightily pleased the Tsar, in spite of his fantastic plans, which were not to be realised and which implied the Russian advance across the Himalayas in order to liberate the oppressed people. This of course increased Tibetan prestige within government circles, and even engaged the attention of the Minister, Count Lamsdorff, who was disinclined towards everything Eastern.[13]

Korostovets maintains that his graceful reception by the Emperor encouraged Dorzhiev, who then called on the Ministry of Foreign Affairs and the General Staff to hand over reports on Tibeto-Russian rapprochement and to try to gain support. Throughout, the Buryat lama 'behaved in a very modest way yet [one] demanding respect', while at the same time being very anxious to avoid attracting the attention of the British. Moreover:

> Judging by his behaviour and flattering ways, one could have mistaken Dorzhiev for a Catholic priest had not his narrow Mongolian eyes and broad cheekbones betrayed his origin. He always wore a long robe, and sometimes on top the dark red outer robe of Buddhist monks.

Initially, Korostovets concludes, Dorzhiev's winning diplomatic overtures did arouse interest to the extent that a special conference was held at which a draft Russo-Tibetan treaty was discussed. The Russian Government finally drew back, however, for while it was interested in undermining the British, the draft treaty threatened the very significant danger of conflict without offering any significant advantages . . .

*

The Russian press was full of news and editorial comment about the Mission. The 17 June (NS 30 June) edition of *Novoye Vremya* spoke in sabre-rattling terms of Russian advances in China, then went on:

> Under the circumstances, a [Tibetan] rapprochment with Russia must seem to him [the Dalai Lama] the most natural step, as Russia is the only power able to counteract the intrigues of Great Britain, who has long been endeavouring to obtain admission, and only awaits an opportunity to force an entrance . . .
> The difficulties encountered by the Tibetan Mission on its journeys through India explain why Tibet, who has already seen the lion's paw raised over it, turns its eyes towards the Emperor of the North.[14]

Ukhtomsky's *St Peterburgskiye Viedomosti* was more moderate:

> Talking about a Protectorate can only have the result of bringing misfortune to our countrymen who may be travelling in these countries, embitter the Chinese and excite the British Indian Government to a more active policy.[15]

One person was much quoted in the press. This was St Petersburg's own semi-official Tibet expert, Dr Piotr Badmayev, who, as a close confederate of Ukhtomsky and Witte in the powerful Eastern Lobby, was undoubtedly playing a very active part behind the scenes. Although he gains no mention in Dorzhiev's autobiography, Badmayev was, like Ukhtomsky, a key figure in this phase of the Buryat lama's career.

*

The Badmayev story[16] begins in 1857 when a Buryat doctor named

Tsultrim Padma – 'Badmayev' is in fact a russification of 'Padma' – arrived in St Petersburg. He is said to have studied Tibetan medicine at Chakpori, the medical college near Lhasa; also at the medical faculty of the Aga Datsan near Chita in eastern Siberia. He subsequently russified himself to the extent of changing his name to Aleksandr Badmayev, and set up a Tibetan pharmacy in the Russian capital, which was the first of its kind in Europe. This was not a great success until his brother Zhamtsaran (1851–1919) began to work there. He possessed a magic touch – in more ways than one – and after Tsultrim's death in 1873 he transformed this 'obscure little shop' into a great 'sanatorium':

> The fame of Badmayev's magical cures spread rapidly, and clients flocked to him from all classes of society, seeking to be cured in his sanatorium. His followers maintained that he could charm away the most stubborn troubles in a marvellous fashion, and that his curative treatment was particularly successful 'in serious cases of stubborn nervous diseases, mental maladies, and disturbances of female physiology'.[17]

Zhamtsaran had been born in the Aga district (Dulidurginsky rayon), where in his youth he had tended his father's large herd of cattle until at the age of twelve he was sent to the gymnasium at Irkutsk. His brother brought him to the capital when he was about twenty, and he later attended two St Petersburg institutes of higher learning: the Military Medical Academy and the University of Eastern Languages. Highly ambitious and able, not to say opportunistic, he got ahead quickly. While still a student, he converted to Orthodoxy – undoubtedly a tactical rather than a spiritual move – his godfather being Emperor Alexander III himself. He thereupon ceased to be simple Zhamtsaran and became Piotr Aleksandrovich. Imperial sponsorship gave him an entrée at Court and the rare privilege of being able to communicate directly with the Emperor.

After completing his university career in 1875, Zhamtsaran Badmayev served in the Asiatic Section of the Ministry of Foreign Affairs until 1893, at the same time holding a lectureship in Mongolian at St Petersburg University and continuing his successful Tibetan medical practice. His political and diplomatic skills, meanwhile, were frequently called upon by the Emperor and he was entrusted with important political commissions. Like Ukhtomsky, Badmayev was an advocate of Russian expansion in Asia. While still at the Ministry of Foreign Affairs, he submitted a memorandum to Alexander III through Count Witte in which he proposed extending Russia's railway links into Chinese territory. He also proposed a plan for extending Russian economic influence in Asia. Some sources go so as far as to suggest this involved encouraging the Mongolians, Chinese Muslims and Tibetans to rise up against their Manchu overlords; these rebels would succeed, he predicted, and would then appeal for the Emperor's protection.[18]

Around 1891, with Russian government backing and a grant from the Treasury of two million rubles in gold, Badmayev departed for the east and remained there until 1896. In November 1893 he opened his trading firm – it had its headquarters in Chita – and during the next few years this concerned itself with organizing large-scale cattle-breeding operations in Trans-Baikalia, leasing land from Russian settlers, purchasing transport animals and opening shops. Then in November 1895, the firm began publishing a newspaper in Chita; it was called *Life on the Eastern Peripheries*, and appeared in both Russian and Mongolian editions; its editor was Budda Rabdanov. It was in fact the first Buryat newspaper and was very popular locally, dealing as it did with the development of the Buryat economy, Buryat culture and aspects of Chinese, Tibetan and Mongolian life. Agents were also dispatched to Mongolia and Tibet to investigate local trading conditions. As we have seen, some of these agents got through to Lhasa and were in touch with Agvan Dorzhiev; others got to Sining.

These activities depleted his financial resources, however, for he eventually applied to the Russian Government for further finance. This was denied, and in 1896/7 his newspaper went bankrupt and ceased to appear. The reasons for this withdrawal of official support are unclear but Badmayev had his detractors. Witte came eventually to regard him as a criminal opportunist, and I. Y. Korostovets, who witnessed his operations in eastern Siberia, believed he had been concerned mainly with feathering his own nest. Beyond acquiring land in his own name and setting up a haberdashery shop, Korotstovets believed Badmayev achieved little; he was, moreover, unpopular with the local Buryat, who disapproved of his conversion to Christianity.

Badmayev continued his political activities afterwards. He published several works on Russia's Asian policy. Also, as a wealthy and influential man, he was able to do much good work on behalf of his fellow Buryats in St Petersburg. He represented Buryat interests to Nicholas II and he arranged for many Buryats to visit the Imperial capital, notably for Nicholas's coronation celebrations in 1896. He sponsored a Buryat school in the Russian capital too; though, according to one source, when in 1896 the Russian Government suppressed the teaching of Buddhism in favour of Orthodoxy, the students revolted and the school was closed down.[19] Finally, he is credited with giving financial support to Aga Buryats wishing to study at St Petersburg University – G. Ts. Tsybikov was one of his beneficiaries.

Badmayev also continued his medical practice, augmenting his Tibetan knowledge by studying western approaches at the Academy of Military Surgery. His favour at court continued into the reign of Nicholas II, whom he treated medically. One report mentions the successful cure of a stomach complaint with a mixture of henbane and hashish – 'the effects of which were marvellous'. During consultations the Emperor often asked Badmayev for political as well as for medical advice, and they discussed the appointment of high officials. The doctor had a marvellous filing system, Fülöp Miller maintains, in which medical and encoded political data were combined.

Tibet therefore figured highly on Badmayev's agenda; in fact, he actively preached its annexation. It is doubtful that he ever travelled there himself, though unconfirmed reports from Paul Möwis, a Darjeeling trader, news-hound and Tibet-watcher, did lead the Government of Bengal to deduce that a certain Baranoff, who might have been Badmayev, possibly led some kind of mission to Lhasa in January 1898. He was certainly in touch with Dorzhiev, however, and when the Tibetan Mission arrived in St Petersburg in 1901 he showed himself extremely well informed, notably about Dorzhiev himself. In general he expounded the official line that the Mission could not be regarded as either political or diplomatic but was rather of a pastoral nature. He did speak, however, of Russia being actively concerned 'to uphold the integrity of China', so the Tibetans, who were subjects of the Emperor of China, were naturally welcomed in Russia when they came 'to pray for assistance against any attack on Tibet'. A summary of an interview in the *St Petersburg Gazette*, also records that he considered 'Tibet is really quite accessible to Russians, but that the object of the Mission is to make it more so. He fears that the English, who have now firmly established themselves in Cashmere, may anticipate Russia in that country.'[20]

*

The British Ambassador in St Petersburg, Sir Charles Scott, conscientiously culled Badmayev's pieces from the Russian press and wired them along with other relevant items to London. He also spoke personally with Count Lamsdorff on 3 July and again on 8 July, having heard in the interim that members of the Tibetan Mission had paid visits to Count Witte as well as to Lamsdorff himself. On both occasions Lamsdorff assured Scott that the mission had no diplomatic status or political purpose, as had been irresponsibly suggested in some quarters of the press. It was 'of the same character as those sent by the Pope to the faithful of foreign lands'. Dorzhiev, a member of the Imperial Russian

Geographical Society, came occasionally to Russia with the object of 'making money collections for his Order from the numerous Buddhists in the Empire'. He had brought Lamsdorff an autograph letter from the Dalai Lama, which on translation had been found merely to contain a simple message to the effect that the Dalai Lama was happy to say that he was well and hoped that Lamsdorff was likewise. As for Dr Badmayev, Lamsdorff dismissed him as an 'eccentric character'.[21]

Lamsdorff's assurances were officially received 'with satisfaction' in London, though at the same time it was made clear that the British Government 'could not regard with indifference any proceeding that might have a tendency to alter the existing status of Tibet'. Beneath the diplomatic niceties, however, both London and Calcutta were alarmed and agreed that a new situation was developing. In the following months their suspicions were to intensify and their attitude to harden.

After 1901, the Dorzhiev phenomenon, whatever the good lama's personal motivations, was no longer marginal but fully integrated into the dynamic pattern of history. There, along with other contributory factors, it served to bring to a head the current phase of the long-standing rivalry of Britain and Russia in Asia.

CHAPTER NINE

Among the Kalmyks and the Buryats
1901 – 1903

In August 1901, bearing the Emperor's letter and gifts, Losang Khechok and Gyaltsen Puntsok set out to return to Lhasa by the overland route, the only safe one as the British were fully aware of their comings and goings. As for Dorzhiev, despite reports that the British received from Chandra Das, Sandberg and other agents to the effect that he returned to Lhasa early in 1902 to a cold reception from the conservatives who disfavoured rapprochement with Russia, he himself records that he remained away from Tibet for the next two years or so, devoting himself mainly to the service of the Buddhists of his native Russia. He had clearly received a mandate from the Thirteenth Dalai Lama to build monasteries, ordain lamas and generally revitalize Buddhism in the Russian Empire. Berlin merely says that he was having 'a rest' during this period. A rest from politics it certainly may have been, but not a time of inactivity by any means; as always, Agvan Dorzhiev was a very busy man.

Between January and March 1902 Dorzhiev paid another visit to the Kalmyks, staying at khuruls in the ulus of Bagatsokhurov, Maloderbet, Ikitsokhurov, Kharakhusov and Erketenov. According to his memoirs, one of the main reasons for this visit was to attend to a particular problem that had arisen. It had been proposed, perhaps by Dorzhiev himself with the Dalai Lama's backing, to establish two choira[1] or colleges of higher Buddhist studies; but an important lama, Shachin Lama, was set against the idea, as were some of the elder monks. Representing the local religious establishment, they may well have felt threatened by the arrival of a prestigious lama from the court of the Dalai Lama, who was not only causing a great stir in the Kalmyk steppe but may moreover have been something of a new broom.

A Kalmyk magnate or noyon whom he calls Tsering Da-ö – perhaps this was Tseren-David Tundutov – disagreed with them, however. 'Even

I [know that] the Buddha, the Second Buddha and others have clearly said in all their teachings that in the Holy Perfection of Wisdom [Prajñaparamita] it is declared that we need to listen [to teachings], reflect and meditate [upon them], and train in the stages of the path', he declared. 'And in the teachings of the Great Dalai Lama it is said that the time has come to establish monastic colleges'.[2]

Having been authorized by the Emperor and his ministers to sort the matter out, Dorzhiev maintains in his memoirs that he did so to his own satisfaction, deciding that Shachin Lama had no authority to impose a veto and that the choira should go ahead. To assist with the task he recruited two Buryat lamas holding the degree of doramba geshe,[3] Gelek Gyatso and Chöjor Chönyingpo, who had received their training at Gomang College and were disciples of another Buryat, Sonam Gyatso, at Padkar Chöling. He also invited a third lama from Tibet, Geshé Shakya Gyeltsen, who had a reputation for having 'practised with great diligence [and] without regard for his cherished life'. And so, Dorzhiev maintains, the two Kalmyk choira were set up according to the noble traditions of Gomang College.

Two choira were in fact established along the lines of Buryat datsans at Amta Burgusta and Sanzyr in the Maloderbet and Ikitsokhurov ulus of Astrakhan province, though work on them did not start until 1906 and 1907 respectively.[4] The Amta Burgusta foundation was situated on the domains of the noyon Prince Tundutov, who had previously donated a house in which a kind of illegal choira had operated. Upon Dorzhiev's arrival in 1906 a 'massive building programme' began.

According to the prospectus:

> The aim of the college is to explain to the students the principles and the will of the Buddha, the Master, in order to show them how to stay away from evil, how to lead a righteous life and how, through correct realisation of the true meaning of an honest conduct in life, one may strive for Nirvana.[5]

Actually, what was taught was Dorzhiev's forte: tsenyi,[6] the traditional programme of Gelugpa dialectics. As at his Alma Mater, Gomang College, the course here was a protracted one, lasting eighteen years. There was no shortage of takers, however. Originally an intake of a hundred students was planned, but soon after opening a hundred more applied, so entry had to be restricted to only the most talented candidates, who were usually monks and novices of fifteen and over recommended by their abbots. Thirty-five houses were built to provide accommodation at a cost of some ninety rubles each. Dorzhiev himself personally donated five thousand rubles; he also generously gave a complete set of the Tibetan Buddhist canon brought from Tibet itself, buddha-rupas, votive vessels and other ecclesiastical objects. Other funds were donated by the Dalai Lama and wealthy local residents; also one ruble was levied from each kibitka (yurt). The actual running expenses were made the responsibility of the local khuruls, the larger ones contributing 214 rubles per annum and the smaller ones 117. Dorzhiev also donated his teaching revenue.[7]

The syllabus included lectures, study and devotional rites, while instruction was in both Kalmyk and Tibetan and also in Russian at the insistence of the Department of Foreign Creeds, with whom Dorzhiev formally negotiated permission for the college. Among the text-books used were F. I. Stcherbatsky's *Theory of Cognition and Logic According to the Teachings of the Early Buddhists*, as well as works and translations by Zaya Pandita and other scholarly Kalmyk lamas.[8]

The house rules were strict: smoking, drinking, playing cards and going to market were prohibited, and students had to dress and furnish their cells, of which there were forty-eight, in a simple manner. Only six hours were allowed for sleep, and meat-eating was forbidden 'according to the ancient Buddhist rules of the Vinaya [monastic code], as it inhibits the faculty of discrimination and leads to somnolence'.[9]

As for the Ikitsokhurov choira, work on this began in the spring of 1907 with the support of wealthy and influential local residents, notably the gelong Dzhomak Gontiev and the zaisan Tseren Badmayev. Funds of about 70,000 rubles were involved. No official permission seems to have been sought, however, for when news of the choira's construction reached the Governor of Astrakhan he sent an official named Kardayev to inspect the place. In August 1907 Kardayev reported on the state of building operations. In addition, there were twenty-five kibitkas to accommodate students when they arrived. They would be under the direction of the gelong Segal'tya Dobdonov; another lama named Dandir Buyuntayev was also brought in from Buryatia to support him. Building work was suspended in the autumn of 1907 but resumed again in the early spring of 1908; the choira was consecrated in the same year. Responsibility for its upkeep was much the same as in the case of the other choira: 300 rubles per annum were to be contributed by the larger khuruls in the area and 150 rubles by the smaller ones; in all, some 1,500 rubles were expected to be required. In addition, a quantity of sheep, cattle, horses and camels were also donated.[10]

*

As instructed by his teacher, Purchok Rinpoché, Dorzhiev also began ordaining Kalmyk monks and novices according to the Lä-chok rite 'which the Dalai Lama had given me'. When writing his memoirs, he believed that he performed the Puja of Accomplishment, the highest offering ceremony at which practitioners give away all spiritual benefit gained through their practice. In addition, because he was concerned that local medical practices offended against the central Buddhist principle of compassion – 'most of the doctors in these lands did not refrain from taking life and practised such things as treating illnesses with the juice of cooked meat' – he invited a doctor of Tibetan medicine, Jangchub Dorji, to help found a medical college. And he also encouraged Padma Tsultrim, a Torgut lama who possessed a Lharampa degree, to train as a teacher with a view to setting up a Kalachakra college. The good geshé eventually accomplished this at a place Dorzhiev calls 'Bagachonu', having studied with Tashi Dönden, who possessed a kachu degree: a lower form of geshé degree awarded at Tashilhunpo, where, as we have noted, there was a Kalachakra college.

In addition to all this, Dorzhiev also carried out much pastoral work among ordinary lay Kalmyks. He dispensed Buddhist layman's vows and 'one-day vows' to pious men and women who wished to submit to a number of strict rules (not to eat after noon, not to sleep on a high or luxurious bed, to refrain from sexual activity, and so forth) for a twenty-four hour period. At such ceremonies, he tells us, up to ten thousand people were in attendance. He also bestowed popular initiations into the practice of the mantra OM MANI PADME HUM, the quintessential mantra of Tibetan Buddhism, as well as into Mig-tse-ma, a practice based on the recitation of a simple four-line verse praising Jé Tsongkhapa as a personification of the great bodhisattvas Mañjushri, Avalokiteshvara and Vajrapani. He stressed to those who received these initiations the benefits that would accrue from reciting the appropriate formulae.

He also gave 'long-life' initiations: common-place tantric ceremonies in which Amitayus, the Buddha of Infinite Life, and other deities connected with longevity – usually White Tara and Usnisha Vijaya – are invoked. Among the accoutrements used by the officiating lama at such rituals is a dish containing long-life pills, a skull cup filled with alcohol and a tse-boum[11] or vase of life, which consists of an elaborately decorated receptacle filled with water imagined to be a 'nectar' or distillation of the essence of deity; above is a rupa or form of the deity in a halo.[12]

Finally, Dorzhiev gave Highest Yoga Tantra (Annutarayogatantra) initiations, again probably to quite large mixed congregations. Technically such initiations should only be given to serious practitioners who have reached a high state of readiness; indeed the consequences of bestowing them on the immature are said to be dire in the extreme – Dorzhiev himself talks of his consciousness being hurled into the Vajra Hell. However, in practice they are dispensed quite freely in the belief that, even if a person has not yet reached tantric maturity, he or she still forms a karmic connection with the relevant tantra that will ripen in a future life. There is also a worldly element: tantric initiations generate large donations, as Dorzhiev himself admits – 'I did this for the sake of profit and fame', he says.

Again in his general discourses he was moved to speak out against the abuse of alcohol and tobacco, both among the clergy and the laity. Even Benjamin Bergman, writing of his travels among the Kalmyks a century before, noted that the drinking of spirits took place among the clergy, particularly the lower clergy, and that tobacco smoke could even be detected in temples. 'I explained to them the negative consequences [of such behaviour],' Dorzhiev writes. 'However, very few paid much attention.'

*

Having done so much among the Kalmyks, Dorzhiev turned his attention to his fellow Buryats. He had it specially in mind to activate Buddhism in Irkutsk province, to the west of Lake Baikal, where his ancestor Ukhin Akhaldayev had gone to live back in the late eighteenth century. Shamanism was still widespread there, though many local Buryats had also converted to Orthodox Christianity. His efforts proved fairly successful in the long run and on the official count there were 335 conversions to Buddhism from both shamanism and Orthodox Christianity.

The authorities were not pleased with his success, however, so when about ten years later he lodged two petitions with the Interior Ministry for permission to build, at his own expense, a datsan at Kirmen in Verkholensk okrug (district), where his family still held land, and for lamas to be allowed to 'reside freely among the Buryats of Irkutsk province in order that they might practise the methods of Tibetan medicine',[13] both were rejected 'because the authorities detected an underlying desire to propagate Lamaism'.[14] Dorzhiev himself always emphatically denied any evangelical zeal, maintaining that the inclination of the shamanistic Buryats of Irkutsk province to Buddhism was not the result of any efforts on his part but represented 'a certain historical and psychological process'; it would moreover be a 'contribution to the general progress of the state'.[15] Despite his petitions being turned down and his also being himself eventually prohibited from visiting the Irkutsk Buryats by the local Governor General, General Selivanov, the Kirmen Datsan was built to a design by Richard Andreyovich Berzen, who also worked at the St Petersburg temple (which it resembled); it was opened around 1912. A second datsan, the Koimor, was also opened in Cis-Baikalia, but much later, probably in the 1920s; it was the first in Irkutsk province to have a tsenyi faculty.

What was special, indeed unique about Dorzhiev as a Buddhist was that he was not, as one might have expected of a person schooled within the Gelugpa church and received into its establishment, an ossified conservative and fundamentalist. Quite the contrary: he was of a modern, progressive turn of mind, concerned on one hand to strengthen the Buddhism of the Buryats and Kalmayks by purging it of the venal abuses that had become endemic and, on the other hand, to expunge the dark, primitive aspects of the religion in order to reconcile it with modern Western thought, notably rationalism.

*

Unfortunately, Dorzhiev arrived back in his homelands at a time of crisis. For many years Russian government policy towards the Buryats (and similar ethnic minorities) had been that enshrined in the enlightened Speransky Statute of 1822, which safeguarded their traditional lifestyle by granting them a high degree of independence. They had their own courts and administrative institutions; also religious freedom and special exemptions. All that changed at about this time when, as part of an assimilation drive, the Speransky system was abandoned in favour of a vigorous russification programme. This culminated in a series of regulations (polozheniye), imposed between 1902 and 1904, which are said to have 'constituted a direct attack on the whole Buryat social structure and landholding pattern'.[16] Buryat courts and administrative institutions were scrapped, military service was threatened (in the event it was not imposed), but worst of all, parcels of Buryat land, which as in all traditionally nomadic societies was held in common, were privatized and handed over to Russian and Ukrainian immigrants, increasing numbers of whom gained access to the region by means of the newly-opened Trans-Siberian Railway.

Concerning himself with these problems, Dorzhiev found it 'difficult to decide what would be best for all the Buryats, whose minds were suffering', but he eventually decided to make an appeal to the government. 'It was like trying to make water flow up a steep hillside', he records.

In the long run, far from destroying Buryat identity, such crude attempts at russification only served to galvanize national, cultural and religious self-consciousness. Pan-Mongolism was also given additional impetus, for many Buryats felt that their salvation lay in their racial links with the other Mongolian peoples.

Attempts by the Orthodox church to convert them to Christianity were another cause of woe for the Buryats. This had been going on for some time, even during the era of the Speransky system. Venyamin, Archbishop of Irkutsk between 1873 and 1890, had been notorious in this respect; and Prince Ukhtomsky had investigated complaints of forcible conversion. The intolerant Christians of the region now turned their attentions to Dorzhiev and made him the butt of various calumnies and false accusations. After three appeals to the Emperor, these intolerant 'long-hairs', as he calls them, called off their smear campaign, but even so the local Buddhists were only able to establish four new datsans. Again, pressure from Orthodoxy tended in the long term to strengthen rather than weaken Buryat Buddhism, which was in any case the central pivot of national identity.[17]

Besides his specifically Buddhist work, Dorzhiev was actively involved in both Buryat (and Kalmyk) nationalism and in Pan-Mongolism, which again brought official displeasure upon him to the extent that he was eventually put under secret surveillance by the Ministry of the Interior. It was his special contribution to expand Pan-Mongolism, which has been called 'the most powerful single idea in Central Asia in the Twentieth Century', into the more expansive Pan-Buddhism, which, as we have already noted, he based upon the Kalachakra myths, including the legend of the messianic kingdom of Shambhala.

A resumé of Dorzhiev's nationalist activities is included in a brief document drawn up by the Interior Ministry 'in connection with the arrival in St Petersburg of a Tibetan representative, Agvan Dorzhiev, with the purpose of petitioning the Russian Government to recognise the sovereignty of Tibet',[18] Dated 1911, this states:

> In the period of the so-called liberation movement, a few of the Buryat intellectuals, under the influence of the new ideas of national self-determination, began, in imitation of other minorities, to organise factions and societies and to lay down a programme of activity. Among the Buryats this movement was generated by two persons – Zhamtsarano, a lecturer at St Petersburg University, and Dorzhiev. Both of them prepared the ground for an active nationalist movement among the Buryats: the former, masquerading as someone engaged in professional business activities, conducted propaganda among Buryat

teachers, and Dorzhiev among the nobility. For this purpose they travelled from one ulus to another in Trans-Baikalia and Irkutsk province. Their activity was primarily directed towards the Buryats of Irkutsk province as these had to a greater extent than the Buryats of Trans-Baikalia, lost their national identity and been assimilated by the Russian population.[19]

These activities probably did not fully come into their own until the revolutionary year of 1905, for the document continues:

> Simultaneous with the generation of a purely nationalist movement among the students and teachers, the narodniks (populists) tried to exploit the 1905 Manifesto to strengthen the foundations of religious tolerance. They recognised lamaism as a national religion and accordingly began to propagate it among the shamanistic and Orthodox Christian Buryats of Irkutsk [province].[20]

Such activities must also have been carried on among the Kalmyks, for the document concludes by observing that Dorzhiev was not only put under surveillance by the Ministry of Internal Affairs but in 1911 the Prime Minister, P. A. Stolypin, issued instructions to the governors of Astrakhan and Stavropol provinces and to the hetman (commanding officer) of the Don Cossacks that he was to be sent away if he appeared in the territories.[21]

Dorzhiev was also, as an extension of his Buryat nationalism, concerned with the promotion and protection of Buryat culture. The Interior Ministry document mentions one of his joint achievements in this field with his colleague Zhamtsarano: the development of a Latin-based alphabet to replace the strange vertical method of writing hitherto used by the Mongol peoples:

> Since the Buryats had no written alphabet of their own and the Ministry of Public Education demanded that they use the Russian alphabet in their schools, the question of an alphabet for these schools was raised. Ultimately, preference was given to a new Buryat-Mongol alphabet created by Dorzhiev with the help of Zhamtsarano for the purpose of unifying all the Mongolian peoples.[22]

In the event, however, few books were published in this alphabet.

Later, in 1910, Dorzhiev was involved in setting up the first Buryat publishing house. It was called Naran (lit. The Sun), and it put out books on 'the social and political history of Buryat thought, philosophical and artistic works'.[23]

Dorzhiev was therefore a multi-faceted person. At base he was a dedicated Buddhist, but one of a progressive and reformist disposition; he was also politically active as a Buryat nationalist; as an intellectual, he furthermore concerned himself with Buryat culture; and in a wider sense he was both a Pan-Mongolist and a Pan-Buddhist. All these were aspects of one and the same man, and they fitted together without tension or contradiction.

*

Dorzhiev's colleague, Tsiben Zhamtsaravich Zhamtsarano (1880–1942?), was a Buryat intellectual from the Aga steppe who was sent to be educated at Irkutsk University, where he developed an interest in socio-political and scientific matters. He then travelled among both the Cis- and Trans-Baikal Buryats as well as in Mongolia, collecting folklore and ethnographical material. Having published a number of books, he was in 1906 awarded the gold medal of the Imperial Russian Geographical Society; he also began to lecture in Mongolian language at St Petersburg University.[24]

During his various field trips, Zhamtsarano amassed a great deal of knowledge and became at the same time acutely aware that the more advanced Buryats were 'searching for an escape from the darkness'; in particular, they were looking for political reform. He subsequently wrote a number of impassioned articles in which he appealed to Buryat intellectuals to strive for the realization of these objectives. In addition he was concerned with popular education and planned an ambitious publication programme that would enlighten his people in the various fields of modern scientific knowledge.

*

Dorzhiev also brought to Trans-Baikalia during this troubled period some four thousand rubles with which he had been entrusted by Prince Ukhtomsky to commission local master-craftsmen to fabricate a dewachen (corrupted in Russian to 'devazhin'): an ambitious model of Sukhavati, the Western Paradise of the compassionate buddha Amitabha where followers of the Pure Land school of Buddhism aspire to be reborn after death. Ukhtomsky wrote to the Chancellery of the Russian Museum in 1905:

> This has long been ready and is kept packed in the home of Bandido Khambo Lama Iroltuev. When I handed over my collection of Buddha-rupas to the Alexander III Museum [he did this in 1902], I also gave them the right to receive this Devazhin, which was to be a supplement to it.[25]

According to Professor Poppe, there were many such models in the

datsans of Trans-Baikalia, and a particularly beautiful one at the Aga
Datsan in Chita:

> This model contained scores of miniature temples, hundreds of statuettes,
> worked in the most delicate filigree, depicting various saints, and an infinity
> of figurines of animals, birds, metal flowers and trees. Each figure was
> made of gilded copper and silver and covered with an extremely fine layer
> of enamel.[26]

*

In January 1902 news reached London that towards the end of the
previous year Dorzhiev had passed through Moscow and had presented
the Imperial Russian Geographical Society with 'interesting Tibetan
antiquities'. It was reported at the same time that he intended to visit
Paris during the coming summer and deliver a collection of Buddhist
objects to the Musée Guimet.[27]

He actually arrived in Paris in October, where according to Joseph
Deniker he commissioned a tse-boum or vase of life, which, as we noted
above, is one of the main ritual objects used in long-life ceremonies.
According to Deniker, this particular tse-boum consisted of an image
of Amitabha, the Buddha of Infinite Light (of whom Amitayus, the
Buddha of Infinite Life, is a bodhisattva reflex), carved in ivory and
tinted red. This was supported by an ivory bowl, again tinted red, which
in its turn rested on a silver platter adorned with two dragons. The
whole object was about eight inches high. Apparently the Dalai Lama,
despite his youth, was rather frail, and handling this two-and-a-quarter
pound object during protracted ceremonies caused him to suffer some
fatigue. Dorzhiev therefore came to Paris to 'find a craftsman sufficiently
skilled to make a similar tse-boum, which would be lighter and more
precious'.[28]

Deniker recommended aluminium for lightness but Dorzhiev, who had
seen a photographer burn aluminium powder, dismissed the suggestion
and opted instead for silver gilt for the lower platter and the two
dragons, which were made detachable (they were in fact only included
as a sop to the Chinese and could be taken off if none were present).
The image of Amitabha and a supporting bowl, meanwhile, were carved
from coral, which Dorzhiev obtained personally from Livorno in Italy.
Various other modifications were also made to the original design. The
image of Amitabha now rested on a lotus of white chalcedony, his head
surrounded by a halo of lapis-lazuli. Above were a chalcedony moon,
a sun of 'yellow stone' and a flame of coral ('symbolizing the radiance
of wisdom'). This beautiful piece, the work of five French craftsmen,

weighed only a pound and three-quarters. Before being shipped to its destination, it was displayed in the Musée Guimet for a week.

*

In Paris in October 1902, Dorzhiev met the exiled neo-Realist poet Maksimilian Aleksandrovich Voloshin (1877–1932), who was one of those Russian intellectuals who were attracted by Eastern religious philosophy.[29] Born in Kiev, Voloshin had, following the early death of his father, moved to the southern Crimea, where he was raised by his mother. He later went on to the Faculty of Law at Moscow University but was expelled for taking part in student unrest. He thereupon decamped to Central Asia in the autumn of 1900, and the six months that he spent there, 'with camel caravans', drastically altered his views and initiated an interest in oriental matters; in particular he was inspired to embark on a critical reappraisal of European culture. He then went to Paris to complete his studies but afterwards, as he told his friend A.M. Peshkovsky,

> I want to set out and explore India, China and Japan on foot. I want to familiarize myself with their cultures, not through European eyes – that would be arrogant and contemptuous – but from an objective point of view.[30]

The young poet's grand plan lost its priority as he fell victim to the charms of fin de siecle Parisian life, at the time at its most gay and bohemian; but the arrival of Agvan Dorzhiev temporarily reawakened it and the two became acquainted. 'Imagine my delight when I was invited to a restaurant by a Tibetan holy man', Voloshin wrote enthusiastically to Y.A. Glotov; 'and I went shopping for the Dalai Lama at the Bon Ma [Bon Marché] with him! On Monday he is coming over to spend the evening with me.'[31]

They talked at length about Buddhism through an interpreter:

> Meeting the Khambo Lama, I developed a passion for Buddhism ... This is my first religious step ... He spoke often about Nirvana, which utterly changed many of my ideas. I learned from him, for example, that Buddhism regards proselytizing with a horror almost equal to that in which it holds violence against the person. How morally admirable this is compared to Christianity, [which is] a religion of propaganda and violence! And the meaning of my tale *Ilimbar Szabba*? You didn't understand it at all. It is not a challenge but a warning. It was composed on the strength of our talks about banning the entry of Europeans to Tibet. Isn't this like encouraging hunting when there is a ban on hunting packs? And Europe is worse than a hunting pack. None has so foully destroyed other cultures as Europe. No other part of the world has such a bloody history.[32]

The picture that Voloshin gives of Dorzhiev himself is of an innocent abroad: 'He appears to have no more idea about Europe than Europeans have about Tibet', he told Glotov – but he was 'very saintly'.

In December 1902, inspired by this meeting, Voloshin announced to his friends that he intended to go to the Far East, visiting the Baikal region on the way, 'where there will be a letter waiting for me at some Buddhist monastery'. He did in fact leave Paris for Russia in January 1903, but he never reached his destination. As V. Kupchenko writes:

> A series of incidents, as much literary as personal in character, deflected him . . . Paris would not give leave of absence to its disciple. It is uncertain whether he was affected by the [subsequent] distant activities of Dorzhiev, who more than once [re]appeared in Russia, and hence in Soviet publications.[33]

Dozhiev probably returned to Trans-Baikalia sometime in 1903. We do not know precisely how long he stayed, but eventually he joined company with a high lama who was going to Tibet. He calls him 'great abbot Tripopa, master of the Kangyur, wise in the sutras, tantras and sciences'.[34] This venerable lama had set up the four new Buryat monasteries mentioned above according to the traditions of Gyu-mé, the Lower Tantric College founded in Lhasa in 1433 by Jé Sherab Sengé, which specialized in training monks in tantric doctrine and practice.

On the way back to Tibet they paused at Urga. There the Jebtsundamba Khutukhtu, in response to their requests, granted them an oral reading of his own collected writings. Curiously, the Khutukhtu's omzé (leader of chanting), a monk named Chog'i Chimé, also told them that the Khutukhtu had declared that the Dalai Lama would soon be coming to Urga and that it was necessary to prepare special quarters for him. Dorzhiev found the suggestion farcical, but in the event the Dalai Lama did arrive in Urga a year or so later, proving that the Khutukhtu either had the gift of second sight – or the luck of the devil. Moreover, when Dorzhiev and Tripopa took their leave of him, the Khutukhtu said, 'Soon we will encounter happiness' – and gave them several silver ingots in protective casings, as well as 'abundant gifts' and of course the obligatory blessings.

For two years or more Dorzhiev had been on the sidelines of power politics. Now, however, he was about to be plunged right back into them for momentous events were under way in the Land of Snows – events which he had unwittingly played no small part in precipitating.

CHAPTER TEN

The Younghusband Mission to Lhasa
1903 – 1904

It had long been known in Britain that the Russians entertained grandiose aspirations to world dominance, something that they had perhaps inherited by reversion from their erstwhile Mongolian conquerors. World domination would of necessity be preceded by dominance in Asia and hence possession of India, the jewel in the British crown. During the eighteenth century, a rumour gained currency that Peter the Great dreamed such dreams and on his death-bed in 1725 willed his successors to realize them. Some Russian emperors appeared to take Peter's injunction seriously. In 1801, the unstable Paul I dispatched twenty-two thousand Cossacks to drive the British out of India, though after he was strangled in his own palace the force was recalled by his successors and so saved from almost certain disaster. Later, Alexander I and Napoleon hatched a scheme for an overland invasion.

During the rest of the nineteenth century, however, the rivalry of Britain and Russia in Asia settled down to a chess-like pattern of move and countermove that became known as the Great Game. The Imperial Russian war-machine advanced remorselessly across the Central Asian chessboard, taking one pawn-like khanate after another – Khiva, Bokhara, Khokhand . . . moving the frontiers of Russia ever closer to those of India. The British could do little about these moves but they did try to prevent the Russians from gaining influence in other key areas. The first was Persia, particularly when it was thought that an invasion could be launched by sea from the Persian Gulf. Later it became clear that the overland route was the only viable one, and then Afghanistan became the crucial area. The British fought two costly wars attempting to establish their influence in Afghanistan and to ensure that the Russians were kept out. Later still, as the Russians advanced into the Pamirs, the British, rushing to plug all possible routes through those high mountains, annexed Hunza, Chitral and Gilgit. The Great

Game was also played in Chinese Sinkiang (Xinjiang), and around the turn of the century, with the declining power of the Manchu Chinese who claimed suzerainty (nominal sovereignty) there, Tibet became an important focus. If the Russians could gain a foothold in the Land of Snows, their armies could come to the Himalayas, India's Great Wall; from there, if they did not actually launch an invasion, they could certainly stir up enough trouble in the Himalayan states and in India itself to pin down large numbers of British troops while they pursued their ambitions elsewhere, notably in the direction of Constantinople.

*

The key figure in the Great Game at the turn of the century was George Nathaniel Curzon (1859–1925). In his younger days a Fellow of All Souls, Oxford, and Tory M P for Southport, he was a brilliant, courageous and highly able man whose career, it was generally agreed, would rise to the heights. Serving as Under Secretary for India (1891–92) and for Foreign Affairs (1895–98), he had taken a special interest in Russian expansion, and in the summer of 1888 rode the new Russian Trans-Caspian Railway through Geok-Tepe, Ashkhabad, Merv and Bokhara to Tashkent in the Islamic south-east, taking copious notes (particularly of a strategic nature) in these areas where the two-headed Imperial Russian Eagle had only recently been hoisted. Curzon, a committed imperialist himself, fully understood and in many ways sympathized with Russian aspirations to dominance in Asia: 'It is a proud and not ignoble aim, and it is well worthy of the supreme moral and material efforts of a vigorous nation', he wrote. However, if Russia was entitled to her ambitions, 'still more so is Britain entitled, nay compelled, to defend that which she has won, and to resist the minor encroachments which are only part of the larger plan'.[1] In other words, he was for a British forward policy in Asia.

One of the first things that Curzon did when he achieved his supreme ambition of becoming Viceroy of India in January 1899 was to change British policy towards Tibet from 'patient waiting' to 'impatient hurry'. What he inherited from his predecessors was, in any case, a highly unsatisfactory situation. For a long time various minor but vexing border and trade disputes had dragged on without resolution because the Tibetans declined to enter into discussions with the Government of India in a statesmanlike way. In fact they stubbornly refused to have any relations at all, explaining that to do so would annoy their Chinese suzerains. Nothing positive came of attempts to deal directly with the Chinese either, for which the Chinese in turn blamed Tibetan intransigence. It was a classic case of passing the buck back and forth ad infinitum and ad absurdum. Concluding that Chinese suzerainty was 'a farce', Curzon decided that 'our dealings must be with Tibet and Tibet alone', for 'it is important that no-one else should seize it, and that it should be turned into a sort of buffer state between the Russian and the Indian Empires'.[2]

So he began a new round of efforts to open communications with the Dalai Lama. A means of doing so was difficult to find, but eventually two letters were dispatched. One of them was handed over to the Dalai Lama's Garpöns or Viceroys in Western Tibet by Captain Kennion, the Assistant Resident in Kashmir; the other was taken directly to Lhasa by Kazi Ugyen Dorji, the Bhutanese Vakil (Agent) in Darjeeling. Both letters were returned unopened. How galling for a supremely proud man like Curzon to receive such a snub – and at about the same time to learn that its perpetrator, the monkish ruler of a backward Oriental country, was freely corresponding with the Emperor of Russia via Lama Dorzhiev. Inevitably, Curzon became more and more convinced that the Russians were beginning to mount their anticipated penetration of Tibet and that a full-blown protectorate might only be a decade away. As for Dorzhiev himself, though Curzon was not precisely sure what he was, he inclined to the view that the Russians were using him as an agent. As he wrote on 11 September 1901 to Lord George Hamilton at the India Office in London: 'I do not myself believe that he [Dorzhiev] is upon a mission, or that he conveys a formal message from the Dalai Lama to the Tsar, but that he will go back with such a mission and such a message, I have not the slightest doubt whatever'.[3]

*

In the months following the Tibetan Mission's reception in St Petersburg, ominous reports reached the British of new and disturbing developments in this particular phase of the Great Game. In January 1902, a Lhasa trader informed Walsh, the Deputy Commissioner at Darjeeling, that an actual treaty existed 'by which Russia undertakes to protect Tibet from any attempt of the British to enter the country'.[4] And in November Charles Hardinge, the British Chargé d'Affaires in St Petersburg, reported that information from a reliable intelligence source led him to believe that, if no formal treaty existed, there was certainly some kind of secret agreement whereby, in return for non-interference in the collection of tithes among the Russian Buddhists, the Dalai Lama would allow the Russians to post a consular officer in Tibet and permit the practice of the Orthodox religion. For fear of antagonizing the

British, the Russians had apparently refrained from sending a consular officer, but would instead send a 'duly-accredited secret agent'. The man selected for this sensitive posting was 'M. Badengieff',[5] though in fact, as we have seen, the man actually selected for this posting was Budda Rabdanov. Some corroboration was given to such reports by information emanating from Lhasa at about the same time that the Chinese Amban had also got wind of a secret Russo-Tibetan agreement and was much annoyed. At his instigation, the Tsongdu (Tibetan National Assembly) had been summoned and had expressed its opposition to 'any protectorate by Russia or interference with the Chinese sovereignty'.

What disturbed Curzon more than Dorzhiev's activities, real or imagined, however, was a series of reports received in 1902 and early 1903, notably from Sir Ernest Satow in Peking and Captain Parr, the Chinese Trade Agent in Yatung. In return for supporting the ailing Manchus in various ways, the Russians would be granted extensive political and commercial rights in Tibet. British official commentators discerned in this the Machiavellian influence of the politically penetrative Russo-Chinese Bank and its gold-mining subsidiary Mongolor – and hence by implication the hands of Prince Ukhtomsky and his man in Mongolia, von Groth, who was believed to have designs on the rich gold fields of Tibet.[6]

For their part, the Russians were equally suspicious of British designs on Tibet. In October 1902, their Chargé d'Affaires in London, Baron Graevenitz, declared that his government had heard that the British were sending troops to Tibet to protect the construction of a railway line, and in December he asked whether the British contemplated a military expedition. Again, in February 1903, he informed Lord Lansdowne, the Foreign Secretary, that his government had heard that a British military expedition had reached 'Komba-Ovaleko' on its way north from the Chumbi valley, and that, viewing the situation with gravity, his government might be forced to take steps to safeguard its interests. In the same month the Russian Ambassador in London, Count Benckendorff, assured Lansdowne that the Russians had no political designs on Tibet, and in April he relayed Count Lamsdorff's categorical assurance that Russia had not concluded any sort of agreement over Tibet, nor had Russian agents been posted there. It was again stressed, however, that the Russian Government could not be indifferent to any change in the status quo vis-à-vis Tibet. Lansdowne in reply gave assurances that Britain had no intention of annexing Tibetan territory, but he left the door open for future military intervention by adding that his government reserved the right to enforce any treaties that the Tibetans might fail to honour. Benckendorff expressed his satisfaction with this.

Such statesman-like pleasantries cut little ice with Curzon. By the end of 1902 he had become convinced of the existence of some kind of secret Russo-Chinese deal over Tibet and was resolved to 'frustrate this little game while there is yet time'. In a letter to Lord George Hamilton of 13 November 1902, he outlined a plan to send to Lhasa a 'pacific mission', accompanied by 'a sufficient force to ensure its safety', to negotiate a 'treaty of friendship and trade with the Tibetan Government'.[7] Unfortunately, though it was agreed that some kind of action was now necessary, the notion did not meet with a very positive response in London. In no mood to add to the white man's burden, the British Government preferred to toy with safer and less potentially unpopular alternatives, such as pressing on with diplomatic efforts or setting the bellicose Gurkhas of Nepal at the throats of the Tibetans. Curzon felt nothing but contempt for the 'inveterate flabbiness' of the politicians and bureaucrats of London and was determined not to be overruled. Imperial history knows many instances of conflict between the men in Whitehall and the men on the spot in the outposts of empire, but what was about to take place was to be a classic of the genre.

*

Throughout the period under discussion the pawn-play of petty border disputes had gone on without pause. Trade had been interfered with, boundary markers set up and thrown down, the Tibetans had occupied Sikkimese territory and been roughly evicted – and of course the vexatious lack of communication continued. Then early in 1903 the Chinese reopened negotiations with the Government of India and agreed to send deputies to participate in discussions, either at Yatung on the Tibetan side of the frontier, or in Sikkim – 'or in some other place as may be decided upon by Your Excellency'. This was enough for Curzon. Placing his own interpretation on the proposal, he obtained permission from London to dispatch a small negotiating party to Khamba Dzong, which lay a few kilometres inside Tibetan territory, on the road to Lhasa.

The Frontier Commission, as it was called, was led by John Claude White, the Political Officer in Sikkim, but Curzon contrived to send along as well a man of similar stripe to himself, who soon eclipsed White. This was Colonel Francis Younghusband (1863–1942), born at Meerut on the turbulent North-West Frontier and a man of action in the best Kipling tradition – the type who tackled a difficult situation by seizing the most dangerous option. At the tender age of twenty-four he had won the Gold Medal of the Royal Geographical Society by making an epic east-west journey across China by a route not hitherto attempted by any European; it culminated in a perilous winter crossing of the Mustagh Pass between Sinkiang and Kashmir. Later, in 1889 and 1890, he proved himself no slouch at the Great Game when he became a front-line player in British moves to block Russian penetration of the mountainous no-man's-land in the remote north-west. High in the Pamirs he twice met, and socialized affably enough in the manner of the military men of the period, with armed Russian parties, one led by Captain Grombchevsky, the other by Colonel Yanov, who left him in no doubt at all as to Russian intentions. He and Curzon subsequently began to correspond and eventually met up in Chitral in October 1894, when Curzon, still an M P but out of office, was on a tour that also included Hunza and the Pamirs. Curzon's cocksureness and argumentative House of Commons debating manner initially grated on Younghusband, who was the local Political Agent, but nevertheless they opened up to each other and the rugged frontier man eventually discovered that the sleek Tory M P's views on frontier matters were in perfect accord with his own.

Eight years later, having more lately been confined to a humdrum job as Resident at Indore, the prospect of a mission in Tibet was meat and drink to Younghusband:

> I was proud indeed to have been selected for this task . . . I was suddenly myself again, and all the exotic life of Maharajahs and Durbars and gold chairs and scarlet chaprassies[8] a sickly dream. Hardships and dangers I knew I should have. The whole enterprise was risky. But men always prefer risk to ease. Comfort only lulls and softens their capacities, whereas danger tautens every faculty. And Lord Curzon was risking much in pressing his scheme forward against so much opposition.[9]

London had only agreed with reluctance to the move to Khamba Dzong and hemmed Curzon around with all kinds of restrictions, notably that he should not allow the Commission to proceed any further. So there it stayed from July to November 1903, camped behind fortified earthworks. Nearby, a typical Tibetan dzong or fort surmounted the crest of a sharp hill; around stretched a barren plain separated by a range of low hills from the snow-clad Himalayas; Everest was visible in the far distance. 'Life was not unpleasant', wrote one observer, 'but no business was done' − for both sides were stalling. The Tibetans wanted to get the British out and to return to the former status quo; Curzon and Younghusband were playing for time in order to build up a strong enough case for pushing on to Lhasa. As for the Chinese, none of sufficient consequence showed up.

In camp at Khamba Dzong in October 1903, Younghusband, who understood clearly that his job was about frustrating Russia in Tibet rather than resolving piffling trade and border problems, reviewed current British knowledge of Dorzhiev and his Russian associates. What had become of the Buryat lama was difficult to say, he wrote, but 'I am inclined to think that Dorjieff was "worked" by some agent such as Badmaieff or Von Groot, an ex-official of the Chinese Customs service, who resides at Urga and is known to have great influence with the lamas both of Peking and Tibet'.[10]

*

By November 1903 the Viceroy had the ammunition he needed. A few petty infractions by the Tibetans were blown up into instances of 'outrageous conduct' to convince a still reluctant British Government of the need for an advance deeper into Tibetan territory. So in December 1903, as sole head of a reconstituted Commission, Younghusband crossed the Jelap-La with the advance guard of his military escort, which Brigadier-General J R L. Macdonald had been appointed to command, marched up the Chumbi Valley and set up camp at Tuna on the edge of the Tibetan plateau. All that the Russians did was lodge a vigorous protest through Count Benckendorff, who in reply was politely reminded of his country's encroachments elsewhere in Asia, and also asked whether Russia would have shown patience if provoked by Tibet as Britain had been. Confronted by such ineluctable logic, Benckendorff was obliged to bow to the necessity for the British move, with the reassurance that its objectives were strictly limited.

In December, Younghusband reported to Curzon that he had heard from several independent sources that the Tibetans were relying on Russian support and that Russian arms had entered the country. He went on: 'It may be assumed as certain that Dorjieff . . . is at present in Lhasa; that a promise of Russian support has been given by him to the Tibetans; and that the Tibetans believe that this promised support will be given to them.'[11]

Younghusband was surely mistaken on all counts. That Dorzhiev was back in Tibet at this time is unlikely, as indeed is the notion that the Tibetans were sanguine of Russian support. Had support been forthcoming, which it was not, it would in any case have been passionately opposed by the traditionally xenophobic ultra-conservatives in the great monasteries, and sought only by the Dalai Lama and his pro-Russian faction. Prominent among these, the British identified the Kalön (Cabinet Minister) Paljor Dorji Shatra, but he had been removed from office, before Anglo-Tibetan hostilities began in earnest, for advocating a conciliatory line. As for Russian shipments of arms

to Tibet, reports of these had been made by Ekai Kawaguchi, the
Japanese Buddhist monk who was in Lhasa in 1901 and early 1902,[12]
but in the heightened atmosphere of actual engagement they inevitably
proliferated – and not only of war materials but of 'skilled assistance'
being sent to Tibet and of Tibetan forces being led by Russians. There
was even a Reuter report, mentioned by Curzon in a letter to Hamilton,
that 'several hundred cossacks have been sent to Tibet'.[13]

In actual fact, no Russian arms or personnel were ever discovered.
Ironically, the Tibetans themselves gave Younghusband a truer account
of affairs when he actually met their leaders face-to-face a few months
later.

*

While the Commission was camped at Tuna, suffering all the rigours of
the Tibetan winter, Tibetan troops under Lhading Depön, a general from
Lhasa, began to mass at Guru a few miles to the north. Monastic officials
were with them. Younghusband boldly decided in February to ride over
there, accompanied by only two fellow officers, to hold informal talks.
Years before he had attempted a similar exploit at a dacoits' lair in
Hunza and brought it off – just. Having been cordially welcomed by the
Tibetans, he asked why they were on friendly terms with the Russians
but continued to keep the British at arm's length. They assured him that
his suspicions were unfounded: they had no dealings with the Russians,
there was no Russian near Lhasa and Dorzhiev merely followed the
customs of his Mongolian people in making offerings at monasteries.
The reason they debarred Westerners from their country, they explained,
was to protect their religion.

Things went well up to a certain point; then the monks present, who
appeared surly to Younghusband and intent on fomenting trouble, began
to demand that he name a date on which he would retire his forces
from Tuna. 'The atmosphere became electric', he wrote; 'the forces of
all became set; a General left the room; trumpets outside sounded and
attendants closed round us. It was necessary to keep extremely cool in
the circumstances.'[14]

But cool he remained and he lived to lead his mission on from
Tuna on 30 March – and straight into the first inevitable and tragic
confrontation with the Tibetans. At Guru, the Tibetan force had built
a sangar (defensive wall) and dug itself in at a strategically good
place where a rocky spur met a marsh fed by a spring. Further
discussions between the two sides were held here, then British troops
moved forward to the wall and began to try to disarm the Tibetans.

Suddenly a shot rang out. It is unclear who fired it but it precipitated a pitched battle. The Tibetans, armed only with matchlocks and swords, stood absolutely no chance against superior British firepower. Estimates vary, but perhaps five hundred or even seven hundred of them were simply mown down, including Lhading Depön. As Edmund Candler, the *Daily Mail* special correspondent, who was badly hacked about in the engagement, wrote:

> Perhaps no British victory has been greeted with less enthusiasm . . . Certainly the officers, who did their duty so thoroughly, had no heart in the business at all. After the first futile rush the Tibetans made no further resistance. There was no more fighting, only the slaughter of helpless men.[15]

*

After one more engagement, in which the Tibetans again suffered heavy losses, the Mission pushed on to Gyantsé, which was as far as London permitted Younghusband to go at this stage. Gyantsé is dominated by an imposing crag rising some four or five thousand feet above the surrounding plain, which is ribbed with defensive walls and surmounted by an 'almost impregnable' dzong. The buildings of the township, many of them monastic, cluster below, dominated by the great gold-capped Kum-bum, a many-storied chörten (stupa) honeycombed with chapels.

Younghusband did not occupy Gyantsé; instead he installed himself in a nearby village while Macdonald went back with the main force to fetch reinforcements. Many of the Mission's difficulties were attributed to Macdonald's hesitancies, for which he earned the nickname 'Retiring Mad'. This time he erred on the side of incaution, however, for soon Younghusband's small escort found itself under attack. Some sources say, though on what grounds it is not clear, that Dorzhiev masterminded this – a highly unlikely possibility. The escort managed to beat off the attackers, but it was now clear that the Tibetans had themselves brought up reinforcements and were prepared to make a vigorous stand. They took possession of the dzong, which the British had unwisely failed to occupy, and from there ineffectively pounded Younghusband's main position with primitive artillery.

By this time Younghusband's morale had reached a low ebb. In a sense he had outcurzon'd Curzon, who had by now gone home on leave, for while he had grown ever more convinced of the necessity for pushing on to Lhasa, Whitehall stubbornly refused to give him free rein to take what his martial instincts told him would be the most effective course. Wider considerations, including relations with Russia and public popularity, seemed to matter more in the corridors of power than the success of the mission or the well-being of his men. Frustrated, he had been brusque in some of his communications, which he was later to regret. He received an official slap on the wrist for impertinence and was told to stay one month more in Gyantsé in order to give the Tibetans time to negotiate.

Younghusband managed to fob off Tibetan attempts at negotiation and at the end of the month was reluctantly given the official go-ahead to advance on Lhasa. First, however, he had to dislodge the Tibetan force from the dzong. After a dummy manoeuvre, the main attack was launched before daylight on 6 July 1904 on the eastern flank, where the rock was steepest. The British battery first pounded the walls until a large breach was made, then, supported by energetic fire from below, the Gurkhas and Royal Fusiliers of the storming party began to clamber up towards the dzong. Looking in the far distance like a swarm of ants, they finally streamed through the breach and began to fight their way through tier upon tier of fortifications, until at last they could be seen raising the Union Jack on the topmost pinnacle in best Peninsula War style. The road to Lhasa now lay open.

*

By this time Russia herself was deeply embroiled in a war with Japan, the culmination of a long-standing rivalry in East Asia that seemed destined to end in conflict. The Japanese tried at the eleventh hour to avoid a conflict by offering to recognize Russian interests in Manchuria in return for Russian recognition of their interests in Korea, but the Russians arrogantly disdained to accept their proposal, and at a crucial moment the Emperor dismissed Witte, his ablest minister; so, without a proper policy or leadership, they blundered into a war that was to prove disastrous.

Dorzhiev records that he returned to Tibet 'when Russia and Japan were at war', which means sometime after January 1904, most likely March or April. As usual he made offerings – he mentions 'raiments' – to the Dalai and Panchen Lamas, to other lamas and to the venerated statues of Shakyamuni Buddha in the Jokhang and Ramoché temples. Ekai Kawaguchi reports hearing that he brought from the Emperor a suit of Episcopal robes: 'It was a splendid garment glittering with gold and was accepted, I was told, with gratitude by the Grand Lama.'[16] At Ganden, meanwhile, he offered a canopy for the tomb of Jé Tsongkhapa, and at Gomang College embroidered hangings with pendant strings. He then considered returning to Russia but, after consulting the Dalai Lama, remained in Tibet for the time being.

Surprisingly, Dorzhiev's advice to the Tibetans at this critical time was the same as that of ex-Kalön Shatra and the Chinese Amban: to act with restraint since the British were powerful and the Tibetans weak. He reiterated this moderate line several times but it went unheeded, for the Tibetans had blind faith in the occult power of their dharmapalas, those Buddhist transformations of the old gods of India and Tibet who may be ritually invoked to defend faith and fatherland in times of danger. Though he fully appreciated the great spiritual wisdom of the Tibetans, from his knowledge of the world Dorzhiev knew that superstitions like these could not stop a well-equipped modern fighting force. Not wishing to be caught up in the impending nemesis – he talks somewhat platitudinously of having too much bad karma to be able to die yet – he started preparing mules for a prompt departure via Drigung, to the north-east of Lhasa; but he was again asked to stay.

According to the Filchner-Tserempil adventure story, Dorzhiev, who had returned to Tibet in 1902, served as War Minister during the Anglo-Tibetan hostilities and organized the procurement and shipment of armaments. Under his orders his protege, Tserempil, who had directed the Tibetan resistance to date, was able to start one Indian rifle factory with the help of some Moslems; small cannon and gunpowder were also made.

The lama's own account is more modest: that he served the Tibetan cause by helping to construct a water-powered mint. Hitherto the process whereby Tibetan coins were struck had been extremely arduous. According to Tsybikov, who witnessed it at the large hardware manufactory and mint at Dodpal at the foot of the Potala during his visit of 1900/1, thin bars of copper-silver alloy were first beaten out by hand on stone anvils, then discs were cut with shears and finally these were struck in a vice with an engraved die.[17] Water-power could speed up the process, Dorzhiev believed, especially at the beating stage.

The new water-driven mint was at Dodé,[18] where there were waterfalls. The site was visited in 1904 by Brevett-Major W. J. Ottley:

> Proceeding up the Lhasa valley, we rounded a spur east of the Sara [sic] monastery . . . About four miles up, the valley divided into two, one going north-east and the other north. We followed the latter, which soon became narrower and narrower, and steeper and steeper. Further on was a Chinese joss-house, and at about six miles the new Tibetan Mint, which had just been built for the purpose of a new coinage. The machinery had not yet been put in, and probably never will be now.[19]

Ottley was wrong; when Sir Charles Bell and Lieutenant-Colonel R. Kennedy visited the Dodé Mint in 1921, they noted about thirty or forty machines of local manufacture there. They were all hand-operated bar two, which were harnessed to a twelve-foot water-wheel. Bell noted: 'It would seem that by using belts a good many more of the machines could be harnessed to the water-wheel.'[20]

L. Berlin corroborates much of this, but adds that Dorzhiev also 'worked for defence', specifically on reconstructing antiquated Chinese guns, 'which made it possible for the Tibetans to offer the British more serious resistance'. The British also picked up rumours that Dorzhiev was in charge of the 'Lhasa arsenal', which at the time was situated at Tip, on the south bank of the Kyi-Chu.[21] However, these rumours were soon supplanted by others to the effect that he was 'devoting the whole of his attention to the minting of silver coins', and it was extrapolated from this that 'he meditates flight from Lhasa before the arrival of the Mission'.[22] It would appear, therefore, that Dorzhiev's contribution at this critical point in Tibetan history was mainly numismatic.

*

Younghusband, meanwhile, in his advance on Lhasa from Gyantsé, had anticipated some Tibetan resistance at the Karo-La. But that soon fizzled out and his Mission, which by now included some eight thousand troops, officials and camp followers, proceeded comparatively unhindered to the lake of Yamdrok-Tso. Nearby, at the village of Nagartsé, Yuthok Kalön, the Chikyab Khenpo or Lord Chamberlain, a member of the Kashag (Tibetan Cabinet), arrived with several monastic representatives to try to halt his advance by gentle persuasion. It was to no avail: Younghusband forged on into the fertile valley of the wide, deep and fast-flowing Tsangpo river. It took a week to ferry personnel and equipment across at Chaksam, using abandoned Tibetan ferry-boats and two canvas Berthon boats. Here more high officials arrived from Lhasa, now only about three days' march away, with urgent letters and further entreaties that the British call a halt – but again to no avail.

With the British so near, there must have been extreme panic in the holy city. What the Tibetans had feared most for over a century was on the verge of happening. The Dalai Lama, who had been engaged for over a year in a nyen-chen or long retreat – it should have lasted three or four years – at a monastery about eighteen miles from Lhasa, had not been directly involved in events so far.[23] The Tibetan Government, unsure of precisely what course to take at this critical juncture, consulted the Nechung Oracle who, having gone into an awesome ritual trance in which he was possessed by the powerful protector spirit, Dorji Drakden, duly pronounced that the Lama should emerge from his seclusion and leave for Mongolia.[24]

Dorzhiev, naturally concerned too for his old pupil's safety, had arrived at a similar conclusion. Protocol prevented him from saying as much directly, so he sent the Lama a letter 'asking how I would know if it came time to leave for Mongolia'.[25] The next evening, 29 July, the British still at Chaksam, he was summoned to the Dalai Lama's summer palace, the Norbulingka, which lies in pleasant grounds about four kilometres west of Lhasa. Here he was informed by His Holiness's personal staff that preparations had been made for his departure. The decision may have been taken or at least endorsed by a joint meeting of the Tsongdu and the Kashag; their concern, according to Tsepön W.D. Shakabpa, being not so much for the Dalai Lama's safety as that there was a danger of 'his being forced to sign an agreement harmful to the long range interests of Tibet'.[26] More unproductive letters had in the meantime been dispatched to Younghusband, including one from the Dalai Lama himself, which had been delivered by the Lord Chamberlain.

At about two o'clock in the early hours of 30 July 1904, Dorzhiev presented himself at the Potala. There, probably in the Dalai Lama's own private apartments at the top of this majestic mountain of a building, the final preparations were made. Then, in the first dawn light, the Dalai Lama left Lhasa with eight companions and headed northwards on horseback towards the Go-La pass. Dorzhiev of course was with him.

CHAPTER ELEVEN

The Dalai Lama in Exile
1904 – 1908

When the British arrived at Lhasa early in August 1904, they were not without their apprehensions. At Gyantsé they had learned that the Tibetans could fight, and there were some who grimly imagined that at Lhasa they would now find themselves attacked by forty thousand fanatical monks armed with Russian rifles – 'We saw them mown down by Maxims, lanes of dead, a hopeless struggle and an ugly page in military history.'[1] But as things worked out, the mission reached the holy city on 3 August without a fight, and during the whole of its six-week stay there no blood was spilled, except by a hefty dop-dop (fighting monk) who went berserk with a broadsword and was duly hanged as an example. No substantial evidence of Russian arms, advisers or troops was found either, proving that reports of such had been largely chimerical, or else exaggerated in the interests of making political capital.

Nor, of course, did the British find any trace of the Dalai Lama and Agvan Dorzhiev. Their small party was by that time travelling northwards via the monasteries of Talung and Reting, which lie about sixty-five and a hundred kilometres north of Lhasa respectively, to Nagchukha. Messages were sent after them by the Amban and the Tsongdu – 'said to be angry with him in consequence of his flight', Younghusband recorded – requesting His Holiness to return to Lhasa. One was brought by Yuthok Kalön who, according to Dorzhiev, told the Dalai Lama, 'If you return to Lhasa you will be received with tributes and respect and come to no harm.' The Lama did not buy this, however, and promptly took the high road to Urga.[2] Younghusband was therefore obliged to negotiate with the Tsongdu and with the Regent, the Tri Rinpoché of Ganden, to whom the Dalai Lama had transferred power before leaving Lhasa. It has been maintained, however, that the seals of office with which the venerable Ganden Tripa had been entrusted were the Lama's religious ones, not those used for transacting temporal affairs,[3] so His Holiness may have had it in mind to repudiate any agreement that was negotiated.

*

In Russia, meanwhile, the antiquarian and scholarly susceptibilities of Prince Esper Ukhtomsky had been aroused at the prospect of the profanation of the hallowed shrines of Tibet by the brutish British:

> What is the chief danger of the movement of the English armies to the 'land of the Lamas'? The Tibetan monasteries are exceedingly rich, and form real treasure-houses of ancient culture; they contain religious objects of the highest artistic value, and the rarest literary memorials. If the Sepoys reach Teshu-Lunpo [sic] and Lhasa, with their fanatical passion for loot, which was so signally exhibited in the recent Boxer campaign, it is beyond all doubt that the most precious treasures on the altars and in the libraries of the Lamas will be in danger. It is impossible even to tell how great an injury may thus be caused to Orientalism, how the solution of many scientific problems may be put off, problems which are closely bound up with the gradual revelation of the secrets of Tibet. The vandalism which was a disgrace to our age, when Pekin [sic] was recently ransacked and looted, will pale before what the English will probably do by the hands of their dusky mercenaries.[4]

He went on to lament that Russia had been too late 'with her obscurely felt inclination to enter into closer relations with the realm of the Dalai-Lama' — but there was hope that some future Dalai or Panchen Lama might be reborn 'within the sphere of Russian influence'; thus, 'England may gain territorial control of the Lamaist world, but to win it spiritually and to bring it closer to them will be given only to those who will not raise a destroying hand against the shrines of Buddhism.'

Given his views, Ukhtomsky's feelings are perhaps understandable, though his specific fears proved unfounded. The discipline of the Indian troops, who included Pathans, Sikhs, Gurkhas and Punjabi Moslems, was, according to Younghusband, 'excellent', though he conceded that 'in their natural state, under their own leaders, and uncontrolled by British officers, they would have played havoc in Lhasa'.[5]

*

By the middle of August the Dalai Lama was reported to have left Nagchukha and to be travelling across the Chang-Tang towards Tsaidam. Even in Lhasa, according to Sir Charles Bell, he would often discard the ceremonial palanquin for a pony or mule; now he rode fast, putting a good distance between himself and British troops. At one point, when both men and horses felt a severe earth tremor, His Holiness explained that they were on the border of Shambhala.[6]

The Ganden Tripa was meanwhile proving himself a skilful diplomatist. He got on well with Younghusband and a formal treaty was rapidly negotiated, ratified by the Tsongdu (though not by the Chinese Amban) and signed on 7 September with all due pomp and ceremony in the great Audience Hall of the Potala. This so-called Lhasa Convention settled various outstanding trade and frontier problems, provided for the establishment of trade marts at Gyantsé and Gartok, imposed an indemnity of Rs 7,500,000/- on the Tibetans to be paid over a seventy-five-year period (during which time British troops would occupy the Chumbi Valley), and bound the Tibetans to have no dealings with any other foreign power without British consent. An addendum allowed for the British Trade Agent at Gyantsé to visit Lhasa.

Afterwards, able to relax at last after weeks of tension, Younghusband rode off alone into the hills outside Lhasa and received a profoundly transformative mystical experience:

> My task was over and every anxiety was passed. The scenery was in sympathy with my feelings; the unclouded sky a heavenly blue; the mountains softly merging into violet; and as I looked towards that mysterious purply haze in which the sacred city was once more wrapped, I no longer had cause to dread the hatred it might hide. From it came only the echoes of the Lama's words of peace. And with all the warmth still on me of that impressive farewell message, and bathed in the insinuating influences of the dreamy autumn evening, I was insensibly suffused with an almost intoxicating sense of elation and good-will. This exhilaration of the moment grew and grew till it thrilled through me with overpowering intensity. Never again could I think evil, or ever again be at enmity with any man. All nature and all humanity were bathed in a rosy glowing radiancy; and life for the future seemed nought but buoyancy and light.[7]

Unfortunately all was not buoyancy and light when Younghusband got back to London. Despite being popular with King and country, the men in Whitehall, notably Sir John Brodrick who had replaced Lord Lansdowne at the India Office, were annoyed that he had overstepped his mandate and were bent on emasculating his treaty. With only a KCIE, a less prestigious order of knighthood than might have been expected, he soon returned to India, where he served as Resident in Kashmir from 1906 until his retirement in 1909, after which he allowed scope to the religious side of his nature, going on to found the World Congress of Faiths, a forward-looking organization concerned with bringing the great religions of the world into harmony with one another.

As for his mentor, Lord Curzon, he had been on leave in England during the negotiations in Lhasa and subsequently had also to grit his teeth and watch his cherished Tibetan policy pulled apart. Such was the fate of two of the last of the classic breed of imperialists.

*

From Tsaidam, the Dalai Lama and his party travelled into the domains of the Kurluk Mongols on the northern edge of Tsaidam, where he was received with 'respects, tribute and glory' by the local beise and others, who were devoted Gelugpas. Indeed, taking advantage of a rare opportunity, the faithful came out all along his route to make offerings and to receive blessings, even when he was passing through bandit country. In several places stone thrones were erected in his honour, and a stream once known as 'The Bad Spring' was renamed 'The Holy Spring'. Such things served for long afterwards as memorials of his transit.

When His Holiness eventually reached the lands of the Khalkha Mongols, he and his party were hospitably entertained for some days by 'the tulkus, lamas and teachers who illuminate the Dharma at the monastery of Yungdrung Pai-se', which may be the Yum-beise küren referred to by Yuri Roerich, a monastery situated in the southernmost part of Mongolia, consisting of two dukhangs or assembly halls surrounded by a cluster of white houses.[8] From there His Holiness proceeded to the monastery of the 'Great Abbot Nomonhan', and then into the aimaks or provinces of Sain Noyön Khan and Tushetu Khan. When the Jebtsundamba Khutukhtu got wind of his approach, he dispatched his brother and two ministers with a palanquin to escort him for the last twenty-eight days of his journey. By the time he reached Urga in November 1904, after three gruelling months in the deserts and mountains of Central Asia, his party had grown to several hundred persons and his baggage was carried by a small army of camels.

Why did the Dalai Lama chose to flee to Mongolia in 1904? Tibetan hagiography tends to portray events in a pious light, untainted by worldly considerations. So, if we are to believe such contemporary Tibetan historical accounts as *The String of Wondrous Gems*, for instance, the coming of the British to Lhasa merely gave His Holiness opportunity to embark on an extended pastoral visit to his Mongolian and Chinese flocks, and at the same time to fulfil a long-standing desire to see two of the great sights of the Buddhist world: the birth-place of Jé Tsongkhapa at Kum-Bum and Wu T'ai Shan, the Buddhist sacred mountain in China.[9] Although this is not a merely fanciful reading – in view of the importance attached to spiritual considerations in the life of a Dalai Lama – it would be unrealistic to imagine that political considerations did not loom large in this particular instance. Urga was after all on the very doorstep of the Russian empire, so it was a convenient place from which to communicate with the Russian Government, or even to make a dash for Russian territory – there is evidence that he initially had this in mind.

The Russians certainly gave His Holiness a warm welcome when he arrived in Urga. Fifty Cossacks from Kyakhta fired a salute, and during his stay he enjoyed the protection of the Russian consul[10] (British sources merely say that he was 'carefully shepherded') whom Dorzhiev visited almost at once on His Holiness's orders. Through him, Nicholas II was informed of recent events in Tibet and that 'the direct aim of his arrival in Urga was the wish to receive help from Russia against the British'.[11] Then in June 1905 Dmitri Pokotilov, the new Russian Minister to Peking, visited him en route to his new posting, bearing gifts from the Emperor and promises of support despite the war with Japan. As a former Director of the Russo-Chinese Bank in Peking and afterwards a member of its Directory Council in St Petersburg, Pokotilov would have at one time worked closely with Prince Ukhtomsky. Like the prince, he was also an Orientalist.[12]

*

According to Berlin, Dorzhiev left Urga for St Petersburg in March 1905 with the Dalai Lama's Secretary, Tseren Damba Dobdanov, and, through the good offices of the Foreign Minister, Aleksandr Izvolsky, was granted an audience with the Emperor. As Izvolsky did not become Foreign Minister until May 1906, there is some confusion here. Berlin goes on to say that as well as outlining recent events in Tibet and relaying the Dalai Lama's wish for Russian support, Dorzhiev also informed the Russian Government that the Dalai Lama wished to visit Peking. The official reply to this was that it would be best if the Lama stayed in Mongolia for the summer of 1905, but when he did go to Peking the Russian Minister there would be given the 'necessary directives'.[13]

In Dorzhiev's own account it is clear that the audience took place much later. Nicholas II and his ministers then agreed that assistance be given to Tibet, though because of Russia's defeat in the war with Japan this would necessarily have to be of a gradual nature. Specifically, they promised to help by negotiating with China and Britain.

Dorzhiev was also at pains to clarify certain matters concerning the Panchen Lama. The press, he suggests, had been putting it about that the Dalai Lama had transmitted his powers to the Panchen Lama – and not merely his temporal powers but perhaps the very spiritual principle that incarnates in the line of the Dalai Lamas. By describing the way in which tulkus (reincarnating lamas) are recognized in Tibet, Dorzhiev showed the Emperor and his ministers that the Dalai Lama could not make such transfers.[14]

All this in fact makes good sense, for in January 1906 the Panchen Lama had visited Calcutta and met the new Viceroy, Lord Minto, though the idea had originated with Curzon, who believed that the Panchen could be used as a medium for maintaining British influence in Tibet following the emasculation of the Lhasa Convention. This of course would have entailed building up the Panchen's powers at the expense of those of the Dalai Lama, a policy against which the Russians, who at the time saw their interests as lying with His Holiness, warned the British. The British in their turn protested about reports that a Buryat escort would accompany the Dalai Lama when he returned to Tibet; the Chinese were also concerned about this.

No report of an audience appears in the British records until 14 March 1906, while Lamsdorff was still Foreign Minister. Cecil Spring-Rice, the Chargé d'Affaires in St Petersburg, then reported to Sir Edward Grey at the Foreign Office in London that he had been told by M. Hartwig, Director of the Asiatic Department, that Dorzhiev had recently arrived in the capital and requested an audience with the Emperor in order to present a message and gifts from the Dalai Lama. Nicholas had subsequently seen him and accepted the gifts, which consisted of an image of the Buddha, a Buddhist text and some fabric.

> The message was to the effect that the Lama had the utmost respect and devotion for the 'Great White Tsar' and that he looked to His Majesty for protection from the dangers which threatened his life if he returned to Lhassa [sic], which was his intention and duty. The answer returned to him was of a friendly character, consisting of an expression of His Majesty's thanks for his message and of his interest in his welfare.
>
> M. Hartwing said that he wished His Majesty's Government should hear exactly what had occurred, as the press would probably make out that the audience had a political character.[15]

Following the audience, the Emperor sent a friendly and vaguely supportive telegram to the Dalai Lama, the text of which was published in the Russian *Méssager Officiel* of 5 April 1906:

> My numerous subjects professing the Buddhist faith had the happiness of saluting their spiritual chief during his sojourn in the north of Mongolia on the borders of the Russian Empire. Rejoicing that my subjects were able to receive a beneficent spiritual influence from Your Holiness, I beg you to believe my feeling of sincere gratitude and esteem towards you.[16]

This and other recent developments further alarmed the Chinese Government, which sent a special mission to warn the Dalai Lama against intrigue with Russian officials and that disregard of this would entail his being deposed.[17]

*

Putting all the evidence together, it is almost certain that Dorzhiev's audience with the Emperor took place in February or early March 1906. As this was towards the end of the Dalai Lama's stay in Mongolia, why the delay? The explanation must lie in the fact that 1905 was an acute crisis year for the Russian autocracy – a full dress rehearsal for 1917. In May Russia received the coup de grâce at the hands of the Japanese when her Baltic Fleet was sunk off the island of Tsushima – the first time that a European power was defeated by an Asiatic one. At home, meanwhile, the year started with Bloody Sunday (22 January), when troops in St. Petersburg opened fire on a crowd of striking workers led by Father Gapon, killing many. It continued with strikes and revolutionary strife, obliging Nicholas, with extreme reluctance, to summon a Duma or National Assembly and to concede what amounted to a constitution, the so-called October Manifesto, which was generally seen as a faltering but positive first step towards representative government.

Thus beset, had Dorzhiev arrived in the capital some time in the first part of 1905, Nicholas would understandably have been in no mood to address himself to the problems of the Dalai Lama, especially if the Lama was declaring his desire to enter the Russian empire.[18] So Nicholas probably temporized and Dorzhiev was for the moment unable to fulfil his mission.

But it is hardly likely that Dorzhiev spent the whole of 1905 idly kicking his heels in St Petersburg. Instead he probably got involved in the upsurge of nationalist activity that took place in Buryatia during that momentous year. This included the election of a Buryat congress, which demanded autonomy, judicial reforms and use of the indigenous language in local government and education,[19] while at the end of the year there was a boycott of the Russian administration and the election of local officials.

The evidence is slender on this point, but it includes the Russian Interior Ministry document of 1911 to which we have already referred. This records that 'during the period of the so-called Liberation Movement', Agvan Dorzhiev and the Buryat scholar and folklorist Ts. Zh. Zhamtsarano were prime movers in nationalist activities. When the document mentions Zhamtsarano conducting nationalist propaganda among Buryat teachers, we can be fairly certain that it is referring to the Banner of the Buryat People, an underground union of Buryat teachers and educationalists that he set up in 1906 with the aim of promoting a Buryat national renaissance, giving the Buryat people a broad education, nationalizing the schools and working for some measure of national autonomy and democracy.[20] These aims were not essentially anti-Russian; nor could they be strictly described as revolutionary but rather what the communists would later term bourgeois-democratic. Slightly earlier, Zhamtsarano had criticized the provocative remarks of the War Minister, General Kuropatkin, who had threatened to obliterate the Buryats from the face of the earth if they raised the slightest resistance to imperial authority.

*

The rip-roaring *Sturm über Asien* naturally has a far more exciting tale to tell. It maintains that during 1905 Dorzhiev remained in Urga while, through his agent Zerempil, he attempted to foment insurrection against the Chinese in the Koko-Nor region of north-eastern Tibet and adjacent areas. In furtherance of this, he procured and shipped arms, mainly Russian and Japanese, across the Gobi to east Tsaidam, and also managed to dispatch a number of Russian deserters and adventures. His notion was to use the Kum-Bum monastery as the starting-point for the planned revolt, which indeed did break out, though in the event it was ruthlessly suppressed by the Chinese. Eventually, at the insistence of the British, Dorzhiev was ordered by the Chinese to leave Urga and was sent by the Russians to Kalmykia. For a time he stayed at the spa of Pyatigorsk 'for recreation'. All this, which reads like an imaginitive resuscitation of Dr Badmaev's old scheme for fomenting rebellion in Chinese dominated territory, must be treated with caution.

*

More dependably, the doyen of Russian Buddhologists, Fyodor Ippolitovich Stcherbatsky (1866–1942), records in a personal article that he met Dorzhiev in eastern Siberia in May 1905. Intending to meet the Dalai Lama, Stcherbatsky had left St Petersburg on 26 April and travelled as far as Troitskosavsk near Khyahkta. There he was delayed for a week, unable to travel the last leg of his journey to Urga, as the Chinese authorities had commandeered all available transport animals for Prince Friedrich Leopold of Prussia and his entourage. It was while waiting that Stcherbatsky met Dorzhiev, who, he interestingly reports, was in hiding, though why and from whom he does not say.[21]

Born at Kielce in Poland into the family of a Russian Army general, Stcherbatsky had been a pupil of the great Russian pioneer orientalist, I.P. Minayev (1840–90), and later of Georg Bühler in Vienna and Hermann Jacobi in Bonn. Rising eventually to the rank of a world authority on Buddhist philosophy, he produced a number of influential studies, some of which, notably his *Buddhist Logic* (two volumes, 1930–32), a study of the epistemology of the ancient Indian pandits Dharmakirti and Dignaga, are still in print. Strangely, he wrote his major works in English, and when asked why this was so answered that he wrote exclusively for 'those Russian noblemen who know only English'[22] – an élitist reply if ever there was one, indicating that he was only interested in high intellectuals with a world or universalist view-point. Later, under the Communists, he more prudently said that it was so that his books could be read in India. He taught at St Petersburg (later Leningrad) University from 1900 to 1941, and trained a generation of eminent Buddhologists, including E. E. Obermiller and A.I. Vostrikov. His teaching methods, which were uniquely his own, were based on classical Eastern and Western approaches that laid primary stress on the teacher-pupil relationship. He was also on the construction committee of Dorzhiev's temple in St Petersburg, in which connection it has been suggested that he merely saw the temple as a convenient laboratory in which he could conduct research. This is perhaps a little cynical, for he was certainly very sympathetic to Buddhism, though not a card-carrying Buddhist like his pupils Obermiller and Vladimirtsov. Obermiller suffered from a hereditary disease for which he sought treatment from Tibetan doctors and believed his life thereby prolonged; Tibetan Buddhism was always for him a very close personal matter. Vladimirtsov, on the other hand, caused something of a scandal in the twenties when Soviet papers revealed that he was a practising Buddhist.[23]

Around 1905, Stcherbatsky was concerned to vitalize his book knowledge of Buddhist philosophy by exposing himself to its living traditions. Dorzhiev, he wrote, gave him a letter of introduction to influential individuals among the Mongolian priesthood, which later gave him an entrée to the court of the Dalai Lama as well as the chance of meeting him personally:

> Finally on 12 May [OS] I was able to get horses, with which we reached Urga in five days. There at first I experienced great difficulty owing to my lack of familiarity with the Mongolian language ... Not without some difficulty, I succeeded in finding a Tibetan, who had been with the Kalmyks and knew some Russian. With his help, I began to familiarize myself with

the spoken Tibetan language. Meanwhile, I was able to arrange a meeting with the Dalai Lama's Soibon Khambo [guardian], Agvan Choi-dag'u, and the Emchi Khambo [physician], Tub-van'u, with the letter of recommendation from Dorzheyev, and a date was arranged for my first audience with the Dalai Lama.[24]

The Dalai Lama urged both Stcherbatsky and his pupil, the Buryat intellectual Badzar Baradinevich Baradin (1878–1937), to return to Lhasa with him, assuring them that they would be afforded every facility to pursue their researches. Stcherbatsky himself would have eagerly snapped up this unique offer – he was extremely keen to find the Sanskrit manuscripts that Sarat Chandra Das had told his teacher Minayev existed in the libraries of the monastic universities of Tibet – but the Acting Foreign Minister, Obolensky, squashed the plan by telling the Committee for the Study of Central and East Asia, under whose auspices Stcherbatsky was travelling, not to authorize the visit.[25] Stcherbatsky was, however, able to further his studies by travelling in both Mongolia and Trans-Baikalia. Baradin, meanwhile, who was in the employ of the Committee for the Study of Central and East Asia and had been specially trained to travel to Tibet, was able to proceed to north-east Tibet, where he collected a quantity of Tibetan Buddhist texts which were later taken back to St Petersburg. He also visited the monastery at Labrang near Lanzhou and subsequently wrote a monograph on the Temple of Maitreya there.

*

Another eminent Russian to visit Urga was the explorer P.K. Kozlov, who came to greet the Dalai Lama on behalf of the Imperial Russian Geographical Society; he had several audiences with His Holiness. A portrait of His Holiness was also made by the St Petersburg artist, N. Ya. Kozhevnikov, who was with Kozlov's party.[26] From the Aga steppe, meanwhile, came G. Ts. Tsybikov and his wife Lkhama Norboevna (1881–1960), who travelled by relay horses accompanied by a farrier. When he saw him again, the Dalai Lama recognized Tsybikov, and asked to know who he was and where he had seen him before. 'I am a Russian professor', Tsybikov replied. 'I am a Buddhist and I saw you when you condescended to touch me with your rosary in your palace in Lhasa.'

*

The Dalai Lama spent just under two years in Mongolia. During this time he was feted both by the aristocracy and the ordinary people, and pilgrims flocked to him from Buryatia and even from as far away as the Kalmyk steppe for blessings. He performed this ritual mechanically, sitting in an arm chair in a palanquin outside which there was a handle from which some holy books hung by silk cord. Every time a devotee passed beneath the palanquin, the handle was set in motion and the book touched each of them as they made their prostrations.[27]

His Holiness stayed initially at the Gandan monastery in Urga, to which the most philosophically inclined lamas were attached. Here, according to Dorzhiev, 'the fine students and sages at the two colleges ... posed a number of questions to His Holiness about the Five Treatises, the Sutras and the Tantras. He answered them with no difficulty at all and so was praised with immeasurable admiration and respect as an omniscient being.'[28] In addition he travelled into the hinterland to dispense initiations and teachings; and thousands saw him celebrate Monlam Chenmo in Urga in February 1905 and February 1906.

Unfortunately, though pious Lamaist sources tend to play it down, friction developed between the Dalai Lama and the debauched Eighth Jebtsundamba Khutukhtu, probably because the Khutukhtu became jealous of the veneration heaped upon His Holiness, who was also technically his preceptor. Certainly during his stay in Urga, coming more closely to know of the wayward young Khutukhtu's peccadillos, His Holiness formed the opinion that he was 'a man of indifferent character who does not follow the tenets of Lamaist doctrine'.[29] It seems, moreover, that local subscriptions were raised to support the Lama and his sizeable entourage, which included a large number of Russian Buddhists, and this may have formed an additional cause of resentment.

Towards the end of his time in Mongolia, the Dalai Lama left Urga for Uliasutai and elsewhere in Sain Noyon Khan Aimak, where he was entertained by local princes. The Chinese were particularly alarmed when they heard that he had visited Van-Khüren, which lay perilously close to the Russian frontier.

*

The Chinese had of course been greatly humiliated by the signing of the Lhasa Convention over their heads. After 1904 they therefore began an aggressive campaign to restore their prestige and power in the Land of Snows. They were assisted in this by the weakness of British policy towards Tibet in the immediate post-Curzonian years. As it was felt by some pertinent British politicians and officials that Chinese assent to the Lhasa Convention was advisable, discussions were held that resulted in the signing in 1906 of an Anglo-Chinese Convention; this de facto recognized Chinese authority over Tibet. In the same year Chang Yin-T'ang was appointed Imperial Commissioner for Tibet; his aim was to diminish British influence and authority and bring Tibet, reorganized into two Chinese provinces, under indirect Chinese rule. By the time he left Tibet in 1908 he had effectively paved the way for possible future Chinese domination. There was also military activity on the eastern marches of Tibet, where from 1905, Chao Erh-feng, Viceroy of Szechuan (Sichuan), waged war against the swashbuckling Tibetan frontier tribes. Chao was to be appointed Resident in Tibet in 1908.

As for the return of the Dalai Lama to Lhasa, by 1906 the Chinese were thought to favour it, though their primary concern was to keep His Holiness away from the Russians. The former Russian Foreign Minister, Count Lamsdorff, who found the Lama's presence in Mongolia an embarrassment, had been in favour too, but his successor, Izvolsky, thought otherwise. Conferring in July 1906 with Sir Arthur Nicolson, the British Ambassador at St Petersburg, he expressed the belief that in Tibet the Lama 'might prove an element of danger and of trouble in that country'. Nicolson agreed with this.[30]

*

Regardless of what these great powers deemed desirable, the Dalai Lama left Mongolia towards the end of September 1906. According to Dorzhiev, he travelled to Kandrowang and Dzaya monasteries, and in October arrived at Sining (Xining), where he was delayed by the faithful who as ever came in crowds seeking blessings. A number of Mongolian princes and a guard from Uliasutai attended him, but no Russian Buddhists. The Chinese then stepped in and took him to 'Kanchow' or 'Hanchow' (Lanzhou?), ostensibly, so their officials informed their British counterparts, to remove him from Russian influence. In the next month, November, he was at Kum-Bum. The monastery there, a vast sprawling complex of buildings, was founded in 1516 amid the green hills of what was once the Tibetan province of Amdo but, since the Chinese redrew the map, now lies in Qinghai. It was (and still is) a great centre of pilgrimage, its special attraction being a miraculous tree said to have sprung from the placental blood of Tsongkhapa's birth; on its leaves a hundred thousand images or else Tibetan letters are said to appear, hence its name.[31]

*

Dorzhiev was meanwhile still in Russia. In November he was reported to have been 'in consultation with officials of the Ministry of Foreign Affairs as to Mongolian matters'. Izvolsky, who privately informed Nicolson of this, said he had not seen the Buryat Lama himself.[32]

Dorzhiev also at this time submitted a report, dated 20 November 1907, to the Vice-President of the imperial Russian Geographical Society, P.P. Semyonov-Shansky, entitled 'On a Rapprochement between Russia, Mongolia and Tibet'. In this he rehashed the old arguments of the Eastern Lobby: that 'Russia must be in every way a kind and constant friend, teacher and protector of the Mongols and Tibetans, and defend them against exploitation and oppression by China and Britain', and that 'we must undertake a peaceful cultural and economic conquest of these countries'. In a manner highly reminiscent of Dr Badmayev, moreover, he went on to propose the formation of a private commercial and industrial enterprise with a network of affiliated offices in these countries; its economic activities would be supplemented with cultural and educational work.[33]

*

The Dalai Lama had passed many months at Kum-Bum when, on 31 August 1907, a diplomatic event of deep significance for him took place.

After the humiliating defeat by Japan, the Russians wished to avoid further confrontation with the British in Asia. The new Liberal Government that came to power in Britain late in 1905 was also of a non-contentious disposition. Accordingly, lengthy discussions were held in St Petersburg between Nicolson and Izvolsky which resulted in the signing of an Anglo-Russian Convention. By its five articles concerning Tibet the two parties agreed to respect the territorial integrity of Tibet, to respect Chinese suzerainty and to deal with the Tibetans only through Chinese mediation except where the British enjoyed special rights under the Lhasa Convention. Furthermore, Russian and British Buddhists might maintain their spiritual contacts with the Lamaist church but there should be no representatives in Lhasa, no commercial concessions in Tibet and no interference with Tibetan revenues.

This Convention finally quashed His Holiness's hopes of receiving Russian succour and inevitably exercised an important influence on the ensuing course of events.

*

Sometime during 1907 or early in 1908 the Lama seems to have abandoned the idea of returning to Lhasa and begun to think instead of visiting Peking. Dorzhiev suggests that this was a free decision:

> After staying for some weeks in Kum-Bum, he wished to go to Peking. When requests were made to the Chinese Emperor and his ministers, some listened and some did not. With the sole intention to devour [Tibet], they made him wait.[34]

The American Minister in Peking, William Woodville Rockhill, took a contrary view. This man, who had a keen interest in matters Tibetan – in 1888 he had resigned his diplomatic post and made an unsuccessful attempt to reach Lhasa – says that the Dalai Lama went to Peking only 'After much hesitation, with much misgiving, and only after repeated and peremptory representations from Peking'.[35] Chinese ambitions in Tibet would of course have been immensely assisted if the Lama appeared, or was made to seem to appear, as a humble vassal come to pay homage to his sovereign, the Manchu Emperor.

Whether through indecision or because permission to proceed was withheld, His Holiness lingered in Kum-Bum until early in 1908, during which time he was again visited by Kozlov, who was then on his Mongolia-Szechuan expedition of 1907–09, during which he discovered the ancient city of Khara-Koto. A British observer noted that the explorer appeared to be on 'very friendly terms' with the Lama.

His Holiness and his considerable entourage then moved, causing much local dislocation, via Sining and Sian (Xi'an) to Wu T'ai Shan, where they arrived in April 1908. According to the hagiographers, during the five months that he stayed at the sacred mountain at considerable expense to the Government of Shansi (Shanxi), he had visions and performed miracles. Various foreign visitors also came to see him, including in June W.W. Rockhill, to whom he had sent an envoy from Mongolia in August 1905.

Late in September 1908, his way, according to Dorzhiev, diplomatically smoothed by the new Russian Minister in Peking, I. Y. Korostovets – Pokotilov had died at his post on 7 March 1908 – the Dalai Lama was at last given permission to proceed. His party then travelled to Tingchou, where they boarded a special train for Peking.

A new and particularly sensitive phase in the saga of his exile was about to begin.

CHAPTER TWELVE

A Heathen Temple in Christian Petersburg
1908 – 1910

Vexingly, our two main sources for the next phases of Dorzhiev's life are occasionally at variance with one another. The first, the 'History of the St Petersburg Buddhist Temple' by Aleksandr Andreyev, is impeccably based on painstaking research in Russian State and other archives; the other, the biography of a Latvian Buddhist monk named Karlis Alexis Mikhailovich Tennisons by his loyal but somewhat eccentric devotee Friedrich V. Lustig (Ashin Ananda), is somewhat less reliable.

Born in Narva, Estonia in 1912, Lustig became Tennisons' principal disciple and, after his death, inherited his mentor's grandiose titles of Buddhist Archbishop of Latvia, Sangharaja [Senior Buddhist] of Estonia, Latvia and Lithuania. His biography of Tennisons is a massive typescript running to nearly a thousand pages; it contains a mass of information, some of it bearing on aspects of Agvan Dorzhiev's career not covered elsewhere. Though much of the biography, including a few fine details, is verifiably correct, parts of it contain small errors, exaggerations and that kind of romantic exuberance that is often impatient of the constraints of accuracy. One hopes one is not doing the late Revd Lustig a grave injustice, but the ineluctable conclusion after reading his text and comparing it with others is that what we have is an attempt to magnify the importance of Karlis Tennisons, and that in this enterprise Lustig was probably faithfully following the example of his preceptor. To give an example: Lustig cites a letter published in the May 1961 issue of *The Maha Bodhi*, a Buddhist journal published in India, in which Tennisons claimed to have been 'a former Lord Abbot of the magnificent Buddhist cathedral Church in Petrograd (now Leningrad)'; modern Buddhists from the Baltic states, on the other hand, have assured me that he was in fact no more than the caretaker at a time when the building was deserted. However, even if Lustig's text is slightly suspect, it cannot be overlooked, though the reader should bear the foregoing caveats in mind.

Lustig maintains that Karlis Alexis Mikhailovich Tennisons (1873–1962)[1], the 'Mahatma of the Baltic', was born at Laura in the Latvian province of Livonia, into a landowning family that had 'professed Buddhism for generations'. This for a start has been contradicted by a Baltic Buddhist who told me personally in Leningrad in May 1991 that Tennisons was in fact an Estonian. But to continue . . . Having received a sound education and travelled widely with his father, he was at seventeen selected with several other lads to accompany Nicholas Romanov on his tour of the Far East (1890–01). This exposed the young Tennisons to living Buddhism, which must have affected him deeply, for in 1892 he travelled to Trans-Baikalia and at the Barguzin Datsan,[2] near the eastern edge of Lake Baikal, he became a pupil of Mahacharya Ratnavajra. This eighty-five-year-old monk, who had once been attached to the Tibetan monasteries of Ganden, Kum-Bum and Lhabrang, had been born Kunigaikshtis Gedyminas, the scion of a Lithuanian royal house. In 1893, on his twentieth birthday, Tennisons was himself ordained a monk. After finishing his brief training in Trans-Baikalia, he embarked on Buddhist missionary work in northern Siberia among such peoples as the Eskimos, Yakuts and Samoyeds. In 1900 he was researching into Buddhist texts in Peking when the Boxer Uprising broke out; during the Russo-Japanese War he performed humanitarian work with the Russian Army in Manchuria. Later he wandered back to Europe via the Altai region and Tannu-Tuva, a Buddhist enclave which at the time was ruled by China as a province of Mongolia.

In the second week of May 1907, this great walker wanders into Astrakhan, the great trading city on the banks of the Volga, and finds accommodation at the local Buddhist temple, where he is treated with great kindness by the Kalmyk in charge, who speaks excellent Russian. As chance would have it, the room next to his is occupied by Agvan Dorzhiev, who has arrived in Astrakhan two days before from visiting his choira in the local province. They talk. Dorzhiev reveals that he is building a Buddhist temple in St Petersburg and asks Tennisons to meet him in the capital in July. This Tennisons does, and both lodge at the house of the beautiful Princess Olizetta Begaliyevna Tundutova, a lady of Kalmyk origin whose patronymic suggests that her father's name was Beg-Ali. Her husband, Tseren-David Tundutov, who had recently died, had been an enlightened noyön of the Maloderbet clan. After being educated in Moscow, he had returned to his people and worked for the abolition of serfdom; this was achieved in 1892. He also donated funds towards the construction of the choira that Dorzhiev organized in his district.[3]

Princess Tundutova holds glittering salons which are attended by such luminaries as Prince Ukhtomsky and Anna Vryubova, the lady-in-waiting and confidante of the Empress.[4] Having visited the site of the Buddhist temple, on 4 August 1907, Tennisons accompanies Dorzhiev and a Tibetan lama of Sera monastery, who is acting as Dorzhiev's secretary, to an audience with Nicholas II at Tsarskoye Selo (now Pushkin). At this, the finance and construction of the temple are discussed in some detail;[5] also Orthodox objections to the project. After inquiring after the Dalai Lama and being told that he is presently at Kum-Bum, Nicholas II informs Dorzhiev of the forthcoming Anglo-Russian Convention, assuring him, however, that 'Russia would continue to regard Tibet as an independent state and do all it could for the preservation of the status quo; and that His Holiness the Dalai Lama would be a most welcome guest if he ever decided to visit St Petersburg'. The three Buddhists then take tea with the Empress, Aleksandra Fyodorovna. Subsequently, having been warned by the Okhrana – the infamous Third Section, precursor of the Cheka, GPU, NKVD and KGB – that British secret agents are shadowing him and might make an attempt on his life, Dorzhiev moves to another address in the city.

Dorzhiev finally leaves for Trans-Baikalia on 24 August. On 1 September Tennisons, who has been left in charge of work at the temple site, discovers that construction has stopped on the orders of Piotr Stolypin, the Prime Minister. He at once telegraphs Dorzhiev in Trans-Baikalia, and receives a telegram back telling him not to worry, that Dorzhiev is now on his way to Kum-Bum to see the Dalai Lama but will return to St Petersburg early the following summer. In the meantime Tennisons has an audience with the Emperor and Stolypin's ban is lifted. Work on the temple cannot begin again, however, because the contractor and architects have decamped. Dorzhiev is back in the second week of June 1908, bringing five Tibetan and Buryat lamas with him. He now receives full protection from the Okhrana. Three days later he has another audience with the Emperor at Tsarskoye Selo, from which he returns in high spirits. Later he and Tennisons go to Peterhof and find the missing contractor and architects working there on the orders of the Holy Synod. They are, however, persuaded to return to the site of the Buddhist temple and work there begins again. During Dorzhiev's frequent absences from the capital Tennisons oversees the ongoing construction of the temple . . .

*

According to Aleksandr Andreyev's more scholarly account, which makes no mention of Tennisons, Dorzhiev did not set off to see the

Dalai Lama at Wu T'ai Shan until January 1908. Up to that time the site for the temple had not been acquired. Dorzhiev himself merely says that he had an interview with the Dalai Lama at Wu T'ai Shan. He then returned to St Petersburg and registered with the police as having taken up residence in Apartment No. 20, 13 Marlaya Morskaya Ulitsa (now Ulitsa Gogolya – Gogol Street).[6] It was in fact unusual for him to take an apartment in the centre of town – Ulitsa Gogolya is just off Nevsky Prospekt – for he usually gravitated to the Petrograd district, where prices were cheaper. As always, however, he would probably have reserved one room as a shrine room.

Dorzhiev brought with him to St Petersburg two petitions from the Dalai Lama. One was a request for a loan from the Russian Government; the other was a new petition that permission be given for a Buddhist temple to be built in the Russian capital. He managed successfully to negotiate the loan at the Finance Ministry and some 110,000 yuan were lent to His Holiness, repayable in three instalments over six months at six and a half per cent interest. This effectively financed His Holiness' visit to Peking. Further loans of 250,000 and 40,000 lan were subsequently requested but turned down on the grounds that the first had not been repaid (it never was in full).[7] The second petition, meanwhile, was received in the Foreign Ministry by Aleksandr Izvolsky, who on 12 July 1908 wrote a confidential letter to Piotr Stolypin:

> Taking into consideration that the Dalai lama is well disposed towards Russia and that the preservation of good relations with him holds vital significance for us with regard to our political interests in China as well as giving us the possibility of successfully exploiting his influence over our Lamaist subjects, I am paying special attention to the petition of His Holiness. As for the request for the building of a temple, I consider it a duty to support this before Your Excellency in the belief that our good intentions towards the wishes of the Dalai Lama will produce a deep impression which will be to our advantage as well as to his and that of the countless Lamaists within the confines of Russia.[8]

Stolypin responded 'completely sympathetically' to this and gave his permission for the temple to be built. Nothing was done immediately, however, for Dorzhiev was soon on his way back to rejoin the Dalai Lama in Peking.

*

The Europeans who witnessed the state entry of the Dalai Lama into Peking in late September 1908 might have been watching a scene from the Middle Ages. He was formally met at the railway station by high

Chinese officials and ceremonially carried into the city through the Ch'ien Men Gate on a yellow state palanquin with sixteen bearers. He was then escorted by Buddhist monks in dark red robes, a military guard of honour, musicians and standard-bearers to the Huang-ssu or Yellow Temple, where he was to stay. This had been built for the state visit of his illustrious predecessor, the Great Fifth, in 1653, and recently renovated.

An audience was fixed for the 6 October but was cancelled because, it was rumoured, His Holiness refused to make the full kow-tow, a demeaning symbol of subservience. He saw himself as coming to the Emperor as the Great Fifth had done, as priest to patron, not as vassal to overlord. Dorzhiev arrived at about the same time, and perhaps it was on his advice that His Holiness then began petitioning various foreign diplomats. The Buryat lama was himself very active in this respect, first visiting Korostovets, who informed him that the time when Russia was concerned with advising or supporting Eastern rulers was at an end. Dorzhiev thereupon remarked that if Russia would not help he had no alternative but to go to the British. Korostovets had conferred with his British counterpart, Sir John Jordan, so he was able to assure Dorzhiev that he would find no consolation in that quarter either. He did suggest, however, that Dorzhiev might visit W. W. Rockhill, who as the American representative might furnish him with disinterested advice. A meeting, arranged by Korostovets, took place on 2 October, Dorzhiev being accompanied by 'another Khenpo, a confidential adviser of the Dalai Lama'. Rockhill found Dorzhiev 'a quiet, well-mannered man, impressionable like all Mongols, and apparently but very little less ignorant of politics and the world in general than the Tibetans'. Clearly devoted to his religion and the person of the Dalai Lama, he was definitely not the sinister intriguer he had been made out to be. Rockhill wrote to President Theodore Roosevelt:

> Dorjieff told me that the Dalai Lama had heard said that the Chinese Government was making certain important changes in the internal administration of Thibet. He did not know their nature and extent. He wished to know whether in my opinion it were better for him to remain in Peking until the changes were made or to return at once to Lhasa. He was without any of his advisers on temporal matters; he felt unable to cope with the questions which might be raised without their assistance; but he feared to go until the programme of Thibetan reforms had been settled, for he apprehended that the Chinese Government sought to curtail the temporal power he and his predecessors had wielded before the Manchus came to the throne of China.[9]

Rockhill replied that whatever the situation had once been, the Dalai Lama's present position was that of a vassal prince. The Chinese furthermore intended to carry out certain administrative, educational, military and other reforms in Tibet, to which he could not see that the Dalai Lama could have any objection. Dorzhiev agreed that there could be no objection to educational and military reforms; the Dalai Lama was moreover quite satisfied with the various treaties that had recently been concluded; his main fear was that China might encroach upon his temporal authority. He also wished to place two matters before the Emperor which he considered of paramount importance; firstly, that the Gelug Church be maintained in all its honours, and secondly, that the right be given him to submit memorials (petitions) directly to the Throne and not through the good offices of the Viceroy of Szechuan and the Board of Dependencies, 'either of which might pigeon-hole them'. Before taking his leave, Dorzhiev told Rockhill that he would report to the Dalai Lama and then return with a draft of a letter that he wished to submit to the Emperor concerning the two points mentioned above. Once these were settled the Lama could leave for Lhasa.

It was also at this time that a British official at last got to meet Dorzhiev face to face. This was the genial Major W. F. T. O'Connor, who had been with Younghusband in 1904 and subsequently served as the first British Trade Agent at Gyantsé, though now he was chaperoning Sidkeong Namgyal, the Heir Apparent of Sikkim, on an educational tour of North America and the Far East. In his memoirs, Frederick O'Connor describes Dorzhiev as a 'cheery looking monk of stereotyped description, about forty-five years of age, a voluble speaker, and evidently a man of intellect and character'. In a private letter he also wrote of their first meeting, which took place at Korostovets' residence after dark one evening:

> I went and we had a three-cornered conversation lasting an hour. It was an amusing anti-climax to all our Tibetan schemes – our Mission, our military expedition, the fighting, destruction of property, heart-burnings and hard work. Here we were sitting quietly round a table in the Russian legation at Peking – the Russian Minister, Dorjieff, the sinister figure who loomed so large in Central Asian politics a few years ago, and nearly set three great powers by the ears, and poor I, who was caught up in great events and used for a time – chatting amicably over the dry bones of a dead policy – Dorjieff and Korostovets in Russian, Korostovets and I in English and French, and Dorjieff and I in Tibetan. Korostovets talked a good deal (he is a voluble man) and, as I say, his sentiments were beyond cavil. I said as little as possible: told Dorjieff I was pleased to meet him, but that England had now no policy in Tibet except to remain on friendly terms with Tibet and China. Poor Dorjieff quite sees the point of view. There is no doubt that he and the Lama dislike the Chinese and would be delighted to see the last of them. But as there is no-one else to turn to and Tibet cannot stand alone, they must swallow their pill and be good boys under the Amban's dictation.

I enclose a photo of Dorjieff (taken some years ago) which Rockhill gave me. He looks much the same now but a good deal older (he is 55). He is still the chief adviser and confidant of the Dalai Lama and is apparently on very intimate terms with the Russians. He says he is not going back to Lhasa with the Lama . . .[10]

A day or two later Dorzhiev visited O'Connor at the British Legation and they had a long private conversation. He had in the meantime reported their previous conversation to the Dalai Lama, who, he said, would feel more equanimous about returning to Lhasa (when he fully anticipated trouble from the Chinese) if he was assured that the British Government bore him no hard feelings. His Holiness had been particularly impressed, Dorzhiev went on, by the friendly reception given in Calcutta to the Panchen Lama by the Prince of Wales and the Viceroy, of which he had received full reports. O'Connor did not have authority to give any assurances, but he did say that the British Government had no objection to His Holiness returning to Lhasa, that they harboured no resentments against him, and that 'they would be prepared to enter into the most friendly relations with him – subject of course to any Treaty by which we were bound'.[11]

*

Ongoing Chinese efforts to pressure the Dalai Lama into submission culminated in a seventy-fifth birthday edict issued on 3 November in the name of the Empress Dowager, who was the real power behind the throne. This exchanged his official title to a longer but more demeaning form, granted him an annual allowance of ten thousand taels and ordered him to return to Tibet, whereafter 'he must be reverentially submissive to the Regulations of the Sovereign State' and report to the Amban.[12] No wonder that Rockhill remarked, 'His pride has suffered terribly while here, and he leaves Peking with his dislike for the Chinese intensified.'[13]

Ironically, China was in fact not only replacing Britain as the source of all evils in the Lama's eyes (and those of Dorzhiev) but Britain was at the same time coming to be regarded as a possible new patron-protector of Tibet. Times were changing . . .

In December, the ineffectual Emperor departed for the 'Western Paradise'. Sir Charles Bell wrote ominously: 'Such evidence as is available of the happenings in the grim prison chamber within the high walls of the Forbidden City – at that time really forbidden – points strongly to the conclusion she [the Empress Dowager] poisoned him.'[14] The machiavellian lady died herself shortly afterwards, also a victim of poison, it was mooted, though in her case self-administered. As the Manchus still venerated Buddhism (after a fashion), they were gratified when the Dalai Lama conducted religious rites for the deceased at the Yellow Temple. He is also reported to have been present at the enthronement of the boy successor, the last of the Manchu Emperors. But these were his final acts in Peking. Realizing that nothing positive could be accomplished there, he prepared to leave for Tibet, sending Dorzhiev to pay proxy farewells to Korostovets and the 'Chinese minister', and offer them the obligatory gifts.[15]

*

When the Dalai Lama left Peking on 21 December Dorzhiev did not go with him. Two representatives of His Holiness who called at the British Legation on the day he left (23 December) with presents and a khada for the King, told British officials that he proposed to remain for some time in Trans-Baikalia before proceeding to St Petersburg, where he intended to continue his work on his Buddhist temple project.[16]

He was certainly back in the Russian capital by 16 March 1909, for on that day he bought for 18,000 rubles a plot of land of some 648.51 square sazheny – one sazhen equals seven English feet – from the wife of a businessman named Isayev. This was at number 11 Blagoveshchyenskaya Ulitsa (now Primorsky Prospekt – Maritime Avenue), near the intersection with Lipovaya Alley. He also bought a quantity of building materials. The site suited some of the traditional requirements for a Buddhist temple [17] being in the quiet northern village of Staraya, overlooking the Greater Nevka; the Yelagin Bridge leading to the pleasant green parks of Yelagin Island was opposite. On the negative side, it was rather too close for comfort to the Orthodox Blagoveshchyenskaya Church (Church of the Annunciation – an interesting domed rotunda, now sadly in a very dilapidated state), which offended some Christians. Andreyev suggests that Dorzhiev may have been recommended this particular piece of land by the Russian consul in Urga, Y. P. Shishmarev, whose relations once owned it.[18]

At the beginning of 1909 Dorzhiev created a construction committee for the temple. It consisted of an architect and eight prestigious European Orientalists and artists: V. V. Radlov (Chairman), S. F. Ol'denburg, E. E. Ukhtomsky, G. V. Baranovsky, V. P. Schneider, N. K. Roerich, V. L. Kotvich, A. D. Rudnev and F. I. Stcherbatsky.[19]

Vasily Vasilyevich Radlov (1837–1918) and Sergey Feodorovich Ol'denburg (1863–1934) were members of the Academy of Sciences and co-founders of the Russian Committee for the Study of Central and East Asia. Radlov was a specialist in the language and literature of the Turkic peoples. Ol'denburg was mainly a Buddhologist with a special interest in Buddhist art and legends; he is also credited as main initiator of the Biblioteca Buddhica, which was founded around 1897 to publish Sanskrit texts and translations. Vladislav Lyudvigovich Kotvich (or Kotwicz, 1872–1944), who was Polish by origin, and Andrey Dmitrievich Rudnev (died c. 1919?), were both lecturers at St Petersburg University specializing in Mongolian studies.

Though Gavriil Vasilyevich Baranovsky is usually given as the official architect, at least two other hands worked on the project. Initially Nicholas Matveyevich Berezovsky was employed. He was still a student when first retained, so his fees were modest; but more importantly he had visited Sinkiang and so knew something of Buddhist art and architecture. Though he probably contributed the seed of the design, being unqualified at the commencement he could not supervise actual construction, so Baranovsky was made the official architect. He was well-known in the first two decades of the century and, among other buildings, designed the Eliseyev house at 56 Nevsky Prospekt, opposite the Pushkin Theatre: an Art Nouveau exercise in Finnish granite (the same pinkish-grey variety as the temple) decorated with muscular statuary and a splendid frontal stained glass window. Eliseyev's shop still does business on the ground floor and now resembles what Harrods' Food Hall would probably look like if Britain had experienced seventy years of Marxist austerity. The Komediya Theatre functions in the building too.

Dorzhiev is thought to have provided the specialist knowledge of Buryat-Mongol-Tibetan temple architecture, Baranovsky to have interpreted this 'in the spirit of European architecture and building technology'. In other words, this was to be a Buddhist temple built with European methods and materials. Unfortunately, late in 1911 Baranovsky clashed with the Construction Committee and with Dorzhiev – he was blamed for on-site pilfering, for one thing – and he felt obliged to resign. He was replaced by Richard Andreyovich Berzen.

Varvara P. Schneider, a niece of the great Indologist, I. P. Minaev (1840–1890), was an artist.[20] It was in the apartment she shared with her sister, A. P. Schneider, also an artist, at 3 Masterskaya Ulitsa, that meetings of the committee were held. The other artist on the committee is far more widely known nowadays for his later collaboration as set and costume designer with Stravinsky and Diaghilev on the ballet, *The Rite of Spring* (1913). Nikolai Konstantinovich Roerich (1874–1947) was a mystical painter and poet. His earliest canvases had been evocations of Russia's past; later his subjects came from Russian legends and fairy tales; later still he attempted works in the manner of ancient Russian church paintings. Meeting Dorzhiev, however, opened up exciting new spiritual vistas for him:

> It was during the construction of a Buddhist temple in the Russian capital that I first heard of Shambhala. Being a member of the committee, I met with a very learned Buriat lama who was the first to pronounce the name of Chang Shambhala. It will be known one day why this name pronounced under such circumstances had a great significance.[21]

With additional influence from Theosophy, to which he was introduced by his wife, Helena Ivanovna (she translated *The Secret Doctrine* into Russian), we may say that Roerich became intoxicated with the romance of Eastern spirituality and, in particular, obsessed with the myths of Shambhala and Maitreya, whose predicted advent he seems to have conflated with the Second Coming of Christ and similar myths in Islam and Hinduism. This inspired a completely new phase in his painting, culminating in his wonderful luminous evocations of the Himalaya and of Tibetan monasteries that seem organic extensions of the mountain crags on which they stand. It also inspired a grandiose messianic vision of the inauguration of a New Age of peace, brotherhood and enlightenment which he expounded in his cloyingly effusive visionary writings.

*

The initial estimate of the overall cost of the temple was 90,000 rubles. Of this, 50,000 was pledged by the Dalai Lama (it was for this that he had applied to the Ministry of Finance for the second and third loans), and 30,000 was given by Dorzhiev. As it was proposed to raise the remaining 10,000 rubles among the Kalmyks and Buryats, Dorzhiev established an appeal committee at the same time as he set up the Construction Committee. This was headed by two shiretuis (abbots): Garmayev of the Atsagat Datsan and Soktoyev of the Tsulgin.

*

The distinguished alternative doctor and power-broker, Piotr Badmayev, was one of the contributors to the temple fund, though he had to be so anonymously as he was ostensibly a Christian. Since last figuring in our story, Badmayev's name had become linked with that of the dissolute staretz, Grigory Efimovich Rasputin, who shot to a position of unprecedented influence with the Empress, initially because of his mysterious ability to relieve the distressing symptoms of the Heir Apparent's haemophilia. In Buddhism such paranormal powers, known as rddhis, are recognized as incidental by-products of spiritual practice; they are not, however, measures of any degree of spiritual attainment, and practitioners are warned not to be seduced by them. Rasputin, it would seem, did not receive such wise counsel, for he freely, licentiously used his powers to secure venal advantages. However, even though he openly indulged his proclivities for sex, drink, power and money (he accepted bribes), the Empress refused to hear a word said against him, preferring to see him as a shining example of the loyal and devoted muzhik (peasant) whom she believed collectively formed a solid body of devoted support for the throne.

Inevitably, Rasputin's rising fortunes gained him many enemies, one of the most bitter being the Orthodox monk Ilidor (Sergey Trufanov), who ironically had at first been one of his staunchest supporters. Ilidor later composed a scurrilous pamphlet entitled 'The Holy Devil', in which he fancifully alleged that Badmayev, Rasputin and Anna Vryubova, the Empress' confidante, were combined in a sinister conspiracy. The Buryat doctor would first secretly administer a poisonous 'yellow powder' to the Heir Apparent so that Rasputin could come along later and pretend to effect a miraculous healing. We can fairly discount this allegation, for Badmayev was actually opposed to Rasputin until around the outbreak of the First World War, when they did begin to conspire together both on the political front and in business deals. There is evidence, for instance, that in 1916 Badmayev offered Rasputin a 50,000 ruble bribe to use his influence with the Emperor to have an 'affair', in which he was involved with a certain General Krulov, approved and funded.[22]

Such was the machiavellian world in which Badmayev moved for many years, yet he was nevertheless a benefactor of the temple.

*

According to a plan registered with the Building Department of the St Petersburg Council on 15 April 1909, building was scheduled to start at Dorzhiev's temple at the end of April/beginning of May that year. Local brick-layers and workmen were engaged as well as ones from Kostroma province, none of whom were probably aware of what they were in fact helping to erect. The pace of work was at first brisk, for by 13 May the foundations had been laid and part of the ground floor. Then came the first of a series of official obstructions. On 16 May D. V. Drachevsky, the municipal chief, issued a directive that work be halted. This had originated at the Department of Foreign Creeds, whose Deputy Director, A. N. Charuzin, had sent a letter marked 'secret and emergency' to the effect that 'no lawful permission has been received from the relevant authorities for the erection of this building in the place stated'.[23] Dorzhiev was away at the time, so on 7 June Stcherbatsky applied directly to Stolypin for permission: firstly, to set up a construction committee, secondly, to build the temple on the site bought for the purpose, and, thirdly, to accommodate Buddhist religious at the temple. From this petition it is clear that what Dorzhiev had in mind was not a simple temple but a monastic complex of the traditional kind containing accommodation for monks and educational facilities in addition to areas reserved for religious rites and practices. Dependent on permission being given, a complement of twenty-one people was envisaged: the shiretui (abbot), ten gelong (monks), and ten getsül and khuvarak (novices).[24]

This was problematic, for existing Russian legislation drastically limited the number of religious that could reside in any Buddhist establishment, and in any case one situated in the capital itself had never been envisaged. Accordingly, Stolypin in his report to the Emperor on Stcherbatsky's petition agreed with the Department of Foreign Creeds that the present site was not suitable 'in view of its distance from the centre of the city and the difficulty of supervising the community house'. He did, however, in consideration of the growing number of Buddhists in the capital, recommend that a Buddhist temple be in principle approved, though not in Staraya Derevnya. To this the Emperor appended a laconic 'S' for 'soglasen' – 'I agree'.[25]

This was bad news for the Construction Committee. With such a large part of the available funds already spent, it was out of the question to think of buying another plot of land and starting over again in the centre of the city, where costs would anyway be far higher. Not deterred, however, Radlov again petitioned Stolypin, informing him that at its meeting of 22 June the Committee had decided to limit itself to building a temple only, with no ancillary accommodation; he also mentioned the expenses already incurred and attached a revised sketch plan drawn up by Baranovsky. The Emperor, who was then at Livadia, found this compromise acceptable. When official ratification from the Ministry of Internal Affairs arrived on 1 November, building began again at the previous brisk pace, and in a year the temple was well advanced towards completion.

*

It is difficult to believe that the initial embargo by the Department of Foreign Creeds, as well as subsequent obstructions, were not in part at least influenced by the strident and vituperative protests of the Orthodox faithful. Dorzhiev himself expatiates passionately on this subject:

Permission had already been granted to my request for a Buddhist temple to be built in the capital; but when it came time to begin the construction, the long-hairs were unable to tolerate this and from all corners of the country appealed to the Tsar, asking him to please give an order that 'no filthy Buddhist temple ever be erected in our celestial city of Petersburg'. In response the Tsar upheld his [previous] order for the temple to be built. Communities of long-hairs in Kiev, Kazan and Irkutsk then made this appeal: 'This inauspicious man called "Dorzhiev", an adherent of the Kalmyk and Buryat Bön [shamanistic] sect, is infiltrating our religion and spreading the doctrine of the Buddha. In particular, this construction of a Buddhist temple in the great capital is most unworthy. Having punished this man by exiling him far away and so on, it should be decreed that he never reside in this country [again].'

In response, no such decree was given and I stayed where I was. However, every day the long-hairs sent many kinds of letters to me. Some threatened that they would kill me and destroy the temple. Others informed me that within so many days I should run far away and out of sight, that I should die from a certain poisonous substance and that members of their notorious 'Bluebird Society' had the means [to carry out these threats]. In spite of all this, I relied upon the Three Jewels and the power of truth and remained equanimous and content. But when a monastery started being built in a place called 'Tungkhung' [probably Tunka, on the Irkut river south-west of Irkutsk] in the part of Buryatia where Bön [shamanism] prevailed, certain long-hairs including Makhashikhiev and others interfered and halted the construction of the temple. But even though they managed to have the doors [officially] sealed shut, they caused no real harm and [finally the monastery] flourished.[26]

The Orthodox polemics were to continue and, if a batch of yellowing pages typewritten in fuzzy Cyrillic and headed 'Documents, Articles & Materials Relating to the Buddhist Temple in Leningrad' is anything to go by, during 1910 and 1911 they became particularly nasty – as we shall see in due course.

*

Far away in Tibet, meanwhile, the Dalai Lama was approaching his holy city of Lhasa. He had been on the long road from Peking for nearly a year. But if his exile of five years was nearly over, his troubles were certainly not.

CHAPTER THIRTEEN

The Turning Point
1909 – 1913

On 25 December 1909 the Dalai Lama took up residence again at the Potala in Lhasa. Within two months he was forced to flee for a second time as the advance guard of a Chinese force reached the holy city, thus fulfilling an ancient Tibetan prophecy: 'In the Year of the Male Iron Dog, a war with China will occur'. On this occasion – a sign of the times and a portent for the future – he sought refuge in the south: in British India. Where else could he turn? The Russians, it was manifestly clear, were no longer interested in dabbling in Tibetan politics; but back in Peking, he and Dorzhiev had already begun radically to revise their view of the old British bogey. Not only had the sahibs treated the Panchen Lama hospitably but they had promptly withdrawn their troops following the signing of the Lhasa Convention, so they obviously had no intention of devouring the Land of Snows; they had also very honourably kept to the terms of the Convention.

Once he had made his dramatic escape across the Himalayas, though informed that the British Government could do nothing to help the Tibetan cause on account of the policy of non-interference, the Lama was treated in a very friendly manner. He and his ministers were accommodated at Government expense in Darjeeling; his security was organized by the Deputy Commissioner; he was allowed to go on pilgrimage to Buddhist holy places; and he formed a cordial relationship with his British liaison officer, Charles Bell, the Political Officer in Sikkim, who was to become an ardent Tibetophile. He was also received with honour in Calcutta by the Viceroy, Lord Minto, to whom, when putting his case, he gave the most earnest assurances that Dorzhiev had been solely a religious adviser – surely an example of the phenomenon of economy with the truth.

Besides appealing to the British for help, the Dalai Lama directed similar appeals to the King of Nepal and the Emperor of Russia.

Nicholas II's reply, to the Lama's embarrassment, was communicated through the British Government. It was according to type – cordial but non-committal.

There was also correspondence with Dorzhiev, who could not accompany His Holiness into this second exile. One letter was delivered by Fyodor Stcherbatsky, then on a year's academic visit to India, who gave it to the Lama's chief secretary when they met on the path above 'Hillside', the secluded house set in woodland where His Holiness was staying. At a subsequent interview at which Bell was present, the 'Russian professor' first presented the seated Dalai Lama with a khada and laid Rs 20/- before him; then he thanked His Holiness for the gifts he had already made to the Buddhist Temple in St Petersburg, reported that there were plans to build a Buddhist hostel and library there, and asked for help in obtaining copies of old Sanskrit manuscripts from Reting monastery to the north of Lhasa and from an un-named monastery near Lake Manasarovar in Western Tibet.

His Holiness made a clean breast of the contents of Dorzhiev's letter to Bell a few days later. Its gist was much the same as that of the interview: a request for Stcherbatsky to be given permission to visit Lhasa and to be assisted in procuring sacred texts. 'It would have been difficult to grant the request, as the Chinese would not have liked a European to come to Lhasa', the Dalai Lama allegedly told Bell; 'but as I have come to Darjeeling, the matter has been made easy for me'.[1]

Bell ingenuously took this to be a shining example of the Dalai Lama's frankness. In reality, His Holiness was again being economical with the truth, for he was, as in 1905, very happy for Stcherbatsky to go to Tibet. Nor were the British authorities averse to the idea. It was the narrow-minded bureaucrats at the Russian Foreign Ministry who, to his lasting resentment, again contrived to block Stcherbatsky's way by failing to process his application for a Chinese visa. Russian officials in India even tried to stop him visiting the Dalai Lama. Stcherbatsky never did visit Tibet but some of his precious manuscripts were obtained for him by the Indian scholar Rahula Sankrityayana; others were collected by the Italian Buddhologist, Professor Giuseppe Tucci.

Other communications that the Dalai Lama preferred not to reveal to Bell must have passed between himself and Dorzhiev, either via Stcherbatsky or by some other avenue, for in the same year, 1910, with unusual haste, building work was pushed forward on a four-storey house on the temple site in St Petersburg in anticipation of His Holiness' arrival early the following year.[2] He also planned to visit London on the way. Neither of these projected visits came off, though exactly why is not clear.

*

Stcherbatsky spent a fruitful year in India. He wrote in his report that 'besides an overall acquaintance with the country', the purpose of his sojourn

> was primarily a quest after the relics of Buddhist philosophical literature, both the works of the Buddhists themselves and in those of the Brahmanas and the Jainas, inasmuch as these latter reflected – directly or indirectly – the period (fifth to tenth centuries A.D.) when Buddhism flourished . . . At the same time I also wanted to familiarise myself with the present state of the study of Sanskrit language and literature in India . . .[3]

What he did, in fact, was to live in a house with an Indian pandit adept in Nyaya philosophy and spend several months speaking only Sanskrit and studying for many hours each day. On his return to St Petersburg in 1911, he proposed to the temple construction committee that a Hindu temple be transported from Rajasthan to Russia by sea. This plan was not taken up but parts of the temple did reach the Russian capital and are still preserved there.

*

The construction of the stone house alongside the St Petersburg temple of course flew in the face of the directives of the authorities, and it goes to show how bold and determined a man Dorzhiev was – determined in this instance to fulfil his original plan of creating a functioning monastery rather than just a show-piece temple. As the Dalai Lama never arrived, he took up residence there himself on 30 November 1910, to be at hand personally to supervise building operations. Ovshe Norzunov, who was to manage the place, moved in too. Later occupants included Rinchen Zhanchatov, the Buryat master joiner who worked on the interior of the temple, the Buryat Cossack, Tsokto Badmazhapov, and Chöpel, a Tibetan assistant to Dorzhiev. In 1913 it accommodated the Mongolian Embassy to St Petersburg.

The years 1910 and 1911 saw Orthodox and ultra-reactionary fanatics attacking Dorzhiev's blasphemous temple with unrestrained venom. In the vanguard was the unsavoury Union of the Russian People, a faction of the Chernyi Sotnyi or so-called 'Black Hundreds' gangs, who were usually more noted for their violent anti-Semitism. Somehow the Petrograd Buddhists managed to arouse their hatred – probably no difficult task – for there appeared in its bulletin, *The Russian Banner*, a series of diatribes like the following:

SOME MORE WORDS ON THE SUBJECT OF THE BUILDING OF A PAGAN TEMPLE IN ST PETERSBURG
   . . . At the very same time that people on the Don are so zealously trying to stamp out the last traces of paganism and purge the area of the temples and statues of devilish idolatry,[4] in the capital of our Orthodox Fatherland – under our very bells, you might say – diabolical works are being wrought, [ones] fit only for the one enemy of our Saviour – the Devil. Our capital has not followed the Christian Path; it has yielded to some wild call . . . Do not forget that you are the City of St Peter, who has lived among your citizens from century to century, from generation to generation, handing down prophetic utterances that your future will be akin to that of Sodom. In view of the recent happenings, is not the time at hand for the fulfilment of that terrible prophecy – that you will be swallowed into the earth or into the watery depths?[5]

A group of religious students at the St Petersburg Clerical Academy were meanwhile calling with equal ferocity for the destruction of the statue of the Buddha that had lately been brought to the city. A wag with the pen-name of Willy went so far as to cobble together a vituperative poem entitled, 'The Buddha and the Seminarist', to express their views (or rather prejudices). In this weird pastiche, Tiberius Gorobets, rhetorician, Khalyava, religious enthusiast, and Brut Khoma, philosopher – valiant spirits who had already 'toppled Darwin and demolished the heresies of Copernicus' – now set out to do likewise with the statue of the Buddha. In straight prose the poem ends:

   – What do we need a premise for! howls Tiberius the Rhetorician. From A to J, that most sacred of letters, we have a whole list of arguments that the idol Buddha is a blockhead! . . . Just as the saintly Prince Vladimir acted when he toppled the head of Perun [the ancient Russian God of Thunder] into the dust, so we shall demonstrate that the spirit of Russia is not dead and throw the [Buddha] idol into the Neva![6]

There were also distorted reports that the cost of the temple – inflated to an entirely imaginary ten million rubles – would be borne by English masons. This may have some vague connection with an old report in the St Petersburg press than a certain Sir Edward Champley or Chumley,[7] who moved in St Petersburg high society circles, became so enthusiastic about the temple that he sent to England for contributions, and even at one stage proposed bringing over an English architect.[8] The basic fear behind the attacks was that the temple, assisted by new legislation granting greater freedom in religious matters, would drag Holy Russia into the black sloughs of Buddhism, Islam, paganism and the other non-Orthodox persuasions. All was not unalloyed prejudice, however: the temple had a fair-minded defender in Bishop Andrey of Ufa, a relative of Prince Ukhtomsky, who declared, 'First of all close down the heathen temples on the Nevsky Prospekt!' He also pointed out that Christian and especially Orthodox churches had been built in Buddhist lands: in China, Japan and Mongolia.[9]

*

Meanwhile in Tibet, the Chinese earnestly set about establishing their power over the Tibetan people, who greatly resented their impositions. Then in October 1911, as though the gods were on the Tibetan side, revolution broke out in China, toppling the decadent Manchus and quickly spreading to Lhasa, where Chinese troops mutinied. The Tibetans, notably the monks of Sera and Ganden monasteries (the monks of Drepung and Tengye Ling were pro-Chinese), seized their opportunity to rise up against the occupying forces.

The Dalai Lama and his court-in-exile fully supported these Tibetan actions, which embarrassed the British, who ordered His Holiness not to encourage resistance. But by June 1912, though many Chinese troops remained and sporadic fighting continued, the Chinese hold on Tibet was essentially broken. Having been advised of an auspicious time and date by his astrologers, His Holiness then left Kalimpong, where he had for the past few months been staying at the house of the Bhutanese Vakil, Urgyen Kazi, and set out on a slow return to Lhasa.

'Soon after their departure daybreak broke,' wrote Charles Bell, an eye-witness to the event; 'and we could behold a gorgeous procession of men, joyful and determined, returning to govern their very own land, very different from the forlorn arrival of tired men on tired ponies that was witnessed two years before.'[10]

*

Dorzhiev, who no doubt had been keenly watching developments, had by now also set out for the Land of Snows, bearing many 'precious things' for His Holiness as well as the usual letters and telegrams. As he approached Tibet he began to hear ominous reports of atrocities by retreating Chinese troops, and at Tsaidam he was told that there was still fighting in Lhasa. From Nagchukha, therefore, which he reached in the spring of 1912, he took a roundabout route along what he calls 'the northern Tsang road'. This brought him to Gyantsé, and thence to Phari, a settlement at the foot of the sacred Mount Chomolhari which used to have a reputation among British travellers of being the dirtiest in the world. There he was reunited with the Dalai Lama who, tired from travelling, had paused at the Chatsa monastery at the request of the local people.

David Macdonald, a British official of Sikkimese-Scottish extraction who was the Trade Agent at Yatung in the Chumbi Valley, from where he had escorted His Holiness, was watching the ceremony of blessing the people on the morning of 7 July when a stoutly built man with an extraordinarily large head stepped out of the crowd and offered him a khada. The man revealed that he was Dorzhiev. They talked, and Dorzhiev was keen to impress upon Macdonald that his reason for being in Tibet was entirely unpolitical. The next day Dorzhiev called on Macdonald at the Phari dak-bungalow, and during conversation he related his adventurous life history. Afterwards they discussed politics, and Dorzhiev seemed most anxious to convince his host that he was in no way anti-British:

> I asked him if he had incited the Tibetans to fight against us in 1904, but he vehemently denied this, laying all the blame on the Chinese . . . He stated that he now wished to return to his own country, and asked me if I would permit him to travel via India. This, of course, was beyond my powers, but I suggested he should apply to the Government of India through me. This he never did, and had he done so, I doubt very much if permission would have been granted.
>
> This man seemed to be, even at that time, high in the favour of the Dalai Lama and lived with the ministers as one of themselves.[11]

Dorzhiev was also seen a few days later by Sonam Wangfel Laden-la (1876–1936), an officer in the Darjeeling Police of mixed Sikkimese and Tibetan extraction. While stressing his devotion to the Dalai Lama and his determination, no matter what the personal risk to himself, to help restore him to his former position, Dorzhiev also expressed his delight at seeing how friendly the British Government were towards His Holiness. He doubted, however, whether the present difficulties in Lhasa could be resolved without British mediation, so he proposed to write to the Russian Government, suggesting that the Anglo-Russian Convention of 1907 be amended so as to allow this. 'It was not the case, he added, that he was a Russian agent, though he knew he was suspected of being one', Laden-la reported.[12]

It may have had nothing to do with Dorzhiev's suggestion, but the British did shortly afterwards moot a relaxation of the terms of the 1907 convention. The Russians were not averse to the notion either, though wanted some kind of quid pro quo.

*

Old fears of the Russian bogey were revived in Indian Government circles by news of Dorzhiev's return to Tibet and prompted the Viceroy, Lord Hardinge, to send instructions to B. J. Gould, the British Trade Agent at Gyantsé, who had taken over the task of escorting the Dalai Lama from Macdonald, to warn His Holiness that 'trouble would inevitably ensue from his intriguing with foreign Powers'. In other words, His Holiness was to be politely pressured to break with Dorzhiev. Gould duly conveyed the message during a long private interview at Kangena on the evening of 14 July. His Holiness, who listened attentively, took the hint, promising that he would 'take such action in respect of Dorjieff' as would dispel any apprehensions of intrigue.[13]

On 21 July, the Dalai Lama, with Dorzhiev still in attendance, arrived at Samding monastery on the lake of Namdrok-Tso. His Holiness intended to stay here until it was safe to return to Lhasa, but Dorzhiev could not linger as he was eager to be on his way to Mongolia before the winter set in. He says in his memoirs that when he told His Holiness this, he was given fifty thousand gold coins for the St Petersburg Temple and blessings for the journey. Berlin adds that he took decorations for the temple and new instructions.

We can have a fair idea what those instructions were. The two lamas undoubtedly discussed political prospects extensively during their time together, particularly the future independence of Tibet, which His Holiness was now more than ever determined to secure. High in both their minds was the model of Outer Mongolia, which had lately taken advantage of the revolution in China to proclaim its own independence under the sovereignty of the Jebtsundamba Khutukhtu; a treaty had also been negotiated with Russia which gave qualified recognition to Mongolian autonomy. The Dalai Lama therefore invested Dorzhiev with plenipotentiary powers to negotiate and finalize a rapprochement between Mongolia and Tibet as sovereign states. He also entrusted him with gifts and a letter for Nicholas II, and instructed him to find out whether the Russians seriously wished to maintain relations with Tibet and, if so, whether they might be interested in re-negotiating the 1907 convention with a view to becoming, with the British, joint protectors of a fully autonomous Tibet. Trading concessions were to be offered as an inducement.

When the Dalai Lama and Dorzhiev eventually took leave of each other at Samding sometime in early August 1912, it was for the last time. It is unlikely that they were conscious of this, unless of course either was endowed with paranormal powers. Certainly both were agreed that the British wish that they separate had to be seen to be taken seriously, for each wrote independently to Hardinge on 27 July, His Holiness stating that Dorzhiev had been given orders to leave Tibet without delay, and Dorzhiev himself that he would definitely be returning to Russia via Chengri and the Chang-Tang. However, they probably regarded this move as just a temporary expedient. In any case, their relationship was a substantial one: it spanned nearly a quarter of a century and ran deep and through many levels; they had been through many crises and accomplished much together. Any British official, however lofty, who therefore believed that it could be easily terminated was deluding himself. Though they never saw each other again, these two powerful personalities remained in touch until the Dalai Lama died in 1933.

*

Dorzhiev left Samding on 2 August and travelled to Lhasa – a dangerous undertaking, for there were still unpacified Chinese troops in the holy city. The Chinese strongholds were at Trapchi, Tip monastery, and Tengyé Ling, which was later destroyed for its perfidy. According to Macdonald, Dorzhiev distributed 'very large presents to the great monasteries, the real seats of power in Tibet, funds for this being supplied by his Russian masters'.[14] Dorzhiev himself merely says that he collected offerings for the Jebtsundamba Khutukhtu and Nicholas II, and for their respective ministers.[15] British official sources report him staying firstly at Drepung and later at Ganden, where he was reported to be 'spending a large sum on religious ceremonies'.[16]

Towards the end of August fighting died down and steps began to be taken to evacuate the remaining Chinese troops from Lhasa and repatriate them by way of British India. Shortly afterwards, in early September, Dorzhiev was again on Central Asian trails, for on the 4th he wrote again to the British, on whom he was now clearly intent on impressing his bona fides, to let them know that he was on the road to Russia. He expected to arrive early the following year, he said, and 'Buddha's Temple, St Petersburgh' would be his address. This letter prompted the surmise that Dorzhiev could both speak and write English.[17]

*

At the end of November Dorzhiev turned up in Urga, having had a good journey from Tibet via Koko-Nor. He was seen there by his old acquaintance, I.Y. Korostovets, who had left the Russian Legation in Peking in 1911 and, as Special Representative, signed the Russo-Mongolian Agreement and Protocol on 21 October (OS). Dorzhiev, who carried a letter for the Emperor and claimed to be authorized to negotiate with Russia on behalf of Tibet, told Korostovets:

> The Dalai Lama had been misled about England, for the English were on the side of the Chinese and aimed at a final annexation of Tibet. Therefore the Dalai Lama wanted to break with China. He had already been proclaimed secular ruler, had appointed new ministers and wanted to enter into a new pact with Russia similar to the Russo-Mongolian one. The basis for this pact or treaty could be a mutual Russo-English protectorate over Tibet and the elimination of Chinese sovereignty. The conditions of the treaty would be as follows: Russia and England to get freedom of entry to Tibet; the Tibetan Government to consult Russian and English advisers and instructors on the organization of its financial and military systems. Russia to get the right of duty-free trade and a concession for exploiting the natural resources of the land. In exchange Russia to grant Tibet a financial loan, with its gold deposits as surety. Russia and England to provide arms for Tibet.[18]

Korostovets doubted that such a sophisticated scheme could have been devised by the Tibetans alone but must have been drawn up with Dorzhiev's assistance. It was, however, unacceptable insofar as its aim was clearly to involve Russia in Tibet and win its support against the Chinese, thereby infringing both the Russo-British Treaty and a later Russo-Chinese one. He therefore advised Dorzhiev that it would be better if the Dalai Lama abandoned these ideas and instead tried to reach an understanding with the British.

Dorzhiev then revealed that the Dalai Lama's Government was presently seeking a rapprochement with Mongolia. Tibet, he argued (displaying a somewhat sanguine understanding of the treaty that Korostovets had just concluded), had just as much right to declare its independence and deal directly with foreign states as the newly autonomous Mongolia, which was recognized by Russia. He added that the draft of an agreement had already been given to the Khalkha princes.

Though sometimes doubted, this Tibet-Mongolia Treaty certainly existed. It was signed on 29 December 1912 (OS) by Dorzhiev and two Tibetans on behalf of the Dalai Lama, and by two Mongolians for the Jebtsundamba Khutukhtu. It stated:

> Mongolia and Tibet, having freed themselves from the dynasty of the Manchus and separated from China, have formed their own independent States, and, having in view that both States from time immemorial have professed one and the same religion, with a view to strengthening their historic and mutual friendship

the Minister of Foreign Affairs, Nikta Biliktu Da-Lama Rabdan, and the Assistant Minister, General and Manlai Baatyr Beiseh Damdinsurun, as plenipotentiaries of the Government of the Ruler of the Mongolian people, and Gudjir Tsanshib Kanchen Lubsan-Agvan ['Assistant Tutor, Great Abbot Losang Ngawang'. i.e. Dorzhiev], Donir Agvan Choinzin, Director of the bank Ishichjamtso, and the clerk Gendun Galsan, have made the following agreement:-

1. The Ruler of Tibet, the Dalai Lama, approves and recognises the formation of an independent Mongol State, and the proclamation of the 9th day of the 11th month of Year of the Pig of Chjebzun Damba Lama of the Yellow Faith [i.e. the Jebtsundamba Khutukhtu] as Ruler of the country.

2. The Ruler of the Mongolian people, Chjebzun Damba Lama, approves and recognises the formation of an independent [Tibetan] State and the proclamation of the Dalai Lama as Ruler of Tibet.

3. Both States, by joint consideration, will work for the well-being of the Buddhist Faith.

4. Both States, Mongolia and Tibet, from now and for all time, will afford each other assistance against external and internal dangers.

5. Each State within its own territory will afford assistance to the subjects of the other travelling officially or privately on affairs of religion or State.

6. Both States, Mongolia and Tibet, as formerly, will carry on a reciprocal trade in the products of their respective countries in wares, cattle, &c., and will also open industrial establishments.

7. From now the granting of credit to anyone will be permitted only with the knowledge and sanction of official institutions. Without such sanction Government institutions will not consider claims.

As regards contracts made previous to the conclusion of the present Treaty, where serious loss is being incurred through the inability of the two parties to come to terms, such debts may be recovered by [Government] institutions, but in no case shall the debt concern shabinars or khoshuns.

8. Should it prove necessary to supplement the articles of the present treaty, the Mongolian and Tibetan Governments must appoint special delegates who will conclude such agreements as the conditions of the time shall demand.

9. The present Treaty shall come into force on the date of its signature. Plenipotentiaries from the Mongolian Government for the conclusion of the Treaty:- Nikta Biliktu Da-Lama Rabdan, Minister of Foreign Affairs; and General and Manlai Baatyr Beiseh Damdinsurun, Assistant Minister.

Plenipotentiaries from the Dalai Lama, the Ruler of Tibet, for the conclusion of the Treaty:-

Gudjir Tsanshib Kanchen Lubsan-Agvan, Choinzin, the Director of the bank Ishichjamtso, and the clerk, Gendun Galsan.

Signed [by Mongol reckoning] in the fourth day of the twelfth month of the second year of the Raised-by-the-Many, and by the Tibetan reckoning on the same day and month of the year of the Water-Mouse.[19]

It is of course quite possible to discern here the rudiments of Dorzhiev's Shambhala Project: his grand design for a Pan-Buddhist confederation in Central Asia. He must therefore have felt a considerable sense of achievement when in January 1913, having dispatched a copy of the treaty to the Dalai Lama for formal approval, he left Urga and began the long haul back to St Petersburg. After so many years of what would now be called shuttle diplomacy, he at last had something solid in his hands. A dynamic new movement was stirring in the dormant heart of that great Buddhist Central Asia. The auguries for the future must have looked promising.

*

On 14 February *Novoye Vremya* reported that a caravan from Tibet was approaching St Petersburg. It included some young Tibetans who were to be educated in Russian schools. This report is not confirmed elsewhere, though oral reports suggest that Dorzhiev did bring a boy back to be educated in the Russian capital, though whether he was a Buryat, a Mongol or a Tibetan is unclear. Having subsequently been with Dorzhiev at the Buddhist temple, he disappeared from Leningrad in the thirties but reappeared again in Buryatia in the sixties, having in the interim been a 'secret lama'; he died in the late eighties. *Novoye Vremya* also reported that Dorzhiev, who had left the caravan and travelled on ahead, was planning to stay in Europe until May, 'when the grass will be growing in Mongolia', and to visit London.[20]

At the Buddhist temple, construction had long since been halted due to lack of funds, but as Dorzhiev had brought back with him the Dalai Lama's pledged contribution, which had been held up, as well as an additional sum from the Treasury of the Jebtsundamba Khutukhtu, work could begin again. Though still incomplete, the first religious ceremony was held on 21 February 1913 to mark the tercentenary of the House of Romanov. It was also no doubt to demonstrate to benefactors that their money had been well used. For the occasion the portico was decorated with the national flags of Russia and Tibet as well as with prayer flags embroidered with Buddhist emblems. As the shrine was not yet ready, one was prepared in the vestibule; it had on it a Buddha-rupa 'in royal attire', water bowls and a gold candelabrum. On the wall behind there were portraits of the Emperor, the Empress and the Heir Apparent, whom the Dalai Lama had lately declared to be a bodhisattva because all attempts to give him a Christian baptism had mysteriously failed. 'All the clergy wore picturesque robes of red and yellow, and brocaded head-dresses in the shape of Phrygian caps', wrote the *Novoe Vremya* reporter. 'The ceremony consisted of prayers accompanied by [the ringing of] small bells.'

Among those in attendance were Bandido Khambo Lama Itigelov, P.K. Kozlov and his wife E. V. Kozlova-Pushkaryova, Princess Tundutova and her son Dansan, various Russian Buddhists, several military officers including a certain General E, two pupils of the School of Jurisprudence, and the Mongolian Prince Khandadorji, who had first been sent on a mission to St Petersburg in 1911 and again in 1912. After the ceremony, Itigelov and Dorzhiev made speeches in which they attributed all credit for the occasion to the beneficence of the Russian Emperor.[21]

*

On the temporal level things did not go so well, for the current Russian Foreign Minister, Sergey Dmirtievich Sazonov (1861–1927),[22] was very much in favour of rapprochement with the British. He had visited England in September 1912 and later repeatedly declared his solemn intention of keeping His Majesty's Government informed of all developments regarding Tibet. The British were particularly concerned at this point by rumours of the Tibet-Mongolia Treaty, which, if it existed and was recognized, might lure Tibet into the Russian ambit. Sazonov assured Sir George Buchanan, the British Ambassador, that he attached no importance whatever to what Dorzhiev had done. He indeed doubted whether Dorzhiev – of whom he spoke in 'very uncomplimentary terms' – had any authority to sign such a treaty. Both the British and Russian Governments eventually decided that the treaty could not be recognized 'in view of the absence of legal rights of the signatories'.[23]

Not surprisingly, when on 11 February Dorzhiev called at the Foreign Ministry to present a memorandum, he met with a cool reception. Officials told him that since he was a Russian national he could not be officially recognized as a representative of the Dalai Lama; and when he went on to reveal that he had a letter from the Dalai Lama to the Emperor suggesting a joint Anglo-Russian protectorate over Tibet, he was told that Russia, who was bound by the terms of the 1907 convention, had no desire to enter into such an arrangement, nor was there any reason to suppose that Britain did either.[24]

Undeterred, in April he handed another memorandum to the Prime Minister, Count Vladimir Nicholaevich Kokovstov, which contained the proposals that he had outlined to Korostovets in Urga. We can safely assume that his overtures fell on equally stony ground here.

But still this indefatigable man would not give up. He next set off for Western Europe, intending to try to drum up support in various capitals, including Paris – where he renewed his acquaintance with his old friend Deniker – Berlin, Rome and London.[25] He certainly got to Paris and perhaps Rome and Berlin, but London, as we have already discussed, is problematic. In any case, his efforts in Western Europe were as unfruitful as those in Russia had been, which is not at all surprising since war clouds were gathering and soon the dogs of war would be loose all over Europe. Remote Tibet, a speck on the periphery of the Western consciousness at the best of times – something perhaps to dabble with if you had nothing better to do – now summarily vanished from all agendas.

Thus Agvan Dorzhiev's Tibet diplomacy was finally defeated by that most inexorable of adversaries: history itself.

*

Last rites were celebrated over the bones of the Tibet-Mongolia Treaty at Simla in 1913–14, when Britain, China and Tibet finally gathered around the conference table to attempt to settle the vexatious Tibetan question. China and Britain were for different reasons very apprehensive about the implications of the treaty, though Charles Bell, an assistant to the British plenipotentiary, Sir Henry McMahon, was sceptical that it even existed. He asked for clarification from the Tibetan plenipotentiary, Lönchen Paljor Dorji Shatra – once deposed from high political office but now reinstated.

The gist of Shatra's reply was that the Dalai Lama never authorized Dorzhiev to conclude any treaty with Mongolia. The letter given to Dorzhiev was of a general nature, asking him merely to work for the benefit of the Buddhist religion.

'It is the custom for us Tibetans to write to everybody asking for help, for instance, in letters written to you yourself we frequently made requests similar to that which the Dalai Lama made to Dorjieff. Unfortunately, the draft of this letter cannot be traced now, and it is feared that it was destroyed when the Yuthok house was burnt down, as the Chikyab Khenpo [Yuthok Kalön] was in charge of the records relating to the tour of the Dalai Lama in Mongolia and China.'[26]

Bell seems to have taken Shatra's spiel as solemn truth – another instance of his naïveté where Tibetans were concerned. Clearly the treaty did exist, and Dorzhiev had been given plenipotentiary powers to negotiate and sign it: why then did the Tibetans repudiate it? Perhaps for pragmatic reasons – in which case they would not necessarily have seen tnemselves as lying so much as deferring to the honourable oriental convention of telling others what they want to hear.

Lev Berlin makes the somewhat startling claim that the Dalai Lama and the Tibetan Government invited Dorzhiev to take part in the Simla Conference.[27] He was unable to attend due to pastoral commitments in

Buryatia and Kalmykia, which is perhaps just as well, for he might have heard himself vilified by the Chinese plenipotentiary, Ivan Chen, who blamed the Younghusband Mission on the fact that the Dalai Lama had given ear to the advice of his Buryat 'assistant' rather than to that of the Amban, Yü-Kang.[28]

But by and large things went rather well for the Tibetans at Simla. The Chinese naturally prevaricated and tried all manner of slippery tactics. Their basic argument was that Tibet had been an integral part of China ever since it had been conquered by Genghis Khan. (The fact that the khan had been a Mongol, not a Chinese, does not seem to have been a problem for them.) The British and the Tibetans could not accept this. Eventually a draft convention was drawn up which divided Tibet into two zones: Outer Tibet, to which the strict terms of the treaty applied, comprised the massive area west of the Yangtze frontier which was traditionally the ambit of the Lhasa Government, and Inner Tibet, where the Chinese could have a freer hand, consisted of various peripheral regions. Britain and China recognized the autonomy of Outer Tibet under Chinese suzerainty or nominal overlordship; the Tibetans there would be free to conduct their own internal affairs without Chinese interference, and whilst an Amban might be posted in Lhasa with a small escort, large numbers of Chinese troops should not be sent. As regards trade, Britain was to have most-favoured-nation status, new regulations would be negotiated and the British Trade Agent in Gyantsé would be entitled to make periodic visits to Lhasa 'in connection with matters arising out of the 1904 Treaty'. Britain was also to arbitrate in the event of any disputes arising from the convention.

Ivan Chen strove until the eleventh hour to get a better deal for China but was finally obliged to capitulate and initialled the draft agreement. His government at once repudiated his action, however, thereby cutting themselves out of the negotiations for the British and the Tibetans went on to make a direct agreement between themselves. This marked the beginning of a close relationship between Britain and Tibet that was to last right down until Indian Independence in 1948. During that time Tibet enjoyed a long and fruitful period of relatively untroubled autonomy. Credit for this is usually attributed to the strength of character of the Great Thirteenth Dalai Lama – who had returned at last to Lhasa, never to be driven out again, in January 1913 – but much credit must also go to his chief adviser, Agvan Dorzhiev. Without Dorzhiev's tireless efforts, Tibetan history would have taken a very different course.

*

1913 was a turning point for Dorzhiev. In the changing circumstances of the times, his efforts as a shuttle diplomatist were no longer required. Fading from the Tibetan scene, he subsequently turned his main attention to his native Russia and his ambitious schemes for developing Buddhism there.

CHAPTER FOURTEEN

The Fall of the House of Romanov
1914 – 1917

On 1 August 1914 Germany declared war on Russia. The confrontation had been building up for some time, for Germany needed to break up the Russian empire and gain access to its vast resources if she was to fulfil her own global ambitions. For Russia, a state already in internal disarray, a crisis of this magnitude was hardly to be welcomed, but at the very outset of hostilities the prospects looked favourable enough, for her war machine was, in terms of sheer manpower resources, second to none.

Agvan Dorzhiev responded patriotically to the new situation by joining forces with Bandido Khambo Lama Itigelov to head a committee to raise funds for the war effort among the Buryats and the Kalmyks.[1] A year later, in 1915, their 'All-Buryat Committee for Collecting Funds for War Needs' carried out a large amount of propaganda work in the East; this included the release of a document to the Buryats in their own language intended to 'explain the importance of the war for the people and the whole State'.[2] A number of datsans in both Buryatia and Kalmykia were moreover 'equipped' – presumably as hospitals or convalescent homes[3] – and throughout the war zhud-khurals or ceremonies for the success of Russian forces were held regularly at the Buddhist temple in Petrograd (as St Petersburg was renamed in 1915).[4] Ironically, such activities were later held against Dorzhiev and cited as proof of alleged complicity with the imperial régime.

Otherwise, it was the good lama's habit at this time to spend each winter engaged in religious and nationalist activities among the Buryats, and the rest of the year either in Kalmykia or in Petrograd.

*

Problems had continued to beset the temple even after building work was resumed in 1913, among them being the objection of the Department of Foreign Creeds to certain aspects of the decoration of the facade. V. V. Radlov argued strongly that a Buddhist temple without decoration would be a stark and styleless one, but as early as 1910 the architect Baranovsky had been obliged to tone down the original plan, exchanging the gilded bronze doors that he had initially specified for plain wooden ones, and subduing the capitals of the portico columns from golden to dark bronze. Most of all, however, officialdom objected to certain typical Tibetan Buddhist decorative motifs, for it feared that anything overly demonstrative might offend or even lead the local Orthodox astray. The main brunt of disapproval fell on the gyeltsen, the gilded barrel-shaped ornaments that characteristically adorn the roofs of Tibetan and Mongolian temples and which probably date back to the remote nomadic past; also the frieze of bronze-gilt mirror discs (tolli) intended to frighten away evil spirits, and the gilded eight-spoked Wheel of the Dharma flanked by two standing fallow deer that symbolizes the Buddha's first sermon at Isipatana. The latter was not put up over the portico until 1915, when a ganjira (pinnacle) was also placed on the roof of the rear tower section.[5]

Problems concerning the number of religious allowed to reside at the temple had also continued. In a letter of 15 March 1912 to A. A. Makarov, the recently appointed Director of the Department of Foreign Creeds, Radlov tried to explain the essential nature of Buddhist religious buildings: 'In the Buddhist world there is in general no separate meditation hall unlinked to a monastic community, since apart from a community a building of that kind would possess no raison d'être', he wrote. 'Buddhist ceremonies are not conducted apart from religious persons and have to be carried out by the whole community.'[6]

His entreaties fell on deaf ears. The number of religious was finally fixed on 2 May 1914, by special order of Nicholas II himself, at nine lamas, including five monks, one of them the shiretui or abbot; all should reside at the temple 'without the establishment . . . of a monastic community according to the forms of the Lamaist cult'. In the same year, on Dorzhiev's recommendation, three lamas were brought in from Trans-Baikalia, four from Astrakhan province and two from Stavropol province; thus 'the Petersburg Buddhist Community was at last formed, being a union of Lamaist monks and Lamaist lay-people, for the most part drawn from the Buryats and Kalmyks who lived in Petersburg'.[7] There is reason for believing, however, that Dorzhiev had no intention of observing the official limitation on residents, for W. A. Unkrig maintains that in 1914 twelve lamas were lodged in the temple and an increase of up to forty was planned.[8]

The temple was finally consecrated on 10 August 1915. No detailed account of the event is available apart from one by Friedrich Lustig, which is problematic for the usual reasons. According to the eccentric Estonian bhikshu (monk), there was more than one ceremony, all of which were 'on a grand scale'. For two weeks beforehand, the place was overwhelmed with 'lavish gifts of flowers', and a panoply of distinguished monks participated in preliminary daily chanting. The Petrograd Mint also struck 25,108 gold, silver and bronze commemorative medals. The Dalai Lama could not personally attend but sent a 'powerful delegation' from Tibet 'to represent the Buddhist Papacy and assist the Tibetan Envoy Dorzhiev'. The Jebtsundamba Khutukhtu also sent a delegation of five monks from Urga; and more 'monks of high standing' came from Siberia. King Rama VI was represented by the Siamese Minister in Petrograd, and the Emperor, Nicholas II, who, together with members of his family had been shown over the building by Dorzhiev a few days earlier, was represented by the Prime Minister, I. L. Goremykin; N. Shcherbatov, the Minister of the Interior, also put in an appearance. In addition there were Kalmyk Cossacks and distinguished academics like S. F. Ol'denburg, O. O. Rosenberg, V. L. Kotvich, F. I. Stcherbatsky, B. Y. Vladimirtsov and A. D. Rudnev.[9]

The 'invocation and benediction service' was chanted by Dorzhiev assisted by three lamas from Tibet: 'May the body, speech and mind of every sentient being be offered to the Buddhas of the ten directions! May all beings be firmly established in Righteousness until they attain the great final Deliverance! May they be free from pain and keep all their faculties unimpaired! May they never turn back from the quest of Supreme Enlightenment!' chanted the great lama – or so Lustig would have us believe – sprinkling the congregation with holy water and scattering coloured grains of rice, while his 'unforgettable words echoed through the immense cathedral in one continuous stream of majesty and obeisance'.[10]

There are certainly some elements of truth in all this, but they are obscured in the usual froth of exaggeration. For instance, commemorative medals were indeed struck but they were of bronze, not of silver or gold, and bore the Tibetan name of the temple: Kun la brtse mdzad thub dbang dam chhos 'byung b'ai gnas' – 'Source of the Holy Teaching of the Buddha, Who is All-Compassionate'.[11] W.A. Unkrig also confirms that Dorzhiev presided at the ceremony, but he makes no mention of any other distinguished participants besides 'two monks and a high official', who were representatives 'of the only country in the world where Buddhism is the state religion', by which he seems to mean Siam (modern Thailand).[12] It is moreover highly unlikely that the consecration was as ostentatious as Lustig makes out for we know that deep prejudice still persisted and both Dorzhiev and his colleagues received death threats through the post as well as threats to blow up the temple. They were therefore concerned to preserve a low profile and, for at least five years after the consecration, ceremonies were held at the temple only irregularly for fear of attracting hostile attention.[13]

*

Dorzhiev's temple, which is believed to have been dedicated to Kalachakra, still stands in the bleak northern suburbs of Leningrad. One comes across it almost by surprise: a solid little edifice faced in dusky Finnish granite sitting demurely in its own minuscule compound. It is surrounded by monotonously uniform residential buildings and a few high-rise blocks put up since World War II. Restless motor traffic roars around it all day. To have come through some seventy-five years of neglect and mistreatment by an unsympathetic régime surely proves that it must possess at least some of the positive characteristics of its great founder, notably his tenacity and ability to survive.

Russian accounts describe the temple as a dugan or dukhang. 'Dukhang' is a Tibetan word denoting the large halls in which monastic assemblies take place, but in Mongolia and Buryatia it seems to be applied to rather more complex structures also including educational facilities, of which this is an example. The temple is in fact composed of two distinct parts. There is what we might call the dugan proper, using the word in its Buryat-Mongol sense, which is a two storey structure that includes the main assembly hall. Behind that there is a narrow tower section of four storeys. The whole structure is clad in dark reddish-violet granite quarried in Finland and is aligned on a north-south axis as is characteristic of Tibetan buildings. Another Tibetan feature is that its walls and windows taper upwards, which is what lends it its very solid appearance.

At the southern end of the dugan, approached through a tree-filled garden and up a flight of granite steps, is an imposing portico consisting of four square pillars with elaborate capitals surmounted by an ornamented pediment on which stands the Wheel of Life and fallow deer motif. Behind, on the front facade of the building, the casings, jambs and lintels of the eight windows have been finished off in grey granite. The crowning entablature is of red brick with horizontal bands of blue glazed bricks decorated with white circles. There are two gilded gyeltsen on the roof, one at each corner of the facade. The topmost storey of the gonkhang tower is also of red brick decorated with bands of glazed tiles and was once crowned by the gilded ganjira. It is said that during the construction of this tower Dorzhiev used to urge the workmen, 'Make it higher – still a bit higher!'[14] Unfortunately it was built too high and in 1910 the authorities decreed that it be pulled down and rebuilt.

The doors of the main portico lead into a vestibule and from there into the main assembly hall, down which run two rows of square columns, again with elaborately decorated capitals. These in effect divide the interior space into three parts. In the temple's heyday, the columns, which like everything else in the building would have been painted in bright colours, were adorned with rich brocaded hangings and thangka paintings depicting Tantric deities. Immediately in front of them were the padded seats upon which the lamas sat during ceremonies, the highest seats, which were reserved for the highest lamas, being at the front (north) end, near the shrine. On small tables in front of the shrine votive objects, offerings, holy books and other Lamaist paraphernalia would have been placed.

Though the assembly hall is devoid of windows, a mystic half-light originating in a skylight on the roof diffuses down into the room through a series of glazed skylights. From the start, however, unlike its Tibeto-Mongolian prototypes, the building enjoyed the benefit of electric light – in 'rather stylish fittings',[15] though nowadays these have been replaced by modern strip-lighting. An elaborate cornice tricked out in many vivid colours runs around the room, while on the floor a lotus motif is depicted in glazed tiles. There was also once a swastika motif but that was smashed up early in World War II because of its Nazi associations.

On the floor above the main assembly hall there is a large, open area in which is to be found a glazed partition surrounding one of the skylights; this is decorated with the Eight Auspicious Symbols,[16] said to have been designed by Nicholas Roerich. Along the east and west walls, meanwhile, there are cells for the resident lamas.

At the front of the building, on the mezzanine behind the portico, there are some rooms which, according to Unkrig, were originally reserved for Khambo Bandido Lama Itigelov. Two shuttered internal windows here enable activities in the main assembly hall to be discreetly viewed from above.

The main shrine, though apparently a large niche in the north wall of the assembly hall, is in fact situated on the ground floor of the tower section. Around its external periphery runs a frieze with a legend in stylized Sanskrit lettering. In the early years, it was dominated by a great Buddha-rupa some three metres high, with an ornamental surround, which would have been copiously draped with khada. It is rumoured to have been made in Hamburg and was of clay or plaster, though there were plans to replace it with a bronze or gilded replica.[17] To the right and left of the rupa stood wooden cases containing smaller figures and various sacred objects, and all around were more elaborate hangings.

To one side of the shrine there is a smaller room, while on the other side stairs give access to the upper storeys of the tower. Andreyev maintains that immediately above the main shrine there was a second, smaller shrine room in which were to be found a sandalwood figure of a seated Shakyamuni Buddha, donated by King Rama VI of Siam, and one of Maitreya, the Coming Buddha, donated by G. A. Planson, the Russian Consul in Bangkok. Both subsequently found their way into the collection at the Museum of the History of Religion and Atheism at Kazan Cathedral on the Nevsky Prospekt. The Maitreya, which was recently discovered in the museum's attics, unfortunately missing its pedestal and head, has now been returned to the temple.[18] There are hopes that other treasures will be returned in due course.[19]

There is another room above this second shrine room, which is currently used as a classroom and dining-room for novices. Then, at the top, about the level of the dugan roof, there is the gonkhang or protector chapel itself, to which access would have been restricted. This had thangka paintings on its walls depicting wrathful deities like Mahakala and Yamantaka or Vajrabhairava; also a shrine upon which stood a figure of Pelden Lhamo who, along with Mahakala, was one the temple's most important dharmapalas. Finally, set high in the east and west walls are windowless cells reached by fixed metal ladders; these were put in for retreat purposes.

According to Unkrig, the temple had the unique facility of a 'steam kitchen' in which offerings of butter, flour and sweets were prepared, these 'in their varying forms' being such as would 'do any of our confectioners credit'.[20] It was also provided with a central heating system – oral reports talk of a hot-air rather than a hot-water system – run from a boiler in the extensive and cavernous cellars, where reputedly during World War II hand-grenades were manufactured. There was also a library – Dorzhiev's own archives were lodged here – and store-rooms for 'utensils, pictures and musical instruments'. The temple's ritual objects were in fact ordered by Dorzhiev himself from specialist workshops in Peking and Dolon-Nor and paid for with 'his own family gold'; they arrived in St Petersburg in two sizeable consignments in June and November 1910.[21]

*

After the consecration of the temple, Dorzhiev went into retreat to perform the sadhanas (yogic practices) of Manjuvajra, Guhyasamaja, the Medicine Buddha and Kalachakra.[22] He does not specify where this took place, but it could conceivably have been at the Petrograd temple itself, possibly in one of the retreat cells in the gonkhang.

Then in the autumn he went east to adjudicate in a monastic disagreement that had blown up around what in his memoirs he calls the 'Tungkhen Khering Monastery'. He almost certainly means the Kiren Datsan, founded in 1817 in or near the Cis-Baikalian village of Tungka, which lies south-west of Irkutsk in the direction of Tannu-Tuva. The main cause of controversy seems to have been the question of relocating the monastery at some new site. Out of three possibilities, Dorzhiev himself favoured a 'quiet and radiant place in front of Mondarga', greatly appreciated by local yogis for its wholesome orientation and penchant for manifesting miraculous signs. 'I think it would be good to go there', he suggested.

Local opinion, however, divided into two factions, conservatives and progressives: the one whipping up confusion through wild talk bred of fear of 'losing their monastic lineage and sponsors', the other simply getting on with preparations for moving to a new site. Dorzhiev says that some of the latter were connected with the 'Kh'oi-mo faction', which suggests that they became sponsors of the Koimor Datsan, actually built in the early twenties on the other side of the Irkut river from the Kiren; it is usually described as Dorzhiev's own second Cis-Baikalian foundation.

The fracas was not easily resolved: quarrels broke out and malicious things were said. Even when some sort of reconciliation was eventually achieved, bad feeling continued to fester beneath the surface, and it was only when some sacred images were damaged that the contending factions were jerked to their senses.[23]

*

Unfortunately, just as the Buddhists of Petrograd were rejoicing in the consecration of their temple, Russian fortunes in the world war were undergoing a dramatic decline. In 1915, after the enemy had launched a successful offensive in May, the public at home were shocked to hear of terrible reversals and troop losses at the front. Many concerned and patriotic groups rallied to help the legions of wounded that were returned home, including the Petrograd Buddhists, for the four-storey stone house in the temple grounds was turned into a hospital for Buryat servicemen.

There was also a general clamour to pinpoint the causes of the débâcle – and to find scapegoats. It quickly became clear that there had been gross mismanagement, in particular a serious failure in the supply of munitions – Russian troops had even on occasion been pitched into battle armed only with bayonets – but, looked at in the broader context, this was just one of a concatenation of secondary ailments that devolved from one central miasma: the imperial regime itself.

During the Cold War era, popular opinion in the West has been in the habit of thinking of Soviet Russia as a repressive and politically flawed state. What we tend to forget is that its precursor, Imperial Russia, was regarded in much the same way by our ancestors. After all, most Western European nations, if they had not actually abandoned monarchy, had by the turn of the century at least restricted its powers, bowed to basic notions of human rights and established the rudiments of representative government. Not so Russia. The Emperor doggedly continued to rule his gigantic swathe of territory, with its ethnically diverse millions, as though it were a private estate. He was like some Eastern pasha: beholden to no-one (except in theory God), advised by whoever gained his favour, his utterances enjoying the status of law, his whims and caprices sacrosanct; and just as he was unnaturally elevated, so the vast mass of his ordinary subjects were correspondingly degraded. Even though freed from formal serfdom in 1861, the muzhik or Russian peasant was still at the turn of the present century bound to his local commune and debarred from moving elsewhere without permission.

Like its successor, the imperial regime was also maintained by fear, and control exercised through a highly developed apparatus of administration and repression which included a police force augmented by a Corps of Gendarmes and a security police, the Okhrana; a colossal army; periodic censorship; a harsh system of punishments for anyone daring to defy the autocracy; a regional network of governors appointed directly by the throne; and a hierarchic bureaucracy, responsible directly to the Emperor, which not only loyally ran the country according to his ukazyi (dictats) but monitored, supervised and regulated every aspect of its life.

This system of government just had to change if Imperial Russia, essentially a rural country populated by millions of backward and apathetic peasants, was to be pulled into the twentieth century. Nor was this just the insight of a few revolutionary extremists – though these naturally attracted most attention with their dramatic terrorist actions – but ran right across the social spectrum. Unfortunately, Nicholas II, though by no means a natural autocrat, had his head resolutely turned in the opposite direction. He believed that he had, on assuming the throne, been invested with a sacred duty to maintain the absolute powers of the monarchy intact. In this he was wholeheartedly endorsed by his wife, Alexandra Fyodorovna, a retiring but proud and passionate woman, devoted to her family, but unable to bear the thought of her son, the Tsarevich Alexey, being deprived of the slightest portion of his birthright. Thus Nicholas and Alexandra studiously spurned the advice of their more forward-looking advisors and strove instead to fend off the inevitable.

The first rude awakening came in 1905. The revolutionary events of that year forced Nicholas to make political concessions; but, strangely perverse man that he was, he afterwards refused to face the reality of what he had done and tried to go on playing the autocrat. He was particularly concerned to outwit or limit the effectiveness of the Duma. It was hardly to be wondered, then, that even the more moderate elements there were driven over to the left out of sheer frustration, and its early sessions, seething with dissent, often degenerated into little more than a platform for the dissemination of radical and even revolutionary propaganda.

During the years immediately following, up to the outbreak of war, Russia enjoyed a period of relative stability. The economy was relatively healthy; the rural folk were relatively prosperous and happy; there was a rapid advance in industrialization in a few places; and there was even something of a renaissance in the arts. But the old root problems lay dormant beneath the bland facade, and it only needed the military reverses of 1915 to reactivate them fully. Unfortunately, after the assassination of the last prime minister of ability, Piotr Stolypin, the imperial couple, deeply suspicious by nature and so inclined to value sycophancy above ability, appointed lesser men to high office – men like I. L. Goremykin, B. V. Stürmer and A. D. Protopopov, who were utterly wanting in the strong qualities required to handle the deteriorating situation.

*

But the shock of 1915 did initially have some salutary effects. Much needed military reforms did take place and, as a consequence, Russian fortunes improved at the front. Unfortunately serious problems then began to assert themselves at the rear as the cities were hit by economic inflation and acute shortages of food and fuel. This led to intense social discontent.

Rejecting all advice, Nicholas responded to the events of 1915 by making himself Commander-in-Chief of the Army, which caused him to be away from Petrograd at army headquarters at Moghilev for long periods. There he began to suffer from insomnia, depression and anxiety, for which in 1916 the Empress sent him a sedative concocted by Dr Badmayev. This again was thought to contain hashish,[24] in which case the Russian Army during World War I would have been under the technical command of a 'stoned' man.

With the Emperor away from the capital, the Empress was able to have a freer hand in politics. This was disastrous, for she was highly unpopular with the Russian people on account of her German birth and at the same time ever more under the domination of her dubious 'friend', Grigori Rasputin. This in turn allowed the philandering staretz to begin to interfere directly in politics himself, to the extent of influencing the appointment of ministers – Stürmer and Protopopov were his appointees – and also of affecting the conduct of the war, which from the start he had opposed. This provoked much annoyance in a society already in crisis, particularly among monarchists who viewed the unsavoury commoner's closeness to the Empress as a dishonour. A plot was therefore hatched and the staretz was murdered in highly dramatic circumstances by the dandyish Prince Yusupov, aided and abetted by a most distinguished gang of fellow conspirators.

Nicholas, who returned from the capital towards the end of 1916, was deeply shocked to find so many close friends and even family members involved in the murder. He severed ties with many and retired with his wife and children, to a reclusive existence at Tsarskoye Selo. There he lingered, a confused and tormented man, protected by the sycophantic Protopopov from the almost universal clamour for his removal.

*

Naturally, life at the temple was not untouched by these events. An interesting though perhaps not entirely objective picture of what things were like there in 1916 is provided by a letter which the British Trade Agent in Gyantsé in southern Tibet intercepted in November. It had been sent to the Dalai Lama by a retired Russian Army officer, Staff Captain Mikhail Yakovich Orlov, asking for permission to live and study the 'wisdom of the ages' in Lhasa – and please to send financial help too. For the past two and a half years, Orlov wrote, he had been living in Petrograd on a small government pension and had frequently visited the 'pagoda', not to attend services but to pray. However:

... lately, when I went to the director of the house, I was refused by him to enter the pagoda, his refusal being based on the fact that they had a commission in the Academy of Sciences under the Presidency of Mr Radlovim [sic], to whom I should make application ... I do not know on what grounds the above-mentioned monk based his answer, but I must state that I never received such an answer when the lamas DJIK DJAT and DODJIEF (who was born beyond the Baikals) lived there ...

There is here only one Buddhist monk. A hostile and serious attitude is being taken up by the female sex, which strives to appear in all respects similar to the male sex, and introduces disturbances, which are most irritating to the monks and make life in the Shrine meaningless. Both religious services and life in the Shrine are impossible. Under the excuse, at one time of repairs, at another of attendance of the sick [undoubtedly a reference to the use of the temple as a hospital for the Buryat wounded], the Shrine can in no way fulfil its lofty purpose.[25]

'DJIK DJAT' must be Sodnom Zhigzhitov, the abbot of the temple, who died mysteriously of typhus in the early twenties; 'DODJIEF' must of course, as the British authorities surmised, be Dorzhiev. The obstreperous women may have been feminists of some kind or other, not one would imagine pious Buryat ladies but perhaps radical or revolutionary ones. As for the presence of only one monk at the temple, this is explained by the fact that during the winter of 1916/17 most of the lamas had returned to their homelands as they were unable to bear the high cost of living brought about by the ongoing shortages.[26]

*

Not all Petrograders could leave the city, however, and their discontent, focused not only against the shortages but against war itself and the Emperor's government, began to intensify to bursting point. In February 1917, open demonstrations broke out in the streets of Petrograd, which were soon joined by dissident workers from the industrial Vyborg district. Soldiers, mostly raw recruits from the country temporarily garrisoned in the city, were detailed to quell the unrest, but they refused to carry out orders and began to fraternize with the demonstrators, whose grievances they understood and in many cases shared.

Karlis Tennisons sampled the atmosphere of these turbulent times when he walked through the city some days later:

On March 10, dismays were most real and pressing. By noon, tens of thousands of people filled the streets near the Kazan Cathedral, and around Alexander III monument there was political speech-making. The mounted police opened fire. There were screams and groans, and the crowd dispersed.[27]

Approaching Liteinyi Prospekt, he noticed that the cinemas were still

crowded and that many workers, who had just received their pay, were
drunk and uttering 'unprintable' oaths. Later he found Dr Badmayev
sitting in a sombre, thoughtful mood in his office. 'Some of our leading
politicians are persons with a natural tendency to evade the truth',
Badmayev declared. 'They play into the hands of the cruel enemy. I
fear it is too late to right the wrong. The flaming utterances of Skobelev
and Kerensky, the Duma representatives, can only ruin Russia.'

'Have you told anyone about these ideas of yours?' Tennisons asked.

'Of course, I told Mr Protopopov. I told Mr Dobrovolsky. I told Mr
Shcheglovitov [President of the Council of State]. But no one seems to
be capable of formulating a constructive programme.'[28]

*

Early in the crisis, the Emperor, estranged from reality as ever, unwisely
chose to leave the capital for consultations at army headquarters. While
there, he initially refused to believe reports of mounting chaos in the
capital, and even when at last convinced of its reality, he vacillated,
causing a power vacuum to open up. The Duma was best placed and
qualified to fill it, but even though its members had been clamouring for
fuller political powers for years, when offered them they too dithered,
daunted by the sheer enormity of the responsibility – and afraid too
that if the imperial regime regained control its wrath would descend
upon them.

The Duma also now had a rival for power in the Petrograd Soviet, a
loose convention of local socialist workers and soldiers, augmented by
unelected sympathizers from various parts of Russia – the prototype,
in fact, of numerous other soviets that quickly began springing up all
over the country. This body was reluctant to seize power too, but for
a different reason: its members believed that the right moment for full-
scale revolution had not yet arrived. Though the Duma and the Soviet
were by no means of one mind in their political objectives, the leaders of
the Duma decided that they must gain the Soviet's support if they were
to make the bold step of seizing some measure of power. They managed
to do this – or, more precisely, they gained the support of the Soviet's
executive committee, Ispolkom, which was dominated by Mensheviks
(a faction of the Social Democrats). A Provisional Government was
then established under the chairmanship of Prince Georgii Evgenevich
Lvov. Unfortunately, this quiet, grey-bearded man, who had done much
good work in the zemstvo movement – the zemstva were district and
provincial councils – was not made of the stuff of revolutionary prime
ministers. As the British agent R. H. Bruce Lockhart put it, 'A man of

great charm, he would have made an excellent chairman of London County Council.'29

The Provisional Government was essentially a stopgap body intended to rule the country until a proper Constituent Assembly, elected on an universal franchise, could be convened. Unfortunately, while its members were very adept at voicing dissent and bandying hypothetical political proposals and programmes, they had little grasp of the practicalities of government; so, while they freely axed large sections of the old apparatus, including the police, they set up nothing substantial in their place. Though support rallied to them from all walks of Russian life, even from former stalwarts of the old regime, what actually now happened was that the country began to fall apart – which, considering that it was still at war, was dire indeed.

There was also a high price to pay for the Soviet's support: Ispolkom began to play an increasingly intrusive role in affairs. It even drafted and circulated its own radical directives to the army, which profoundly affected the already shaky discipline at the front – there had been large numbers of desertions for some time. Also, to please Ispolkom, a general political amnesty was announced, so terrorists and hardened professional revolutionaries, many of whom were in internal exile or abroad, were free to return to Petrograd. In his dingy lodgings on the Spiegelgasse in Zurich, Vladimir Ilich Ulyanov began to organize his transit across German territory; in New York, Lev Davidovich Bronstein began to pack his bags.

*

The Emperor did not return directly to Petrograd from army head-quarters. His special train was diverted to Pskov, where pressure was brought to bear on him by high military officers, notably General Alekseyev, to recognize the Provisional Government and to abdicate. Searching his conscience, he was initially reluctant to take this fateful step, but after agonizing for some time, finally did so, naming his brother, Grand Duke Mikhail Aleksandrovich, as his successor. In the event, Mikhail, whose shoulders were no broader than those of his brother, bowed out too, so the monarchy effectively came to an end.

On one hand filled with a deep sense of shame and failure, on the other relieved that the incubus of absolute responsibility had been removed, it was plain Colonel Nicholas Romanov who was reunited with his family at Tsarskoye Selo some time afterwards. Unfortunately, though the Provisional Government favoured sending him out of the country, the increasingly powerful Ispolkom insisted that the imperial family be detained lest they become a focus for counter-revolution; it was therefore to the indignity of house arrest that the former Emperor returned.

*

Having personally known him and fully, if not fulsomely, extolled his virtues at the consecration of the Buddhist temple less that two years before, one might in fact have expected Agvan Dorzhiev to have shed a compassionate Buddhist tear for the fate of Nicholas Romanov. Not so, if we are to believe the evidence of his memoirs: these suggest that he accepted the news with total dispassion, laying the blame directly on the association with Rasputin. He even writes with sympathy of 'the worthy Kerensky [who took over the premiership from Lvov in July 1917] and other honest men who seized the capital';[30] and he inserts an apocalyptic meditation on the evils of monarchy (and government in general), which is loaded with distinct resonances of contemporary radical propaganda:

> From the time of King Mangkut[31] until the present day, kings and their subjects have not managed to live in a harmonious way, with [the subjects] honouring those above them and [the rulers] loving those below. Latterly governments ... have overpowered [their subjects] with the sole desire to oppress, torment and devour them. This intolerable situation prevails over most of the world. The subjects too do not hold their lords in high regard, and [consequently] evil behaviour increases greatly. In particular, hunger [for power] between governments grows and they come to rely on jealousy and competitiveness alone. They drive their innocent subjects into the hands of their enemies and let them be killed. And as the seas of blood rise, wrong-minded and heartless governments proliferate. Whenever those who are honest start to work for the suffering people with compassion and no regard for their own life, they are subjected to such intolerable things as murder and imprisonment.[32]

Friedrich Lustig paints an entirely contradictory picture. According to him, Dorzhiev was away from Petrograd until 2 May 1917. As he seems to have amended his dates to the Gregorian Calendar (NS), this would have been towards the end of April according to the Julian (OS). When Karlis Tennisons met him at the railway station that day, he seemed outwardly in good humour, but it soon became apparent that he was inwardly troubled and 'quite heartbroken' by the calamity which had befallen the Imperial House of Romanov. The first thing he wished to do was present the Dalai Lama's compliments to Nicholas, and to this end he went to see Paul Milyukov, the Minister of Foreign Affairs in the new Provisional Government.[33] Milyukov received Dorzhiev, who no doubt presented himself as the official representative of the Dalai Lama, and told him that the Dalai Lama's compliments would be conveyed to Nicholas by A. F. Kerensky, currently Minister of Justice, who went periodically to Tsarskoye Selo.

The interview must have taken place within about ten days of Dorzhiev's return, for Milyukov, a leading supporter of the war, was forced to resign on the night of 4/5 May (O S). The Kadet leader had been in the forefront of liberal agitation for many years; he was a patriotic and scholarly man, and he was noted for his energy. But he had lately been under intense pressure – there had actually been demonstrations against him – and his feelings must have rubbed off on Agvan Dorzhiev, for the lama returned sombre-faced from the interview, surrounded by clouds of foreboding for the future of Russia.

Shortly afterwards, Lustig maintains, Dorzhiev and Tennisons were actually invited to a reception given by Prince Lvov at which the sanguine Prime Minister explained to a 'smirking' Dorzhiev that 'an era of real progress has come to our great Motherland' – until surges of strident music drowned his monologue. '"How perfectly calm and contented Prince Lvov felt as he spoke to me," Dorzhiev exclaimed, laughing uproariously, when they had returned to the temple. "What a wonderful man! So there are no crises in Petrograd, no mobs yelling imprecations, and no German agents preaching defeatism. Good heavens! What a frame of mind!"'[34]

Lustig's account, clearly subject to its own pro-monarchist biases, must be treated with the usual caution; but even so it is a useful foil to Dorzhiev's own record, which has its biases too, for he wrote it at a time when he was anxious to present himself as a loyal supporter of the new order with few regrets for the passing of the old. Taking everything into account, it is doubtful that he felt no pity for the personal fate of Nicholas II, though at the same time it is quite likely that he had been entertaining mixed feelings about the imperial regime for some time. After all, Nicholas had done nothing very positive to help the Tibetan cause – indeed he had finally abandoned it – and the imperial bureaucracy had certainly hindered the completion of the Petrograd temple. The autocracy was furthermore closely aligned with the Orthodox Church, which had consistently thrown obstacles in the way of his Buddhist missionary efforts.

'Especially in this country of Russia', Dorzhiev wrote in one of his rare vituperative moments, 'the long-haired followers of the Christian religion were, with their growing power, persecuting all the adherents of the countless other religions . . . *Even the Tsar and his ministers were deceived by these people.*'[35]

But it was probably not merely dissatisfaction with the old order that influenced his thinking at this crucial time. Despite the prevailing political chaos, the shortages and the suffering, a revolution had taken place, and revolutions have a buoyant, hopeful, liberational aspect that touches those millennial yearnings to which most people with any imagination are susceptible. In this case, moreover, the deadening hand of an iron autocracy was being released, so energies that had been thwarted for centuries could at last begin to express themselves. The air was full of exciting possibilities . . .

From the time of his first visit to Europe, Agvan Dorzhiev had shown that he was not an ossified reactionary, hostile to all change, but a progressive, interested in the modern Western world and concerned to work with it. Even at around the age of sixty-three he probably retained enough visionary imagination to respond positively to the liberational spirit of the times – and he would also have been heartened by the enlightened stance that the Provisional Government had adopted on the issue of religion. The preferential status of the Orthodox Church was to go, opening up prospects for what looked like a new era of spiritual freedom and tolerance; at the same time there was official sympathy for the aspirations of the national minorities.

So a subtle transformation began to become apparent around 1917. The Buddhist monk Agvan Dorzhiev, who had at one time hob-nobbed with great autocrats like the Dalai Lama of Tibet, the Jebtsundamba Khutukhtu of Urga and Emperor Nicholas II, was changing – not into an out-and-out revolutionary on the left wing of the Social Democrat or Socialist Revolutionary parties, but at least into some kind of liberal, committed to forward thinking notions like democracy, social justice, reform and the 'scientific' viewpoint currently fashionable among Russian intellectuals.

CHAPTER FIFTEEN

The World Turned on Its Head
1917 – 1918

Dorzhiev was not content to remain on the sidelines during the momentous revolutionary year of 1917. He firstly joined with Badzar Baradin and Sodnom Zhigzhitov, the abbot of the Petrograd temple, in the establishment of a Buryat-Kalmyk Committee in Petrograd.

This short-lived initiative, which proclaimed itself 'the central body administering the affairs of state construction in Buryatia and Kalmykia',[1] had a rival in the Buryat National Committee (Burnatskom), which was founded in March 1917 with the aim of 'uniting the leading Irkutsk and Trans-Baikal Buryats in their struggle for "national autonomy" and protection of their lands from confiscation by Russians'.[2] Burnatskom's members included most of the leading Buryat intellectuals – Zhamtsarano, Tsybikov, Rinchino, Bogdanov and, so one source maintains, Baradin – and established its headquarters at Chita, with a branch at Irkutsk and a representative in Petrograd. It was this representative, Dashi Sampilon, who reported at a Burnatskom congress, held at Chita between 23 and 25 April, that the Buryat-Kalmyk Committee maintained a conservative agent in Petrograd, a wealthy Irkutsk Buryat named Khankhasaev, who did not represent Burnatskom's interests but merely lobbied for a return to the principles of the old Speransky legislation and the reconstruction of the steppe dumas. Burnatskom's platform was more radical: it wanted an entirely new internal order and an entirely new relationship with the Russian Government. Also it seems that Khankhasaev maintained no relationship with the soviets. On the basis of Sampilon's report, Burnatskom sent a telegraph to Prince Lvov informing him that the Buryat-Kalmyk Committee did not represent them.

It is clear, therefore, that the Buryat-Kalmyk Committee was not a radical group but well to the right of Burnatskom, which itself was a middle-of-the-road organization, acceptable to most Buryats but definitely not radical enough for those on the far Left, including the

Bolsheviks, who had their own organization, the Central Executive Committee of Siberian Soviets (Tsentrosibir), though this and its main rivals were composed primarily of Russians rather than Buryats.

*

It may have been in connection with his work for the Buryat-Kalmyk Committee that Agvan Dorzhiev made the journey to the lower Volga region which Friedrich Lustig describes.

Tennisons, who as a Buddhist chaplain to the Russian Army had been at the front – he had witnessed, among others, the famous Battle of Tannenberg – and was going, at Dorzhiev's suggestion, to recuperate at a mountain spa in Georgia, travelled with Dorzhiev to Rostov-on-Don via Moscow, Orel, Kursk and Kharkov. Frustratingly, the trains they used were sometimes slow and usually very crowded, mainly with military personnel; also, though Dorzhiev had managed to procure first-class tickets, first-class facilities were often not available – further evidence of the breakdown caused by the February Revolution. Having, however, learned the 'technique of acceptance' as part of the Buddhist monastic discipline, the two bhikshus 'yielded themselves to the situation'; though Tennisons admits that the journey was not completely devoid of charming interludes; on one slow train with creaking axles a Ukrainian lad played an accordion memorably, and there was also the temptingly prepared tea of the Ukraine to savour.

During the journey, Dorzhiev took the opportunity to sketch out his latest views on the future of Buddhism in Russia:

> In the opinion of the learned Patriarch, Buddhist monasticism would not be able to remain merely contemplative, self-centred, or aloof, but, taking into account time, place, and circumstance, would have to move on with the vital current of our modern age.[3]

Arriving at last at Rostov-on-Don, the bustling industrial centre and wheat port near where the quietly flowing Don enters the Sea of Azov, Dorzhiev and Tennisons put up at a local hotel: a place distinguished, in Lustig's account, for the lavishness of its floral displays and the mild manners of its waiters. The great lama planned to stay for two or three days here in his 'pretty suite of rooms' before going on to visit his choira in Astrakhan province. Tennisons, on the other hand, resumed his journey to Georgia the following day after an emotional farewell with his mentor. They did not in fact see each other again until 1920.

*

Very soon afterwards, Dorzhiev showed up in eastern Siberia to take part in the second of four All-Buryat Congresses that took place that year. At these, various administrative, legislative, judicial, cultural, economic and religious matters were debated in anticipation of the convening of the long-awaited Constituent Assembly.[4] This second one was convened at Gusinoye Ozero Datsan by the two Buryat leaders, Elbek Dorji Rinchino (c. 1885–1937) and Mikhail Nicholaevich Bogdanov (1878–1919).[5] It ran from 7 to 15 June (O S) and followed an earlier conference held at Chita in May, which, according to the British communist, G. D. R. Phillips, 'put forward very mild demands for the establishment of a Buryat steppe "duma" or "parliament" and certain educational and land reforms'.[6]

By Dorzhiev's account, religion rather than politics dominated the agenda at the Gusinoye Ozero congress; in fact, he maintains that the event was convened to stem a general decline in spiritual standards among the clergy:

> even among the Sangha [Community of Buddhist monks], there were those who, out of desire for wealth and enjoyment, would terrorize households, take possession of their goods and make the people their servants. They did not engage in the activities of learning, reflection or meditation, but wasted their lives for the sake of worldly pleasures. Moreover, they did not teach their students, so that although the mere name [of student] was used, in fact students were in such decline that they were virtually non-existent. The majority of teachers were interested only in honours and food; and, in most instances, no effort was made to improve the quality of training and students. Thus [my country] had become a place of which in all respects I could only be ashamed.[7]

Specifically, the congress raised the notion that a committee be set up in Petrograd to look after the interests of the Buddhist church, and it was hoped that the orientalists of the capital would lend their support to it.[8] Also, probably because of fears of what might happen to it in the currently lawless climate, the Petrograd temple was declared a property of the Buryat-Mongol people, while the two ancillary houses on the site, built by Dorzhiev himself but technically belonging to the Tibetan Mission, were earmarked as hostels for Buryats and Kalmyks studying in the capital. Nothing was done to implement these decisions until the following year due to the further political upheavals in the capital, but then Dorzhiev did contact the architect Richard Berzen about building a third house and a crematorium at the rear of the temple.[9]

Though Dorzhiev must have had a hand in some of these measures himself, he does not seem to have been too impressed with the proceedings: 'Certain people who did not want this to happen caused disturbances', he says, 'and the event was a fiasco'.[10] It is tempting to assume that he means hard leftist elements, particularly Bolsheviks and their fellow travellers, who were natural rivals to the bourgeois nationalists, liberals and Buddhists that had dominated developments in the Buryat lands since the February Revolution. In fact, he is more likely to mean the conservative Buddhist clergy and their right-wing allies at the other extreme of the political spectrum: the predatory 'noyons and lamas' of whom G. D. R. Phillips writes so disparagingly. These would undoubtedly have objected to the reformist views that he no doubt expounded with some force.

Also discussed at the Second All-Buryat Congress was the intention of the Provisional Government to overhaul the statutes that regulated the Buddhist lamas of eastern Siberia in order to bring them in line with the new liberal spirit. A commission was to be set up under Professor S. A. Kotlariyevsky, the Minister of Foreign Creeds in the Provisional Government, and would include Professor S. F. Ol'denburg, then Minister of Public Education, and representatives of various government departments and of the Buddhist clergy and laity.[11] The congress elected Agvan Dorzhiev to the staff of the commission along with D. Sampilon, R. Bimbayev, S. Zhigzhitov, S. Tsybiktarov and B. Baradin, and they were furnished with instructions 'defining the will of the Buryat people as to their religious affairs', which they were to submit to the commission. These advocated the liberation of the Buryat Buddhist church from state interference and control (to as great an extent as the law permitted); also the establishment of more democratic procedures of self-government for both the church as a whole and for the individual datsans based on freely and secretly elected congresses, councils and committees.

Dorzhiev seems to have been generally pleased with the outcome of the Kotlariyevsky Commission's work. 'Without [indulging in] close-minded pettiness about our doctrines, we were able to revise our customs while conforming to our precepts', he wrote.[12]

His hopes that the national aspirations of his Buryat people would also have been encouraged when in August the Provisional Government's Foreign Minister, M. I. Tereshchenko, chaired a special conference on the oppressed indigenous peoples of Siberia. S. F. Ol'denburg is reported as taking part in this body too.[13]

*

In the autumn of 1917, Dorzhiev made his usual annual pilgrimage back to his Buryat homeland and spent the winter of 1917/18 there. In

1 Agvan Dorzhiev as a young lama.

2 The broad valley of the River Uda, near Naryn Astagat in the Buryat region of Trans-Baikalia (Eastern Siberia).

3 Jilginsky/Olkinsky Datsan, founded in the early 19th century. A Buryat steppe temple similar to the now ruined Atsagat Datsan where Dorzhiev spent his formative years.

4 The 13th Dalai Lama, Tubten Gyatso.

5 The distinguished Russian Buddhist scholar Fyodor Stcherbatsky in Urga, Trans-Baikalia, after his meeting there with the 13th Dalai Lama in 1905.

6 The Buddhist scholar
E.E. Obermiller, a pupil of
Stcherbatsky, with the Buryat
lama Losang bstampi Nima.

7 Dorzhiev leaving the
Tsarskoye Selo Palace after
his audience with Tsar
Nicholas II, August 1907.

8 The Great Image of Lord Buddha in the St. Petersburg Temple.

9 A Prayer Service at the St. Petersburg Temple in 1916. Dorzhiev is seated in the front row with, on his left, Ovshe Norzunov. Stcherbatsky (with moustache) is in the second-from-back row, facing the camera, beside a group of distinguished Orientalists, members of the Building Committee. During the First World War the Temple was used partly as a hospital and a small group of nursing sisters can be seen to the right of the photograph. In the back row are Buryat soldiers.

10 Dorzhiev in 1922.

11 First Great Mongolian Congress (Khural), Urga, 8th November 1924. Dorzhiev is in the centre. Others present include Tsyren Dorzhi (to the left of Dorzhiev), later arrested during the pogrom of 1935, Zhamtsarrano, Baradin, and P.K. Kozlov.

12 Thangka painting of *The Wheel of Life* (Bhavachakra), commissioned by Dorzhiev in 1925 from Osir Badayev.

13 Detail from *The Wheel of Life*.

14 Dorzhiev at the Second All-Buryat
Buddhist Congress, 22nd December 1925.

Ⅰ-Всесоюзный Духовный Будийский Собор. Москва-19 $\frac{20-28}{1}$ 27-

15 The First All-Soviet Congress of Buddhists, Moscow, 20th–28th January 1927. Dorzhiev is seated in the centre. Ovshe Norzunov is on his left.

16 Danzan Norboyev, sixth incarnation of Ganzhirva-Gegen, on the high lama's throne in the Leningrad Temple.

21 Lama Zhaltsanov, one of the lamas arrested at the Leningrad temple in 1935.

22 Dorzhiev photographed in his native Trans-Baikalia shortly before his death.

23 Yuri (George N.) Roerich (seated centre) in Ulan Udé in 1958. The group includes Bidya Dandaron (far left, back row), and K.M. Gerasimova (at right of standing group). Photograph probably taken at the Institue of Scientific Research.

24 A group of lamas photographed outside the Aginsky Datsan, near Chita, Trans-Baikalia, in 1978.

25 Friedrich Lustig (Ashin Ananda), Buddhist Archbishop of Latvia and biographer of Karlis Tennisons. (Photograph by Kate Wheeler.)

26 The Leningrad temple as it is today.

27 Ivolginsky Datsan: Stupa.

28 Ivolginsky Datsan: Prayer Wheels.

29 The Dalai Lama at Ivolginsky Datsan in 1979, during his first visit to Russia.

30 Great Khural or Maitreya Festival, Ivolginsky Datsan 1985. The late Abbot is seated under the Rupa.

Red Petrograd, meanwhile, the political tumult went through new and momentous phases that resulted in the Bolshevik Revolution of October 1917 and its world-shaking aftermath.

The leading Bolsheviks had begun to return to the capital in the spring of 1917. The foremost of them, Lenin (Vladimir Ilyich Ulyanov, 1870–1924), made his legendary arrival at the Finland Station on 3 April (OS). Now, after frustrating years in both internal and external exile, of splitting doctrinal hairs at socialist conferences all over Europe and living the often hand-to-mouth existence of a professional revolutionary, he at last had the chance to get to grips with a real revolution. The core of his overt political agenda was unveiled the next day in his so-called April Theses: to move the revolution on from its bourgeois phase to that of full-blown proletarian-peasant revolution as quickly as possible. This meant ousting the Provisional Government and transferring power to the soviets. Lenin also called for a withdrawal of support for the war, the creation of a popular militia to replace the army, the nationalization of land, and soviet control of production and distribution. His hidden agenda was to seize power; so, when he called for the transfer of power to the soviets, what he had in mind was not soviets as constituted in the spring of 1917 with a majority of Mensheviks and Socialist Revolutionaries (SRs), but soviets dominated by his own Bolshevik party. Actually his aspirations did not stop there: once the revolution had been established in Russia, he wanted to see it spread internationally like a raging forest fire.

Lenin's extreme stance alarmed many left-wingers (and even some Bolsheviks) and temporarily put him out on a limb; but he was not a man to be disheartened by a little opposition. Of all the personalities that had either stumbled or strutted onto the revolutionary stage so far, he was far and away the most clear-headed, authoritative and coldly practical. He was also the most ruthless. Concepts like honesty, fair-play, justice and sticking by agreements were, in his view, contemptible bourgeois indulgences; a member of the dedicated revolutionary elite had to be prepared to use any means, fair or foul, to realize his ends.

Over the following months, this physically unprepossessing but intellectually commanding man pursued his political goals with single-minded determination. His party was at first marginal, just one among a medley of groupings competing for power and influence; but, with its aggressive revolutionary posture, its propaganda machine churning out a plethora of incendiary papers and pamphlets, and its catchy slogans of 'Bread, Peace and Freedom!', 'Down with the war!' and 'All Power to the soviets!', it began to win grass roots support among the Petrograd workers, soldiers and sailors, who were increasingly impatient of the inability of either the Provisional Government or the Petrograd Soviet to radicalize fully the revolution. Exploiting their frustration, Lenin and the Bolsheviks were able to call out large-scale demonstrations, some of which have been characterized as attempts at putsch. Alarmed, the acting authorities struck back and Lenin had actually to go into hiding a couple of times, but on the whole they were more afraid of counter-revolution from the right than of the revolution being hi-jacked from the left, so they failed to act decisively too.

In this atmosphere of escalating subversion, social breakdown and unrest, the Provisional Government in May entered into a functional coalition with the Petrograd Soviet, which brought six socialists into the Cabinet. Then in July, Aleksandr Fedorovich Kerensky, an SR who had recently taken over the portfolio of the Ministry of War, replaced the exhausted Lvov as Prime Minister.

Highly popular at the outset, Kerensky was ambitious and possessed great talent as an orator, which as War Minister he had deployed to considerable effect raising the morale of troops at the front, though it was really oratory of an emotional or even histrionic kind, not notable for its content or logic. Essentially, he saw his mission as being to save the revolution by acting as a bridge between right and left; instead he found himself hopelessly caught in the cross-fire from the two cardinal political directions.

In August, Kerensky had to deal with an attempted coup by his Commander-in-Chief, General Kornilov, though some commentators maintain that in reality Kornilov, a staunch patriot, merely wanted to restore order at home and discipline at the front, and was inveigled into mutiny by a paranoid Kerensky. Kerensky afterwards assumed virtual dictatorial powers, but the affair was not only damaging to his credibility as prime minister, but also put his relationship with the Army out of joint. At the same time the German war machine was inexorably advancing, Riga was taken and Petrograd itself came under threat.

The Bolsheviks, exploiting this crisis to the full, came fully into their own as autumn approached. Not only were the Provisional Government's power and prestige at their lowest ebb, but their own power was increasing steadily and they had recruited their own Red Guards; while in Trotsky (Lev Davidovich Bronstein, 1879–1940) they enjoyed the services of a tactician and propagandist of considerable flair. By October, though opinion was divided among the party leadership, Lenin, who had recently emerged again from hiding, was resolved to seize power. The strategy devised was brilliant. The Provisional Government had planned to elect and convene the long-awaited Constituent Assembly in November (OS), but the Bolsheviks decided on their own initiative to call an All Russian Congress of Soviets, packed with their own supporters. This would legitimize their coup, which would be made, not in their own name, but in that of the Petrograd Soviet and its Military Revolutionary Committee.

*

And so to the dramatic days and nights in late October 1917 (OS) that proverbially shook the world. The hagiographers of Lenin and the Bolshevik leaders have mythologized their rapid seizure of power as a heroic struggle of epic proportions; actually it initially went off amazingly easily. Encountering very little resistance, Bolshevik forces merely took over various key points in Petrograd, culminating in the Winter Palace, which they eventually took with only minimal contention. The radical American journalist John Reed was there and later recalled a great crowd containing a few Red Guards moving through the Red Arch 'like a black river' into the great open space in front of the palace. Fearful that the Provisional Government's troops inside would start firing, they stooped low and ran towards the minimal shelter of the Alexander Column. They huddled there for a few minutes until, reassured, they began to advance again:

> By this time, in the light that streamed out of all the Winter Palace windows, I could see that the first two or three hundred men were Red Guards, with only a few scattered soldiers. Over the barricade of fire-wood we clambered, and leaping down inside gave a triumphant shout as we stumbled on a heap of rifles thrown down by the *yunkers* [cadets] who had stood there. On both sides of the main gateway, the doors stood wide open, light streamed out, and from the huge pile came not the slightest sound.[14]

Lenin's faction then declared in the name of the Military Revolutionary Committee of the Petrograd Soviet of Workers' and Soldiers' Deputies that the Provisional Government was deposed, and the Bolshevik-dominated Congress of Soviets gathered at the Smolnyi Institute, which in pre-revolutionary days had been an educational establishment for aristocratic young ladies. Besides ratifying decrees on peace and land redistribution, it was also decided to replace Ispolkom with a Council of People's Commissars (Sovrarkom). Under Lenin's reluctant chairmanship, this body, which was theoretically to exercise authority only until the arrival of the long-awaited Constituent Assembly, was also packed with Bolsheviks.

*

Agvan Dorzhiev was almost certainly back among the Buryats when the October Revolution took place, but according to his memoirs his response was positive. He singles Lenin for particular praise:

> At this point, out of compassion for the weak and oppressed, Lenin, the leader of the Bolsheviks, whose motivation was to take good care of the weak, together with many others beneath him, completely overcame the government officials, the rich and the traders who were tormenting the oppressed people that lived in great misery and hunger, and took over the government.[15]

In Buddhist terms, however, for a person to have become motivated by altruistic compassion (Skt karuna) implies a lofty degree of spiritual development. True, some accounts suggest that there was something almost ascetic about the way in which Lenin dedicated his life to his chosen cause of communist revolution; and he is moreover said to have regarded himself, not as a man with ordinary egotistical motivations, but as a channel through which the impersonal laws of history (in the grandest Marxian sense) could operate. But it would be naive to read too much into this kind of thing. He was essentially a politician, and for all the noble rhetoric that he declaimed in his speeches and writings, he was a conspiratorial, distrustful and, on occasion, coldly cruel man – and moreover an ideological atheist with a deep loathing for all religion. Lacking a real spiritual dimension, therefore, his compassion would have been essentially theoretical, something of the head rather than the heart, while the real well-springs of his motivation lay down in the depths of his unreconstructed subconscious, where in the Buddhist view the three fires of greed, hatred and delusion hold sway unless transformed through conscious spiritual practice. In his specific case there would have been greed for power, hatred of the former ruling and middle classes, and delusion as to his own true nature and motivation.

*

If seizing the rudiments of power had been easy for Lenin and the Bolsheviks, consolidating it proved very much more difficult. During the weeks following their coup, they ran into much hostility and resistance in Petrograd, for not only were ousted politicians understandably vocal in protest and militant in attempts to claw back lost power, but many workers were angered that the other radical parties had been excluded from Sovnarkom. There was even opposition at the core of the Bolshevik Party itself. What remained of the administrative machine, furthermore, threatened to grind to a halt because the banks refused to release funds and the chinoviks in the ministries went on strike. On top of all that, Kerensky, who had fled the city after the first abortive attack on the Winter Palace, arrived at Gatchina near Tsarskoye Selo with a Cossack force.

The Kerensky threat evaporated almost of its own accord, but Lenin tackled the other problems with tough decisiveness. He issued threats; he closed down opposition newspapers; he published vituperative denunciations of his enemies and detractors; he nationalized the banks; he set up revolutionary tribunals to try arrested dissidents; and he attempted to appease popular dissatisfaction by encouraging workers to take over factories and peasants to seize land. He also whipped up class hatred by blaming continuing shortages and high prices on hoarding and profiteering by speculators, kulaks (Bolshevik newspeak for enterprising peasants), landowners and other enemies of the people.

These tough policies – an augury of even greater toughness to come – worked to a degree. The Bolshevik Revolution survived its first crucial phases and even spread beyond Petrograd to Moscow and beyond as soviets and military revolutionary committees in cities, towns and villages right across the land began attempting to displace existing organs of government. These seismic pulses even reached distant Trans-Baikalia, where a soviet replaced the Verkhneudinsk Committee of Social Organizations.

As a first step towards laying the foundations of the one party state, the Bolsheviks dissolved the long-awaited Constituent Assembly when it finally convened in January 1918 (OS) – a great irony this, for they had once posed as its champions. Then they gradually eliminated all other political parties and factions, not only enemies and rivals but eventually even many former friends and allies, like the Left SRs and the Anarchists. When this had been accomplished, they attempted to impose their communist programme on the shattered remains of the old system.

But the process was not by any means the easy inevitability that Soviet historians would have us believe. Following the October Revolution, soviet power established itself only fitfully and precariously in many areas, while the Ukraine, the Baltic States, Poland, Finland, Transcaucasia and other parts of the old empire took proclaimed Bolshevik ideology on the rights of nations to self-determination at face value to declare independence and secede. Furthermore, from the summer of 1918 onwards, following the humiliating Peace of Brest-Litovsk that the Bolsheviks signed with Germany and her allies, British, French, Japanese and American troops intervened on the soil of the newly-declared RSFSR (Russian Soviet Federative Socialist Republic[16]), supporting White or anti-Bolshevik resistance fighters, with the result that the advancing tide of Bolshevik revolution was temporarily driven back. A long and bloody Civil War lasting from mid-1918 until 1920 had to be fought before effective opposition was finally subdued, the seceding regions repossessed and the Bolshevik communists were at last able to impose their will upon the vast swathe of territory that had once fallen beneath the sway of the two-headed imperial eagle.

*

Having returned to Buryatia late in 1917, Agvan Dorzhiev was present at a fourth Buryat congress held at Verkhneudinsk between 11 and 18 December 1917, when a twelve-man Central National Committee under the chairmanship of Zhamtsarano was elected, a new Khambo Lama chosen – this was the shiretui Laidanov – and a new Petrograd delegate, Ts. Badmazhapov, delegated to replace Sampilon.[17] The fellow-travelling G. D. R. Phillips detected in all this a set of sinister stratagems to reinforce the malign influence of Lamaism.

Afterwards, over the following winter, it is likely that Dorzhiev kept in touch with ongoing political developments and discussed them at length with friends like Baradin and Zhamtsarano. He may also well have been bandying ideology with local Bolsheviks, for he mentions in his memoirs knowing Yakov Davidovich Yanson (Hanama, born 1886), a Latvian Bolshevik who, having spent some years of exile in Siberia during the final phases of the imperial regime, was active in the Irkutsk area following the February Revolution, becoming Chairman of the party's Eastern Siberian branch, and, between 1918 and 1920, the representative of Narkomindel (Peoples' Commissariat for Foreign Affairs) in Irkutsk.[18] These meetings and discussions may well have started to carry his thinking even further to the left, and he probably began to speculate whether it would be possible to work with the Bolsheviks if they managed to establish themselves succesfully as the new power in the land. This would have been very much an open question at the time, however, not least because the precarious soviet power in the region was about to be seriously challenge. Not only did the Japanese begin landings at Vladivostok in April 1918, but a swashbuckling local Cossack named Ataman Semenov,[19] having collected a raggle-taggle army in Harbin over the winter, marched into Siberia with French, and later Japanese, support in the spring of 1918, and by the summer had established himself in Chita, from where he dominated a considerable part of Trans-Baikalia for many months to come.

*

Before the Semenov depradations got fully under way, Dorzhiev had again departed westward on the Trans-Siberian, probably planning to supervise the new construction work at the Petrograd Buddhist Temple, which was scheduled to begin in the summer. A cholera epidemic was now added to the agonies of the 'conquered city', however, so with two attendants, Togme Droltar and Chakdor, both monks of the 'Kalota' monastery,[20] he headed south for the Kalmyk steppe with the funds he had collected and the intention no doubt of collecting more.

Southern Russia was not a zone of tranquility in the early months of 1918. Indeed, for the next two years it was to be a major cockpit of the Civil War. White resistance centred on the Volunteer Army, founded late in 1917 by Generals Kornilov and Alekseyev, but later commanded by General Anton Ivanovich Denikin (1872–1947). Many Cossack forces rallied to this, including the Kuban and Don Cossacks, and for a time it was able to build strong bridgeheads and disperse the Reds in the north Caucasus, the Caspian steppes, on the lower Don and Manitsch. There were also Kalmyk soldiers in the ranks of the Volunteer army, for loyalty to the old regime persisted among many of them.[21] Among them were Kalmyk Cossacks commanded by Princess Tundutova's son, Danzan, who fought the Reds with General Tumen until he was defeated and disappeared some time in 1918.[22] Many Kalmyks also participated with other Cossack and anti-Bolshevik forces in a South-East Union, which during its brief life developed into a secessionist movement.

Dorzhiev says in his memoirs that he had it in mind to visit a Kalmyk monastery that had been damaged in recent fighting; also to see doctors, which is convincing because we know he drank kumiss (fermented mare's milk) for the sake of his health in Kalmykia, and took mud baths too. Having completed his business in the late spring or early summer, he and his attendants then left the Kalmyks, intending almost certainly to return to Buryatia on the Trans-Siberian. Actually, the railway was by now in the hands of some 45,000 Czech deserters from the Austrian Army, who, while on their way to Vladivostok and repatriation, had resisted when the Reds tried to disarm them and, joining forces with interventionist Allied forces and anti-Bolshevik Whites, had effectively terminated Bolshevik power east of the Urals for the time being.

Before Dorzhiev and his attendants actually reached the main line, however, they arrived at the railway junction near Urbach (or Urbakh),[23] an old German settlement in the Saratov region, just east of the Volga and to the south of the Urals. Here the line coming up from Astrakhan meets one coming from the east and another going west to Saratov. At this remote waystation the unthinkable happened: they were arrested by Red Army personnel and handed over to the local Cheka.

*

The Extraordinary Commission (for Repression against Counter-revolution), better known by its acronym of Cheka, was set up as early as November 1917 by a hawk-faced Polish zealot named Feliks Dzerzhinky. It appropriated wide-ranging powers, not merely to root out but also to try, sentence and execute counter-revolutionaries and saboteurs. Over the following months this remit was considerably widened to include criminal and semi-criminal elements like speculators, hooligans and bandits. From the start it was a tool, not of bourgeois justice with its nice concern to separate the guilty from the innocent, but of revolutionary justice; in short, it became a conscious instrument of state terror whereby often blameless victims were killed in large numbers to impress upon the population at large the foolishness of resisting Bolshevik power.

It was the local Chekists in Ekaterinberg (Sverdlovsk) in western Siberia who, panicked into precipitate action by fear of the westward-advancing Czech forces, murdered the entire Romanov family on the fateful night of 16/17 July 1918 (NS) at the Ipatiev House, where they had lately been confined. One might have expected Agvan Dorzhiev to have mentioned this barbarous event in his memoirs and to have expressed grief and disapproval, for to take life is to flaunt the first and most important of the Buddhist precepts; but for some reason he chooses to remain silent.

According to A. Andreyev, the Urbakh Chekists accused Dorzhiev and his attendants of attempting to smuggle state valuables out of the country; that is, they were taken as speculators. Dorzhiev himself, on the other hand, intimates that he was suspected of being a counter-revolutionary: fighting had recently broken out in the region between the Reds and 'an alliance of Ural Kalmyks, Cossacks and Russians' – he may by this mean either forces attached to the South-East Union or General Denikin's Volunteer Army – and he was suspected of being in sympathy with them.[24]

No doubt deeply baffled as well as highly apprehensive, he was bundled onto a prison train for Moscow, which had lately been declared the new capital of the RSFSR, and on arrival was incarcerated behind the brick walls of the infamous Butyrki prison.

The origins of this grim bastion near the old Butyrki Gate go back to the reign of Catherine II, when it was used both as a barracks and as a prison. The great rebel Pugachev was kept in chains in one of its towers, later known as the Silo. According to Aleksandr Solzhenitsyn, it then lay empty for many years before undergoing, in more 'enlightened' times, a radical conversion.

'The mason's chisel and the plasterer's trowel enabled the suites of rooms to be divided up into hundreds of spacious and comfortable cells,' writes the author of *The First Circle* with black Russian humour; 'while the unrivalled skills of Russia's blacksmiths forged unbendable bars to go over the windows and made the tubular frames of the beds, which were let down at night and pulled up in the daytime . . .'[25]

Twenty-five beds were fixed to the walls of each cell, so that there were a hundred prisoners to every four cells and two hundred prisoners to a corridor. 'And so this salubrious establishment flourished . . .' serving the old regime well until 1917, when in a wave of revolutionary idealism the inmates were released. It afterwards quickly reverted to its old function, however, becoming primarily a place of detention for those under investigation by the Cheka.[26] It still exists (and is probably in use) – take the Metro to Novoslobodskaya: it is opposite Savyelovsky railway station.[27]

*

The summer of 1918 was a most inauspicious time in which to fall into Chekist hands, for in that month there was the build up to the unprecedented orgy of paranoid bloodletting known as the Red Terror, which was officially unleashed in September. The immediate causes of this were not only foreign intervention and increasing White resistance, but also an attempted coup initiated by Marya Spiridonova's Left SR faction and a number of politically inspired murders or attempted murders of prominent figures. On a single day in August, Fanya Kaplan made an attempt on Lenin's life and M. S. Uritsky, the head of the Petrograd Cheka, was assassinated. The Bolshevik response, executed mainly by the Cheka, was draconian. Tens of thousands of Russians at a conservative estimate were arrested and liquidated; also the practice of taking hostages was begun and, a little later, the foundations of the Gulag were laid with the opening of the first prison camps for dissidents. Disturbing developments like these, as the Anarchists[28] – arguably the true if impractical custodians of that spirit of freedom that is elemental to authentic revolution – were not slow to point out, proved that the Bolshevik Communists, for all their revolutionary rhetoric, were in fact constructing a new and even more repressive autocracy on the ruins of the old one; in this sense they were themselves the real counter-revolutionaries.

His sojourn in Butyrki was an extremely dark period for Dorzhiev: his passage through the Valley of the Shadow. He knew no-one in Moscow and there was no way he could get a message out to his friends in Petrograd. As for the food, that amounted to little more than starvation rations, with virtually no water, while ironically he was himself eaten alive by lice. 'Even the mere sight of the metal windows and doors were enough to give one extraordinary mental anguish', he wrote later; and the jailers reminded him forcibly of the dread guardians of the Buddhist hells, who heap excruciating (and, it must be added, highly imaginative) tortures upon their hapless victims without cease over vast aeons of time. Worst of all, from time to time someone in his cell would be called away. This usually happened at night and the pretext tended to be 'for questioning', but in fact everyone was aware what was going to happen.

Strangely, however, imprisonment in such conditions is sometimes not without spiritual benefits. The thought that he is to be hanged, Dr Johnson informs us, concentrates a man's mind wonderfully; so too in his Butyrki cell Dorzhiev meditated deeply upon the most profound issues of life and death, of this world and the beyond:

> Upon deeper reflection, [freedom from this place] seemed as good as freedom from the prison of samsara [the endless cycle of birth and death]; yet it would be possible to leave that prison but hard to leave the prison of samsara. If one gave one of those jailers just a small gift, it was certain that they would be more gentle with one; but if one gave such a gift to the guardians of hell, it is possible that one would continue to suffer. Although one got no [decent] food and starved, at least one was given a little each day; but if one were born as a hungry ghost, for many thousands of years one would not even hear the word 'food . . .' In that place there was not any certainty of being sent somewhere and not being killed; [likewise] it is the very nature of things that one day one will be dispatched to Yama [the Lord of Death] and certainly killed. In prison one lives quietly and is free to do as one likes; but in samsara one wanders without any freedom at all. By thinking of things in this way, I then understood how very foolish it was to be unafraid of samsara, [and] the thought arose that I had to try by every means to free myself from samsara.[29]

Then one night – he does not say so himself, but about one o'clock in the morning was usual for such things – the door was flung open and the officers who entered the cell stared long and hard at one person: Dorzhiev himself. Dazed, he was probably marched outside, either into the corridor or to an interrogation room. There his worst fear was confirmed: he too was about to be shot.

CHAPTER SIXTEEN

Fellow Traveller
1918 – 1920

Sometimes those with power of life and death play cruel hoaxes upon their victims. It happened to the 28-year-old Fyodor Dostoyevsky in Semenovsky Square, St Petersburg on a bitterly cold day in December 1849. Having heard the sentence of death read out, he was blindfolded and bound to a wooden stake alongside two others. The detail of soldiers present raised their rifles . . . but nothing happened. A few moments later he was told that he had actually been sentenced to exile and penal labour in Siberia.

Though the details may have been different, psychologically and spiritually Dorzhiev must have gone through much the same kind of ordeal in Butyrki, for though told he would be shot his life too was spared – and indeed not only that: shortly afterwards he also managed to bribe one of the guards to smuggle a letter to V. L. Kotvich, who, as well as being a scholar, had long worked for the Ministry of Finance, and so still had influence in official places even after the Revolution. Kotvich alerted Ol'denburg, Vladimirtsov, Stcherbatsky and Dorzhiev's other Petrograd orientalist friends: men endowed, the lama writes, with a kindness rare to find in samsara. An emergency meeting of the temple construction committee was then convened on 10 September with Stcherbatsky in the chair, when a petition was drawn up and sent to the Cheka. It argued that Dorzhiev had 'betrayed neither Buddhism nor the [Bolshevik] government'. With additional help from Y. D. Yanson – and perhaps even, through him, from even more exalted officials in the collegium of Narkomindel – both Dorzhiev and his attendants were released.

*

Dorzhiev was unable to return immediately to Buryatia after regaining his liberty because, as he puts it, 'the eastern road . . . was disrupted'.

This is an understatement. Because of the Czech uprising, all of Russia east of the Urals was now out of Bolshevik control. Independent governments had been set up at Samara, Omsk and Vladivostok, which quickly united in a Provisional All Russian Government with its seat at Omsk. Though this was overthrown by the Reds in November, in that same month, with foreign support and finance, Admiral Aleksandr Vasilyevich Kolchak (1873–1920), the former commander of the Black Sea Fleet, was declared Supreme Ruler and began his struggle for control of the area between the Urals and Lake Baikal. Further east, meanwhile, Ataman Semenov, still virtual master of Trans-Baikalia, refused to submit to Kolchak, but there was little the admiral could do since Semenov enjoyed the protection of the powerful Japanese, who by now had thousands of troops in eastern Siberia.

Dorzhiev therefore had little alternative but to beat a retreat to Astrakhan, even though the Civil War continued to rage in the south. Monasteries had been destroyed, he reports, and lamas had taken to growing their hair, wearing laymens' clothes and drifting back into lay life. The people were understandably unhappy; but before he would listen to any complaints, he distributed to each monastery – there were about seventy of them, with a lama population of around 1,600 – a strict ordinance forbidding looting and destruction of any kind. Then he actually visited each in the company of 'fine working people' and 'proclaimed the kinds of laws that would operate in the new country'.

Dorzhiev's view of monastic life in the Kalmyk region was broadly similar to his view of monastic life in Buryatia: that it was in a decadent state. Because of the complacency and indulgence of the majority of lamas, monasteries tended to impoverish the localities in which they were situated rather than enrich them; as a result, it had become impossible to maintain all the monasteries, so they had all been contracted into a single foundation, which was situated at a place called 'Khetsebolak'. Dorzhiev advocated that lamas and laity get together to build new monasteries, and there were many who felt that in the prevailing situation this was the best they could do, but others demurred.[1]

Naturally Dorzhiev took the opportunity to propound his new views to the Kalmyks. 'In former and in later times', he told them, 'if one asked either lamas or their students about the customs of study in small monasteries or about the need for the noble wisdom to be studied in the larger monasteries, because things have remained [as they were] from the past until the present, they would say that there was no need for various innovations.'[2]

Clearly there was need for such innovation, however, because 'the Dharma traditions of the Doctrine were declining', and

> Whatever appears in the mind of [a monk these days] becomes a condition for increasing attachment to wealth and enjoyment. Some even exceed worldly householders in accumulating clothing and property . . . Through their shameless and inconsiderate behaviour, some monks do not reserve even a corner of their minds for thinking about the vows laid down by the Buddha. When non-Buddhists see such monks, they assume that the Buddha's Doctrine is defiled. Moreover, the teachings of lamas who are sympathetic to the Bön [shamanistic] traditions are particularly confusing for benefactors. The monks now have many detractors, who say that they just collect the offerings made to the monasteries and then do nothing but enjoy themselves.[3]

Such views antagonized many older and poorly motivated lamas and a split between conservatives and reformers, between old lamas and young, began to open up. Dorzhiev was particularly critical of the Shachin Lama, though whether the person fulfilling this role in 1918 was the same as in 1901, when he previously had a disagreement with a lama of that name, is not clear. The present incumbent had, it appears, taken to the peripatetic life, wandering from place to place, no doubt relieving the faithful of munificent offerings while dispensing little substantial in return. In other words, he had become the typical parasitic priest leeching the blood of the toiling masses that the Bolsheviks singled out for their most scathing criticism.

With his keenly practical outlook, Dorzhiev would have been fully aware that in the new Russia Buddhism would not survive long if lamas continued to behave like this. The two dhorampa geshés whom Dorzhiev had brought in to run his choira, both of whom were 'motivated by the best of intentions', had some words with the Shachin Lama on behalf of 'the monks and lay people'. One would imagine, however, that this high religious dignitary, used so long to uncritical veneration and obedience, would not have been pleased to have had his behaviour criticized – and one would somehow doubt that he mended his ways.

The Civil War stranded Dorzhiev in Kalmykia for the winter of 1918/19 as well as for part of the following year. It would be entirely wrong, however, to imagine that he spent this time of forced exile embroiled in parochial church affairs or even that he made good the resolution forged in Butyrki to apply himself more wholeheartedly to Dharma practice. Quite the contrary: he began dabbling again in political affairs – and ones of a kind one would least have expected him to favour.

*

In March 1920 (NS), having had spent much of the Civil War in a retreat high among the dark mountains of the Caucasus, Karlis Tennisons determined to emerge from solitude and return to Petrograd even if it meant facing a firing squad. Still weak and giddy from undernourishment, he falteringly took the downward path that brought him at length to a tiny mountain village of flat-roofed hovels. Here he was told that the Bolsheviks had begun their final Trans-Caucasian offensive and were inflicting crippling defeats on Denikin's Whites.

At the end of April he arrived in Stavropol to find the atmosphere of this once prosperous trading city poisoned by suspicion. Its citizens had been reduced to abject poverty, while the efficient troops of General O. I. Gorodovikov, the local Kalmyk military commander, strutted about everywhere. Naturally, Tennisons sought out the local Buddhists, who told him that their loyalty to the imperial regime had brought the full wrath of the Reds down upon them:

> The Communist agitators abused the Buddhists of the lower Don and Stavropol until they were hoarse. Hard-working and simple, the Buddhists of those parts tried to live up to Buddhist ideas and learn to forebear and accept life as it came. When the Communists eventually became masters of the region, they ordered the massacre of the Buddhist monks. The land was ravaged with unprecedented savagery. In an orgy of spoliation and incendiarism, the monasteries were reduced to ashes, and the once flourishing villages were desolate.[4]

This is, characteristically, something of an exaggeration: some Kalmyk monasteries were destroyed during the Civil War, though in 1921 the majority were still standing; some monks also suffered, but only Lustig speaks of actual massacres. Whatever the truth of the matter, Tennisons was overwhelmed with grief and subsequently wandered about the city in a state of disorientation, convinced that the end of the world had come. It was thus, as he was entering a tea-house in a side street near the market place, that he was arrested by two Chekists, marched to a large building in the centre of the city and handed over to a 25 year-old Red Army officer for interrogation.

> 'People say you're a newcomer here in Stavropol, citizen. All newcomers have to be questioned', he said, motioning Tennisons to a chair. 'Now tell me your story – briefly.' Tennisons was not far into his story, however, when a commotion was raised in an ante-room and, after a flurry of excited whispers, an obviously important Bolshevik strode into the room.
>   'Comrade Amur-Sanan!' said the Red Army man, leaping to his feet. 'What can I do for you?'
>   'I've a few matters of great urgency,' Amur-Sanan replied, handing over several

type-written pages. 'These are deciphered telegrams . . .' Seeing Tennisons, a look of astonishment came over his face: 'What's this man here for?'

'We're checking his story.'

'I know him,' Amur-Sanan said, frowning pensively. 'He's a friend of Gorodovikov and a student of Khambo-Lama Agvan Dorzhiev, who's now a member of TsIK. Please issue him the necessary identity papers.'

The Red Army officer blushed. 'Aren't you making some mistake, comrade?' he asked politely, wiping his brow.

'No, no, there's no mistake,' Amur-Sanan retorted without hesitation, looking across at the bewildered Tennisons with a shrewd twinkle in his eye. 'Please stop the interrogation and write out an identity card . . .'[5]

Tennisons later discovered that this enlightened Kalmyk Bolshevik 'had the gift of popular eloquence'; he had also succeeded in saving the lives of many Buddhist monks. But who was he?

'Amur-Sanan' is in fact a Kalmyk variant of 'Amursana', the name of an ambitious Dzungarian nobleman of the eighteenth century who passed into Mongolian legend as a hero of the struggle to throw off the Chinese yoke. Later a renegade lama named Danbi-Dzhaltsan, also known as Ja-Lama, who was possibly of Kalmyk origin, claimed that he was the grandson and afterwards the reincarnation of Amursana. Though for political reasons Ja-Lama has more or less been written out of Mongolian history, he played a considerable part in the modern freedom struggle. Combining fighting prowess with ruthless cruelty (he had a penchant for ripping out the living hearts of his enemies) and quasi-occult manipulative talents, he arrived in Mongolia 'with only two camels' but won financial support from Mongol princes, who sent their sons to fight with him. In 1912 he helped liberate the city of Kobdo from the Chinese and then established himself as a major power in the western region until 1914, when he was arrested by the Russians. After having been imprisoned in Tomsk and Yakutsk, he was, as the orientalist B. Y. Vladimirtsov recorded in a letter dated 2 September 1916, transferred at his own request back to Astrakhan province: 'to the Kalmyks, to his alleged homeland . . .' Moreover, Vladimirtsov wrote:

> I am certain that Agvan Dorzhiev was somehow involved in this . . . He was here again not long ago and came to see me and persistently questioned me about Ja-Lama – where he is now, what the official attitude is to him, etc.? Then Agvan went to Trans-Baikalia via Irkutsk, and now yesterday I learn about Ja-Lama's transfer. Isn't it curious? I wouldn't be surprised if Ja-Lama appeared again somewhere in Tibet or Mongolia.[6]

He did indeed spirit himself back to Mongolia by 1918, and soon re-established himself as a freelance warlord until he was treacherously assassinated at the behest of the new Urga government, with Russian support, in his lair in the Gobi late in 1922. His head was then cut off, smoked according to a 'Mongolian method' and brought to Leningrad in 1925 by V. A. Kazakievich. It is still preserved in a glass jar in the Museum of Anthropology and Ethnology (Kunsthammer) – accession number 3394.[7]

When I started to make inquiries about the Kalmyk Amur-Sanan in Leningrad, my Russian friends, for all their dedication to rigorous 'scientific' investigation, at once exclaimed 'Ja-Lama!' Actually, this is not remotely feasible. There was, however, a prominent Kalmyk Bolshevik named Anton Mudrenovich Amur-Sanan (1880–1939), who participated in the struggle to establish a Soviet regime in Kalmykia. He was born in the Bagaburulovsky aimak (now Gorodovikovsk rayon), studied between 1915 and 1917 at Shanyavsky Public University in Moscow, and became a member of the Communist Party in 1918. Around 1919 he was the chairman of the Kalmyk section of Narkomnats (the Commissariat for Nationalities). In later years he distinguished himself in letters, writing (in Russian) the autobiographical *Mudreshkin Syn* ('Son of Mudresh', 1928), which 'shows a man's path from herdsman to state figure', and the novella *Aranzal* (1932), which presents a portrait of a Kalmyk village of pre-Revolutionary times.[8] On the available evidence, it would seem that this was the man whom Tennisons met in Stavropol in 1919, though Aleksandr Andreyev, who has read *Son of Mudresh*, says that he does not show any great sympathies for lamas in the book.

As for TsIK, this was the Central Executive Committee (of the Soviets), a governmental body consisting of five or six hundred members elected from the All Russia Congress of Soviets and divided into two councils: the Union Council and the Council of Nationalities. As it was more like a parliament than a committee and met only rarely, however, it elected from among its members a more compact presidium. Lustig's contention that Dorzhiev was elected to TsIK by the Buddhists of Trans-Baikalia is not corroborated elsewhere, though the implication that he had become a fellow traveller is indeed true.

It would appear then that Dorzhiev began to collaborate with the Bolsheviks while he was in Kalmykia in 1918 and 1919. Further corroboration of this comes from a document published by Amur-Sanan in 1919 under the title, 'The Importance of Buddhist Mongolia to World Revolution'.[9] Basically a foreign policy document addressed to Narkomindel, it urges that use be made of Kalmyk (and also Buryat) Buddhists to transmit 'the whole idea of the soviet government' to their other Mongol kinsmen, and through them to bring Tibet 'into the sphere of Soviet influence'. Mention is made of Norzunov and Dambo Ulyanov; also of Tsybikov; then:

> The Kalmuk [sic] intelligentsia has a particularly important task to perform in this tremendous undertaking, a task which can be made easier by such well-known Eastern specialists as Agwan Dorji [sic], the founder of the Buddhist temple in Petersburg [some years back] which greatly displeased England, and a supporter of a rapprochement between Mongolia and Russia . . . He is at present in the Kalmuk steppes carrying on agitation in favour of soviets among the Kalmuks. He is ready to proceed to the east any time. Britain once offered large sums of gold for the head of this dangerous revolutionary. The temple mentioned above was actually built for political reasons, namely to distract the attention of Mongolia and Tibet from Britain's advances.[10]

One would certainly have thought that after his experiences at the hands of the Chekists and the agony of imprisonment in Butyrki Dorzhiev would have become thoroughly disenchanted with the Bolsheviks; but evidently not so. What, however, had brought this astonishing conversion about? Had something crucial happened in Moscow during the summer of 1918 – something he was not prepared to divulge in his memoirs? Did he make some kind of a deal with the Bolsheviks, agreeing to work for them in exchange for his life and liberty? Or was he somehow persuaded that they were genuine idealists with every intention of creating a more just society – and that moreover they were actually sympathetic towards Buddhism and the just aspirations of national minorities like the Buryats and Kalmyks? Aleksandr Andreyev believes this to have been the case, though, as usual with Dorzhiev, a pragmatic element was not lacking either:

> Strange as it may seem, Dorzhiev showed genuine loyalty to the Bolshevik regime, taking the pompous declarations of the new ideologues of Communism in all good faith. It was in this post-October period that he came up with the peculiar statement that 'the Buddhist doctrine is largely compatible with current Communist thinking', which later became one of the corner-stones of the new religious 'Obnovlenchestvo' (Revival of Faith) Movement, of which he was one of the primary inspirations. Today it is very difficult even to imagine the euphoric atmosphere of the days when such statements were loudly proclaimed, let alone be able to offer some kind of evaluation. Some of the first decrees of the Soviets after they came to power, especially the one issued on 23 January 1918 (The Decree of Freedom of Conscience and Creed) were indeed warmly acclaimed by many, including Dorzhiev himself, who still earnestly believed that Buddhism would flourish in Russia in the not too distant future. Harsh realities would very soon disillusion him, though for pragmatic reasons, working for 'essia' [?], he carried on his 'flirtation' with the atheistical Soviet authorities until the late 1920s. Was there, however, any alternative if Buddhism was to survive under the brutal Bolshevik rule?[11]

Stcherbatsky is another protagonist in our story who initially welcomed the Bolsheviks. He had become deeply prejudiced against the narrow-minded bureaucrats of the old regime, believing that they had placed unnecessary obstacles in the path of his plans to visit Tibet. He therefore had high hopes that the new breed of official would adopt a different attitude. Indeed, almost the first thing he did after the October Revolution was re-present his proposal for a Tibetan expedition, and he received a positive response from the suave Deputy Commissar at Narkomindel, Lev Mikhailovich Karakhan (1889–1937), a Bolshevik of Armenian origin who was very interested in Oriental affairs (he served as Soviet Ambassador to China in the years 1924–27).[12] There was a condition, however: the professor should take a radio transmitter to Tibet with him. Stcherbatsky does not seem to have been averse to this proposal, and preparations went ahead to the extent of ammunition being collected, but ultimately the expedition never came off because the Civil War blocked all overland routes to Tibet.[13]

Later Stcherbatsky helped Narkomindel by translating reports from an agent they managed to insinuate into one of the great monasteries of Lhasa. These were written on very small pieces of paper in Tibetan cursive script and contained lists of important lamas, socio-economic conditions and suchlike.

*

After spending about five days in Stavropol, Tennisons resumed his journey, travelling on to Moscow by way of Tsaritsyn. He had hoped to meet Agvan Dorzhiev in the new capital but, as the lama was in Trans-Baikalia, he telegraphed him there. Three days later an answer came back:

BUDDHIST MONK TENNISONS: OVERJOYED BY NEWS FROM YOU STOP HEREWITH YOU ARE APPOINTED ABBOT OF OUR TEMPLE IN PETROGRAD AS FROM 17 JULY 1920 [STOP] PLEASE PROCEED TO YOUR POST AS SOON AS POSSIBLE [STOP] KHAMBO DORZHIEV[14]

Getting out of the train at last in Petrograd, Tennisons found the people looking out emptily on a completely new and alien world. But he had business to do; so, the sun burning low in the sky, he made his way to Staraya Derevnya. At the temple gate, which was slightly ajar, he paused, sensing that something was amiss. No sound came from the building. He waited a moment and listened; then he walked up and saw with a sickening chill that the sacred place had been ransacked and abandoned.

Shortly afterwards he went to see Stcherbatsky, who had lately been put in charge of the building. It was a hot summer day and the professor was taking a bath. Despite the desperate conditions in Petrograd, he did not seem to have lost any weight over the winter and was looking 'supine'.

'You are looking very well, sir,' the Baltic bhikshu said icily. 'When did you last visit the Buddhist temple?' Stcherbatsky became highly embarrassed. 'I'm sorry', he confessed. 'I'm afraid to go there. What can I do? They'd dismiss me from the Academy of Sciences . . . Yes, I'm afraid of losing my job! You know, people are so cruel these days.'

Tennisons, horrified to find that self-interest loomed so large in the great scholar's thinking, rebuked him soundly. Stcherbatsky, stricken with contrition, humbly begged his pardon, which was magnanimously given.[15]

Later, when militant communists broke into the temple and smashed the large figure of the Buddha in the main shrine, the intrepid Tennisons risked being shot by going directly to confront the well-known Bolshevik, Grigori Yeveseyevich Zinov'iev (1883–1936). This man, who had once shared exile with Lenin himself in Poland and Switzerland, was now president of the Petrograd Soviet. He listened to Tennisons with a 'look of mute submissive inquiry'. Subsequently the Buddha-rupa was rebuilt by 'the best Soviet sculptors at the expense of the Communists'.[16]

*

One source[17] maintains that Dorzhiev was invited to attend a special session of the Politburo – Lenin, Stalin and Bukharin also took part – held to discuss the nationalities question; this followed the Baku Congress of the Nations of the Orient in the summer of 1920, the theme of which was the promotion of socialist revolution among the 800 million people of Asia. It is unclear whether he took up this invitation, but he was back in Petrograd in late September, when he saw for himself what had befallen his beloved temple. His response was to write a forceful letter of protest in his official capacity as Tibetan representative in the RSFSR. Dated 1 October 1920, this was addressed to his acquaintance Y. D. Yanson, who was now Head of Narkomindel's Eastern Department, and fully described the circumstances and extent of the loss and damage:

> Before the war, Tibetan, Mongolian, Buryat-Mongolian and Kalmyk lamas lived at the temple, but during the war they had to leave for their native lands because the cost of living rose too high for them. After the departure of the lamas, Stcherbatsky, the Sanskrit professor, was entrusted with the management of the temple, its library and the temple property. However, in

1919, a unit of the Red Army was quartered in the houses attached to the
temple, the commander of which, having assured Mr Stcherbatsky that the
temple was not in any danger, sealed its doors and evicted Stcherbatsky from
his apartment. In this way, [responsibility for] the security of the temple and
its property was assumed by the said military unit or its commander, who had
evicted Mr Stcherbatsky and [thereby] replaced him as manager and keeper
of the temple. Soon after the eviction of Mr Stcherbatsky, the temple was
subjected to unprecedented profanity, pogrom and looting. This was made
clear by the Examining Emergency Committee [Cheka], which arrested seven
Red Army soldiers and relieved them of their duties. The head was ripped off
the main plaster statue of the Buddha, which was one sazhen high, and a great
hole smashed in the chest through which sacred scrolls were extracted and later
sold on the black market as cigarette papers.

He then goes on to enumerate the items looted from the temple.[18] They
included large and small figures of Buddhist deities in bronze, gilt or
copper; silver offering vases; temple drapes and decorations of Chinese
brocade; a quantity of sacred mirrors of gilded copper; the metal stand
for a sacred timepiece; two gilded metal volutes for the sacred cylinders
(gyeltsen) on the temple roof; a number of thangka paintings; fox furs,
lynx furs, bearskins and quantities of various fine fabrics, including
silks; chairs, beds, cupboards, ottomans and vessels of porcelain and
copper; and a sizeable quantity of wood and anthracite designated for
heating purposes. Furthermore, all metal door and window handles and
the decorations of the locks had gone, while the doors and shutters
had been smashed to pieces or otherwise damaged. Also, because all
the panes of glass were taken from the roof, rain was getting in and
damaging the interior of the temple. Dorzhiev goes on:

> The library, in which were lodged valuable and rare books in European as well
> as the Tibetan and Mongolian languages, was completely destroyed. Books in
> European languages were looted, while those in Tibetan and Mongolian were
> torn to pieces and used for domestic and toilet purposes. Also treated in this
> way were extremely rare archives of secret and non-secret documents and letters
> concerning the relations between Russia, England, Tibet and China over the past
> thirty years.

Even his own personal belongings had not been respected. European,
Tibetan and Mongolian fur clothing and non-fur clothing had been
taken; 'also all my underwear, as a result of which I remain completely
without clothes and have no means of acquiring new ones'.

Such 'profanation and looting' was 'completely and absolutely
insupportable from every point of view', he declared, because:

> Firstly, the temple is the only example of Indo-Tibetan art and architecture

in Russia and Europe; secondly, at this time when Soviet Russia is trying to forge more or less close links with the Buddhist East ... through the Buryat-Mongols, the Kalmyks, the pure Mongols and even the Tibetans, this pillage and profanation of the Petersburg Temple, which is without doubt regarded as a holy place by all Buddhists and falls under the special supervision of the Dalai Lama, will be especially detrimental ... especially taking into account their backward views and lack of political culture, as well as their domination by religious hierarchs ... This plunder of the Buddhist temple in Petrograd, the heart of revolutionary Russia, makes the situation even more sensitive, especially as representatives from Buddhist countries, who now often come to Russia, watch the political situation closely [and] often still with distrust. Thirdly, according to the decree passed by the Peoples' Congress at Gusinoye Ozero Datsan in July 1917,[19] the temple has become the property of the Buryat-Mongol people and its houses and communal dwellings will provide accommodation for Buryat-Mongol students and the stipendiaries of all nations attending Petersburg educational establishments. Attached to the Petersburg temple are two houses belonging to the Buryat-Mongol people.[20] In these houses a military unit is at present quartered, and it is for some reason mercilessly destroying the wooden fence around the temple and its houses, as well as the wooden parts around the building right up to the very doors, for the purpose of obtaining fire-wood, thereby making these buildings unfit for use. Moreover, in connection with the opening of the Eastern Institute[21] in Petrograd and the decision to accept Buryat-Mongol, Tibetan, Mongol and Kalmyk students for instruction there [they would pursue two-year courses in elementary Russian], the above-mentioned house will be needed. There is, on the neighbouring plot owned by Isayev, whose whereabouts are presently unknown, a house which was transferred to the ownership of the state and temporarily occupied as a shelter, and on the rear side of the temple there is an empty, unused plot which might be turned into a garden in which a crematorium could be built.

[On the basis of the foregoing] I ask and insist in the common interests of Soviet Russia and the peoples of the Buddhist East:

1. That funds be made available both for the restoration of the Petrograd Temple and for its upkeep until such a time as it may be brought under the management of concerned Buddhist peoples, such as the Buryat-Mongols, the Mongols and the Kalmyks, etc., and turned into a revolutionary centre for such peoples.

2. The liberation of the aforementioned houses from the military unit so that they can be speedily repaired and returned to residential use.

3. The transfer of the vacant plot of land at the rear of the temple so that it can be turned into a garden for the hostel and used for the building of a crematorium, and that the former Isayev house and its garden be made available to serve as a Buddhist hostel.[22]

On 4 October this letter was handed to Zinov'iev; Yanson and Karakhan supplied a covering letter in which they not only called Zinov'iev's attention to the 'terrible destruction of the Buddhist Temple' but reiterated Dorzhiev's argument that if news of it leaked to the Buddhist world it might undermine trust in the Soviet Union. Subsequently, the Senior Inspector at the Bureau of Complaints and Declarations of the Workers' and Peasants' Inspectorate in Petrograd, G. L. Pinkus, formally registered the fact of the looting and desecration of the temple, noting in addition that the Cheka had also investigated the matter but with no results.[23]

*

The looting and gutting of buildings – even splendid baroque palaces – for firewood was not in fact at all unusual in Petrograd at this time because of the ongoing winter shortages of fuel added to general lawlessness. The revolutionary writer, Victor Serge, gives a vivid picture in his novel *Conquered City* of how Petrograders lived in frozen dwellings 'where each habitable corner was like a corner in an animal's lair', rarely taking off their pungent fur-lined clothing and only occasionally venturing into the next room 'to pry up a few floor boards in order to keep the fire going' or to empty the night's excretions at the end of the corridor.[24]

Despite such terrible conditions, the Bolsheviks permitted an exhibition of Buddhist art to be opened at the Russian Museum in August 1919; it was organized under the auspices of the Board for Museums and the Preservation of Ancient Monuments, a body set up by Anatoly Vasilyevich Lunacharky (1875–1933), the enlightened Commissar for Education. The new authorities would have regarded it as a revolutionary event – a blow against conservatism and the Orthodox Church – while for Buddhists and Orientalists it must have seemed a token that they were living in a new, free world.

Besides the exhibition proper, which displayed many items of oriental Buddhist art from the collections of Ukhtomsky and Kozlov, a series of important lectures was put on. Ol'denburg and Stcherbatsky gave the opening lectures; their subjects were 'The Life of the Buddha, the Great Teacher of Life' and 'The Philosophical Doctrine of Buddhism' respectively; later the Mongolist B. Y. Vladimirtsov, spoke on 'Buddhism in Tibet and Mongolia' and the Buddhologist, O. O. Rosenberg,[25] on 'The World Outlook of Contemporary Buddhism in the Far East'.[26] All were concerned to demonstrate the compatibility of Buddhism and Bolshevism:

S. F. Oldeburg referred to the importance of Buddhism in advancing the brotherhood of nations and thus to its role as a harbinger of Soviet ideals . . . O. O. Rozenberg [sic] described Buddhism as a religion of the oppressed; it had established the principles of the equality of all living things . . . F. I. Shcherbatskoi even ventured to claim that the basic idea behind the Buddhist religion came extraordinarily close to the modern, scientifically-based *Weltanschauung*.[27]

*

Dorzhiev's letter had some effect. The Red Army unit was withdrawn from the temple precincts and Narkomindel agreed both to take the temple 'under its management and protection' and to repair it as quickly as possible. But when he arrived in Petrograd in May 1921 – he had with him four Buryat lamas and, because of the food shortage, had brought brick tea, bottled Siberian butter and other provisions,[28] Dorzhiev found that the work had been only roughly carried out. He therefore wrote another strong letter to Narkomindel, dated 18 July 1921, in which he maintains that, despite the fact that since August of the preceding year some two million rubles had been spent, all that had happened was that

> . . . a few locks on doors have been replaced, the cellar has been cleaned, in some places the re-painting of the walls has been begun, and the upper lantern, by which the temple is lit, instead of being glazed is covered with some kind of boarding so that when there is heavy rain, water freely penetrates the interior . . . Although the central statue of the Buddha is repaired, because of the lack of knowledge and art of the workmen, it has been done very unskilfully, so the head of the statue must be done again.

According to the local Narkomindel man in Petrograd, Dorzhiev continued, the poorness of the work was due to the lack of a proper directive from the centre, scarcity of building materials and the fact that supervision of the work had not been delegated to someone with a proper knowledge of oriental architecture. He then resorted to a little more diplomatic arm-twisting, reiterating almost verbatim his previous argument that the looting and profanation of the temple could only have a detrimental effect on Soviet Russia's image in the Buddhist East. This was a pity, he suggested, because at that moment those efforts seemed to be meeting with success: the Red Army, in alliance with the Army of the People's Republic of Mongolia, had just retaken Urga from Baron Ungern-Sternberg – this happened on 6 July 1921 – and a Tibetan Mission was expected the following spring.[29] In these circumstances:

> It could lead to distrust in my words and . . . show them that the Government of Soviet Russia is quite indifferent to the fact of the attack on the temple and

the destruction of a Buddhist holy place ... Therefore, it is necessary before next May to bring the temple into order, both internally and externally, and to fill its interior with the appropriate statues, pictures, brocades, silken decorations and effects. For this purpose I have ordered from Tibet all the necessary statues and pictures for the interior of the temple. I could have taken the repair upon myself without bothering the Commissariat for Foreign Affairs if up to this time links with Tibet had not been broken. At this particular time, [however,] it is not possible for me to receive funds, not only for the repair of the temple but also for my own personal future upkeep, from the Tibetan Government. On the basis of the foregoing I have the honour to ask in the general interests of the strengthening of relations between the Soviet Union and the peoples of the East:

1. That firm instructions be given to the executive of the Peoples' Commissariat for Foreign Affairs in Petrograd that the Buddhist Temple be repaired, and to entrust the work to the engineer of the Peoples' Commissariat for Foreign Affairs, Krichinsky. To help Krichinsky, they should appoint the civil engineer Berzen, who as the architect who built this temple is a man who knows all about its details and construction ...

2. To supply the architect with every necessity for the speedy implementation of the work, with funds, materials and labour.

3. To allow 882 arshins of brocade for the interior decor.[30]

In conclusion, he ventured to insinuate that if Stolypin, a prime minister under the benighted imperial regime, had recognized the importance of the temple in the face of enormous public outcry, the new Soviet Government would be showing itself highly remiss if it failed to fulfil his requests in full.

This letter also had some limited effect. Krichinsky, who was the architect of the Petrograd mosque, was engaged to supervise the repair work, which was carried out around 1922 under the auspices of the Petrograd branch of the Board for Museums and the Preservation of Ancient Monuments with funds collected by Dorzhiev himself. A full restoration was not completed until 1926, however, and for much of the intervening period the temple was unoccupied by monks and hence inoperative as a working monastery. It also lost its former abbot: Sodnom Zhigzhitov, having returned to Trans-Baikalia, died there of typhus in 1921.

*

By 1920, Amur-Sanan's proposal that Dorzhiev's good offices with the Tibetans be used by Narkomindel had been fully taken up. He was then known to the highest officials in the commissariat: L. M. Karakhan and his superior, Commissar Giorgy Vasil'ievich Chicherin (1872–1936), a man of aristocratic birth who had joined the Social

Democratic party shortly after graduating from St Petersburg University and afterwards spent many years in exile. These officials recognized Dorzhiev as the official representative of Tibet and accorded him diplomatic privileges. The Buddhist temple in Petrograd moreover became an unofficial Tibetan mission, with the St Petersburg-educated Buryat, Galan Nindakov, as its secretary.[31]

Dorzhiev himself records in a letter to Chicherin of 24 April 1925 that he had worked for the Soviet cause from the time of his release from Butyrki Prison:

> During these years there was hardly a single caravan and not a single pilgrim travelling to Tibet and certain corners of Mongolia by whom I did not forward letters and information about the situation in Soviet Russia. By doing so I continually indicated to the Dalai Lama and other exalted officials in the Buddhist hierarchy that Russia, by proclaiming the principles of liberty in the new life, not only put them into practice at home but carried the banner of freedom to all the oppressed nations of the world, especially to the peoples of the East.[32]

It was almost as though the Great Game had started all over again – with one of its key players, Agvan Dorzhiev, restored to his old role as shadowy go-between. Perhaps a key to the enigma of the man lies here. Did he have such an irrepressible penchant for dabbling in power politics and mixing with the high and mighty that, when the opportunity arose again, he just could not let it pass? Since his political connections gave him considerable leverage with the Soviet Government – his letters, after all, are not weak or truckling by any means – was he from his side perhaps also hoping to exploit this to further the cause of Buddhism in Russia? Or was he at this time so infatuated with the new ideology that he was convinced that whatever appeared good for Bolshevism must also be good for Buddhism?

As is usual with human beings, his real motivation was probably a mixture of these and other elements of which he himself was probably not fully aware. Perhaps too, trying to find his bearings in a chaotic situation, he was more than a little confused, as he indeed suggests in the closing passages of his memoirs:

> As for my own angle on what the future will bring, because of the mental confusion of my consciousness, I do not know what good and bad will ensue. I would [only] offer the following homily: 'Don't be a monkey; think things out for yourself.'[33]

But it was an extremely dangerous game that he was playing – and as time went on it was to become more rather than less tortuous.

CHAPTER SEVENTEEN

Reform and Renaissance
1920 – 1924

As the Civil War began to wind down, the political situation in Siberia became considerably more favourable for the Bolsheviks. In 1920 Admiral Kolchak's forces disintegrated, and the Supreme Ruler himself, having formally relinquished power in January, was shot on 7 February. The Czech Legion was also evacuated, and the interventionist British and French forces pulled out as well, leaving the Japanese and the Red Army confronting each other. But the mood of the Japanese had become considerably less bellicose too. The result was that they abandoned Ataman Semenov and began to withdraw as well – though slowly and with incidents.

This superficial success was mirrored elsewhere, though what by 1921 the Bolsheviks had mastered was a blackened and bloodied remnant of an empire. Six years of war, revolution and civil war had killed millions, divided the people, smashed the economy, and brought chaos and suffering on an unprecedented scale. 'War Communism' whereby they had attempted to forcibly impose their ideological programme on the people, had provoked extreme resistance and resentment. Then in 1921 the sailors at Kronstadt, who had been some of the most ardent supporters of the original revolution, rose up, this time against the Bolsheviks that they had helped install in power. 'Soviets Without Communists' was their slogan. In the same year a terrible famine swept the Volga region.

Lenin and his colleagues were sufficiently astute to realize that if they were to stay in power and rebuild the country they would have to modify their strategy. They therefore retreated and inaugurated a New Economic Policy (NEP) which permitted a measure of private property holding and individual trading enterprise. This was, however, a tactical retreat so as to make a more effective advance later on.

*

The Kalmyks, for whom an autonomous oblast was created within the RSFSR in 1920, suffered particularly during the Civil War and in the great famine that had followed it. Responding to this with a characteristically good heart, Agvan Dorzhiev 'devoted his exceptional energy and organizational initiative to the collection of donations for the Kalmyks, and the dispatch of food and money, both of which were of considerable help to them'.[1]

He was also, as we have noted, in Petrograd during the summer of 1921, and again for two months in 1922, when he officiated at the ordination in September of Mikhail Ivanovich Popov-Loeffler, the son of a Petrograd property millionaire who had lost everything in the Revolution; Popov-Loeffler took the Tibetan Buddhist name Sonam Namgyal. According to Lustig, Dorzhiev also sent a letter to the Dalai Lama, requesting him to confer the status of Buddhist archbishop on Karlis Tennisons with respect to Latvia, Lithuania and Estonia, then independent states.

While waiting for confirmation to arrive – it took a year – Tennisons moved to a sovkhoz (soviet farm) near Moscow managed by Vladimir Dmitrievich Bonch-Bruevich (1873–1955), a prominent Bolshevik with a deep interest in religious sects. Towards the end of 1923, however, Dorzhiev summoned him back to Petrograd as the anticipated letter from Lhasa had arrived. Duly elevated, Archbishop Tennisons now passes out of our story. He spent some time in the Baltic States during the twenties, but eventually left for Western Europe and, later, the East. He was in China in the mid-thirties, and latterly lived in Thailand and Burma, dying in Rangoon on 9 May 1962. Friedrich Lustig, who inherited his preceptor's titles, continued to live at the north gate of the Shwedagon Pagoda, Rangoon, until his death in May 1991.

*

Various other distinguished characters who have graced our stage departed permanently into the wings around the turn of the twenties. Prince Ukhtomsky died peacefully after a spell of ill health in 1921. He had survived the Bolshevik Revolution better than many, continuing to pursue his scholarly-aesthetic interests as Assistant Curator of the Far Eastern Department of the Russian Museum and as a fellow worker of other museums and academies. Both his great collections of oriental art had long since been donated to the state: the original Lamaist one to the Ethnographical Department of the Russian Museum in 1905 (it passed to the Hermitage in 1933), and a later one, consisting of some 2,000 pieces of Chinese art, to the Museum of the Ethnography of the Peoples of the World. After the October Revolution he was allowed to retain custodianship of the latter in his flat at Oranzhreinoia 5/34 in Pushkin (formerly Tsarskoye Selo), as it could not be accommodated at the museum.[2] His son, D. E. Ukhtomsky, followed his interest in Oriental ethnography as a worker at the Russian Museum until his untimely death in 1918.[3]

Ukhtomsky's one time political ally, Dr Piotr Badmayev, had passed away in Petrograd some two years earlier. Shortly before his death, he called at the hotel in Tashkent at which the British agent, Colonel F. M. Bailey, was staying. Bailey was out at the time but later wrote that he was sorry to have missed meeting the famous doctor of Tibetan medicine, about whose medical skills he was sceptical. 'Later when I was in Lhasa I made inquiries about Badmaiev', Bailey records, 'but no one had heard of him there'.[4] Subsequently, Badmayev's lucrative Tibetan medical practice was successfully continued by his nephew, N. N. Badmayev, whose patients included the writer, Aleksey Tolstoy, and prominent Bolsheviks like N. I. Bukharin and A. I. Rykov. He was also held in high regard by G. N. Kaminsky, the Commissar for Health, a great enthusiast who opened a short-lived department of Tibetan medicine at the All-Union Institute for Experimental Medicine. N. N. Badmayev is even said to have attended Stalin on several occasions, which may ultimately have been a bad thing for him, for he was liquidated in the late thirties.[5] Another relative continued to practise in Warsaw; descendants of the family still live in St Petersburg today.

*

Despite their recent successes, the Bolsheviks were not confident of their ability to take on and hold the vast territories of eastern Siberia while the Japanese presence there continued, so they agreed to the establishment of a fellow-travelling buffer state, known as the Far Eastern Republic (FER): 'a characteristic attempt to build a half-way house between Bolshevism and the bourgeois world'.[6] Under the premiership of a moderate Bolshevik named A. M. Krasnoshchekov, this ostensibly indepedendent democracy was formally recognized by the RSFSR on 14 May 1920.

The authority of the FER started east of Lake Baikal and encompassed the Buryats of Trans-Baikalia, whose national aspirations it tried to placate by establishing an autonomous Buryat oblast. It also adopted a liberal policy towards Buddhism. Against all the auguries, then, Trans-Baikalian Buddhism began to flourish as never before. Old monasteries were repaired, new ones were built and many new lamas were ordained. In 1916, there had been 16,000 lamas and 36 datsans, but both these figures increased substantially.[7] Unfortunately, the Buryats of Cis-Baikalia, who fell under the aegis of Soviet Russia, fared rather less well.

Despite visits elsewhere, Dorzhiev was primarily based in Buryatia during the twenties. During this period he and fellow intellectuals like Baradin, Zhamtsarano and Rinchino attempted to engineer a reconciliation between Buddhism and Bolshevism. Incorporating and expanding progressive ideas that they had been developing for some time, this soon blossomed into a full-blown reform movement (obnovlencheskoye) within the Russian Buddhist Church. Dorzhiev himself argued that the 'Buddhist doctrine is largely compatible with current communist tradition' because

> [both maintain] that the weak should not be oppressed but cared for; that everyone should be regarded as though they were a [close] relative; that non-virtues, such as stealing, should be avoided; that the various kinds of avarice and magic should not be allowed; [and] that one should engage in a truthful and upright livelihood.[8]

He also ingeniously proposed the consonance of Buddhism with dialectical materialism on the grounds that it did not doctrinally assert the existence of God and so was a 'religion of atheism'. He was concerned to rebut the criticism that Buddhism was 'unscientific' too. Certainly Buddhism does not demand a leap of faith (except in the case of the Pure Land school); rather it encourages practitioners to investigate phenomena thoroughly and accept as true only that which they have satisfactorily proven for themselves. Some of the more enthusiastic devotees of the reform movement went even further than Dorzhiev. They declared that the ideals of Bolshevism were prefigured in Buddhism – so Shakyamuni Buddha was in fact a proto-Bolshevik . . . and indeed his spirit was alive in V.I. Lenin![9]

Dorzhiev was also a great enthusiast for Tibetan medicine, which as a spiritually based system is not separate from Buddhism. He established a Central Council for Tibetan Medicine, which ran a manba or medical school at the Atsagat Datsan. He therefore defended this form of healing against the attacks of its detractors:

> Some of our physicians, in return for mere food and clothing, carry with them some superb medicines that treat [people] with both positive and negative

results. Due to this, certain European doctors, either out of jealousy or
competitiveness, have tried to prohibit them by claiming that they are
harming people. But since it is evident that there are many illnesses which
these doctors cannot cure, it is amazing that they should say [our physicians]
cause harm. Moreover, to prohibit we followers of the supreme teacher
[from practising] these [medical] teachings, which are expressly given for
the benefit of others, is equivalent to prohibiting the practice of Buddhism
itself.[10]

Central to the practical programme of the reform movement was that
lamas should bring their lifestyle into harmony with that of the
'toiling masses' by renouncing wealth and privilege, and returning
to the austerity and simplicity of a kind of idealized early Buddhism.
Similar arguments were at the same time being enunciated within the
Orthodox Church by the followers of the Living Church movement,
which in its journal castigated 'the idleness, self-interest, mendacity
and gluttony of the clergy', called for the communization of clerical
life on the lines of the early Christian communities, and advocated
that the clergy cease avoiding physical labour, a thing declared to be
'a joyful manifestation of the fullness of life and a guarantee of social
well-being'.[11]

Dorzhiev's hope then, as he expressed it in his memoirs, was that the
Buddhist monastic way of life, 'which will not tyrannize the people',
should continue. Indeed, allowing himself a supreme flourish of the
imagination, he went so far as to envisage that, under the benign
patronage of the Bolshevik regime, Russia would become a land worthy
of the noble title 'Supreme Place' – that is, one in which the Buddhist
religion thrives.[12]

Though there was no doubt an element of sincerity in Dorzhiev's
reforming zeal, there was also a pragmatic one too. As he had travelled
beyond the confines of Buryatia and moved within Bolshevik circles,
he knew only too well how hostile the new ideology was to religion
and what happened to conservative religious who refused to mend their
ways. In the Volga region, for instance, a metropolitan and several
archbishops had been shot for opposing the use of church assets for
the relief of famine victims; and all over the country anti-religious
pogroms were going on – great bells and crosses were being cast down,
spires and cupolas toppled, churches and monasteries dynamited, holy
icons and other religious objects desecrated, and clergy subjected to
humiliation and harassment.[13] The Lamaist Church therefore had to
reform itself radically and work with the new regime; the alternative
was destruction.

*

Of course there were many conservative Buryat lamas and laymen who thought otherwise. Dorzhiev and his colleagues were to clash with them at the very first All-Buryat Buddhist Congress, which was convened under his chairmanship at the Atsagat Datsan on 15 October 1922, shortly before the absorption of the Far Eastern Republic into the RSFSR. The purpose of this congress, which was attended by both Trans-Baikal and Cis-Baikal Buryats, was to discuss new regulations proposed by the reformists; these dealt with the general administration of the Buryat Lamaist Church, the administration of the various datsans and the monastic code by which lamas and khuvarak (novices) should live. Apparently, the way in which the reformers presented these proposals suggested that they were acting on behalf of the authorities of the FER; those authorities, for their part, stood back and allowed the clergy a free hand to define their relationship vis-à-vis the new system.

Essentially what the proposed new regulations and rules did was to enlarge upon the democratic reforms of the Kotlaryev Commission of 1917. It was proposed, for instance, to curtail the powers of the Khambo Lama and instead make the elected Congress of Clergy the supreme organ of church government. The Central Clerical Council, presided over by the Khambo Lama, would at the same time become the supreme executive organ, while the running of datsans was to be entrusted to datsan councils presided over by shiretuis (abbots). Thus the Khambo Lama and the shiretuis would become subject to the central and monastic councils, and had no right to make independent decisions except in minor day-to-day matters.

These new reforms were passed without much demur; but passionate quarrels broke out when the functions of parish councils and datsan councils came up for discussion. The conservatives violently opposed the proposal that monastic councils be subordinated to parish councils, in which lay delegates would be in the majority; also that lay people might call lamas to account, override their decisions and subject them to criticism. After 'stormy disagreements', a compromise was reached which toned down the powers of the parish councils and so made the lamas less susceptible to lay domination.

Even more heat was generated when the congress went on to discuss reforms designed to bring the way of life of the lamas more in harmony with that of the toiling masses. In this connection, the reformers had already published their programme in the newspaper, *Shene Baidal*. They proposed that the congress should:

1. Manifest the means of establishing a communal way of life without private property. Lamas who wish to enter the new way of life must completely repudiate private possessions; their houses and all their private property must be transferred to the monastic commune. They should also renounce property lodged in the homes of their relations; personal books must be given to the monastery library and turned over to collective use. A communal dining-room must be organised, based on the rules of the commune, and living-quarters, food, clothing and other necessities must be used strictly in accordance with the Vinaya [Monastic Code of Discipline]. The norms set out in the Vinaya must be observed. The accumulation by lamas of donations solicited on their personal initiative is strictly forbidden. It is especially important to pay attention to the continuing practice of collecting donations under the pretext of commissioning the making of Buddha-rupas and [other] cult objects, by means of which the lamas appropriate a portion of these funds or waste collective funds.

This situation must be stopped at root. Moreover, the receiving of a gebzhi or gabzhi [geshé] degree involves the collection of donations and the establishment of a procedure for the distribution of donations of property to the lama-khuvarak commune. This situation must [also] be stopped. In the holy book, *A Guide to the Bodhisattva's Way of Life*,[14] it is written, 'Our great teacher did not permit the donation of property for the attainment of the highest paths.' The lamas' procedure for raising funds for the Buddhist community must be established with the sanction of the existing organs of authority. Religious services for the laity, such as fortune-telling, the swearing of oaths, healing, giving readings for the gaining of material happiness, prayers for the dead, and the reading of prophecies and precepts must be carried out [only] by such persons who have been especially appointed for such purposes; the arbitary performance of rites by individual lamas acting on their own account is not to take place; property received for the celebration of such rites must be handed over to the monastic commune. There must be established a procedure for the exclusion from the congregation of lamas those who break the general rules of the Vinaya and also [offend against] the accepted conventions of the Buryat-Mongol people.

2. There must be established a procedure for keeping and maintaining the property of Lamaist communities that is not opposed to the interests of the toiling masses and the policy of the state, and detailed accounts of income and expenditure must also be set up. It is furthermore necessary to establish that all the property of a monastic community is to be considered the social property of the Buryat-Mongol people. It must [as well] be clarified whether or not the property of a monastic community is liable to tax assessment.

3. Lamas abiding by the aforementioned rules of life must [also] follow the general rules of society in conformity with other citizens.[15]

It is impossible not to detect here the antiseptic odour of an unappealing puritanism. Something similar is present in early Bolshevism too. Evidently spiritual and political idealists – and perhaps other sorts as well – have this tendency, as though their aspiration for higher, more perfect forms induces a concomitant contempt for worldly things, and especially anything that gives comfort and pleasure to the body and the ego.

Two special reports were read at the congress: 'On Putting the Clergy's Way of Life into Good Order According to the Rules of the Dulva-Vinaya' by Lharamba Nimbo, and 'On Procedures for Ordaining Young People in Monasteries' by Zhigzhitzhap Batotsirenov. These were then handed over to four special sub-committees charged with the duty of working out detailed proposals on matters relating to administration, regulations, religious education and Tibetan medicine. Dorzhiev sat on the sub-committee for regulations with Khambo Itigelov, Ayurzana Tsibenov and Zhigzhitzhap Batotsirenov. Gombozhab Tsybikov, the Buryat scholar who had been in Lhasa in 1900 and 1901, sat on the sub-committee for administrative matters.

Batotsirenov's report reproached the lamas in hell-fire terms for a lifestyle which had become so brazen that, if it was not radically and speedily reformed, the authorities would be compelled to step in and 'call things to order by force'. As the root of the lamas' corruption lay in their 'unbridled thirst for private property', Batotsirenov suggested that all money, possessions and income be transferred to monastic communes. When new regulations to this effect were proposed and debated, what provoked particular controversy, however, was the censure of luxury implicit in proposed Article 13, which forbade lamas from owning gold and silver articles, silk and carpeted bed-furnishings, and clothing made of expensive materials like silk, sable and otter fur.[16] The 'endless disputes' that this generated forced the congress into an impasse and caused Baradin, Tsybikov, Rinchino, Batotsirenov and a few other intellectuals to walk out of the conference hall, leaving behind a written declaration that again warned the lamas that, if they were not prepared to abandon the 'insatiable desire for the ownership of property', then 'the end is unforeseen and hope is lost'.

Far from bringing the congress to its senses, disagreement subsequently became even more intense; so, in an effort to hasten a decision, the chairman, Agvan Dorzhiev, reminded those present of the sad fate of those Orthodox hierarchs in the Volga region who had not been prepared to allow church treasures to be used for famine relief. When this stern warning also fell on deaf ears, he too walked out, declaring that he could not preside over such a gathering. In his absence he was promptly accused by Budazhap Dorzhiev of insulting the Soviet authorities and the Communist Party. 'In the Soviet Union there exists religious freedom', declared this other Dorzhiev, no doubt with some passion – and then he too left the hall.

After some deliberation, the remaining delegates went out to persuade those who had left the hall to return. It was then agreed that Agvan Dorzhiev had not in fact insulted the authorities or the party, and Article 13 was passed in an amended form that allowed lamas to retain any personal property (including livestock) in their possession prior to the enactment of the new regulations, but not any that they might acquire afterwards. It was also agreed that fences around individual lamas' plots of land be replaced by a common fence around the whole monastery, and that traders should be forbidden from entering monastic precincts, which would be closed at sunset, by which time women should also have left. Furthermore, for infractions of the monastic code, such as trading, speculation, smuggling, drunkenness, playing games of chance, sexual misconduct and fomenting strife and discord, lamas would be subject to punishments ranging from a rebuke to disrobement.

Batotsirenov was also concerned about the quality of lamas. Due to the practices of ordaining very young boys as khuvarak and accepting almost anyone who wanted to join it, the sangha had become flooded with people who were simply not up to the ethical, intellectual and spiritual demands of the religious life. He wanted to restrict khuvarak ordination to boys of fifteen and over, but the combined sub-committees on monastic rules and education preferred an age limit of seven or eight years, government regulations permitting. This was because there were plans in hand to set up combined elementary schools for both khuvarak and lay children in the monasteries, and entry into schools of higher religious training would only be possible after graduation from one of these. Furthermore, it was agreed that teachers trained in Europe would be employed in the new elementary schools, and European methods would be used, but teaching would be conducted through the medium of the local language. The 'precious teaching on religion', meanwhile, would become 'the property of the national culture'.

It was also planned to reorganize colleges of tsenyi and schools of medicine (manba). Entry to the former would be more selective; methods, programmes and resources would be reviewed; and more rigorous examination requirements would be set, so that in future, candidates would not be able to acquire degrees through bribery and other forms of corruption. The manba, meanwhile, would seek to combine the Tibetan and European medical systems by introducing the teaching of anatomy, physiology and European diagnostic techniques, and in future only those qualified in this new programme would be allowed to practise. Entry to manba would also be open to both monks and lay people – even women might apply! – and healing would be given free of charge (some lamas objected to this) and only by means of pharmaceutical medicines. There would, however, be no attempt to separate medicine from religion. Finally, in order to raise the 'cultural level' of religion, it was agreed to ban the cults of incarnate lamas (Tib. tulku) and oracles.

For all the passion spent in the conference hall, this first All-Buryat Buddhist Congress did not have any great effect. The situation in eastern Siberia was still very unclear, so the rank and file of lamas were able to go on soliciting donations and generally behaving much as before. It was not, however, an isolated phenomenon. As Gerasimova points out, 'throughout the land there was a wave of legal clerical conferences that discussed the matter of loyalty to the powers-that-be and the forms that religious life would take under the new conditions'.[17]

*

The absorption of the FER into the RSFSR took place shortly after the congress, on 10 November 1922, for its usefulness as a buffer state had ceased with the final withdrawal of the Japanese from Siberia. The move added a sizeable swathe of territory to the RSFSR, for, once its forces had crushed those of Ataman Semenov, the FER extended all the way to the Pacific.

Almost at once the Soviet authorities had to decide what to do about the Buryats. Naturally, the Buryats themselves wished the Soviet Government to grant them the same kind of autonomy that had been granted to the Kalmyks and other national minorities. In this, however, they were strongly opposed by the Russian communists living within their national homeland. The final decision rested with Stalin (Iosif Vissarionovich Dzhugashvili, 1879–1953), the Soviet Commissar for Nationalities. In uncharacteristically enlightened mood, the dark Georgian ruled that both the Trans-Baikalian and the Cis-Baikalian Buryats be united in a single Buryat-Mongol Autonomous Soviet Socialist Republic (BMASSR), though, as elsewhere, it was clear that autonomy did not imply freedom to secede from the RSFSR or to deviate substantially from its ideology and policies.

Despite their ideological aversion to religion, the policy makers at the centre were at this stage undecided as to how to treat Buddhism. Officials in the BMASSR were therefore initially allowed to adopt a relatively liberal policy, and as a result the Buddhist revival that had begun during the lifetime of the FER continued for a few short years. This was by no means a benign aberration on the part of the Soviet Government; as we have noted, they wanted to use 'progressive' Buryat Buddhists to carry revolutionary ideas to the 'oppressed peoples' of Buddhist Asia.[18]

And of course no one was more useful to them in this respect than Agvan Dorzhiev, who continued to work closely with Narkomindel during the twenties. Around 1921, for instance, he was involved in the formulation of a sinister plot to send weapons and foment revolution in Tibet. An exploratory expedition masquerading as a pilgrim group would be sent first; this would carry a radio transmitter (there are resonances of Karakhan's proposal to Stcherbatsky here). If it was successful, a second and highly secret expedition – every effort would have to be made to ensure that the British did not catch wind of it – again posing as a pilgrim group, would take in the weapons. According to Russian sources, Dorzhiev even supplied the names of Buryats and Mongols who could take part: one was Dashi Sampilon.[19]

That Dorzhiev was prepared to go so far as to connive in fomenting revolution in Tibet was one of the most surprising discoveries during the research for this book – and one of the most difficult to explain. On the face of it, it looks like extreme disloyalty to his old friend and pupil, the Thirteenth Dalai Lama. After all, Dorzhiev had seen what the Bolsheviks had done to an unreconstructed autocrat like Nicholas Romanov; did he wish a similar fate on Tubten Gyatso?

British intelligence, which at this period at least was highly efficient, was quickly alerted to what the Bolsheviks and Dorzhiev were up to. Sir Charles Bell, in Lhasa on an official visit between November 1920 and October 1921, reported to the Government of India in a letter dated 6 February 1921 that, while there were no signs of serious Bolshevik activity in Tibet, an agent of Dorzhiev was living at Drepung. The man, a Mongol who was masquerading as an anti-Bolshevik, was in Lhasa ostensibly to sell watches, gold and so forth.[20]

Dorzhiev also helped organize the secret delegation that arrived in Lhasa disguised as a pilgrim party in 1922. One of its principal members was Sergey Stepanovich Borisov, an Oirat from the Altai region – he was in fact ethnically Turkic – who at the time held an important post in the Peoples' Commissariat of Internal affairs.[21] According to Robert Rupen, he also worked as a Comintern agent in Mongolia in the early twenties, later going on to deal with Narkomindel's Mongolian, Tibetan and Tannu-Tuvan business, and winding up as deputy head of the Far Eastern Section in 1928. Borisov's colleague was a Buryat lawyer named Vampilon. The delegation achieved nothing, according to N. Poppe, because it had nothing acceptable to offer the Tibetans – aside from an offer of help against the British.

This last assertion sounds a little strange, for the British were at this juncture on very cordial terms with the Tibetans. Among other things, they were giving the much-needed military and technical assistance to secure Tibet's precarious independence from the Chinese. British political officers were also paying periodic visits to Lhasa. Besides Bell, Colonel F. M. Bailey went there in 1924, and one of his official objectives was to advise the Tibetans on 'the exclusion from Tibet of Bolshevist and anti-British propagandists',[22] which indicates that the Government of India was by this time aware of and concerned about Bolshevik activities in the Land of the Snows.

In 1923, the Narkomindel official, Lev Efimovich Berlin, published his article on Dorzhiev in *Novy Vostok*, a journal set up in 1922 by the Peoples' Commissariat for Nationalities through the All-Russian Scientific Association of Oriental Studies to promote Soviet political aspirations in the East.[23] Berlin's unconcealed intention was to pose Russia as the benefactor of Tibet, and to show how the diplomatic efforts of Agvan Dorzhiev, who was now fully converted to the Bolshevik cause, had significantly helped the Tibetans to liberate themselves from centuries of Chinese overlordship and at the same time had foiled the schemes of the British to undermine that hard-won independence. He concluded that, though at that juncture the British might have managed to achieve their aims in Tibet by resorting to military machinations and secret imperialist deals, the day of reckoning was at hand when the growth of class conflict and the national liberation movements would reverse the apparent 'victories' of British policy, just as it would ring the death knell on world imperialism in general.[24]

In the following year, when he was seventy, Dorzhiev wrote his own Tibetan memoirs. It is tempting to think, because these were produced so soon after the Berlin article, which also contains much biographical data, that there was a link between the two – perhaps even that the memoirs were produced for propaganda purposes. Both these speculations do not hold up on deeper consideration, however. In the first place, Dorzhiev states quite clearly in the colophon that he was persuaded to record the main events of his life by a rabjampa geshé named Tubten Dondrup, who had made the obligatory offerings. Furthermore, though he does say some positive things about Lenin, he is quite frank about his low opinion of many elements within the Bolshevik Party. Communism was a fine system, he concedes, but few Bolsheviks lived up to its high ideals; indeed, within their ranks there were 'a number of evil-intentioned [people], who had stolen from or subdued the weak', and the system moreover gave power to many 'bad people or sexual perverts who thought only of their own well-being'; thus both Bolsheviks and Communism gained a bad reputation world-wide . . .[25] Hardly the words of a propagandist.

*

We know that his political work for Narkomindel brought Dorzhiev into contact with Chicherin and Karakhan, but did he know or meet any other of the early Bolshevik leaders?

Friedrich Lustig maintains that he did, and that his 'prodigious strength of character, even in its trivial aspects' impressed many of them, including Aleksandra Mikhailovna Kollontai (1872–1952), a lady of noble origins who played a prominent part in the revolution and later went on to become a diplomat and campaigner for womens' rights. Anatoly Lunacharsky also came to have a deep respect for the Buryat lama's intellectual acumen.

'When we talk to the Khambo Lama, we Bolsheviks require the full possession of our intelligence to do justice to ourselves', he declared with 'loud theatrical emphasis and gesticulation' at a meeting of intellectuals.[26]

More interestingly, though, did Dorzhiev meet Lenin? – who, incidentally, had a Kalmyk grandmother on his father's side of the family. While there are oral reports that he did, solid, documentary proof is entirely lacking. The only person within the wider Buddhist ambit who certainly did meet the Bolshevik leader was S. F. Ol'denburg, who had once been in the same student group at St Petersburg University as Aleksandr Ulyanov, Lenin's elder brother, who was executed in the Petropavlovsk Fortress in 1887 at the tender age of twenty-one for his involvement in a plot to assassinate Alexander III. Ol'denburg and Lenin met for the first time before the Revolution and spoke about Aleksandr, who had been a gifted student of zoology;[27] they met again in January 1918 when Ol'denburg was with a party of scholars involved in the reconstitution of the Academy of Sciences. By then, like Stcherbatsky and many other orientalists, he was prepared to go along with the new regime and put his knowledge of the East at its disposal for revolutionary purposes.

'Go to the masses', Lenin allegedly told Ol'denburg, 'and tell them about the history of India, about the age-old sufferings of the vast masses who have been enslaved and oppressed by the British. You will find yourself surprised by the response of our proletarian masses – and you will draw inspiration from it . . .'[28] Ol'denburg was apparently deeply impressed.

Lenin is also reported as having inquired of Lunacharsky about Stcherbatsky. 'He is a wonderful scholar', replied the Commissar for Education, 'who has written a splendid brochure in which he treats Buddhism from the socialist point of view (rejection of individualism and private property, acquisition of peace of mind and attainment of joy through social harmony)'.[29]

Lunacharsky, who was himself very interested in Buddhist philosophy, sent Stcherbatsky to the West in 1921 to buy books for the Academy of Sciences. The Sanskritist visited France, Germany and Czechoslovakia; also Britain, where he developed an extensive network of contacts with whom he later corresponded. These included the writer, H. G. Wells; the pioneer of Pali studies, T. W. Rhys-Davids; E. Denison Ross, the director of the School of Oriental Studies; E. D. McLaggan, the president of the Royal Asiatic Society; the Buddhist scholar, F. W. Thomas; and many others.[30] He also, towards the end of the decade, corresponded with the philosopher, Bertrand Russell, in the hope of persuading him that, as Indian philosophy was an independent living tradition and the equal of European philosophy, both could fruitfully interact with each other. His arguments fell on stony ground. Russell could hardly believe that Indian philosophy had not been to some extent influenced by Greek philosophy.[31]

Despite his political entanglements, the 1920s were Stcherbatsky's most prolific period. It was then that he produced his most important works, including *Buddhist Logic*. The first volume appeared in 1929, but the appearance of the second was initially frustrated by the authorities and only finally came out due to pressure from Sergey Ol'denburg, who was then still Secretary of the Academy of Sciences.

*

In Mongolia, following the defeat of the White forces of Baron Ungern-Sternberg, a constitutional monarchy with curtailed powers was restored under the Jebtsundamba Khutukhtu. The land was now very much in the Soviet ambit – where else could it look for support against the Chinese? – but the communists, though they had a role in the new government, were unable to assume power because they were just one faction among many in a society in which the Buddhist church was still protected and enormously influential, where the broad masses were educationally extremely backward, and where economic development was at an extremely primitive stage. What was needed therefore was time – time to build up party organization and lay the necessary economic and social foundations for a communist revolution that could take place at a later date.

Many Buryats and Kalmyks came to Mongolia during the Civil War and afterwards, either as refugees or to act as intermediaries between the Comintern and the Mongolians. Among them was Dorzhiev's friend,

Zhamtsarano, who had already done much useful educational work in Mongolia in the period 1911 to 1919. In 1921 he put together two important documents articulating the Mongolian People's Party's platform for the First Party Congress held in Kyakhta; in the same year he became the Deputy Minister of Internal Affairs in the new government.

Following the transmigration of the dissolute Jebtsundamba Khutukhtu to his next life on 20 May 1924, a Great Khural was summoned to determine the future constitution of the recently declared Mongolian People's Republic. It convened in Urga on 8 November and was attended by Agvan Dorzhiev as the representative of Tibet; also by Rinchino, Zhamtsarano, Baradin and P. K. Kozlov.[32]

Naturally, a great deal of Pan-Mongol sentiment was expressed at the khural: 'We must be the cultural centre of our race; we must attract to ourselves the Inner Mongolians, the Barga Mongolians [and so on] . . .', declared Rinchino. Agvan Dorzhiev, meanwhile, when greeting the khural on behalf of Tibet, welcomed the new independent Mongolian state and recalled the times when, under Genghis Khan, the Mongols had ruled a great empire. 'I note this with satisfaction', he said, 'and hope that Mongolia grows and thrives'. He then went on to recall how Mongolia and Tibet had been united for centuries by bonds of true friendship based on their devotion to the Gelug school of Tibetan Buddhism:

> We [will] strive to make our centuries-long relations still more firm and deep. We wish to help the Mongol people in their cause of liberation. Even though they say that the Tibetan nation is small and backward, we also disseminate in our own country the ideal of liberation from foreign oppression. Let the cause of liberation and the flourishing of the Mongol and Tibetan peoples triumph! Let the teachings of Shakyamuni shine [forth] like the rays of the sun! Let our peoples be strong and inviolable from [both] inner and outer enemies like Mount Sumeru![33]

On 10 December he presided over an evening session of the khural. In a friendly and genuine atmosphere, the problems of national minorities and outlying regions were discussed. Dorzhiev himself declared that he devoutly hoped that the Tibetans would some day be able to rid themselves of foreign oppression and become masters in their own land.[34]

In the same year Dorzhiev also began negotiations with the Mongolian Government with a view to making the Petrograd Buddhist Temple a joint Tibeto-Mongolian responsibility. This process, in which Zhamtsarano must have been involved, would secure the temple by bringing it under the protection of diplomatic privilege. The arrangement was not finalized until 1926, however.

*

Lenin died on 24 January 1924. He had been ill for some time, and had also showed signs (as well he might) of dissatisfaction with the way the new state he had brought into being was going. His departure, of course, left a huge vacuum at the heart of the Soviet power structure, and during the next few years there was a contest to fill it. On the face of things, Trotsky looked like the obvious successor; but there were also Zinov'ev and Kamanev, and, on the right wing of the party, Bukharin.

Things were going to change, then – but in 1924 no one could have said precisely how.

CHAPTER EIGHTEEN

Gathering Clouds
1925 – 1929

It was none of the obvious candidates who won the struggle for the Soviet leadership but the hitherto unfancied Iosif Stalin, the mediocrity of the party. He alone had the stomach for the necessary intrigue and ruthless manoeuvring; as General Secretary of the Communist Party, which had grown immensely in membership and influence in recent years, he moreover had a viable power base. It took him several years to overcome his opponents and consolidate his own power, however, so the draconian historical phenomenon known as Stalinism did not come fully into being until the end of the decade. In any case, it was not the decision of Stalin alone to create Stalinism; like many if not all other political leaders, he basically expressed tendencies that were already gestating at the grass roots level, in his case among the rank and file party members, who, now that Lenin's New Economic Policy had to a large extent fulfilled its object of righting the economy and restoring social stability, wanted to see the implementation of a full communist programme. The period under examination in this chapter could therefore be called the prelude to Stalinism.

As we have noted, Dorzhiev was showing signs of disillusionment with the Bolsheviks as early as 1924, when he was writing his memoirs. He expressed them more forcibly in a letter of 24 April 1925 to G. V. Chicherin, which was written in Moscow.[1] In this he complains that current Soviet legislation prohibiting anyone under the age of eighteen from embarking upon a religious career was radically undermining the foundation of Buddhism, which depended upon its monastic sangha, entry to which was elsewhere open to boys of between eight and ten years of age. 'With this law in force', he declared, 'the Soviet Government's solemn declaration of religious freedom [i.e. the decree of 23 January 1918] becomes, with respect to Buddhism, a mere fiction'.

This legislation was further aggravated, he contends, by systematic anti-religious propaganda conducted by party organizations, including Komsomol, the Soviet youth league, which were not only armed with the 'theses of militant materialism' but also enjoyed official support. It was a further mockery, he maintains, for the authorities to declare full religious freedom on the one hand and to condone anti-religious activities on the other.

He then drew Chicherin's attention to the fact that, alongside the pro-Soviet propaganda that he was transmitting, Buryat and Kalmyk visitors to Lhasa were relaying another and very different message about conditions in Soviet Russia: one concerning what he calls 'funeral of the gods':

> Although this information is not transmitted around the world by radio waves or through the wires of the telegraph and does not appear in the newspapers, it still in a quiet and invisible way performs its evil work by raising doubts in the minds and consciousness of the masses and the upper echelons about the correctness of my information concerning the situation in Russia.[2]

The paltry advantages to be derived from anti-religious propaganda among the Buryats and Kalmyks would therefore be more than offset by damage inflicted to the Soviet image in Tibet and Mongolia. It was furthermore his experience that Komsomol activities in the villages tended to strengthen rather than diminish faith in religion.

He then played his strongest card:

> In the past four or five years I have tried, to the best of my ability, to help you with your work as far as this relates to Tibet; and, if in future there will be a need for my participation, I would always be pleased to offer you my humble services. But I must alert you to the fact that I no longer have the enthusiasm, inspiration and ardent faith I once had for this work because all my petitions to the Soviet government concerning the principal issues bearing upon the religious life of my Buryat and Kalmyk co-religionists have gone by unnoticed and [have] not been put into practice. Under such conditions [my efforts] lose their meaning and purpose, for I am not a politician but a man of religion.

He concludes by asking Chicherin to lay four proposals before the appropriate official bodies, requesting them: to allow young males of eighteen and under to be accepted into the Buddhist Sangha; to free the practice of Tibetan medicine from legal sanctions (except where practitioners committed crimes through the application of their remedies); to exempt Kalmyk and Buryat lamas from military service; and to change the substance of anti-religious propaganda among the Buryats and Kalmyks, if for any reason it could not be temporarily halted.

There is no record that this letter either prompted the authorities to

action or even evinced a reply. Indeed, most of his private letters of
protest during the twenties fell on stony ground, though for the moment
he still enjoyed a protected existence, carrying special Narkomindel
papers that required that the bearer 'shall not be subjected to search
or detention without prior notification of the People's Commissariat for
Foreign Affairs'.[3] Later, however, when he began to voice his complaints
more openly, things would get difficult for him.'

*

There are few records of Soviet missions to Lhasa in the mid-twenties –
an outcome, perhaps, of the loss of enthusiasm to which Dorzhiev alludes
above; also, when one composed of 'Mongolians' (which may mean
Buryats) did arrive in 1927, though it carried a letter of commendation
from Dorzhiev, the Tibetan authorities informed their friends in the
Government of India that he had at the same time written privately
to the Dalai Lama advising him to have nothing to do with the group.
This suggests that by this juncture Dorzhiev may have been playing a
double game: outwardly appearing to help Narkomindel but at the same
secretly warning the Dalai Lama of Narkomindel machinations.

These 'Mongolians', who according to British records, left Lhasa in
December 1927, after having had an audience with His Holiness,[4]
may be identical to a similar group mentioned by Tsepon W. D.
Shakabpa: it was, he says, composed of Buryat lamas led by a certain
Zangpo, and its aim was to promote Tibeto-Soviet friendship and spread
propaganda. Shakabpa also mentions a 'Soviet-Mongol' mission arriving
the following year, 1928,[5] while British sources talk of a mysterious
figure, believed to be a 'high military official of the Soviet', living in
considerable style in the holy city for over a year. He was a large,
rubicund man, perhaps a Buryat, whose name was Po-lo-te; he was
on intimate terms with a number of important Tibetan officials and
was also received by the Dalai Lama. In March 1930, though initially
reported to be travelling towards India, he disappeared in the direction
of Nagchukha.[6]

There is every reason to believe that all these missions went away
as empty-handed as the Borisov-Vampilon mission, for by the middle
of the decade, with or without Dorzhiev's help, it must have become
abundantly clear to the Dalai Lama that Bolshevik ideology was
totally inimical to his political and spiritual order, not to mention
his own position. Certainly when, shortly before his death in 1933,
he wrote his so-called Final Testament, he issued the strongest possible
warning against the dangers of 'the barbaric red communists', who

by that time had robbed and destroyed the monasteries of Mongolia, and either forced the lamas to enlist in their armies or else killed them outright:

> It will not be long before we find the red onslaught at our own front door . . . And when that happens, we must be ready to defend ourselves, otherwise our spiritual and cultural traditions will be completely eradicated. Even the names of the Dalai and Panchen Lamas will be erased, as well as those of other lamas, lineage holders and holy beings. The monasteries will be looted and destroyed, and the monks and nuns killed or chased away . . . The birthrights and property of the people will be stolen; we will become like slaves to our conquerors, and will be made to wander helplessly like beggars. Everyone will be forced to live in misery, and the days and nights will pass slowly, and with great suffering and terror.[7]

Uncannily accurate prophecies – though in fact it was the Communists of China rather than those of Soviet Russia that in the end brought them to pass.

*

Towards the end of 1924, the reform movement had gathered momentum in the BMASSR with attempts to elect datsan councils and implement the statutes and regulations promulgated in 1922. These efforts were strongly opposed by those rich abbots who objected to the limitation of private property.

Further contention was set off in 1925 and 1926 by the publication of new Buryat republic laws concerning the separation of church and state, which at the same time invalidated all existing Buddhist statutes and regulations on the grounds that they were 'not responsible to Soviet jurisdiction'. To settle matters, the reformers decided to call a Second All-Buryat Buddhist Congress in 1926, and accordingly officials were sent out to the datsans to supervise the election of delegates. The conservatives chose largely to ignore these elections: the lamas of the Egituev, Tsongol and Tsugol datsans, for instance, declared that they 'had need of neither the TsDS [Central Datsan Council?], nor the congress, nor the Khambo-Lama'. As a result, only fourteen conservative delegates were elected as against fifty-two reformers. Later, however, realizing that they had put themselves at a serious disadvantage, they tried to 'unite their forces, reach a level of agreement and work out a united platform'; if this failed, they planned to disrupt the congress. After conspiratorial meetings in private quarters in Verkhneudinsk, they finally came up with two hundred unofficial candidates drawn mainly from Khorinsk aimak. These were headed by

Zhigzhit Galsanov, Erdenyi Shoirodov, Tsibik-Dorzhi Badmayev, Nima Darmayev, Bal'zhir Naidanov and Erdenyi Vambotsirenov.

The conservative platform, for which popular support was claimed, was based on objections to the separation of church and state, the call up of lamas for military service, the raising of age limits for entry into the monastic sangha, the opening of secular schools in the datsans, and to all the resolutions of the 1922 congress. They were strongly against the socialization of property and income, the doing away with lamas' private plots of land, and the organization of agricultural communes. As they had furthermore decided to push their own candidates for the position of Khambo Lama, they began a smear campaign against Khambos Munkuzhapov and Agvan Dorzhiev: during the elections for the presidency of the congress, Guru-Darma Tsirempilov went so far as to accuse Munkuzhapov of being a speculator and smuggler, as well as a man completely ignorant of Buddhist philosophy.

The reformers, meanwhile, held their own private meetings in Agvan Dorzhiev's quarters, when they discussed the problems that were likely to arise at the congress and the various candidates for the position of president. Those who took part in these discussions included Khambo Lama Munkuzhapov, Tsiren Sosorov, Badzar Baradin, Gombozhab Tsybikov and B. H. Badmazhapov.

When the congress opened on 22 December 1925, the reformers were able to engineer the disqualification of the conservative candidates who had not been properly elected; then, after various minor matters had been discussed, the main business of the meeting was broached: the revision of the statutes and regulations of 1922. This began with addresses by Agvan Dorzhiev; Khambo Lama Munkuzhapov; Lubsan Shirab Tiepkin, the head of the Don Kalmyks, who had taken refuge at the Leningrad temple; and Bato-Dalai Ochirov, the representative of the Leningrad temple. They called upon congress members to 'create a religious union based on the pure teachings of the Buddha and in harmony with the laws of the Soviet Socialist republic'.[8]

According to Gerasimova, 'Agvan Dorzhiev delivered a fiery [and] extremely expressive speech on how religion would be destroyed by the decline in morality among the clergy'. Discipline in the datsans was lax, he said, and the lamas failed to follow the holy teachings of the Buddha, which taught them 'wholeheartedly to listen, think and contemplate; instead they amassed money, cattle and other valuables, built houses and mansions for themselves, and busied themselves with trade and speculation, all of which impoverished the laity. Moreover:

Many depraved persons now hold high office in the khids [datsans]. In these circumstances, one wonders: to whom does the religion belong? Significant depraved and criminal elements, with the object of strengthening their position, falsely slander those who keep the precepts properly before the mass of the faithful in an attempt to transfer their sins to others ... Such lamas are rightly called parasites; they are like ticks which, though appearing to be small insects, increase themselves twentyfold by drinking the blood of other animals. Understand what we have come to! Is it not time to put aside the past and reform our lives in line with the holy teachings of the Buddha? Only by accepting the new situation and establishing strict discipline among the novices, the pupils of the Buddha, can we reach the point where Buddhism will shine [forth] like the sun. Only in this way can we save the religion from self-annihilation, which is inevitable in five to fifteen years if the clergy do not adopt measures [to save it].[9]

When the article in the statutes concerning money-grubbing by the lamas was discussed, Dorzhiev told them baldly: 'There has been enough riding on the backs of the population ... The time has come for lamas to live a communal life [and] to try and turn to farming. This is not at odds with the Buddha's teachings.' In other words, he was advocating that the datsans transform themselves into kolkhoz: agricultural communes. To this Zhambo Zhalayev, the abbot of Kizhinga Datsan, replied that it would take the lives of a thousand buddhas – that is, an inconceivable length of time – to establish lamaist life in full conformity with the Buddha's teachings.

The delegates then argued over whether the lamas should hold property and become involved in farming. The conservatives were able to quote the Vinaya to show that it was permissible for them to accept donations and to buy clothing and buildings with them (existing Russian law also allowed this), but not to occupy themselves with manual labour, for digging the ground would lead to the killing of numerous tiny insects and so would transgress the first precept: that against killing sentient beings. Zhambo Zhalayev added that to involve the lamas in communal agricultural activities would anyway signify the end of their 'happy life'. Dorzhiev, the realist, replied that under socialism it was not expedient to live by the labours of others, for the state would not give land to non-labouring elements.

*

Between 1926 and 1929 the controversy between the reformist and conservative lamas within the Buryat Buddhist church reached its deepest depths of acrimony. Two modern Buryat historians have written:

It is probably difficult for the reader to imagine the struggle between the reformers and the conservatives, so we will briefly explain that this was a struggle typical of church schisms. In its course the dirtiest methods were employed: mutual murders, diversions, profanation of temples and all possible mutual exposure of all different kinds of vices. Besides the publication of articles in the periodicals from one side or another, there were also many complaints of the most litigious kind of party, soviet and law enforcement organs.[10]

Standing in the centre of it all, Dorzhiev himself inevitably came in for special personal attack. In 1926, for instance, lamas of the Atsagat, Egituev and Kizhinga datsans composed a scurrilous tract entitled 'Some Words About Lamas', in which, among other things, they accused him of considering himself the Second Buddha, of propagating reformist ideas and of fomenting division between the sangha and its lay devotees. The tract was circulated to Chita, Verkhneudinsk and Moscow newspapers.[11]

Then in the summer of 1926 came an event of the highest significance, which further exacerbated the struggle. This was the nationalization of the Buryat datsans, which in effect meant the transfer of their administration into the hands of groups of lay devotees. The conservatives showed themselves utterly unable to handle this situation, whereas the reformers were actually able to lend a hand in the reorganization process and so to advance their cause still further. It was not easy for them, however, because many datsans had a preponderance of conservatives. In the Egituev Datsan, for instance, Dorzhiev had a hard struggle to save the monastery from actually being closed down due to the intransigence of the opposition. He was finally able to do so by setting up a special group named Tasak-Bugulmi.

After nationalization, the conservative lamas held religious assemblies in ad hoc places like barns, under awnings, granaries and private houses.[12]

*

In Leningrad – to which the old capital's name was changed from Petrograd after Lenin's death in 1924 – Dorzhiev's temple languished, still neither fully repaired nor fully functional as a religious shrine. Many of its problems were temporarily resolved, however, by an agreement that Dorzhiev signed in Moscow on 1 June 1926 with Bolgan-Chulgan, the representative of the Mongolian People's Republic in the USSR. This made the temple and its ancillary buildings the joint property of Tibet and Mongolia. The Mongolian plenipotentiary furthermore undertook to 'take upon himself the management, upkeep, repair and care of the said buildings'.

Bearing in mind that 'the function of the temple is to further cultural relations between the Buddhist East and the USSR', it was also agreed that the temple should be available to Buddhists wishing to study the teachings or to perform services and rites, and that there should also be accommodation for monks. The main dwelling house in the precincts, meanwhile, was to be put to the use of the Mongolian plenipotentiary, while the rest of the building would be at the disposal of Mongolian and Tibetan officials, and would also provide accommodation for Tibetans, Mongols, Kalmyks and Buryats visiting the city. Dorzhiev was designated manager of the temple complex.[13]

So, in effect, the temple became an official Tibeto-Mongolian Mission, which is what Dorzhiev afterwards called it. As such, it enjoyed a measure of diplomatic immunity, which was useful a few years later when the situation began to deteriorate and it could serve as a sanctuary for lamas from Buryatia and Kalmykia. The new arrangement also prompted the Mongolians to stump up funds from the treasury of the late Jebtsundamba Khutukhtu for the full restoration of the building, thereby enabling it to discharge its spiritual function again. Lamas then began studying and practising there again, and, until the early thirties, Mongolian and Tibetan lamas came every year in mid-August to celebrate religious rites; there is record too of a Cham dance being performed by lamas from the Aga Datsan in June 1930.[14]

The impression is therefore of the temple being relatively active during the late twenties. In addition to its religious and diplomatic activities, it provided accommodation for students and visitors as well as serving as a haven for scholars and a metropolitan headquarters for members of the Buddhist reform movement. It was also a Tibetan medical centre and dispensary; the two rabzhi (doctors of Tibetan medicine), Balzheer Zodboyev and Shchoyshee Dhaba Tamirgonov, based there won a certain fame in the locality for their ability to perform cures. Two small shops in the adjacent buildings moreover did trade in rice, spices, incense sticks, religious images and cult objects.[15]

Connections were also kept up with Stcherbatsky and the other Leningrad orientalists, and indeed it was one of Dorzhiev's aspirations to turn the temple into an important East-West cultural centre – 'culture' being something that the communists could tolerate, as opposed to religion, which they loathed. Having tried and failed to hold the Buddhist Exhibition of 1919 there, he planned another for 1926, to be grandly called the First International Buddhist Exhibition, and got Baradin to help him draft the main theses of his opening address. The main object of 'Buddhism as an Oriental Culture' is quite clearly to impress the authorities, for he not only stresses (or restresses) the cultural aspect of Buddhism but also its atheistical basis (actually non-theistical would be better: the Buddha maintained the proverbial noble silence on the matter of God and gods, or declared it to be a useless field of inquiry), its consonance with the discoveries of modern European science and its origins in Indian national culture (the communists were very anxious to ingratiate themselves with the Indians).

Having surveyed the enormous extent of the Buddhist penetration of Asia and argued that Buddhism brilliantly reflects the genius of the Indian people 'not only with respect to religon but, to an even greater degree, to philosophy, psychology, epistemology, general methodology, linguistics and the others arts and sciences', Dorzhiev's theses single out four key humanistic ideas originated by the Buddha that, he maintains, are highly relevant to modern European man:

7(i) Shakyamuni Buddha was the first in human history to proclaim the notion of the vital unity of life, not only of human life by itself but of all living creatures on earth and also in the other inhabited worlds of infinite space. The truth of this notion on the global level was scientifically proved by the great English scientist Darwin. Shakyamuni Buddha [moreover] taught that all living creatures have the same aspiration to life and life's benefits, and that service to living creatures is the highest duty of every man. He also taught that, among living creatures, man is the most able to attain the supreme good, this being his sole prerogative.

7(ii) Shakyamuni's second great notion is his atheistical teaching, [in which he] demonstrates that there is no creator god. Instead he advances the concept of an infinite chain of cause-and-effect [Skt pratiya-samutpada], from which it follows that the world is infinite in time and space, [that it] has neither beginning nor end, that nothing can arise from nothing, and that something existent cannot be utterly destroyed. Everything is in a constant state of flux – something that exists in a given moment ceases to be the same in the next moment. In Europe it became possible to speak of such things only after the development of the exact sciences, which emerged as the result of a continuous struggle waged against the theistic ideologies by the European peoples, who still are, on the whole, under the influence of Biblical-Christian theism.

7 (iii) The third great idea of Buddhism is the search for superior methodologies for [dealing with] the mental activity of man. In this sphere Buddhism contributed a great deal to the All-Indian theory of concentration and meditation, as well as to the self control of thought that is required for any human mental activity. To the same area . . . one should also attribute the most profound cognitive theories developed by the great Buddhist philosophers of India . . . These theories led to different methods of reasoning: to classical didactic formulae . . . as well as to examples of syllogisms . . . However, these theories are still unknown in civilized Europe but should certainly be inherited by world science.

7 (iv) Finally, the fourth great notion proclaimed by Shakyamuni Buddha is the relativity of all existence: the idea that there is no absolute, independent and unconditioned being . . . He taught that our sufferings and misfortunes

are produced by ignorance of this great universal law of being, and that in understanding this truth lie the meaning of life and our [attainment of] bliss. The Buddha's teaching on the relativity of all being has been proven in our own time by the relativity theory of the German physicist Einstein . . . The only difference is that the Buddha discovered his theory by the speculative method and made it the basis for his regular everyday world-meditation, whereas the German scientist came to his conclusions as an ordinary modern man of science [working] through scientific experimentation.[16]

Concluding, Dorzhiev points to the possibility of a genuine and egalitarian rapprochement between the peoples of this magnificent Indo-Buddhist culture and those of the scientific West.

Strangely, this is the only text that it has been possible to locate in which Dorzhiev deals with Buddhist philosophy (of which, of course, he was an accredited master), aside from the more homespun remarks that he infiltrates into his memoirs. Whether he in fact wrote philosophical works is uncertain: in Leningrad someone remarked that they had seen two volumes listed under his name in a Tibetan-language catalogue of such works in Ulan-Bator, but subsequent attempts to clarify this proved futile.

The main question, however, is to what extent these views are his own. We know Baradin helped him draft them, but the style of presentation is not at all Asiatic but almost entirely European, with sophisticated allusions to modern Western science and philosophy, so the temptation is to wonder whether the Leningrad orientalists may also have been directly or indirectly influential. Indeed, it is very possible to see, if one is looking for them, the lineaments of many of Stcherbatsky's principal preoccupations – with Buddhist logic, for instance, epistemology, psychology, theories of cognition and causality, and so forth. Not entirely coincidentally, perhaps, the great Sanskritist was working on his *Buddhist Logic* at this time and was also about to publish his *Conception of Buddhist Nirvana* (1927), which deals precisely with relativity as conceived within the Madhyamaka or Central Way school of Mahayana Buddhist philosophy: the school of Nagarjuna and his followers. The main body of *Conception* is a translation of selected portions of Nagarjuna's *Madhyamaka-Shastra*, which Stcherbatsky translates as *Treatise on Relativity*, alongside a translation of Chandrakirti's commentary. Dorzhiev, as a good Gelugpa geshé, would certainly have been well schooled in these works.

It would be as wrong to systematize Nagarjuna and Chandrakirti's views on relativity as it would those of the modern Western philosopher, Ludwig Wittgenstein. All are concerned with philosophy as therapy rather than discourse: that is, with helping the mind escape from the snares and traps created by its own thought processes by showing the ultimate absurdity of all propositions. In basic Buddhism we find the notion of pratityla-samutpada, dependent origination, which is in essence a theory of creation by causes; also the notion that the elements of the phenomenal world are real. Nagarjuna and his followers demolished all this. According to them, all that pratitya-samutpada can mean is that every object in the phenomenal world appears to exist only in relation to all the other objects, but without possessing any inherent reality. To see this is be to see shunyata, emptiness: the lack of inherent being or self-nature – a liberating experience that summarily terminates analytic thought and induces the blissful post-conceptual state of nirvana – the 'quiescence of Plurality' (Nagarjuna). In ultimate terms, though, it should not be thought that samsara and nirvana are separate: nirvana is samsara viewed sub specie aeternitatis.

It is beyond my competence to say in what way the relativity theory of Nagarjuna and Chandrakirti resembles that of Einstein, though it is currently fashionable to look for parallels between Buddhist philosophy and the findings of modern theoretical physics. Stcherbatsky sought parallels too, but mainly in the sphere of Western philosophy (Zeno, Bradley, Spinoza, Hegel); he nowhere mentions Einstein (or Darwin for that matter) in any of his principal works, which argues against the notion that he directly helped Dorzhiev to draft these theses, as is the fact that the drafting was done in Verkhneudinsk, not Leningrad. Even so, it is hard to discount completely the possibility that he and some of the other Leningrad orientalists did not exert at least a strong indirect influence.

As the projected Buddhist exhibition of 1926 never took place, this important speech was never delivered. Clearly, the backing of the Soviet authorities, to which Dorzhiev alludes in the final paragraph, was withdrawn at some stage. This reflects a change in the official attitude towards Buddhism that had taken place since 1919 – and is a portent of things to come.

*

While Dorzhiev was in Moscow in June 1926 for the signing of the agreement on the Leningrad temple with the Mongolian representative, he may have met Nikolai Roerich, who was secretly in the Russian capital at the same time with his wife Helena Ivanovna and son Yuri.

After first meeting Dorzhiev in the early days of the St Petersburg temple, Roerich had left Russia in 1916 and for a short time lived just across the border in Finland, from where he made periodic visits to the Russian capital. His attitude to the revolution seems to have been ambivalent: on one hand he welcomed a (theoretically) progressive new order, but he was also patrician by upbringing and temperament – a very special sort of person. So, while he temporarily headed a commission for the protection of art treasures, a post given him through the good offices of the writer Maxim Gorky, he finally left Russia around the turn of 1918 and headed for England, which he intended to use as a stepping-stone for India. Things did not work out to plan, however, and instead he was lured across the Atlantic to the land of milk and money. He spent the years 1920 to 1923 in the United States, where his guru-like appearance (Gurdjieffian shaven head, achetypal sage's beard) and grandiose ideas perhaps impressed people as much as his often striking paintings and theatrical designs, for he was able to attract support, financial and otherwise, both for himself and for the artistic projects that he spawned, like the Master Institute, the Corona Mundi and the Roerich Museum.

His wife accompanied him to the USA; also his sons Yuri (1902–60) and Svietoslav. Yuri had already begun his career in oriental scholarship by enrolling at the Indo-Iranian Department of the School of Oriental Studies at London University; in the USA, he enrolled at Harvard; later he went on to study in Paris. Svietoslav, on the other hand, followed in his father's footsteps and became an artist.

In 1923 the Roerich family visited India. Roerich then returned briefly to Europe and the United States, and in 1924, having mustered the necessary funds for an ambitious Central Asian expedition, he set off for Berlin to obtain official permission to enter Soviet territory. This does not appear to have been categorically given, but he nevertheless returned to India and organized a caravan. Finally in March 1925, with his family, acolytes and entourage, Roerich began a slow progress up through Ladakh and Chinese Sinkiang. They crossed the Soviet border near Chuguchak at the end of May 1926, and then proceeded directly to Moscow.

An air of great secrecy surrounds Roerich's Moscow venture of June 1926. Indeed all mention of it was suppressed in the accounts subsequently published by himself and by Yuri; but then there was always something mysterious about the man – Igor Stravinsky once remarked that 'He looked as though he ought to have been either a mystic or a spy'.[17] Perhaps he was a bit of both; many indeed thought so. He does, however, seem to have been cordially received by Soviet officials like Chicherin, whom he knew from his university days, and Lunacharsky.

According to one source, Roerich presented Lunacharsky with a number of paintings and discussed with him the possibility of holding an exhibition of his work in Moscow.[18] Another maintains that Roerich broached the notion of his returning to Russia and establishing the kind of artistic institutions he had set up in the USA; these proposals were sympathetically received, but no guarantee could be given of freedom to enter and exit the Soviet Union at will, which Roerich regarded as an essential precondition; in fact, Lunacharsky advised him to leave while he was still able to do so – advice which Roerich heeded.[19] At his meeting with Chicherin on 13 June, on the other hand, he handed the Commissar for Foreign Affairs a casket containing sacred Himalayan soil for Lenin's tomb and a message to the Soviet people from the Mahatmas, the Theosophical masters of wisdom who are reputed to live in a sequestered valley in Tibet. After a string of high-flown eulogies, the message concluded:

> You brought children the full power of the Cosmos. You saw the urgency of building new homes for the Common Good! We stopped an uprising in India when it was premature; likewise, we recognised the timelessness of your movement and send you all our help, in affirmation of the Unity of Asia![20]

Roerich obtained permission from Chicherin for his expedition to proceed through Soviet territory to Mongolia. They may also have discussed religion; in which case, if Roerich did indeed meet Dorzhiev either in Moscow at that time or later in Verkhneudinsk, he may have communicated the (misleading) impression that Chicherin was sympathetic to Buddhism.[21]

The indications are that at this point Roerich had come to believe in his highly imaginative way that Buddhism might flourish in Russia under the new order; indeed, that its advent might be a portent that the predictions concerning Shambhala were about to be realized – and if Lenin was not the Shambhala Kalki incarnate, he at least might be a 'fiery bodhisattva' come to pave the way for the inauguration of the new age. Certainly, a short while later, he was putting it about that Buddhism and communism were 'one thing'. His thinking was therefore not so far removed from that of Dorzhiev and associates. It would in any case seem quite likely that Roerich, through the underground channels of communication that Russians seem to be able to keep open even during the most difficult of times, would have been aware of what they were thinking and doing.

Having left Moscow, Roerich made a side trip to the Altai region, after which his expedition proceeded eastwards via Omsk to Irkutsk and Verkhneudinsk, where it turned southwards for Mongolia. Here a politically pragmatic line was continuing, for the local communists still found themselves obliged to work with class enemies like the lamas and the nobility, and to countenance a measure of foreign capitalist activity; a reform movement similar to that led by Dorzhiev and his friends was also active. It was only after 1928, guided by the steel hand of the Comintern, that a hard Marxist-Leninist line was adopted.

During the few months that he was in Urga, Roerich spent much time with Zhamtsarano, who was then head of the Mongolian Scientific Committee. They would certainly have spent many absorbing hours discussing Buddhism, Pan-Buddhism, Shambhala, the coming of Maitreya and other such fascinating topics. Later, the expedition crossed Mongolia by the classic route through Yum-beise Khuree, visiting en route the lair of the recently murdered Ja-Lama in the Gobi. Having passed through An-hsi, it then proceeded across the Tsaidam region to the Tibetan uplands, where it was delayed in often bitterly cold conditions for many months, awaiting permission to proceed to Lhasa. This was finally denied, but the expedition was allowed to cross Tibet by a circuitous route that took it to the west of the holy city, and to make its exit through Sikkim in 1928. There is a story that while in Tibet Roerich masqueraded as the 'Prince of Shambhala', and wore a suitably sumptuous suit of oriental-style clothing that he had had run up in Urga for the purpose.

In 1929, Roerich promulgated the Roerich Banner of Peace and the Peace Pact, which were concerned with the protection of cultural treasures during wartime. Again, he managed to attract a fair amount of support in high places, for in 1935 the Roerich Pact was signed at the White House by delegates from various American countries, in the presence of President F. D. Roosevelt. Since about 1929 Roerich had also been the guru of Roosevelt's Secretary of Agriculture, Henry Wallace, whose department financed his second expedition to Central Asia in 1934. Officially this was to search for drought-resistant grasses; in fact Roerich was more preoccupied with auguries that the new age of enlightenment and universal brotherhood was at hand. Needless to say, Wallace's involvement with what at the time would commonly be regarded as screwball ideas, though later repudiated, caused a great furore when news of it was eventually leaked in the press in 1948, and his career was effectively finished.

Roerich, on the other hand, still awaiting the realization of his visions, died in 1947 in Kulu in the Himalayan foothills of northern India, which had been his base for many years. There, at Urusvati, Roerich had in 1930 set up his Himalayan Research Institute, where his son Yuri, as director, conducted his scholarly and teaching activities until his eventual return to the land of his forefathers in 1957.

*

The First All-Russian Buddhist Congress was held in Moscow between 20 and 29 January 1927. One piece of encouraging news that the congress received during its session was that an Institute of Buddhist Culture – the first such scholarly foundation in the West – was to be created under the auspices of the Academy of Sciences and that Stcherbatsky was to be its director. The presidium of the academy was promptly telegraphed:

> The first All Union Buddhist Council expresses profound gratitude to the Academy and to orientalists Stcherbatsky, Ol'denburg and Vladimirtsov for their initiative in creating the Institute of Buddhist Studies and cherish the hope that the study of Buddhism will signify a beginning of the right understanding of the latter by the Western cultural world and be a pledge of the future flourishing of our most precious religion.[22]

The news would no doubt have particularly gratified Dorzhiev, who, as we have seen, cherished hopes of East-West cultural cross fertilization through Buddhism. The congress also sent a message of devotion to the Dalai Lama.[23]

*

In 1928, a major debate was held in Verkhneudinsk between Buddhists and Bolshevik anti-religionists. Dorzhiev took part along with Baradin and others, and was probably more adept than most of his co-religionists, being able, as Walter Kolarz says, to 'quote in his support various learned Soviet authorities'.[24] He had also been schooled in Buddhist logic and debate as part of his geshé training.

The debate in Verkhneudinsk was not, however, the kind of stylized affair conducted according to time-honoured rules and procedures as would have taken place in the hallowed courtyards of Gomang College. The anti-religionists waded in forcefully, blasting the Buddhists with raw Marxist-Leninist rhetoric, and it seems likely that proceedings would have become heated or even disorderly, for Dorzhiev afterwards complained that both he and his religion had been insulted.[25]

In the same year, 1928, the Leningrad atheistical journal, *Antireligioznik*, announced the disturbing news that the orientalist, Vladimirtsov, had been converted to Buddhism: 'In the dimly-lit pagoda on Novaya Derevnya, this scholarly academician took Buddhist vows, for which he received a diploma from the Dalai Lama in Lhasa, to the accompaniment of howling lamas and the wild music of ritual instruments'.[26]

*

Writing from Moscow on 12 May 1928, Dorzhiev informed G. V. Chicherin about a high lama named Danzan Norboyev, who was regarded as an incarnation of Ganzhirva-Gegen. As 'Ganzhirva' is the Buryat-Mongol equivalent of the Tibetan 'Kangyur', the local canon of Buddhist scriptures, the title signifies one who knows this whole body of works by heart and can bestow initiations.

The tradition of Ganzhirva-Gegen was associated with the Tsugol Datsan in Trans-Baikalia. It was there that the fourth khubilgan, a Mongol, predicted his next incarnation would take place. Accordingly, when he died, the lamas of Tsugol sent representatives to Tibet to consult the Dalai Lama and receive directions. The fifth incarnation was duly found in the Buryat Sumayev family in 1854. He spent many years studying abroad but returned to Trans-Baikalia in 1877, entered the Tsugol Datsan as a gelong and was quickly made abbot; he died in 1887. Norboyev was discovered as the next, the sixth, khubilgan and confirmed by the Dalai Lama and Agvan Dorzhiev in Urga in 1905, when on his way to Labrang. As the climate of Amdo did not suit him, he returned to his homeland in 1907, but two years later followed the Dalai Lama to Tibet via Peking and Kum-Bum in order to continue his spiritual education. He gained a lharamba geshé degree in Lhasa in 1916, and in 1918 returned to Trans-Baikalia with the Dalai Lama's blessings and a document instructing him to dedicate himself completely to the benefit of others and to the propagation of Buddhism in his homeland, and wherever else he might find himself. He then lived at the Tsugol Datsan until 1929.[27] In 1922, his position was discussed by the First All-Buryat Buddhist Congress, particularly what should be done about his property and how to protect him from people of 'vicious behaviour' in his entourage.[28]

Dorzhiev wrote that it was the Dalai Lama's wish that Norboyev come to Leningrad to learn Russian, and he begged Chicherin to help make this possible. He also expressed the hope that Norboyev would assist the cause of Russo-Tibetan friendship and, in view of his advancing old age, soon replace him as the representative of Tibet.

For the next few years Norboyev indeed effectively acted as Dorzhiev's deputy, co-ordinating the affairs of the Tibet-Mongolia Mission and, according to one source, serving as an unofficial spiritual representative of the Dalai Lama (Dorzhiev being the diplomatic representative).

*

During the years up to 1929, thanks largely to the efforts of Dorzhiev and his friends, Buddhism had enjoyed a special status among the religions of the Soviet Union. True, it had been subjected to a certain amount of anti-religious propaganda that had undoubtedly had a deleterious effect: in particular, many young men were induced to feel that the life of a Buddhist monk was not a socially very useful or laudable one, and this had a considerable effect on the lama population – by 1929 there were under 7,000 as opposed to 16,000 at the height of the recent renaissance. Datsans also began to be heavily taxed and penalized in petty ways, like being denied access to supplies of building materials (in practice this was easily circumvented). But still, Buddhism had been mercifully spared the awful pogroms wreaked upon Orthodox Christianity.

All this was to change drastically in 1928/9. Having exiled Trotsky and gained ascendancy over Bukharin and other rivals, Stalin at last had the reins of the Russian tarantass firmly in his hands and decided, for reasons best know to himself, to release the hell hounds of class war once again. What lay ahead for the Buddhists of the Soviet Union was clearly announced in the party press, which began to publish diatribes in which the dangerous reformist (or neo-Buddhist) notions of Dorzhiev and his friends were singled out for special attack. Buddhist atheism had nothing at all to do with militant atheism based on the Marxist appraisal of the laws of nature and society, it was grimly declared, while Stalin himself denounced 'the absurd theory of the identity of the Communist and Buddhist doctrines'.[29] Lamas meanwhile were stigmatized as 'sworn enemies of socialist reconstruction', and datsans as 'strongholds of the old regime', which made it inevitable that they would soon be closed: the first, the Alar (founded 1814), a small monastic house in Irkutsk province accommodating less than a dozen lamas, was in fact closed in 1929.

The regime's anti-Buddhist operation in the BMASSR was initially spearheaded by the Society of the Militant Godless, the anti-religious arm of the party, which established a local branch in 1929. Its cadres attempted to discredit Buddhism and to undermine the authority of the lamas by creating a negative image of them as money-grubbers, reactionaries and saboteurs. They were lampooned in the press and even in little plays staged in clubs. The anti-religionists also attempted to disrupt festivals and to bring about the formal closure of the datsans and Tibetan medical schools.

*

In January 1929, *Buryat-Mongolskaya Pravda* informed its readers that it had received a cable from Dorzhiev confirming that he would be taking up the challenge of the Militant Godless to participate in a debate scheduled to take place in Verkhneudinsk in late February on the subject of the 'class essence of religion'. He was at the time in Berlin, having gone to Germany to organize the casting in bronze of the great Buddha-rupa in the main shrine of the Leningrad temple at a foundry in Hamburg (it had hitherto been made of alabaster). Despite his previous unhappy experiences, he made good his promise and took part in the debate, which was duly reported in the same newspaper.[30]

*

Dorzhiev was now, at seventy-five, an old, ill and disillusioned man. For most of his life he had worked tirelessly for the cause of Buddhism, yet all his achievements seemed to be slipping away like sand between his wizened fingers. His complaints to the authorities fell on deaf ears; indeed, far from getting better, matters were taking a disturbing turn for the worse, and the current anti-religious drive not only descredited his reform initiative and all his efforts to reconcile Buddhism and Bolshevism, but de facto gave the victory to his conservative opponents. As for his diplomatic services, since world revolution had been officially supplanted by Stalin's doctrine of 'socialism in one country', they hardly counted for much. Clearly his star was waning.

It is completely improbable, however, as was later alleged by his detractors, that he abandoned all notion of reform in favour of anti-Soviet counter-revolutionary activity; rather, he is more likely to have hoped that the lay devotees themselves would carry on the struggle to save Buddhism at the grass-roots level. But it must have been with a heavy heart and a sense of great apprehension – perhaps even of impending cataclysm – that, after in August blessing the spot where the lamas of the Aga Datsan planned to erect a Kalachakra suburgan (stupa), he left Buryatia to pay another visit to Leningrad. Perhaps *in extremis* he hoped that by speaking directly to officials there he could salvage something; Danzan Norboyev went with him.

CHAPTER NINETEEN

The Destruction of Buddhism in the USSR and the Death of Agvan Dorzhiev 1930 – 1938

What Stalin did in the 1930s was to abandon the soft approach of Lenin's New Economic Policy for something like the hard line of War Communism. Centralized control and full collectivization again became the order of the day, whether the people agreed or not, and a remorseless drive was set in motion to transform industry and agriculture and to push them to ever higher levels of productivity. It was hoped in this way that the Soviet economy would quickly catch up with those of the decadent bourgeois democracies of the West. There was also a power-political sub-text: to forge the economic muscle to withstand blockade if the USSR ever again found itself encircled by hostile powers; also to create the necessary armaments industry to secure its defence from actual attack.

The propaganda of the period portrayed Stalin not only as wise patriarchal leader but as great builder and, though admittedly the statistics were cooked, Soviet industry undeniably made amazing leaps forward. But the achievements of the First Five-Year Plan (1928–32) and its successors, like the construction of the Magnitogorsk Metallurgical plant in the southern Urals and the great hydro-electric plant (Europe's largest) on the Dneiper, were bought at great cost in human terms. In the atmosphere of escalating state pressure and paranoia that Stalin orchestrated with the aid of the GPU (later renamed NKVD), failure to meet sometimes impossibly high production targets, not to mention any upset or disaster, laid managers, workers, designers – whoever – vulnerable to charges of wrecking and sabotage. At the same time, class and ideological enemies were persecuted and/or liquidated. In his ruthless drive to collectivize agriculture, for instance, Stalin singled out the more prosperous peasantry as his ideological bête noir. 'Liquidate the kulaks,' he declared; but all the peasantry, rich and poor, were opposed to collectivization and all suffered both in the brutal dispossession process that accompanied it and the terrible famines that followed.

*

Western intellectuals, who were sensitive to the deficiencies of capitalism and so had high hopes that the Soviet Union would evolve something better, were encouraged by the positive propaganda, and were often as a consequence prepared to overlook or explain away the dark side of the communist utopia. In performing radical surgery, one argument ran, one has to be prepared to shed a little blood.

One such positive spirit was G. D. R. Phillips, who in 1943 published a small book in English on the Buryats. Writing with all the enthusiasm of the convert, Phillips waxed rhapsodic about the socialist achievements he found in abundance in Ulan-Udé ('Red Udé'), as Verkhneudinsk was renamed in 1934. Giant factories had been built – a great railway repair works; a meat combinat that 'uses everything except the beasts's last breath'; a mechanized glass factory; a milling combinat; two mechanized bakeries. Large numbers of Buryats had poured into the city to work in these delightful places.[1] One day Phillips caught sight of a group of them: healthy and happy young men and women who, having completely forsaken their old nomadic ways, now wore Western-style clothing. They stopped at a kiosk to buy an ice-cream while they waited for a bus. Nearby stood some dirty and decrepit wooden houses of the old sort; on the other side, however, shone a clean white concrete block with gleaming glass windows – a resplendent symbol of the new Ulan-Udé that was endowed with all the assets of modern science and culture: schools, hospitals and clinics, clubs, theatres, cinemas, radio and a public library where, now that illiteracy was being overcome, 'one could see young Buryats taking from the shelves books in Russian or Buryat on agronomy, mathematics, genetics, sociology, geography, *Othello* in Russian or Buryat; other works of Shakespeare, Dickens and Galsworthy in Russian'.[2] The streets of this socialist elysium, meanwhile, were by day merry with motor traffic and illuminated at night by the wonder of electric light.

In the rural areas efforts were under way to facilitate the 'transition to more cultural forms of life' – that is, to settle the nomads and semi-nomads, to break up old clan relationships and to collectivize the land. The basic aim here was to neutralize the class divisions and abuses that had been re-established during the era of the New Economic Policy. Phillips maintains that mistakes were made during the collectivization process: instead of urging the local peasantry to displace the rich men of the ulus encampment and village themselves, some Buryat Bolsheviks used what Stalin called the 'cavalry raid': 'The "propagandist" called a meeting of the ulus or village, slammed his revolver on the table and announced that the village or ulus was now "collectivised".'[3] But such mistakes were really the work of 'enemies within the Party and Soviet Apparatus' (the party leadership itself was, of course, infallible), and anyway they did not much affect the process, for the collectivized rural population rose from 4.2 per cent in 1929 to 19.5 per cent in 1930 and stood at over 60 per cent by 1932 – and this was mostly achieved, according to Phillips, by positive inducement rather than coercion. When those still attached to the old nomadic ways saw with their own eyes how good things were on the collective farms – when they saw the tax relief benefits, the housing subsidies and the health care facilities, not to mention the bright new tractors, lorries, combine harvesters and other machines, and the technical advice available from agronomists, veterinary surgeons and other experts – they could only ask, 'Why should I not join the collective . . . ?' They could even have a little land and a few animals of their own. Phillips concludes:

> Economically, settlement for the nomads meant immediate reduction in the winter death-roll [sic] of animals. Culturally, it meant that the Buryats themselves learnt the use of soap, of newspapers, of clubs, of music, in that order.[4]

*

In 1930 the campaign against religion was initially stepped up in Buryatia. In February, for instance, measures were taken against the New Year festival, Tsagaansar, and subsequently a decision was made to close twenty datsans within one month. These zealous efforts were ultimately counter-productive, however: local protest thwarted the closing of the datsans, and the Buryat branch of the Militant Godless was disbanded – one source even maintains that many Buddhists had joined its ranks, declaring that they were atheists![5] However, the attacks did not by any means stop.

In the same year, the pioneer Tibetan traveller, Gombozhab Tsybikov, passed peacefully away in his native Aga steppe. He had spent the last years of his life simply: getting up early and walking in the countryside with the local herdsmen. His final illness came on suddenly. 'I know that I will die,' he told his wife when she came to see him in the Aga hospital, 'but the Soviet Government will, I think, preserve my manuscripts and books.' He then asked for a clock to be put at the head of his death-bed and bravely awaited his final hour.[6]

Agvan Dorzhiev returned to the same area (the Aga Steppe) for a

Kalachakra Festival that was held in May 1930 at the Aga Datsan, the largest Buddhist foundation in the region, built between 1811 and 1816 on the lower reaches of the Aga river. In those days it consisted of a central dukhang and six smaller ones, four of which were devoted to philosophical, medical, tantric and Kalachakra studies; of the remainder, one housed a gigantic brass image of Maidari (Maitreya, the Coming Buddha) and the other, the Temple of Amitabha, two models (devazhin) of the Tushita and Sukhavati heavens.[7] It also seems to have been one of the strongholds of the reform movement, and one source maintains that Dorzhiev built an 'obnovlenchesky dugan' (reformist temple) there.[8]

As the Kalachakra stupa had now been completed, Dorzhiev was able to consecrate it himself besides giving Kalachakra initiations to a group of Aginsky lamas, whom he then invited to return to Leningrad with him in order to receive commentarial teachings on Kalachakra. In order to obtain the necessary authorizations to travel, he registered them as a troupe of Mongolian Cham dancers. Most of them stayed in the old capital for about a month before returning home, during which time, besides their studies, they did in fact put on a performance of a Kalachakra Cham dance. A few did elect to stay on, however.[9]

*

The Aga Datsan visit was Dorzhiev's last to Trans-Baikalia for some years. In 1931 he was 'invited' to Moscow by Narkomindel and 'shown' that he was 'exceeding the limits set for diplomatists' by 'stirring up the population of Buryatia against the Soviet state'.[10] It was then 'proposed' that he take up a 'steady place of residence' in Leningrad. In other words, he was being politely placed in a kind of internal exile. Clearly he had no option but to accede.

For the next few years he shared a pleasant wooden house in Ol'gino, just beyond the outer suburbs of Leningrad, with Norboyev. It can be reached by following Primorsky Prospekt westwards past the Buddhist temple. For a few kilometres the road runs through the marshlands of dark water and rustling sedge that flank the northern shore of the Gulf of Finland; then it turns inland. Ol'gino itself is a quiet, dusty village of wooden houses, all individually different but rather run down now, set among the obligatory birches. The house that Dorzhiev shared with Danzan Norboyev, No. 7 Konolakhtinskaya Prospekt, had been built in 1908 by a Finnish jeweller named Andrey Seppenem; he had also built a laundry and workshop in the garden.[11] It is unclear whether the two-storey building that now stands on the site is this original one, though it may well be.

There is little evidence of how Dorzhiev passed his time at Ol'gino. He had visitors, no doubt, and he still kept in touch with what was going on in monastic circles in Buryatia – and, one would assume, in Kalmykia too. But one would hope that he also at last enjoyed periods of relative tranquillity when he could apply himself to his Buddhist practices and so prepared himself for death. After all, he was now a very old man and could only get about with the aid of sticks.

He also continued to write letters of protest to Narkomindel – and quite often in blunt terms – about what was happening to Buddhism in the Soviet Union. Not only did these have no effect but, now that his amazing run of good luck with the authorities was well and truly over, they almost certainly tended to harden the official attitude towards him, and in fact in 1934, a first serious move against him was made. A certain 'O. N.', with whom he had had vague contacts the previous year, alleged to the GPU that under the guise of organizing the Lamaist reform movement he was in fact creating a counter-revolutionary organization. Some forty other people were named at the same time, including D. Sampilon, E. D. Rinchino, Danzan Norboyev, and academics like Stcherbatsky, Ol'denburg, Vostrikov and Obermiller – who were alleged to be part of his intelligence network. O.N. also alleged that in 1924 Dorzhiev had sent a letter to a Tibetan lama at the Tsugol Datsan named Donir Lama, whom he used as a courier. The contents of the letter were not known to O. N. But this did not prevent him from forming the opinion that they were intelligence materials. This imaginitive man also denounced Dorzhiev and his associates as Japanese agents and dangerous Pan-Mongolists.

Fortunately, in the climate of 1934 such flimsy evidence was not sufficient to bring the full machinery of state repression down upon Dorzhiev, so after being held in custody for twenty days he was released. The 'evidence' of O. N. was not, however, consigned to the waste paper basket where it belonged: ominously, it was filed for future use.[12]

*

Clearly Dorzhiev's main reason for choosing to live in Ol'gino was its proximity to the Buddhist temple, where, despite the growing atmosphere of threat, a number of lamas were still living. Indeed, strange as it may seem, many lamas actually sought sanctuary in the city from the persecutions that were visited upon them in the outlying provinces at this time. A very few, like the Buryat lama, Losang Tanpa'i Nyima, were actually officials of the temple and therefore qualified for support; others sought employment in the vicinity, some as gardeners in the parks on nearby Yelagin Island.

A curious little cameo of how the temple appeared to outsiders at this period appears in the novel, *Ospolneniye Zhelanii ('The Fulfilment of Wishes')*, by V. A. Kaverin:

> A strange building appeared on the right-hand side with gilded plates on its pediment.
>
> 'It's a Buddhist temple,' said Trubachevsky.
>
> They peeped in at the gates. There was no one around. The doorway, hidden behind four angled pillars, was open. It was dark inside and probably cool.
>
> 'They'll send us away, won't they?'
>
> 'Of course not.'
>
> The big Buddha was sitting cross-legged in a niche with an enigmatic smile on his lips. He was young, about seventeen years of age, delicately pink, with eyes the colour of lapis lazuli. Bowls filled with rice and sugar had been placed before him. Light played on the coulmns of coloured brocade.
>
> 'He is handsome,' Mashenka whispered under her breath.
>
> 'They brought him from Hamburg. He was manufactured there.'
>
> She looked at him with distrust. 'Was he?'
>
> 'Upon my word.'
>
> Huge paintings rising to the ceiling hung against the walls in the four corners of the temple. Fantastic spirits of good and evil were depicted on them. Wrathful in appearance, they wore bizarre oriental robes reminiscent of the caftans of the Russian boyars of old.[13]

Spiritual life went on in the temple in the form of teaching, study, debate and practice; but ceremonies came to an end when in December 1933 the last was held to honour the death of Dorzhiev's old protégé, the Thirteenth Dalai Lama. This must not only have been a great personal loss but must also have dealt a severe blow to the old lama's diplomatic prestige and status, for these rested precisely upon this strong personal connection. Though he appears to have formally continued to act as the representative of Tibet, it is hard to know how seriously he was taken after 1933.

There is no doubt, notwithstanding the various sinister Narkomindel schemes in which he became embroiled, that Dorzhiev always held the Dalai Lama personally in high regard. In his memoirs, he talks of him as a kind of spiritual sun, casting the rays of his benign influence across the whole of Asia – 'Such activity cannot be understood by the minds of [ordinary] people.'[14] An era was over.

*

In Buryatia, one datsan after another was meanwhile being shut down 'on the popular request of the toiling masses'. The Gusinoye Ozero

Datsan closed in 1930, the Tsongol in 1931, the Kirmen in 1932 – and so it went on. By 1935, the Buryat party secretary could report to the Kremlin that six datsans had been closed and twelve wound up 'voluntarily' by the lamas themselves; the total number of lamas had at the same time been reduced to 900 – and it was to continue to fall.

The main brunt of the pogrom came after December 1934, however, when a general reign of terror was unleashed by Stalin following the murder of Sergey Mironovich Kirov, the popular Leningrad party boss. In Leningrad itself a number of lamas at the Buddhist temple were arrested in May 1935 and, having been condemned as 'socially dangerous elements', were sentenced to terms of three to five years in hard labour camps. The Leningrad branch of the KGB has released a listing of six.[15]

Danzan Norboyev also passed away in mysterious circumstances in August of the same year. When asked, the KGB admitted that his name was mentioned in records of 'the investigatory processes of Buryats living in Leningrad in 1930–40 and connected with Buddhist crimes', and that he was described as the 'closest colleague and representative of Agvan Dorzhiev'; but beyond the fact that he did die in 1935, 'further information is not available'.[16]

*

Most of the Buryat Datsans were closed during the Second Five-Year Plan (1933–37). A few were then turned over to utilitarian purposes but many were totally razed to the ground along with their precious libraries and collections of Buddhist artefacts. The actual destruction was not in the main carried out by imported heavies but, as in Tibet during the Cultural Revolution (1966–76), by local people, particularly young people, who found it all great fun.

Particularly poignant was the destruction of the Aga Datsan, once a great centre of Buddhist philosophical study and xylographic printing, which was closed in 1934 and most of its lamas arrested and sent to concentration camps in Turukhansk Krai. Several months later *The Son of Genghis Khan* was filmed in the locality:

> One episode in the film was a procession of lamas bearing the sacred writings, for which the 108-volume *Gandzhur* [Kanjur] from the monastery library was used. After the scene had been shot and the books were no longer needed, they were thrown into a ditch at the far side of the road and were lost. Soon afterwards, on the orders of the Special Far Eastern Army, work was begun on strengthening the area from the military point of view, and the datsan was marked for destruction. The Academy of Sciences of the USSR contacted Marshall Blücher, at the time

in command of the Far Eastern Army, and requested him to preserve the library and the religious vessels. Blücher promised to co-operate, but asked the Academy to send representatives as soon as possible to receive these objects. This was in 1935. Owing to a delay in obtaining passes from the NKVD, it was the summer of 1938 before the expedition could be sent. All that was collected were pitiful relics of what was once an outstanding Tibetan-Mongolian library. Icons, statues of the Buddha and all the utensils had long been scrapped. Thus, in the Agin [sic] datsan alone many objects of great cultural value which could have made a fine museum of Buddhist culture were destroyed.[17]

Shocked at such gross vandalism, the author of these words, the scholar Nikolai Poppe, was prompted to propose to the local party leadership that steps be taken to preserve at least one datsan as a monument-cum-museum and to hand over the contents of any others that might be closed to the Academy of Sciences. The last request was granted; as for the former, M. N. Yerbanov, the local political boss, replied: 'If we listened to you, professor, you would next be demanding that the lamas be preserved for you. This, however, is not in my power, since the NKVD has taken on the task of preserving the lamas in places not so remote.'

The prison camps to which the lamas were sent, though often largely unguarded, lacked proper food, water and medical facilities, and many soon died from malnutrition, abuse and/or disease. By 1936, Vyacheslav Mikhailovich Molotov could rejoice in the liquidation of the 'parasitical lama class' as one of the achievements of Soviet policy in the BMASSR.[18]

*

The same was happening in Kalmykia. One or both of Dorzhiev's choira was closed in 1932, while the monasteries were again sometimes put to secular uses, but mostly razed to the ground along with their contents. Indeed, sacred Buddhist texts and artefacts were so thoroughly destroyed or vandalized that, when an anti-religious museum was set up in Stepnoi (now Elista), hardly anything could be found to exhibit there. By 1940 nothing remained of Kalmyk monasteries or lamas.[19]

It was a similar story in Mongolia, where Khorloin Choibalsang (1895–1952), the local Stalin replica, urged and assisted by Moscow, set about eradicating the local Buddhist church. Nearly all the monasteries were destroyed and most of the lamas shot. Now in the 1990s, the vast killing fields where they were buried are disgorging their bleached skulls, each with a neat hole in the top of the head. According to one of their surviving executioners, who claims to have dispatched over fifteen thousand, they were simply lined up on the edges of open graves, into which they fell when they were shot.

Both the Soviet and the Mongolian authorities maintained that Buddhist lamas were in league with the Japanese, who were then conducting their brutal imperialistic expansion in Asia. Having over-run Manchuria and established the puppet state of Manchukuo, they began rapidly to extend their power in China itself. They also had designs in Mongolia, and to this end attempted to exploit Mongolian nationalism, which of course was inextricably bound up with Buddhism.

According to our fellow-travelling friend G. D. R. Phillips, Buryat lamas were involved in spreading propaganda in support of a Japanese invasion of the Soviet Union and in a variety of sinister plots. A group in one aimak, for instance, was shown to have been planning to blow up bridges. In a district near the frontier, meanwhile, another group was conspiring to get its own placemen voted onto the local soviet. One of the conspirators, a lama named Gurzhap Abushev, arrived one day at the collective meat-market in Ulan-Udé, ostensibly to sell meat; in reality he was there to rendezvous with a spy named Sanzhidayev, who sold him lost and spoilt party membership cards supplied by a 'spying organization'. 'Both these men were arrested in the act of transaction,' Phillips says; 'one Party card had been sold for 800 roubles.'[20]

Phillips furthermore maintains that in 1935–36, during rituals performed in the datsans of Khorinsk aimak to hasten the intervention of the King of Shambhala, the lamas produced pictures in which the armies of Shambhala were shown emerging from a rising sun – 'an indication of Japan'.

While it is certainly true that the Japanese did try to exploit the Shambhala legends for their own ends, and that they did try to recruit Mongol lamas as agents, it is unclear to what extent the lamas in Buryatia were inveigled into their intrigues – or indeed whether the Soviet authorities seriously believed they were. One oral source maintains that the datsans did become centres of anti-Soviet dissent, that supplies of arms were kept in them and that they were used as bases for emigration out of the USSR; but this quite probably arose from local feeling and had little to do with the Japanese.

It is likely, then, that the Japanese conspiracy connection was first and foremost an excuse for doing what the Soviet authorities were already set upon doing: destroying the lamas and the monasteries. In any case, this was a time when spies and wreckers were being discovered everywhere, even among outwardly impeccable communists. Conspiracies were therefore evidence of the intense paranoia of the moment rather than of actual misdeeds.

The trusting Phillips naively (and wrongly) denies that the authorities took any action against the Buryat lamas; in fact he maintains that they received support in high places – an oblique reference to M. N. Yerbanov, the local party boss, and his colleagues, who were feted in Moscow in January 1936 and then, in the capricious style of the times, accused less than a year later of almost every dark deviation in the Soviet index of infamy; from economic inefficiency to going soft on Buddhism and colluding with the black fascist samurai of Japan. After brief trials, they were speedily executed in October 1937.

Many Old Bolsheviks – that is, the first wave of communist leaders – met with the same fate after having been put on show trial during the terrible purges of this period. Bukharin, Zinov'ev and Kamenev were shot, as were the early Narkomindel officials, Karakhan and Berlin (Chicherin would probably have been shot had he not died of natural causes in 1936). The same fate also befell the Kalmyk Bolshevik, Anton Amur-Sanan. Indeed, a twilight pall of death lay across the Soviet Union: people did not sleep for fear of the midnight knock upon the door; no one was safe, not even the highest officials; and if death spared them, there was still the living death of the prison and labour camps that proliferated like a fungal growth across the land.

By the late thirties, the whole Soviet Union had became one vast Gulag in which all the citizens were slaves of the state, controlled by state terror.

*

During this dark period Agvan Dorzhiev suffered declining health. In 1935 he tried to get permission to visit a health resort on the Black Sea that was frequented by academicians of the Oriental Institute. A year later he felt it necessary to make provision for the Leningrad temple by drawing up his last will and testament. This was written in the form of a letter to his 'near relative' Sandzhe Dantsykovich Dylykov, born in 1912 in Khara-Shibir, who at the time was a post-graduate student at the Oriental Institute specializing in Mongolian studies. Dated Ol'gino, 1 September 1936, the will lays down:

> The Tibetan Government and the Supreme Ruler of Tibet, the Dalai Lama, in 1901 officially appointed me, Khambo Agvan Dorzhiev, to serve as the Plenipotentiary Representative of Tibet at the Government of Great Russia, and after the Revolution of 1917 I continued to work as a diplomatic official at the Government of the Union of Soviet Republics.

My forty-year-long activity as a statesman was directed towards the establishment of better relations between Tibet and Great Russia – the USSR; however, due to the extremely tense situation in the Far East and Europe during the last years and subsequently to the international situation of Tibet, I failed to accomplish much to further the actual independence of the Great Tibetan People, [despite] taking advantage of the assistance of the Great Soviet Union.

Now, being anxious about the future fate of the Buddhist Temple in Leningrad and the houses attached to it, as well as about the property and funds that are intended for dispatch to Tibet, including my own private property on the territory of the USSR – in the town of Ol'gino in the Leningrad area, [and] in the Buryat-Mongol and Kalmyk republics – I feel obliged to appoint you, Sandzhe Dantsykovich Dylykov, as my near relative enjoying my full confidence, [to be] my successor in the affairs of the Tibet-Mongolian Mission and the sole heir to all my property, both moveable and immovable.

As regards my Mission and the future prospects for its activities, I authorize and oblige you, S. D. Dylykov, to enter into negotiations with the NKID [People's Commissariat for Foreign Affairs] [of the] USSR, requesting assistance and protection until the arrival of an authorized representative of Tibet. I am certain in advance that Narkomindel [i.e., the NKID] [of the] USSR will adopt a sympathetic attitude towards you, and hope that after my decease it will not allow any interference from whomsoever in the affairs of the Tibet-Mongolian Mission and/or the management of my property by anyone other than yourself, who is my trustee and official representative to the NKID USSR.

Finally, I am confident that the NKID USSR [will] create all the necessary conditions to allow you to fulfil your duties after my decease in relation to the possession, management and usage of my private property, moveable and immoveable, as you deem fit, as well as with regard to the co-ordination of the affairs of the Tibet-Mongolian Mission, the safe-keeping of the Buddhist Temple and adjacent houses, and the care of the funds intended for dispatch to Tibet, until the arrival of an official representative from Tibet or else the promulgation of a special decree by the Soviet Government for the purpose of equipping an expedition to Tibet, in which you, Sandzhe Dantsykovich Dylykov, must participate.

This letter, signed and sealed by myself with the seal given to me by the Supreme Ruler of Tibet, the Dalai Lama, is officially my last will; it comes into effect immediately upon being signed by myself.

Two copies of this will have been made in the Russian language, one for S. D. Dylykov, the other for the Commissariat of Foreign Affairs of the USSR.[21]

Shortly afterwards, in January 1937, the 85-year-old Agvan Dorzhiev left Leningrad for Ulan-Udé. He stated that he wished to meet Buryat lamas, but other sources suggest that he may have had it in mind to spend the Tsagaansar (new year) celebrations with his relatives in

Buryatia; these would have taken place in mid-February, according to the Tibetan calendar. It is quite likely too that, sensing that the end was drawing near – both his own end and that of Buddhism in Soviet Russia – he wanted to spend his final days with his family, as was customary. He was accompanied by his cook, Dugar Zhimbiev, a lama of the Atsagat Datsan; his relative Sandzhe Dylykov saw him off at the station.

*

One night in August 1937 is still remembered by Russian Buddhists. Black Marias drove up to the house next to the Leningrad temple where the few remaining lamas were still living. NKVD officers got out and banged on the door. Having been admitted, they presented their warrants. Rooms were then searched and afterwards the lamas were driven down to the NKVD headquarters on Liteinyi Prospekt – the new yellow-ochre KGB building stands on the site today, its many aerials spiking the sky. They were then quickly tried in camera before NKVD troikas or three-man tribunals. None of the usual proprieties of justice were honoured. They were all simply sentenced to death and taken down into the sound-proofed cellars of the building the same night to be shot in the back of the head at point-blank range by dehumanized functionaries who probably salved their consciences with the conventional formula that they were purging the Soviet utopia of class enemies.

Later, after certificates of death had been obtained and records made, the bodies were driven away in lorries for burial in unmarked graves on the bleak waste land at Levashovo on the northern peripheries of the city. The place lies west of the local railway station, on the Vyborg road, nearly opposite a military camp. It is nowadays surrounded by a high wooden fence; inside, pine trees have been planted, probably in an attempt to conceal what now has been officially admitted: that this is just one mass graveyard in which at least forty thousand and perhaps as many as a hundred thousand victims of Stalin's terror are buried. Here and there wooden pegs have been driven into the ground to mark a spot where human remains have been located. A grim anonymity hangs over the place: there are no permanent monuments, though here and there pathetic damp-stained photographs in protective plastic coverings have been fixed to tree trunks along with a few scrawled messages of love and pain; also bunches of withered flowers. Whatever the cynics say, human affection can, it seems, endure for half a century and more.

According to the records of the Leningrad KGB, the lamas who were shot on 24 August included: Dorzhi Zhamtsaranovich Zhamtsarano, born 1900 in Chisano in Khorinsk rayon, the head of the Tibet-Mongolian Mission in Leningrad; Balzhir Rodnaevich Zodboev, born 1886 in Yangazhin village, the personal doctor of Agvan Dorzhiev; Ostor Budayevich Budayev, born 1881 in Aga village; and Chaizhi-Dava Tomirgonov, born 1893, a native of Khorinsk rayon and a doctor. The following were shot on 15 November: Zhan Tsybikovich Tsybikov, born 1892, also from Khorinsk rayon; and Namzhil Tsybikovich Tsybenov, born 1896, from Mozhikh village in Eravnen rayon.[22]

The same fate befell many Leningrad orientalists. Along with numerous other intellectuals and scholars – that is, anyone capable of independent thought – they were subjected to isolation, arrest and execution during the thirties. Many were denounced by envious or embittered people, for this was a time when the baser elements in society often triumphed and the noble ones ended up in the NKVD cellars. Dr Yaroslav Vasil'kov of the Oriental Institute of the USSR Academy of Sciences possesses a card index containing information on between four and five hundred orientalists who were liquidated in this way. There are cards for B. B. Baradin, who was shot in 1937, and for Ts. Zh. Zhamtsarano, who, having been forced to leave Mongolia for political reasons around 1932 and afterwards worked at the Institute of Oriental Studies in Leningrad, was arrested in 1937 and died at some unknown later date in prison camp. Vasil'kov also has cards for M. Troitsky, M. I. Tubyansky and A. I. Vostrikov.

Andrey Ivanovich Vostrikov (1904–37), a specialist in Tibetan literature with a particular interest in native Tibetan writers, is a particularly tragic case, for his teacher, Stcherbatsky, pronounced him a finer scholar than himself. He studied both in Leningrad and in Buryatia, and his works include translations of all the basic texts of Hindu Nyaya philosophy, numerous articles, and a study of the logic of Vasubandhu, which was sent to India for publication but unfortunately lost. This brilliant man was arrested on 9 April 1937, accused of absurd political crimes under paragraphs ten and eleven of the notorious Article 58 of the Criminal Code, tried on 26 September and shot the same day. As for his papers, they were hidden in a sofa but later disappeared after his wife was arrested.[23]

Surprisingly, Stcherbatsky was not liquidated, though he played with fire to the extent of writing a concerned letter to Stalin about the deteriorating situation for orientalists, tempering, however, any implied criticism with prudent expressions of loyalty. Perhaps his international reputation saved him; or maybe the authorities wanted to use his network of contacts abroad. But he had to watch much of his work being undone: not only the closure of his Institute of Buddhist Culture in 1930 but the discontinuation of the Biblioteca Buddhica series in 1937, and of course the arrest and dispatch of his pupils and colleagues. He also found it very difficult to publish anything during the thirties after the appearance of the second volume of *Buddhist Logic*. A tired and disillusioned man, Stcherbatsky was evacuated to Kazakhstan during the early phases of the Great Patriotic War against Germany (1941–45), where he lived in comparatively comfortable circumstances until his death on 18 March 1942 at Borovoe in Akmolinksk oblast.[24]

*

Arriving in Trans-Baikalia, Dorzhiev settled in his quarters in the medical school of the Atsagat Datsan. In the prevailing climate of terror, he was not left in peace for long. On 13 November 1937 he was arrested (Order of Arrest number 616) and indicted under various clauses of Article 58 of the Criminal Code:

58–1a: Treason against the state.
58–2:   Armed insurrection with the aim of separating from the Soviet Union some part of its territory.
58–8:   Terrorist acts.
58–9:   Diversion.
58–11: Organizing of counter-revolutionary crimes.[25]

He was interrogated only once: on 26 November. The record of this interview, which is currently lodged in the archives of the Buryat KGB, comprises some two-and-a-half handwritten pages. According to this, he manifestly 'showed that he was one of the leaders of the counter-revolutionary Pan-Mongolian insurrectionary terrorist organization, the ultimate aim of which was the overthrow of the Soviet people'. When pressed as to the aims of this organization, he allegedly said that he could not describe them in detail; however, 'I can say that the final aim . . . was the overthrow of Soviet power, which I personally hated for closing the monasteries; also in general for the attack on religion.'

At that point the interrogation was discontinued and the words 'Because of Illness' inscribed on the record in a different ink.[26] The following day, 27 November 1937, at 16.00 hours, he was moved to the prison hospital in Ulan-Udé.[27] This abrupt deterioration in his health was perhaps due to physical maltreatment: the NKVD were allowed to beat suspects during this period and otherwise subject them to pressure during the course of their interrogations.[28]

A number of depositions attached to the record of the interrogation show that for some months before his actual arrest, the NKVD had been actively trying to build a case against Dorzhiev. They had little initial success. In August 1937 an aging lama doctor who had lately been released from prison camp could only testify that he had had dealings with Dorzhiev to recite a particular prayer. Two other lamas questioned in October knew nothing of any counter-revolutionary activities by Dorzhiev, while a third cross-examined in the same month, though admitting that he had received visitors to Leningrad, informed Dorzhiev of their arrival, and given them letters from Dorzhiev, did not believe that Dorzhiev had personally received them 'with the aim of their becoming conspirators'.[29]

It was only on 2 November that an unemployed gebzhi-lama named B. A. testified that the group named Tasak-Bugulmi that Dorzhiev had set up at the Egituev Datsan around 1926 was not concerned to facilitate the nationalization process but was rather dedicated to the violent overthrow of Soviet authority, the establishment of an independent Mongolian power and the preservation of the Buddhist religion – all patently absurd suggestions. Dorzhiev had in addition collected secret information about military equipment, B. A. went on, and had been involved in stirring up anti-Soviet feeling among collective farm workers. In 1936, moreover, he had issued orders for new members to be recruited into the organization (B.A. gave names) and for new insurgent cells to be set up. Cross-examined, B. A. added that he himself had collected materials for Dorzhiev.[30] Further testimony that Dorzhiev was a leader of a counter-revolutionary organization was provided on 13 November by M. P., a worker 'in a responsible management position'; he named Dorzhiev's fellow counter-revolutionary conspirators as M.N. Yerbanov, A. A. Markizov, B. B. Baradin and Ts. Zh. Zhamtsarano – illustrious company indeed![31]

After Dorzhiev's arrest, the NKVD stepped up its efforts. On 20 November, two lamas, Ts. B. and Sh. R., gave remarkably similar evidence to the effect that they had been members a counter-revolutionary group and had collected intelligence information for Dorzhiev while he was living in Leningrad on such matters as the economic situation in the BMASSR and the feeling of the Buryat people towards the Soviet authorities; they also gave the names of people who were in communication with Dorzhiev. Then on 22 November a certain B. B., who was apparently a nephew of Dr Piotr Badmayev, disclosed under cross-examination that he had been initiated into a counter-revolutionary organization by Dorzhiev in 1927; however, as they had merely spoken about the development of Tibetan medicine, the meaning of the term 'counter-revolutionary' had clearly been stretched to accommodate the needs of the NKVD.[32] More damning 'evidence' implicating Dorzhiev directly with the Japanese bogey was obtained during a cross-examination held on 23 November. According to a certain B. Zh., who claimed to have been led into a counter-revolutionary organization at the Ana Datsan in 1926, Dorzhiev had carried out anti-Soviet propaganda and spoken about war with Japan. Central to these sinister activities, in which about seven other lamas were also implicated, had been lun-duns or mystical prophecies. B. Zh. produced a sheet of paper containing one of these; it had originated in Mongolia and foretold the start of a war in 1937 that 'would lead to better, happier life'.[33] Later, on 24 November, S. M., a former lama of the Atsagat Datsan, and Zh. D., a gebzhi-lama, testified that in 1929, abandoning all hope for the success of the reform movement, Dorzhiev had transferred his energies and allegiance to the active struggle against the Soviet authorities.[34]

The collection of evidence continued even after Dorzhiev was taken to the prison hospital. Most of the lamas interviewed implicated him in the standard counter-revolutionary activities, but perhaps most damning was the testimony of an official, D. D. Dorzhiev, who from 1929 to 1937 served as President of the Buryat Sovnarkom (People's Commissariat). Like leading political figures of the time, he was somehow persuaded or coerced into confessing to quite incredible anti-Soviet crimes, including having been involved with Agvan Dorzhiev, Yerbanov, Dabain, Danilov and various other party bosses in the implementation of the Buryat republic's 'restrained administrative methods in the fight against religion', including the obstruction of the closure of the datsans.

The documents in case number 2768 in Buryat KGB archives also reveal that inventories were at the same time drawn up of Dorzhiev's property. A document dated 27–28 November 1937 lists his personal real estate as including a hut, a house, a barn, a bath-house and a yurt, together comprising some 1703 square metres of living space, and some 78,297 square metres of land; all this plus other items was insured for 58,777 rubles. Subsequently, the regional finance department drew up further inventories with a view to recovering unpaid taxes amounting to 28,346 rubles, 20 kopeks for the years 1935, 1936 and 1937. These list trivial items like shoes, socks and shirts, hinges, screws and taps, cups, spoons, forks and items of furniture. Mentioned also are medicines prescribed for Dorzhiev by Dr P. E. Vinogradov: presumably it was intended to recoup the cost of these as well.[35]

*

The record of the efforts of the NKVD to compile a case against Dorzhiev show that these noble agents of Stalinist power were forced mainly to rely on the testimony of disaffected conservative lamas who still bore umbrage against Dorzhiev for his reformist activities. Some may also have been subjected to physical beatings and other forms of pressure in order to secure their co-operation. Even so, nothing of any real substance was obtained; indeed, much of the so-called evidence is either highly suspect or self-contradictory. It would seem highly unlikely, for instance, that during the twenties, when he was wholeheartedly striving to reconcile Buddhism with the ideology of the Soviet authorities, he would at the same time have actively organized resistance to those authorities. Certainly we can discount Dorzhiev's alleged confession: many prominent early Bolsheviks with impeccable revolutionary credentials similarly confessed to unlikely counter-revolutionary activities.

*

There is a legend that some time after he had been installed in the prison hospital, Dorzhiev was let out under NKVD guard to spend a week in religious devotions and meditation with his relatives in Khara-Shibir or Chelutai.[36] This is highly improbable: the NKVD quite simply never allowed people to go free once they had taken them into custody.

What is certain, however, is that Agvan Dorzhiev died in the prison hospital 'as a result of cardiac arrest and general physical weakness due to old age' on 29 January 1938, having been, according to reports, conscious to the end.[37] His body was subsequently buried at a secret traditional burial place in the forest near Chelutai.[38]

Subsequently, the authorities formally discontinued his case on the basis of Article 204–P–b ('Lack of evidence for bringing the accused to justice according to the provisions of the USSR penal code').[39] Permission was also given to the regional finance department to sell the property that had been inventoried.

In 1956, as part of the anti-Stalinist wave that swept across the USSR during the Khruschev era, the case against Agvan Dorzhiev was investigated and in December 1957 it was curtailed under Statute 204-b due to lack of evidence. Full and final rehabilitation did not come until 14 May 1990, however, when a resolution was passed dismissing the case 'on the grounds of lack of evidence and absence of criminal activity'.[40]

*

Such, then, was the life of one who apparently as W. H. Auden said of Mozart, 'did no harm to our poor earth' – for on the surface at least

Dorzhiev spent his many years working for the cause of Buddhism and it has been effectively impossible to detect any shadowy side to his character: no venal peccadillos, no dirty dealings, nothing in fact to compromise the image of his being a kind of Buddhist paragon beyond, perhaps, that he occasionally indulged in the minor diplomatic sin of saying one thing to one party and something else to another. This, though, in a sense, is what one would expect. In the Buddhist world in which he mainly operated it is simply not done to say anything untoward about anyone, especially a high lama, which is why today some lamas are able to behave outrageously with virtual impunity. I have in fact met two lamas who claimed to have contact with Dorzhiev: former Khambo Bandido Lama Erdineyev and a very old Buryat Dhoramba geshé named Tenzin Gyatsho who, between 1930 and about 1990, spent most of his time in eastern Tibet and China. It was impossible to elicit anything substantial out of either. In both their eyes Dorzhiev was simply a great lama and that was that.

Certainly, though, as a historical figure Dorzhiev stands as a kind of colossus. He made his considerable influence felt across a vast swathe of territory: from Lhasa to St Petersburg, with important extensions into eastern Siberia and Mongolia, down into the Kalmyk lands of southern Russia, and even passingly into western Europe. Moreover, had he not appeared when he did, the course at least of Tibetan history might indeed have been very different: this was the view of Alastair Lamb, the eminent historian of Central Asia, with whom I discussed Dorzhiev in 1988. And the amazing thing is that he was almost always working in the face of large negative factors. Had these not been present, he might indeed have played an even greater role in shaping the destiny of Russia and Central Asia.

As regards the character of the man, from what we know of his outward, worldly activities it is possible to deduce certain things. He must have been endowed with enormous determination and energy as well as being charming and possessing some kind of natural authority that caused a variety of people to respect him. One could go on, and run the risk of crossing that hazy boundary where reasonable extrapolation begins to blur into speculation. The truth is, however, that in the last analysis the real core of Agvan Dorzhiev – the inner man, his spiritual life – remains an enigma. There are brief items that one could take as flashes of self-revelation in the memoirs, but often there is a kind of conventionality about them – obligatory self-deprecation and so forth – that makes them unsound as evidence. I have in places ventured to account for some of the more perplexing changes in his life, notably his decision to work with the Bolsheviks, but no completely satisfactory psychological explanation is possible on the evidence that we presently have. Perhaps now that archives are opening up in the former Soviet Union, new and enlightening material will emerge, notably in Buryatia.

For all the quantities of research I have amassed, I therefore do not feel competent to write an obituary of Agvan Dorzhiev. I will leave that to the German Mongolist, W. A. Unkrig, who was far closer to him in space and time:

> We must take our leave of Agvan Dorzhiev, for whom both as a man and a character we must have the highest regard. He is looked upon in Russia as the very embodiment of the entire lamaistic world and its most worthy representative both within and without that great country. Whatever the Russian Government has given him, he has handed on in full – yes, even enriched – to his co-religionists and fellow Mongolians.[41]

CHAPTER TWENTY

After Dorzhiev
1938 – 1991

Although Stalin had only lately accomplished the destruction of Buddhism in the USSR, the Soviet empire formally acquired a third Buddhist enclave during the Great Patriotic War, though in fact its power there had been long established. This was Tannu-Tuva, or Uryankhai: a remote region in the north-west corner of Outer Mongolia, between the Tannu-Ola and Sayan mountain ranges.

When the Chinese were suzerains in Mongolia, the nomadic people inhabiting Tannu-Tuva had come under their aegis, but from the late nineteenth century numbers of Russian traders, gold prospectors and farmers settled there. By around 1920 these comprised some 20 per cent of the population, which inevitably led to calls for annexation to the Russian empire. Although some politicians, notably Sazonov, were doubtful of the wisdom of such a step, Nicholas II was in favour of it; so following the declaration of Mongolian independence in 1911, a Russian border commissioner was appointed and the way prepared for the declaration of a protectorate. Then came the Revolution and in 1918 Chinese troops briefly reoccupied Tuva. By the early twenties, however, a People's Republic of Tannu-Tuva had been set up under Soviet control, and the region was finally annexed outright to the USSR in 1944.[1]

According to Aleksandr Piatigorsky, Buddhism first came to the Uryankhai region around the sixth century CE, but, as it was not firmly established, it afterwards underwent waves of decline and renaissance. During the Manchu period, when Buddhism became institutionalized in this region, some twenty-two khure (monasteries) were built and the number of monks ran to around four thousand (ten per cent of the male population). Unfortunately, the rise of Soviet-backed communism in the early twenties led to much the same sort of anti-religious repression as in the USSR itself: all lamas were deprived of civil rights in 1929, and in 1931 monastic property was confiscated; there then remained only one khure with fifteen lamas.[2]

What was singular about the Buddhism of Tannu-Tuva, again according to Piatigorsky, was that it forged a working syncretism with shamanism. Graphic evidence of this was observed by P. E. Ostrobskikh towards the end of the nineteenth century among the Todjin clan, who lived in the east of the region:

> They are mostly Buddhists and shamans at the same time. In the dwelling of their chief Lama (Hambu-Lama) I saw, side by side with Tantrist Thangkas, the sacred Shamanistic costume of his consort, the Great Shamaness.[3]

*

In Kalmykia, the Great Patriotic War had particularly tragic consequences. Like many Russian minorities, some Kalmyks at first regarded the invading Germans as liberators and sided with them. A free Kalmyk cavalry corps fought with the Wehrmacht in Russia and the Balkans; but many Kalmyks fought bravely with the Red Army too. Nevertheless, for the sins of the few the full brunt of Stalin's wrath descended upon the whole nation and in 1943 perhaps as many as 10,000 were deported to the frosty wastes of Siberia, where a huge number perished. The surviving remnant was not able to return to the lower Volga region until after the death of Stalin in 1953. Others in the meantime had gone into foreign exile. Some went to Germany, where they settled mainly in the Munich district and set up a temple in a disused barracks at Ludwigsfeld between Munich and Dachau. Ven. Lidshi Agdshulov (1899–1973) was the first incumbent there, while another Kalmyk lama, Ven. Sharapov, lived in Ulm. Other Kalmyks went to France and Belgium, where they found work in mines, but the majority made their way to the United States and established a settlement in New Jersey, where the First Kalmyk Buddhist Temple was established in a converted garage at Freewood Acres in 1952. In 1955, the eminent Kalmyk lama, Geshé Wangyal (1901–83), came to minister there.[4]

The Buryats fared rather better. Stalin was forced to moderate his anti-religious policies in order to secure popular support for the Motherland's heroic war effort. For pragmatic reasons, therefore, though it continued to be illegal elsewhere in the USSR, Buddhism was again tolerated in Trans-Baikalia, and in 1945 permission was given to set up an entirely new foundation, the Ivolga Datsan, some thirty kilometres from Ulan-Udé; later the old Aga Datsan in the Chita oblast was allowed to be reopened as well.

The few monks that were permitted to take up residence in these two datsans were, however, subject to severe restrictions under regulations promulgated in 1946. They could not possess money, give religious instruction to young people under eighteen years of age or perform rituals outside the confines of their monasteries. Church administration was placed in the hands of a congress on which both lay and religious delegates were represented, and monastic heads were elected by datsan councils. The datsans themselves had moreover to be self-financing and detailed accounts had to be submitted for scrutiny.

The state meanwhile exerted overall control of Soviet Buddhism by establishing a Central Buddhist Board of the USSR with its headquarters at Ivolga and a small office to handle foreign relations in Moscow; this last was run by Russians. At the same time the Bandido Khambo Lama, now projecting a distinctly fellow-travelling complexion, became a kind of propaganda agent, turning up at world Buddhist conferences to promote an agit-prop sort of 'peace'.

However, just in case Buddhism might begin to edge ahead of communism in the battle for the hearts and minds of the people, vigorous anti-religious propaganda was kept up as well. The following, couched in the familiar rhetoric of class war, appeared in a Soviet teachers' journal:

> The problem of atheistical education, taking local characteristics into account, must be tackled seriously, and starting with the teacher first of all. To start with there must be a study of Buddhism in all its varieties, of lamaism, the religion widespread over the territory of the Buryat Republic. In order to fight the enemy, you must know him. There must be clear recognition of the way in which the child is affected by the religious observances which it sees.
>
> Finally, the most serious question of selecting the methods for carrying on the fight. They must be more clever, more intricate, more effective than the methods used by religion.
>
> Children must be clearly informed about religious art, making a clear distinction between its two aspects – aesthetic value and the skill of the local craftsmen, and the religious 'outer covering'. You must know how to talk to the children about religion in such a way as to eliminate its influence and at the same time to avoid offending parents who are believers. In such a way that instead of being passive observers, the children should be converted into active opponents, rejecting religion on ideological grounds.[5]

This curious dual policy of theoretical tolerance allied to active discouragement enabled the Soviet authorities to proclaim to the outside world that the Buddhists of the USSR possessed complete freedom of conscience in matters of religion while at the same time limiting their activities and permitting anti-Buddhist activities.

*

In the immediate post-war years, what Buddhism remained in the USSR was, as far as the authorities were concerned, an exclusively Trans-Baikalian affair. It had officially been expunged from the European part of the empire, where of course, if it did not obediently die out, it was forced underground.

As for the temple in Leningrad, that potent symbol of a pan-Russian Buddhism, Dorzhiev had of course entrusted this to S. D. Dylykov. There can be no doubt that the old lama regarded Dylykov as a relative and trusted him; what is open to question in the light of subsequent events is whether he was not misguided in this respect. Certainly Dylykov seems to have been concerned to be seen to be a good Soviet citizen. During the thirties, for instance, he represented Komsomol among the young Buddhist laymen in the house adjacent to the temple, where he also lived; and later, on the fateful night in 1937 when the last of the lamas were taken away to the Big House on Liteinyi Prospekt, he is alleged to have been in the building and to have spoken with the NKVD officers but to have somehow managed to avoid arrest himself. Not surprisingly, therefore, he is suspected by some Buddhists of being a quisling in cahoots with the NKVD. What is beyond speculation, however, is that he failed to carry out Dorzhiev's last wishes, choosing instead to play Pontius Pilate by washing his hands of the trusteeship invested in him and turning the temple and its contents over to the state. Arguably in the prevailing circumstances this was the only option open to him if wanted to stay alive – and unlike many other orientalists he has both stayed alive down to the time of writing and has also enjoyed an academic career of sorts.

The secularization of the temple was formally transacted on 22 April 1938. Its treasures were then transferred to the Museum of the History of Religion and Atheism at Kazan Cathedral on Nevsky Prospekt, itself newly secularized. Unfortunately, the great statue of the Buddha in the main shrine never reached its destination, for it toppled off the cart in which it was being carried and the broken pieces were unceremoniously dumped in the waters of the Little Nevka. Thereafter, for over fifty years, the empty shell of this unique and highly spiritual building suffered the indignity of being put to a number of inappropriate uses. In 1938 it was rented to the Building Workers' Trade Union as a 'facility for physical culture'; then during the Great Patriotic War it served as a military radio station, and as such was both a beacon for Soviet planes and a link with the outside world during the nine hundred day siege. A concrete patch with steel reinforcements on the dukhang floor still marks the spot where the transmitter stood. As for the aerial, this was a steel cable moored to a caterpillar tractor in the grounds and kept aloft by a balloon. Later, up until 1960, the temple was co-opted into the Cold War as a jamming station.

The temple was not forgotten, however, for some Leningrad citizens were concerned to see it, if not fully restored to its original status – at the time that was utterly unthinkable – then at least put to more auspicious uses. As far back as the 1940s various scholars advocated that it be put in the care of the Institute of the Peoples of Asia (a department of the USSR Academy of Sciences) and turned into a museum of Mongolian religion and culture, which would also house a library of rare Tibetan manuscripts and xylographs brought from various plundered datsans in the Chita region. This proposal was eventually turned down by the Presidium of the Academy of Sciences on the grounds that 'it is considered inappropriate to fund a new museum on the history of religion'. Then, towards the end of the 1950s, Yuri Nikolaievich Roerich put forward the idea of turning the building into an Oriental museum which would again serve as a store for Tibetan texts. Unfortunately, nothing came of this plan either.[6]

*

In 1953, the death of Stalin lifted the grotesque pall of fear and misery that had hung over the Soviet people for many years. Basic conditions were then set for a revival of interest in the study and practice of Buddhism in the European part of the USSR. Two crucial events quickened this process: the return of Yuri Nikolaievich Roerich to the USSR, and the release from captivity of the outstanding lama, Bidya Dandaron.

Yuri (George) Roerich (1902–60), a highly educated Mongolist and Tibetologist, the translator of the *Blue Annals*, played a vital part in the regeneration of the decimated tradition of Russian orientalism: the tradition of Ol'denburg and Stcherbatsky. Lured back to the land of his forefathers in 1957 by wily Soviet officials in India, he took up a post at the Oriental Institute of the USSR Academy of Sciences in Moscow and soon gathered around himself a new and talented genera-tion of Indologists and Buddhologists, including Aleksandr Moisevich Piatigorsky, Sirkin, Gerasimov, Glazov and Elizavenkova.

Unfortunately, having spent most of his life in exile, Roerich found the cynical chicanery of Soviet life stressful; he lived there for only three years, but his influence during that time was considerable. One of his final acts in 1960 was to help publish B. Tuparov's Russian translation of the *Dhammapada*, a classic Pali Buddhist text, which was to be the first Biblioteca Buddhica publication since 1937. At the eleventh hour, after the book had gone to press, the authorities slapped a ban on it, but Roerich went to see Dr G. P. Malalasekera, the Ceylonese Ambassador, who promptly announced that there would be a grand reception at his embassy in honour of this historic event, the publication of a Russian version of the *Dhammapada*. The authorities were caught in a very neat trap and had to lift the ban – but Roerich's health failed soon afterwards.

Bidya Dandaron (1914–74), on the other hand, was not only a distinguished classical Buddhologist but a tantric adept and guru.[7] He belonged to a yogic tradition that had grown up in Trans-Baikalia alongside the mainstream monastic Gelug tradition. Its founder was a lama named Lobsang Samdan (also known as Tsedenov; born 1850 or 1855), who had undergone orthodox training at the Kizhinga and Gusinoye Ozero datsans and acquired a geshé degree. Later, deciding that the monastery is still samsara, he retired into a thirty-three-year retreat in a small wooden hut on a hill near the village of Ust-Orot. Emerging eventually from seclusion, which he had devoted to the contemplation of Vajrabhairava, Lobsang Samdan declared himself of the Nyingma tradition (the oldest school of Tibetan Buddhism) and soon gathered a number of followers. One of these was Dorzhi Gabzhi Badmayev (died 1920), who had entered into an unofficial liaison with the widow of a steppe lama named Dandar Bazarov. Bidya Dandaron, who was born out of wedlock to the widow Dandarova on 15 December 1914, was soon recognized to have great spiritual potential, and during a ceremony at the Chesan Datsan in July 1921, was declared to be the heir of Lobsang Samdan, who had by now styled himself tsar of the theocratic state called Balagat that he had established in part of the Kizhinga valley.[8] Naturally Lobsang Samdan's grandiose aspirations alienated many and he and his lama ministers are said to have been arrested by Ataman Semenov at the behest of Burnatskom.[9] He finally disappeared around 1924, after which the surviving members of Balagat movement looked to Dandaron as their leader.

In 1936 Dandaron had come to Leningrad to study at the Institute of Aeronautical Engineering. As he also had aspirations of deepening his Buddhist studies, he visited Agvan Dorzhiev. An old and sick man by this time, Dorzhiev could not undertake to help Dandaron himself, but he wrote a letter of recommendation to the orientalist, A. I. Vostrikov, who arranged for Dandaron to audit his lectures at the university. When Vostrikov was arrested in the following year, Dandaron was arrested too, but perhaps because of his youth he escaped being shot and was instead sentenced to ten years in prison camp under the notorious Article

58 of the Criminal Code. In all, Dardaron spent some twenty-two years of his life in the Gulag, which – a reflection perhaps of his Buddhist fortitude – he regarded as particularly conducive to spiritual practice. He was released from his first term in 1944 and sent to internal exile, but he absconded and returned secretly to Buryatia, where he was rearrested in 1947. During his second term of imprisonment he was able to study with Mongolian lamas from Hailar in the Barga region of Manchuria, who, because they had the misfortune to be living in Japanese-held territory during the war, were subsequently imprisoned as collaborators. Dandaron also organized his own small groups in the camps. The motley membership of one of them consisted of one ex-NKVD colonel, a Japanese military intelligence officer (a specialist in torture), a Gestapo officer, three fallen local party bosses, a German journalist and two Ukrainian Jews.[10]

On his release in 1955 (or 1956), Dandaron obtained a post at the Buryat Institute of Social Sciences in Ulan-Udé, and soon disciples were gravitating to him for spiritual direction, not merely from his native Trans-Baikalia but from Moscow and Leningrad, the Baltic States and the Ukraine. They included Aleksandr Piatigorsky and Oktobrina Volkova, two scholars who had been students of Roerich (who had in fact met Dandaron in Ulan-Udé in 1958), and Vladimir Montlevich and Aleksandr Zheleznov, then employed at the Museum of the History of Religion and Atheism in Leningrad. These developments alarmed the authorities for they proved that the cordon sanitaire that they had thrown around Russian Buddhism, restricting it to Buryat Trans-Baikalia, had been broken. They therefore arrested Dandaron for a third time in 1972 on charges of organizing an illegal religious group; there were also far-fetched accusations at his trial of all kinds of 'black deeds', from fanaticism to blood sacrifice and physical violence.[11] The Buryat scholar K. M. Gerasimova, one of Dandaron's colleagues at the Institute of Social Sciences, also gave 'scientific' evidence that what he was teaching was not authentic Buddhism – an action that has not endeared her to contemporary Russian Buddhists. Dandaron was duly sentenced to five years' imprisonment, while some of his students, who had also been arrested, were subjected to 'ambulatory forensic psychiatric diagnosis', declared insane and temporarily incarcerated in psychological institutions; others lost their jobs.

The Dandaron affair provoked some concern and protest in the outside world, which vexed the Soviet authorities somewhat, particularly that their image might be tarnished in Buddhist Asia. A passionate apologist leapt to their aid – none other that Agvan Dorzhiev's relative and heir S. D. Dylykov, then a Vice-President of the World

Fellowship of Buddhists. In a letter of 12 October 1973 to Aiem
Sankhavasi, the Honorary Secretary General of the World Fellowship
of Buddhists, he wrote:

The reports about alleged 'persecutions' which have appeared in the foreign
press do not reflect the real position of believers in our country. The Buddhist
population of the USSR enjoys full freedom of conscience and is not subjected
to any repressions whatsoever.

The only person brought to trial on criminal offence was the former lama
Bidia Dandaron [sic], who had in the past few years worked as junior scientific
associate of the manuscripts department, Institute of Social Sciences of the
USSR in Ulan-Ude. Dandaron was not so much engaged in scientific work
as in drinking and getting together a group of 'disciples' among whom were
neither any Buryats nor Buddhists. They, naturally, did not have any contacts
with Buddhists in our country.

Dandaron needed his 'disciples' to help him obtain money to continue his idle
and dissipated life. He constantly demanded from his 'disciples' money, valuable
things and vodka, and frequently organized drunken orgies.

Dandaron speculated with various articles of Buddhist worship. He threatened
to kill or to apply violence to those who tried to call him to order and to return
to normal life. Thus, Dandaron together with his 'disciple' [sic] savagely beat
up one of his fellow-countrymen by the name of Dambadorzhiyev, who dared
to criticise Dandaron for his immoral behaviour.

D. Dashiyev, Dandaron's adopted son, who is a student of the Leningrad
University, time and again censured his stepfather for organising gatherings
in his flat and for his regular drinking bouts. Dandaron, a chronic drunk-
ard, became violent on many occasions and beat up Dashiyev's mother.
Dashiyev often had to protect his mother from being beaten up by his
stepfather. Dandaron decided to revenge himself on Dashiyev for disobey-
ing him. In Solnechnaya Street, Ulan-Ude, the student was attacked, and
if not for the interference of passers-by, he would have fallen victim to
the hooligans.

The People's Court of the Oktyabrsky district of Ulan-Ude investigated in an
open trial the case of Dandaron, who was charged with criminal encroachment
on the personality and rights of citizens and, guided by the relevant articles
of the criminal code of the Russian Federation, sentenced Dandaron to three
years' imprisonment in a general regime colony. Dandaron's 'disciples' acted
only as witnesses at the trial. The public of Buryatia met this decision
with approval.

Some organs of the press and propaganda in foreign countries are now
portraying the criminal Dandaron as a 'martyr', presenting his trial as an
alleged persecution of Buddhists. The Buddhists, as well as all other believers
in our country, can freely perform their religious rites.

In May this year the Buddhists of the USSR widely marked Wesaka Day. In
July solemn khurals in honour of Maitreya, the Coming Buddha, were held
in the Buddhist temples of Buryatia. The religious ceremonies were, as always,

headed by the Reverend Bandido Khambo Lama Zhambal-Dorzha Gomboyev, the Chairman of the Buddhist Council of the USSR.

We, the Buddhists of the Soviet Union, do not doubt that the Soviet court has punished Dandaron for his crimes, rather than for his religious convictions.[12]

This is hardly an impartial letter, but even sympathetic commentators have been prepared to concede that Dandaron's influence was 'less ethical than usually demanded' in the strictest traditions of Buddhism.[13] Unfortunately, he was no longer resilient enough to withstand the rigours and abuses to which he was subjected at the Vydrino camp.[14] Forced to carry on working with a broken arm and leg, he died on 26 October 1974.[15]

*

The kind of Buddhism that was being practised in Buryatia at this time was by and large of the popular sort that offers consolation against the pains, woes and difficulties of human existence. It was more concerned with the enactment of rituals, in which shamanistic and even communist elements were mingled, than with doctrinal study or the arduous quest for inner illumination through meditation. In consequence, statistics show that it tended to find its strongest support among the old, the uneducated, women and those living in more remote rural areas, and to be despised by those with a modern, critical, urban outlook.

Local Buddhist rituals had traditionally to do mainly with rites of passage like birth, taking a name, first hair-cutting, marriage, death and transit through the bardo or after-death state, though now lamas were increasingly concerned with only the last two. Certain traditional Buddhist festivals also continued to be celebrated, such as Tsagaansar, the new year celebrations, and the khural of Maidari, whose millennarian cult, mixed up with elements of the Shambhala myths, continued to exert a particular fascination. At this khural, a statue of Maidari sitting in a carriage drawn by a wooden horse would be ceremonially carried around the datsan, and believers would try to touch it.

Observers and scholars travelling in Buryatia at this time noted the prevalence of obos – cairns bristling with prayer-flags and surrounded by inscribed tablets and offerings – where rituals were held to invoke the local spirits. Due to the shortage of lamas, laymen or former lamas often performed these rituals. Sometimes, even those who would not admit to being either believing or practising Buddhists would attend, this in itself suggesting that, for all the government's efforts at anti-religious propaganda, Buddhism still retained a powerful subconscious hold.

*

The Dandaron affair was a shock, particularly for European Russian Buddhists, but it was not a disenabling one. The small groups that had re-emerged in the 1950s and 1960s in Leningrad and other centres continued to function underground through the 1970s and into the 1980s – and often with that special dedication that develops under repression. Some of them contained Dandaron disciples, or disciples of his disciples, but in the absence of fully qualified teachers most had to depend to a large extent on books for instruction. A few managed to persuade academic orientalists to teach them classical Tibetan so that they could have access to basic texts, and a few Buddhist works, deemed to be 'scientific', were published under the noses of the authorities, who did not realize what they were. Mostly, however, Soviet Buddhists had to turn to books in Western European languages, particularly English, which were translated and circulated in samizdat form. This introduced them for the first time to traditions of Buddhism other than the Tibetan, and, through the works of D. T. Suzuki, Zen temporarily became quite the vogue. The popular Buddhism of Alan Watts and other writers of the Californian counter-culture also penetrated the USSR during the Hippie era.

As for Dorzhiev's temple, in 1960 the Leningrad city council had transferred the tenancy to the USSR Academy of Sciences, which placed it in the hands of the Institute of the Peoples of Asia (now the Institute of Oriental Studies). Unfortunately, the building proved unsuitable for the purposes of this institute, which was consequently obliged to cede it to the Zoological Institute. This body located three of its laboratories in the building, where vivisection experiments were reportedly conducted – something particularly offensive to Buddhists. Then in 1970 the temple was transferred to state ownership as an architectural monument of importance, and in 1981 it was again decided to transfer it, this time to the Museum of the History of Religion and Atheism, though this resolution was never implemented.

*

In the freer atmosphere of Mikhail Gorbachev's age of Glasnost, things became considerably easier. Not only could Buddhists from European Russian centres again travel to Trans-Baikalia to receive direct teaching from Buryat lamas but, as Buddhism was now no longer deemed to be politically contentious, it became possible for non-ethnic groups to throw off the stigma of illegality by becoming officially registered with the Council of Religions Affairs of the USSR Council of Ministers.

At a meeting held at the Leningrad Temple in May 1991 to set up an umbrella organization to co-ordinate activities, the groups represented included the Leningrad Religious Society of Buddhists (registered 28 June 1989), the Latvian Buddhist Community of Riga, the Estonian Buddhist Community of Tallinn, the Institute of Mahayana at Tartu University in Estonia (this is led by Linnart Mäll, an orientalist of distinction, direct pupil of Dandaron and currently chairman of UNPO: The Unrepresented Peoples' and Nations' Organization[16]), and the Buddhist Community of Novosibirsk, which was represented by Kungpa Nyimo, a son of Dandaron. There are also believed to be groups in Moscow, Kiev and Kharkov, which may either be registered or in the process of becoming registered; while in Tashkent, perhaps the least likely place one might expect to find one, there is a Korean Zen group.

Buddhism is also now reported to be undergoing a revival in Trans-Baikalia, where two historic datsans are again functioning: the Tsugol Datsan in the Chita oblast, where Zhimba Zhamtso Tsybikovich Tsybenov is shiretui, and the Gusinoye Ozero Datsan, seat of the Khambo Bandido Lama. The Ivolga and Aga Datsans continued to flourish under the shiretuis Sodbo Dorzhiev and Zolsho Zhigmitov respectively, and there have been reports of between seventeen and twenty smaller Buddhist centres in operation as well. Meanwhile in Elista (population around 80,000), the administrative centre of Kalmykia[17], there is a small centre in a local house; its bakshi (resident religious instructor) is Tivan Dardzhi, who is also a member of the Soviet Parliament.

The obstacle to further development in all these places is a general dearth of fully trained lamas. In all, at the time of my visit in May 1991, there were only eight fully ordained gelong (monks) in the whole of the former USSR, and seven of those were over eighty. Fortunately, the more relaxed atmosphere prior to and following the disintegration of the USSR has allowed foreign Buddhist leaders and teachers to visit the region and this has both broken down the long standing isolation of Russian Buddhists from the rest of the Buddhist world and provided much-needed inspiration and, in some cases, instruction. Among those who have made visits are His Holiness the Dalai Lama, who indeed ordained some of the gelong mentioned above; Kusho Bakula Rinpoché, the foremost lama of Ladakh and one-time Indian Ambassador to Mongolia; øle Nydal, a Danish devotee of the late Karmapa, who directs a thriving Karma Kagyu Tibetan group in the Leningrad area;

Joseph Goldstein and Sharon Salzburg of the Insight Meditation Society of Barre, Massachusetts, who have conducted well-attended vipassana (insight) meditation retreats; the late Dr H. Saddhatissa and some monks from the Chiswick Vihara, England; Bernard Tetsugen Glassman, a New York-based Zen priest; and Finnish and British order members of the Friends of the Western Buddhist Order.

The main loyalty remains to the local Tibetan-derived tradition, however, though, as in the contemporary West, it is unclear whether orthodox monasticism will prove as generally attractive to present and future Buddhists as it once did in the traditional East. Dr Bata Bayartuev, a Buryat scholar with whom I spoke in Leningrad in 1991, feels that today many more practitioners are drawn to the yogic tradition of lay practice propagated by Dandaron and his followers than to the strict monasticism of Agvan Dorzhiev and the conservative lamas of the Buryat datsans.

But unarguably of greatest symbolic significance during these exciting times of revival and regeneration has been the return of Dorzhiev's St Petersburg temple to Buddhist hands after over half a century of secularization. Though, at the time of writing, the exact question of legal ownership has not yet been resolved it still technically belongs to the local municipality[18] − it was given back to Buddhist hands in June 1990, and when I visited it in May 1991, though it was still in a bare and dilapidated state, it was again functioning as a working temple as its great founder envisioned it. A complement of shaven-headed Buryat novices, dressed in vivid brocades of scarlet, orange and saffron, were training under the new abbot, Gelong Tenzin-Khetsun Samayev, a vigorous English-speaking lama from southern Cis-Baikalia,[19] who was himself trained at the Gandan Monastery in Ulan-Bator, the School of Buddhist Dialectics in Dharamsala and Drepung Monastic University in south India. Lama Samayev plans to restore and refurbish the temple fully, and repossess its plundered treasures from the Museum of the History of Religion and Atheism; then he hopes to set up a monastic school and a publishing house.

*

Despite the Soviet authorities' attempts to annihilate it, Buddhism was never completely eradicated among the Buryats and the Kalmyks but continued to exert a deep hold, both on the conscious and unconscious levels. Now that the anti-religious propaganda and pressure are removed, we can fairly safely expect a revival.

As for Buddhism among European Russians, the auguries are also positive. Despite the enormous suffering that these people have experienced for so long – perhaps indeed because of that suffering – they still possess a deep and genuine spiritual quality and this, after so many years of denial, urgently craves nourishment. Orthodoxy, which is undergoing a rapid revival, will no doubt provide much of that nourishment; but the world is changing and nowadays many feel the need for new spiritual perspectives. Certainly, when I last spoke with him just before the great changes, Lama Samayev expressed a strong belief that Buddhism has something special to offer in the spiritual and ideological vacuum that now exists. A young Buddhist psychiatrist, Denis Dubrovin, who practises in one of Dorzhiev's old haunts, the Petrograd district of St Petersburg, was of a similar opinion. With his friend, Mikhail Momot, he discussed at length the similarities between certain aspects of Buddhism and Orthodox Christianity, and the fascination that Buddhist philosophy has always held for European Russian intellectuals. 'Even our greatest writer Leo Tolstoy[20] was interested in Buddhism,' he said. 'There is something in this philosophy that is very close to the Russian soul.'

Certainly its ability to rise phoenix-like from the ashes of the Stalinist holocaust has amply demonstrated the spiritual robustness of the 250-year-old tradition of Russian Buddhism. The present modest resurgence is therefore hopefully a harbinger of greater things to come. Indeed, the world is changing so fast at the moment that it no longer seems folly to hope that the noble visions of Agvan Dorzhiev may quite soon be realized – and not just his vision of a Russian Buddhism, but that even more ambitious vision of the the great, traditionally Buddhist, zone of Central Asia as a dynamic new religious, cultural and political centre.

APPENDIX ONE

PRE-1940 DATSANS OF TRANS-BAIKALIA

1. Sartulsky Datsan, founded 1707
2. Tsongolsky Datsan, 1730
3. Gusinoyozersky Datsan, 1741
4. Atsaisky Datsan, 1743
5. Dzhidinsky Datsan, 1749
6. Bultumursky Datsan, 1757
7. Gegetuevsky Datsan, 1769
8. Arakiretsky Datsan, 1769
9. Ichetuevsky Datsan, 1773
10. Zagustaisky Datsan, 1769
11. Iroisky Datsan, 1810
12. Kudarinsky Datsan, 1831
13. Yangazhinsky Datsan, 1830
14. Tsezzhinsky (Burgaltaisky) Datsan, 1830
15. Bulaksky (Sanaginsky) Datsan, 1828
16. Kudunsky Datsan, 1756–8
17. Tugnugaltaisky Datsan, 1758–73
18. Aninsky Datsan, 1775–95
19. Aginsky Datsan, 1811–16
20. Egituevsky Datsan, 1824–6
21. Tsugolsky Datsan, 1826
22. Chesansky Datsan, 1828
23. Khokhyurtaevsky Datsan, 1828
24. Atsagatsky Datsan, 1825–31
25. Tsulginsky Datsan, 1830–1
26. Zugalaevsky (or Eugalaevsky) Datsan, 1826
27. Semiozerny Datsan, 1908
28. Kondinsky Datsan, 1909–10
29. Alkhanaisky Datsan
30. Guninsky Datsan, 1802
31. Tokuinsky Datsan, 1802
32. Khuzhirtaevsky Datsan, 1826
33. Tarbagataisky Datsan, 1825
34. Birtsuevsky Datsan, 1828
35. Ulikhunsky Datsan, 1832
36. Barguzinsky Datsan, 1818
37. Kirensky Datsan, 1817
38. Khoimorsky Datsan, 20th century
39. Alarsky Datsan, 1814
40. Okhinsky (Zhilginsky) Datsan, 19th century
41. Alyatsky Datsan
42. Unginsky Datsan
43. Bil'uirsky Datsan
44. Kirmensky Datsan, 1912
45. Ol'khonsky Datsan
46. Kharatsinsky Datsan, 1918
47. Murinsky Datsan, 1919

APPENDIX TWO

DORZHIEV'S INVENTORY OF ITEMS LOOTED FROM THE
PETROGRAD BUDDHIST TEMPLE IN 1919

1. 20 large and small statues either of bronze or gilt and of Indian or Tibetan origin depicting different deities.
2. 60 of the same made of copper, and gilt statues of Chinese and Mongolian craftsmanship.
3. Silver offering vases and cups weighing 910 lan (1 lan = 10 units of gold).[1]
4. Temple decorations and draperies made of Chinese brocade – 882 arshins.[2]
5. 18 small sacred mirrors of gilded copper, 1 arshin in diameter, which decorated the external facade of the temple.
6. 7 similar large mirrors, each 1.5 arshin in diameter.
7. 1 metal stand for a sacred timepiece.
8. 2 gilded metal volutes for the sacred cylinders [gyeltsen] on the temple roof.
9. 26 sacred paintings on canvas.
10. All metal door and window handles were looted, also the decorations of the locks, and after that the doors and shutters were smashed to pieces or [otherwise] damaged.
11. All the panes of glass from the roof of the temple were looted, as a result of which rain and wind could get in and damage the interior.
12. The library, in which were lodged valuable and rare books in European as well as the Tibetan and Mongolian languages, was completely destroyed. Books in European languages were looted, while those in Tibetan and Mongolian were torn to pieces and used for domestic and toilet purposes. Also treated in this way were extremely rare archives of secret and non-secret documents and letters concerning the relations between Russia, England, Tibet and China over the past thirty years.
13. From the furnishings of the temple and the monks' flats were looted all the porcelain and copper vessels, cupboards, 3 expensive beds and 8 simple iron beds, 2 dozen soft oak chairs, 2 ottomans, etc.
14. From the temple treasury: lynx fur – 25 pieces, fox fur – 18 pieces, 'barsov' and Tibetan cloth – 36 pieces, donated by Tibet for completing the outer decor of the temple; for the same purpose from the Buryat-Mongols – 3 pieces of bearskin, from the Mongols – 11 lengths of blue and brown silk, half-silk and tussore.
15. 80 sazhenes of wood and 500 poods of anthracite, prepared for heating the temple and the adjacent quarters, and wood for completing the construction of the temple.
16. Besides which were also looted things personally belonging to me, [namely] European, Tibetan and Mongolian fur clothing and non-fur clothing, also all my underwear, as a result of which I remain completely without clothes and have no means of acquiring new ones.

NOTES

PREFACE

1. These were apparently made by Pauwels and Bergier in a book published in English translation as *The Morning of the Magicians*. Their thesis that Dorzhiev and Gurdjieff were the same person was firmly put to rest by Alexandra David-Néel in her article 'Gurdjieff et Dordjieff,' *Nouvelles Littéraraires*, 22 April, 1954.

2. The Jesus Prayer – 'Lord Jesus Christ, Son of God, have mercy on me' -is repeated over and over, just as devotees of the Pure Land School of Buddhism repeat 'Namu Amida Butsu' or 'O-mi-to-fo' ('Homage to Amida Buddha'). First propagated on Mt Athos, it was believed to produce hesuchia or inner quietness in the heart, hence its devotees being called Hesychasts. The practice of the Jesus Prayer also possessed psychosomatic aspects: e.g., devotees would concentrate on the heart area when repeating it, and they would exercise forms of breath control. In the fourteenth century, attacks upon Hesychasm were mounted by Barlaam of Calabria, and a defence put up by Gregory Palamas, who discussed various aspects of prayer in his *Triads*, notably that the human body should participate. The movement was revived in the eighteenth century in the *Philokalia* of Makarios of Corinth and Nikodimos of the Holy Mountain, and has since been highly influential on modern Orthodoxy.

1. THE BURYATS

1. James Gilmour, *Among the Mongols* p. 46.
2. Ibid, pp. 47–8.
3. G.D.R.Phillips, *Dawn in Siberia*, pp. 23–4.
4. Lindon Bates Jr., *The Russian Road to China*, p. 151.
5. Rinchen, (ed. and tr.), *Four Mongolian Historical Chronicles*, p. 149.
6. Information in the following section on Lobsan Zhimba Akhaldayev and Damba Darzha Zayayev is drawn mainly from Rinchen, *Four Mongolian Historical Chronicles*; N. Poppe, 'The Buddhists in the USSR'; Bawden, *Shamans, Lamas and Evangelicals*, p. 166–7; and Glava Perbaya, 'Stanovlenie Tserkovnoy Organizatsii Buryatskogo Lamaizma, v XVIII –

pervoy polovine XIX v,' in *Lamaizm v Buryatii, XVIII – nachala XX veka, etc.*, an anthology of the USSR Academy of Sciences, Novosibirsk, 1983, pp. 12 ff.

7. Ratö (founded 1045) is near Lhasa, 'about 5 km behind Drölma Lhakhang'.
8. Foreword by Prof. Dr. Raghu Vira to Rinchen (ed. and tr.) *Four Mongolian Historical Records*, New Delhi, 1959, p. 6.
9. Dr. Raghu Vira in Rinchen (ed.and tr.), op. cit., p.6.
10. Glava Perbaya, op. cit., p. 20.
11. Glava Perbaya, op. cit., pp. 20–1.
12. Rinchen (ed. and tr.), op. cit., p. 152.
13. Dr. Raghu Vira in Rinchen (ed. and tr.), op. cit., pp. 7–8.
14. Rinchen (ed. and tr.), op. cit., p. 150.
15. Glava Perbaya, op. cit., p. 24.
16. Bawden, op. cit., p. 167.
17. For a full listing of classic Buryat datsans, see Appendix 1.
18. N. Poppe, op. cit., p. 169.
19. Tib. mTshan.nyid, sometimes also transcribed as tsanit: the classical dialectical programme of Buddhist doctrinal studies based on the systematic logic and epistemology of the Sautrantika philosophers, Dharmakirti and Dignaga.
20. N. Poppe, 'The Destruction of Buddhism in the USSR', p. 15.
21. Robert Rupen, 'The Buryat Intelligentsia', p. 384.
22. This is mostly based on notes made from an extempore translation of a Russian book (publication details unfortunately not available). Incidentally, the first Russian reputed to have had a grasp of the Mongolian language was Kulvinsky (died 1701), a member of the diplomatic staff, who was many times in Dzungaria and among the Oirat khans.
23. Tents.
24. H. P. Blavatsky, *Isis Unveiled*, vol. II, p. 600.
25. Extract from an article by H. P. Blavatsky, entitled 'Mr A. Lillie's Delusions', quoted in G. Barborka, *H. P. Blavatsky, Tibet and Tulku*, p. 121. The full quote is:

I will tell him [Arthur Lillie] also that I have lived at different periods in Little Tibet as in Great Tibet, and that these combined periods form more than seven years. Yet, I have never stated, either verbally or over my signature, that I had passed seven consecutive years in a convent. What I have said, and repeat now is, that I have stopped in Lamaistic convents; that I have visited Tzi-gadze, the Tashi-Lhünpo territory and its neighbourhood, and that I have been further in, and in such places of Tibet as have never been visited by any other European, and that he can ever hope to visit.

26. G. D. R. Philips mentions in *Dawn in Siberia* that an anti-Tsarist plot was fomented by a lama named Danzhin in 1767. It was this, he claims, that caused the authorities to become more tolerant towards Buddhism and to abandon for the time being any plans they might have had for its suppression.

27. There being no *j* in Cyrillic, 'Dorzhi' is the russification of the Tibetan word/name 'Dorji', which literally signifies the enlightening thunderbolt of the great god Indra.

2. EARLY LIFE

1. Central State Historical Archive, Leningrad, (TsGAOR), f. 560 (Collection of the Ministry of Finance), op. 28, d. 64, II. 11–15, marked with the seal of Ministry of Finance, 3 December 1901. This is a brief resumé of Dorzhiev's life to 1901, probably written by Dorzhiev himself at the request of the Russian Ministry of Foreign Affairs in 1901. It is a Russian text but probably, judging from its vocabulary and idiom, translated from Tibetan. Another copy exists in the Archive of the Foreign Policy of Russia, f. 560 (Kitaiskii stol), op. 491, d. 1448 (1900–1903), II. 162–7. Both documents are in Russian typescript and unsigned. I am indebted to Aleksandr Andreyev for supplying me with an English version.

2. Agvan Dorzhiev, *Chos.brgyad.gdon.gyis.byas.te//rgyal. khams.don.med.nyul.ba.yi/ dam.chos.nor.gyis, dbul.ba'i.sprang/øtsun.gzugs.shig.gi.bgyi.brjod.gtam* (throughout I follow Stephen Batchelor's unpublished translation (1989)) hereafter referred to simply as Dorzhiev, Autobiography, p. 1. [After John Snelling's death another translation of the autobiography was published by Thubten J. Norbu and Dan Martin: *Dorjiev: Memoirs of a Tibetan Diplomat*. The full Tibetan title translates as: 'The story of one who looks like a monk – but really is a beggar deprived of the jewel of the sacred Dharma, in the thrall of the eight worldly winds who slinks meaninglessly around the world.'

3. I am indebted for this and some of the following information to Dr Bata D. Bayartuev, a scientific collaborator of the Institute of Humanities of the Buryat Scientific Centre, Siberian Division, USSR Academy of Sciences, Ulan-Udé, with whom I had an interview in Leningrad in May 1991.

4. W. A. Unkrig. 'Aus letzten Jahrzehnten des Lamaismus in Russland', p. 139.

5. Lindon Bates Jnr., op. cit., p. 271.

6. Machig Drub'pai Gyelmo (Ma.gcig sGrub.pa'i rGyal.mo), also referred to in Tibetan as Kandro Drubpa'i Gyelmo, is credited with the composition of eight of the texts in the Tengyur, the Tibetan collection of works by Indian masters: two Amitayus sadhanas, two Amitayus mandala rites, an Amitayus fire-offering rite, a secret Avalokiteshvara sadhana and a Hayagriva sadhana. For further information, see G. N. Roerich, *The Blue Annals*, pp. 436–41.

7. An oral report has it that when the young Dorzhiev one day joined a queue of people waiting to be given blessings by a famous Buryat yogi who had clairvoyant powers, the yogi picked him out of the crowd and declared that he should become a monk. Letter, Joshua Cutler to Stephen Batchelor, 9

March 1991. Cutler obtained the information from Geshé Dawa Sangbo, a Buryat lama then resident in the USA, in June 1990.

8. See Bazarov, B., and Shagdurov, U., 'Agvan Dorzhiev: Poslednie Stranitsy Zhyzny', p. 122, and Pubayev, R. E., 'Agvan Dorzhiev', p. 94.
9. Dorzhiev, op. cit., p. 77n.
10. Letter from A. Breslavetz, 21 December 1989.
11. R. E. Pubayev, 'Agvan Dorzhiev', in *Natsionalno-osvoboditelnoye Dvizheniye Buryatskogo Naroda*, p. 94.
12. rNam.sNang
13. A. M. Pozdneyev, *Mongolia and the Mongols*, vol. 1 (1892). Most of the detailed information about Urga in this section comes, unless stated otherwise, from Chapter 2 ('Urga or Da Khüree'), pp. 43 ff.
14. G. N. Roerich, *Trails to Inmost Asia*, p. 154. Chapter VII ('Mongolia') contains much helpful information on Urga.
15. See Chapter 2, note 12.
16. Gilmour, op. cit., pp. 150–1.
17. Ibid., Chapter XII ('Urga'), pp. 150 ff.
18. The Jonang school was heretical insofar as its masters were believed to propound some kind of atman or soul theory.
19. Pubayev, op. cit. p. 94.
20. See *Sutra of the Wise and the Foolish, or The Ocean of Narratives*, translated from the Mongolian by Stanley Frye, Dharamsala, 1981.
21. Dorzhiev, op. cit., pp. 3–4.

3. TIBET AND WU T'AI SHAN 1873–1888

1. 'Yungdrung' is Tibetan for 'swastika'.
2. G. N. Roerich, *Trails to Inmost Asia*, pp. 247–8.
3. Ibid., p. 281.
4. Sir Charles Bell, *Tibet Past and Present*, pp. 226–7.
5. Abbé Huc, *Travels in Tartary and Thibet*, tr. W. Hazlitt, 1852 – edited edition London, 1970, p. 276.
6. Ibid., pp. 278–9.
7. Dorzhiev, op. cit., p. 5. Khensur Ngawang Nima comments that a brother of the present Dalai Lama, Tenzin Chögyel Rinpoché, is regarded as an incarnation of Ngari-pa.
8. This supposed visit by Dorzhiev to Wu T'ai Shan was one of the most problematical matters when piecing together his early life story. Only in his *Autobiography* (p. 6) does he mention that he visited the 'Five Peaked Mountain', all the other sources tending to deal very cursorily with this part of his life. However, I am bound to confess that I am still not entirely convinced that he did go there. It is possible, for instance, that when he speaks of the 'Five Peaked Mountain', he means some location in Trans-Baikalia. The term may even be open to metaphorical interpretation. This should be borne in mind when reading what follows.

9. 'Dzasak' was a Mongolian honorific accorded in old Tibet to high dignitaries equal in rank to a shapé or cabinet minister. 'Kusho' is likewise a noble title.
10. Gilmour, op. cit., p. 161.
11. Ibid., p. 167.
12. 'bul sdud
13. Ibid., p. 169.
14. L. Berlin, '*Khambo-Agvan-Dorzhiev, (I Borbe Tibeta Za Nezavicimos)*', p. 141. Robert Rupen maintains in *Mongols of the Twentieth Century* that Lev Efimovich Berlin served as a Narkomindel (i.e. Commissariat for Foreign Affairs) official in charge of the Japanese and Tibetan section from 1925 to 1926, and as Scientific Secretary of the Institute of the Peoples of the Orient. He was also involved in an unsavoury scheme to topple Grumm-Grzhimailo. Aleksandr Andreyev of the Soviet Cultural Foundation, Leningrad, on the other hand, says in a letter to the author of 22 February 1991 that he was a 'political officer with the Narkomindel, in charge of Tibet[an] and Mongolian affairs in the early 1920s', that he wrote two articles for *Novy-Vostok* and another (unsigned) article on Dorzhiev entitled 'The Tibetan Bismarck' in *Krasnaya Gazeta* (May 1925). Andreyev also believes that L. E. Berlin was a member of a Soviet delegation that signed a friendship treaty with Mongolia in Moscow on 5 November 1921, and that in later life he was a professor at the M. V. Lomonosov University, Moscow. An Old Bolshevik, he may well have been shot in the thirties.
15. Dorzhiev, op. cit., p. 9.
16. Ibid. p. 10.
17. Alexander Ular, 'The Policy of the Dalai Lama', p. 42.

4. THE THIRTEENTH DALAI LAMA 1888–1898

1. Based on personal reminiscences of the 13th Dalai Lama given to the author by the late Mrs M. D. Williamson and Mrs J. M. Jehu; also on various written records, notably that of Sir C. Bell.
2. Sir Charles Bell, *Portrait of the Dalai Lama*, pp. 302–6.
3. Kundé Ling, founded 1794, is now destroyed. It used to be situated south-east of Chakpori, the medical college of Lhasa, within the old circumambulation route known as the Lingkor. It was one of four royal colleges in Lhasa, the others being Tengyé Ling, Tsomo Ling and Tsemchok Ling. Their senior incumbents were graced with the honour of the Mongolian title of Khutukhtu. See Stephen Batchelor, *Tibet Guide*, London, 1987, p. 167; Keith Dowman, *The Power Places of Central Tibet*, London, 1988, p. 61; G. Tucci, *To Lhasa & Beyond*, London, 1985, p. 86, etc. Regents were also drawn from three other monasteries, including Reting.

4. G.H. Mullin (tr.), *Path of the Bodhisattva Warrior: The Life and Teachings of the Thirteenth Dalai Lama*, p. 39.

5. mTshan.zhabs

6. Autobiographical text by A. Dorzhiev in the Archive of the Foreign Policy of Russia, f.143 (Kitaiskii stol), op. 491, d. 1448 (1900–03), II. 162–7; a copy also exists in the Central State Historical Archive in St Petersburg (TsGAOR), f.560 (Collection of the Ministry of Finance), op. 28, d. 64, II. 11–15.

7. S. Markov, 'Tibetskye Chetki' ('Tibetan Rosary'), p. 101.

8. Ibid., p. 101.

9. las.rung.

10. tshe.rdas.

11. The kings of Sikkim were Tibetan nobles and had estates in the Chumbi Valley, a wedge of Tibetan territory probing south across the Himalayan crestline.

12. The Torgut were one of the Kalmyk clans.

13. Sarat Chandra Das: born Chittagong, E. Bengal, 1849; educated Presidency College, Calcutta. 1874; appointed head-master of Bhutia Boarding School, Darjeeling; began to study the Tibetan language and established friendly relations with the Maharaja of Sikkim and many leading lamas. 1879: travelled to Tashilhunpo with his colleague Urgyen Gyatso; remained there for six months. 1880: at home in Darjeeling working on 'papers on the history, religion, ethnology and folklore of Tibet, drawn from data collected during his journey'. 1881–82: a second and more extended expedition to Tibet; stayed at Tashilhunpo, mapped Yamdrok-Tso and visited Lhasa. 1882: founded Buddhist Text Society of India. 1885: on Colman Macauley's mission to Peking; subsequently awarded the title Rai Bahadur. 1887: awarded 'back premium' by Royal Geographical Society for his geographical researches. Subsequently employed as chief Tibetan translator to the Indian Government. 1902: resigned from Bengal Civil Service; published *Tibetan-English Dictionary* and *Journey to Lhasa and Central Tibet*; he also published numerous other scholarly books and articles. (Information: W.W. Rockhill's introduction to Das' *Journey to Lhasa and Central Tibet*, 1902.)

14. For an account of this expedition, see G. Bonvalot, *Across Tibet*, New York, 1892.

15. Autobiographical text by A. Dorzhiev in the Archive of the Foreign Policy of Russia, f. 143 (Kitaiskii stol), op. 491, d. 1448 (1900–1903), II. 162–7; a copy also exists in the Central State Historical Archive in St Petersburg (TsGAOR), f.560 (Collection of the Ministry of Finance), op. 28, d. 64, II. 11–15.A.

16. Ular, op. cit. pp. 42–3.

17. Bell, op. cit., p. 62.

18. Wilhelm Filchner is something of an enigma. According to a note in the *Journal of the Royal Central Asian Society (JRCAS)*, (vol. 14, p. 368) based

on the Berlin equivalent of *Who's Who* he was born in 1877, attached to the 'Great General Staff' as captain, retired and became an explorer. He visited the Pamirs in 1900, led a German expedition to Tibet in 1903 and an Antarctic expedition in 1910–12. In the twenties he was involved in mapping parts of north-east Tibet and China. The *JRCAS* note suggests that he was killed in eastern Tibet with a party of missionaries in 1927 or 1928. This must be wrong, however, for according to his one book available in English translation (*A Scientist in Tartary, from the Huang-Lo to the Indus*, trans. E. Lorimer, London, 1939), he continued his explorations in Inmost Asia. 'Let me make it clear that my researches related solely to geophysics,' he wrote; 'I was aiming at nothing less than the magnetic exploration of one of the largest hitherto . . . unexplored regions of the world.' One scientific journey took him from Tashkent to Leh via Kulja, Urumchi, Nagchukha and Gartok. Another, between 1934 and 1938, took him from Langchow to Leh via Koko-Nor, Tsaidam and Khotan.

Though scholars like Robert Rupen seem to accept the accuracy of *Sturm über Asien*, the book is in fact highly problematic. True, its main contours are sound enough, but these were probably provided by Filchner in his editorial capacity. The details we can assume came from Zerempil – and fantastic they are indeed. They make out that Agvan Dorzhiev was supremely powerful in Tibet, variously enjoying ministerial responsibility for foreign affairs, finance and war. It was he, for instance, that advised the Dalai Lama to return Curzon's letters unopened. Unfortunately, much of what is recorded is verifiably incorrect – for instance, that Dorzhiev was 57-years-old in 1900 (he was only 46), that he was born a Russian subject but in Tibet, that besides Gandan he studied at Sera monastic university, that his political activities in Lhasa were supported by Tsybikov who was there for many years (he was in fact there for just over one year – May 1900 to September 1901), etc., etc. The book also maintains that it took Dorzhiev a year to negotiate his Tibet-Mongolia Treaty when in fact he was only in Urga for about a month in 1913 according to reliable sources. Afterwards, Filchner maintains, he returned to Lhasa and stayed there until around 1921, when in fact he never set foot in Tibet after 1913. One could continue . . .

Filchner and Zerempil – who was allegedly recruited to the Russian secret service by Dorzhiev at the Gandan monastery in Urga – juxtapose rip-roaring adventure with political matter, making this truly a 'story of struggle and intrigue in Central Asia'. Was it then a commercially motivated book designed to provide the armchair traveller with a stirring read? Or was there some deeper and more sinister motive? If one wishes to go the road of conspiracy theories, it might be suggested that the book was conceived in the dirty tricks department of some foreign government's intelligence service with a view to re-inflaming Anglo-Russian rivalry in Central Asia.

19. Central State Historical Archive, St Petersburg, (TsGAOR), f. 560 (Collection of the Ministry of Finance), op. 28, d. 64, II. 11–15, marked with

the seal of the Ministry of Finance, 3 December 1901. Letter of 22. 5.78 from Dr P. D. Rayfield to J. Somers.

20. Bell, op. cit., p. 61–2. Unkrig, op. cit., p. 139, writes: 'His knowledge attracted the Dalai Lama, who firstly appointed him soibun (bsoi-dpon), that is personal valet to a high-ranking ecclesiastical dignitary, but later was appointed senechal ("Hofmarschall").'

21. Markov, op. cit., p. 101.

22. Tsepon W. D. Shakabpa: *Tibet: A Political History*, p. 195. and K. Dhondup, op. cit., pp. 7–9. This incident recalls another in 1934 when again a high Tibetan official, Lungshar Shapé, tried to seize power following the death of the Thirteenth Dalai Lama by similar means. Magic papers were found in his boots too – but he suffered a rather more dire punishment, being, among other things, blinded as well as thrown into a dungeon. When he later emerged, his natural pride and arrogance were, according to Hugh Richardson, who saw him, undiminished.

23. Parliamentary Papers, 1904, vol. 67, Cmd. 1920, No. 34: Sir C. Scott to the Marquess of Lansdowne, July 1st 1901, 2nd Enclosure: 'Another Interview with M. Badmeyeff'.

24. Ular, op. cit., p. 43, maintains that in 1896 the Dalai Lama sent Dorzhiev on a scholarly, not a political mission to Trans-Baikalia. He stayed for a year at the Gusinoye Ozero Datsan near Selenginsk, the seat of the Bandido Khambo Lama – 'and during his stay there were elaborated the great lines of the further Russian-Tibetan connivance . . .'

25. Central State Historical Archive, St Petersburg (TsGAOR), f. 560 (Collection of the Ministry of Finance), op. 28, d. 64, II. 11–15. L. Berlin in his *Novy Vostok* article says that the Dalai Lama 'decided to send Dorzhiev to his Russian Homeland to clarify Russia's relations with Tibet and the possibility of real support from Russia'.

26. Kha.btags. – a white silk scarf traditionally offered as a token of greeting by Tibetans and other Lamaist Buddhists.

27. Alternative reading: 'I departed from Lhasa in the company of some endowed with worldly wealth and others with the wealth of the Dharma.'

5. UKHTOMSKY'S SUMMONS 1898

1. Berlin, op. cit., p. 142.

2. Quoted in Rick Fields, *How the Swans Came to the Lake*, p. 115. The Buddhist sites at Bodh-Gaya were not finally restored to Buddhist hands until after Indian Independence.

3. Ular, op. cit. p. 43.

4. According to G. D. R. Phillips, op. cit., p. 113, exiles like Bestuzhev and his brother 'travelled among the ulus encampments as far as the authorities permitted, inquiring and recording all they saw and heard. From their inquiries the Buryat national spirit was given an impetus; a

new value was set by Buryats upon Buryat epics and culture and national life in general.'

5. V. Kupchenko (with E. Demin), 'V Zabaykalye – Cherez Parizh' ('To Trans-Baikalia via Paris'), *Baikal*, p. 144.

6. The principal source of information on Prince Ukhtomsky is G.A. Leonov, 'E. E. Ukhtomskii: K Istorii Lamaistskogo Sobraniya Gosudarstvennogo Ermitazha' ('E. E. Ukhtomskii: On the History of the Lamaist Collection in the State Hermitage Museum') in *Buddizi i limeramurno – chudomestvenie tvorzemvo narogov tschengravioi Azii* ('Buddhism and the Literary-Artistic of the Peoples of Central Asia'), Novosibirsk, 1985. Leonov maintained in conversation in June 1988 that he had never seen the name of Agvan Dorzhiev in any of the Ukhtomsky papers in Russian archives. Dorzhiev's Kalmyk factotum, Ovshe Norzunov, was mentioned, however; also Dr Badmayev. The Narkomindel official, L. Berlin, op. cit., calls Ukhtomsky, 'a man who took bribes to protect Russian Buryats from predatory missionaries'.

7. Albert Grünwedel, *Mythologie du Bouddhisme en Tibet et en Mongolie, basée sur la collection Lamaïque du Prince Oukhtomsky*, Leipzig, 1900, pp. ix-xxxiii.

8. Ukhtomsky in Grünwedel, op. cit., p. 22.

9. Olcott's Fourteen Propositions (or Fourteen Fundamental Buddhist Beliefs) was an early attempt to forge Buddhist unity by enunciating the basic principles essential to all schools and traditions. Ukhtomsky enumerates them in his Introduction to Grünwedel's *Mythologie* (pp. xxiv-xv); in the same piece he also states (p.xxii): 'L'Américain Olcott, président de la société théosophique, cherche avec beaucoup d'énergie, depuis des années, à retrouver les morceaux de la chaîne spirituelle qui unit les différents pays, où l'on adore le Buddha. Il parcourut l'Asie, fit la connaissance des plus célèbres parmi les prêtres indigènes et composa pour les buddhistes du monde entier une sorte de confession.' Olcott and his mentor, Mme Blavatsky, in association with their protégé Anagarika Dharmapala, later played an important part in reviving Sinhalese Buddhism.

10. H.S. Olcott, *Old Diary Leaves*, Madras, 1895–1935, Series 4 and 6, pp. 298–9.

11. The English edition was published as Prince Esper Ukhtomsky: *Travels in the East of Nicholas II, Emperor of Russia, 1890–1*, 2 vols, London, 1896 and 1900.

12. I was told orally that the newspaper's offices were next to Ukhtomsky's St Petersburg town house at 26 Spalernaya, now Ulitsa Voinov. When I visited the street, the house at that number was rather more humble than I had expected, which led me to suspect that the whole street had been renumbered at some stage. However, the building next door was more utilitarian and even in 1991 mechanical noises like those of printing presses were coming from it.

13. Quoted in David Dallin, *The Rise of Russia in Asia*, p. 53.

14. Prince Esper Ukhtomsky, *Travels in the East of Nicholas II, Emperor of Russia, 1890–1*, vol. ii, London, 1900, p. 56.
15. I. Y. Korostovets, *Von Cinggis Khan zur Sowjetrepublik*, p. 187. Korostovets calls Mongolor's manager Herr von Groth. Robert Rupen (*Mongols of the Twentieth Century*) calls him Baron Victor von Grot, while Alastair Lamb (*British India and Tibet*), basing himself on British records, calls him M. von Groot. Peter Fleming, in *Bayonets to Lhasa*, pp. 82–3, meanwhile writes: 'From St Petersburg and other sources came reports suggesting that these elusive, gnome-like characters [Dorzhiev, Norzunov, etc.] were controlled from Urga in Outer Mongolia, by a master-mind variously known as de Groot and von Grot . . .'
16. Alastair Lamb, *British India and Tibet, 1766–1910*, p. 220.
17. Ukhtomsky in Grünwedel, op. cit., p. x.
18. Leonov, op. cit., p. 107.
19. Ukhtomsky in Grünwedel, op. cit., p. x.

6. MISSION TO EUROPE 1898–1899

1. R. E. Bruce Lockhart, *Memoirs of a British Agent*, p. 74.
2. L. E. Berlin, op. cit. p. 142.
3. A. Andreev, 'Iz Istorii Peterburgskogo Buddiystkogo Khrama', ('History of the St Petersburg Buddhist Temple'), *Minovsheye*, Paris, No. 9, undated print-off, p. 385.
4. Ibid. pp. 1–3.
5. Vladimir Nabokov, *Gogol*, reprint London 1989, pp. 16–17.
6. Kalmyk labourers were brought to the site of St Petersburg and worked on the very earliest parts of the city, roughly in the area of the Petropavlovsk Fortress. Thus there have been Buddhists in the city virtually from the day of its first foundation.
7. The term 'khuvarak' seems to have a wide range of connotations – or at least is subject to different usages. It is sometimes used to denote lesser clergy generally, sometimes novice clergy, and sometimes upasaka or lay followers of the Buddhist religion.
8. Article on Kalmyk ASSR in *Great Soviet Encyclopedia*, New York and London, 1973.
9. G. Dorzhiev, 'Svyav' Narodov' (Links of the people), *Baikal* 3, Ulan-Udé, 1991, p. 128.
10. Unkrig, op. cit., p. 141. Unkrig was born in Pomerania and, from 1908, trained for missionary work among the Mongolians at the Religious Academy in Kazan. Later (1912), he became a Russian Orthodox priest. World War I thwarted his theological plans and he returned to Germany, where he became involved in scholarly work. He edited the journal *Sinica* and collaborated with Wilhelm Filchner, author of *Sturm über Asien*, and catalogued Tibetan and Mongolian texts for Sven Hedin. Lamaism and Tibeto-Mongolian medicine were his scholarly fields. In 1943, he

was appointed lecturer in Tibetan and Mongolian at the University of Frankfurt-am-Main. He died in Darmstadt. Obituary by W. Heissig, *Central Asian Journal*, 1957.

11. James Webb, *The Harmonious Circle*, London, 1980, p. 61. Webb's highly readable book is a tour de force of research which, unfortunately, is subjected to highly bizarre interpretation. He argues, brilliantly but perversely, that Norzunov was in fact G. I. Gurdjieff in disguise.

12. Joseph Deniker, 'A Leader of the Tibetans', p. 73.

13. A small amount of information on Budda Rabdanov was published in the article 'Tibetskye Chetki' ('Tibetan Rosary') by Sergey Markov (*Prostor*, No. 1, Alma-Ata, 1976, pp. 93–104). Markov was a Soviet journalist who worked on various journals, including *Soviet Siberia*, where his editor was one Max Garber. He learnt about Rabdanov from another Buryat named Tsybikzhab Baldano. As a boy, Baldano had longed to have a Russian education but his father had not permitted it, so he ran away from home. In Chita he met Rabdanov, who arranged for him to go to a Russian school.

Markov also met Agvan Dorzhiev in Novosibirsk at some unspecified date:

Once when I came to the railway station at Novosibirsk, the station master came up to me and said: 'Go to the fifth wagon. In it you'll find the Tibetan wise man.' I knocked on the door of the compartment and, getting an answer, went in and froze on the spot. There was sitting a Buddhist high priest in a robe and yellow hat, and with him were two lamas with Mausers in a wooden box. I held out my visiting card and pronounced my carefully-learnt English phrase. The old man answered me in Russian:

'Don't make a mess of the English language. What are you interested in?'

'Your business. Who are you?'

'I am the head of the Buddhist church in the Soviet Union: Khambo-Lama Agvan Dorzhiev. Who are you?'

'Sergey Nikolaievich.'

'Well, Seriozha, I'll give you a present.'

He took a Parker pen, which was very rare at the time, and with it wrote something in the book at his side.

'This book was written by my friend Piotr Kuz'mich Kozlov. He will soon be going past your town. If you are interested in Tibet, read this book which Gonbochzhab Tsybikov wrote called *A Buddhist Pilgrim at the Holy Places of Tibet*.'

Then he added:

'Please don't describe, particularly in print, this through journey of mine. Au revoir.'

The Khambo-Lama handed the visiting card back to me. The Manchurian Express went on towards Moscow.

When I got back to the editorial office and told Maks about my unexpected acquaintance, Maks whistled and said:

'Fifteen lines in tomorrow's edition in heavy petite type.'

The Harbin turncoats began to look at the gift of Agvan Dorzhiev. The book was *Tibet and the Dalai Lama* by P. K. Kozlov.

'Ah, it's the man himself!' – cried the turncoats, looking at the picture in the book of Agvan Dorzhiev. In a robe, high-pointed hat and coloured fur boots, he was sitting behind a carved table. With him there was a stuffed peacock and a pot with some flowering begonias.

14. 'Cérémonie Célébré au Musée Guimet le 27 Juin 1898, etc.', (official programme). Museum reference: 1V–9-1V c. 10.
15. Frederick Sachse, 'Alexandra David-Néel, 1868–1969', *The Middle Way*, vol. 59, No. 1, May 1984.
16. A. I. Termen's quotation of Aginsky's remarks are to be found in E. Demin's epilogue to V. Kupchenko, op. cit. p. 144. George Deniker's letter to Jeffrey Somers of 5 Feb. 1981 states that a 'second stay took place in 1913 after the last Ching's [sic] emperor and establish republic (1912). Agwan [Dorzhiev] was making the tour of capitals (Petersbourg, Paris, Berlin, London, also Rome and Vatican) to announce that if Tibet had been vassal of Chinese Emperor, it had no idea of becoming vassal of a new "republic".'
17. Letter from A. Dorzhiev to P.K. Kozlov, Archives of the Geographical Society, St Petersburg, F. 18, op, 13, d. 10, (P.K. Kozlov Collection).
18. A simple unsprung carriage.
19. One lan is a measure of weight equalling 31.2 grams, probably in this case of silver; Norzunov himself estimated it equivalent to forty francs.
20. Ovshe Norzunov, 'Trois Voyages à Lhassa (1898–1901)', p. 222.
21. Berlin, op. cit., p. 142; and Central State Historical Archive, St Petersburg, (TsGAOR), f.560 (Collection of the Ministry of Finance), op. 28, d. 64, II 11–15; copy also exists in Archive of Foreign Policy of Russia, f. 143 (Kitaiskii stol), op. 491, d. 1448 (1900–03), II 162–7.
22. A. Dorzhiev, op. cit., pp. 23–4.
23. Deniker, op. cit., p. 74.
24. Ibid.
25. Berlin, op. cit., p. 142.
26. PRO: FO 17 1551 HM 07974, Appendix III, Missions Between Russia and Tibet, p. 6.

7. THE AFFAIR OF THE STEEL BOWLS 1899–1901

1. Norzunov, op. cit., p. 218.
2. Khensur Ngawang Nima's notes to A. Dorzhiev, op. cit., p. 25.
3. Leonov, op. cit., p. 105. Leonov gives no date for this note from Ukhtomsky to the Emperor. The prince says that Norzunov had 'just completed one very dangerous trip to Lhasa via India . . . and he is shortly going in the next few days to the Dalai Lama via Calcutta and Sikkim'. So far as my research has shown, none of Norzunov's trips to Tibet quite conform to this pattern, so Ukhtomsky would seem to have confused matters a little. On general evidence it would seem that the audience, if in fact it came off, would have taken place around January 1900.

4. Incidentally, the editor of Das's dictionary, Revd Graham Sandberg, a clergyman and Tibetan scholar of Darjeeling, also supplied the British with intelligence.

5. Most of this and the following account is derived from Norzunov, op. cit., and from official British papers, mainly PRO: FO 17 1551; and IOR: L/P & S/11/19S.

6. J. Deniker, op. cit. p. 74.

7. Berlin, op. cit., p. 143.

8. Tib. Da-tse-ndo; modern Kangding near Chengdu.

9. Parliamentary Papers, 1904, vol. 67, Cmd 1920, No. 31, C. Hardinge to the Marquess of Salisbury, St Petersburg, 17 October 1900.

10. IOR: L/P & S/ 11/ 19S, No. 217-G, Khampa Jong, 7 October 1903, Col. F. Younghusband to L. W. Dane.

11. Quoted in Alastair Lamb, op. cit. p. 206.

12. PRO: FO 17 1506, Curzon to Lord G. Hamilton, Simla 13 June 1901: Alleged Tibetan Mission to Russia.

13. The names of the Mission's personnel were kindly clarified for me by Jeremy Russell of the Library of Tibetan Works and Archives in Dharamsala, who consulted the Tibetan edition of W. D. Shakabpa's book. Most sources mention only two Tibetans. Dorzhiev (op. cit., p. 30), says his party consisted of 'Lo-khe and Gyen-pun, the two representatives of the [Lhasa] Government, my travelling companion Jigje, Opashe [Norzunov] and Tsultrim'. Berlin (op. cit. p. 143), talks of 'his [the Dalai Lama's] secretary, Kainchik, and Dzhamsanom [or Jamsanom], chairman of the hoshun'. The *St Petersburgh Gazette* meanwhile mentioned 'the Secretary of the Dalai Lama Chambo Donid Lubson Kaintchok; the Captain of the district of Tibet, Sombu Tsiduron Pundzok; Dorjieff's Secretary and Translator, Owshche Norsunof; and Chief Shigshit Gaszonof' (IOR: Range 1920, vol. 67: Enclosure in No. 34: Summaries of Articles in the Russian Press). The information about Tsultim Gyatso comes from Friedrich Lustig's unpublished biography of K. A. M. Tennisons, p. 210: in October 1899, Tennisons met at a hamlet near Iakutsk the Mongolian Buddhist priest 'Lama Tsultim Gyamtso', who 'was at one time, for a brief period, secretary to . . . Dorzhiev'.

14. This diary, 'a small book in an oilskin binding' of some 400 sides of paper, was located and studied in Tsybikov's birthplace, Urdo-Aga, by the Soviet journalist Sergey Markov, upon whose account much of the following is based.

15. S. Markov, op. cit., p. 99.

16. In Sanskrit 'Vajravarahi' literally means 'Diamond Sow', which resonates with a legend dating from the seventeenth century in which Dorjé Pamo resorted to the somewhat dramatic stratagem of changing her monks into pigs when Samding monastery was threatened by a raiding party of Dzungarians. Sergey Markov also notes that around 1897 the Kalmyk, Baza Bakshi Monkochzhev, had visited Samding In 1897, A.

Pozdneyev published in St Petersburg *The Story of the Journey to Tibet of Baza-Bakshi of Baga Dörbet*, (N. Poppe, 'The Destruction of Buddhism in the USSR', p. 20n).
17. A. Dorzhiev, op. cit., p. 28.
18. The Chinese Representative in Lhasa.

8. THE TIBETAN MISSION OF 1901

1. Ekai Kawaguchi, *Three Years in Tibet*, pp. 499–500.
2. There is in official British records (PRO: FO 17 1551 HM 07974: Appendix II, Dorjieff) a brief account of another pamphlet that Dorzhiev is reputed to have presented to the Dalai Lama. It apparently contained 'an enumeration of the good acts of Emperor Nicholas II, in the direction of furthering the happiness of the world'. It too was in three languages – Russian, Mongolian and Tibetan – and in it Dorzhiev 'explained to the Grand Lama the many advantages which the Buddhist Church would gain by friendship with so great a monarch, and represented that if the Grand Lama visited the Russian capital he might convert the Tsar to the Buddhist faith'. This pamphlet was in addition 'believed to have been largely circulated amongst the Buddhists of Mongolia and Tibet'. This information was obtained by the Deputy Commissioner of Darjeeling from a Mongolian lama named 'Gyeshala'. 'Geshe-la' is the usual respectful mode of address for a geshé or Tibetan Buddhist doctor of divinity, so the name means no more than, say, 'Reverend Sir'. In fact there is no evidence that Dorzhiev ever wrote such a text, though one along apparently similar lines was certainly published by the Kalmyk lama, Dambo Ulyanov, under the title *Predskazaniya Buddha o Dome Romanovih i Kratkii Otcherk Moih Puteschestvii v Tibet v 1904–7*, ('Predictions of the Buddha about the House of Romanov and a Brief Account of my Travels to Tibet in 1904–5'), St Petersburg, 1913.
3. W. A. Unkrig to Dr R. Loewenthal, letter of 17 Dec. 1954, quoted in Rupen, *Mongols of the Twentieth Century*, pp. 106–7.
4. Central State Historical Archive, St Petersburg, (TsGAOR), f. 560, (Collection of Ministry of Finance), op. 28, d. 64, II 11–15, dated 3 (or 23) December 1901; a copy also exists in Archive of the Foreign Policy of Russia, f. 143 (Kitaiskii stol), op. 491, d. 1448 (1900–03), II. 162–7.
5. A. Dorzhiev, op. cit., p. 29.
6. PRO: FO 17 1551 HM 07974, p. 9.
7. Ibid. Appendix III, Missions between Russia and Tibet, p. 9.
8. Leonov, op. cit., p. 111.
9. PRO: FO 65 1631.
10. This Ulyanov is also probably the man reported by British intelligence to have travelled with one 'Menkhondjinoff' from Astrakhan to Lhasa in 1891, returning via Koko-Nor and Peking. Later, on 1 January 1906 (OS), Nicholas II recorded in his diary that he had that day given an audience

to two Buddhist Kalmyks: Ulyanov, and a lama of the same name, who were on their way to Tibet. Finally, A. Grünwedel refers to an 'Ulijanov': a gelong (monk) attached to the Guards Regiment of the Don Cossacks who, he maintains, wrote a voluminous book in Russian in which he attempted to 'prove from the Kalachakra that the Romanov dynasty would be the future rulers of the world, and he traced their genealogy back to the ancient dynasty of [the] Suchandra [kings of Shambhala]'.

References: PRO: FO 228 1186: India to Peking, 16 February 1895; Hugh Seton-Watson, *The Decline of Imperial Russia*, p. 327; W. A. Unkrig, op. cit., p. 148; A. Grünwedel, *Der Weg nach Shambhala*, pp. 3–4.

11. A. Dorzhiev, op. cit., p. 31.
12. C. Nabokov, *Contemporary Review*, vol. 130, 1926, p. 480.
13. I. Y. Korostovets, op. cit., pp. 208–9.
14. IOR: Range 1920, vol. 67, Item No. 34, Sir C. Scott to the Marquess of Lansdowne, 1 July 1901, enclosure.
15. Ibid., Item No. 35, Sir C. Scott to the Marquess of Lansdowne, 4 July 1901, enclosure.
16. Much of the following information is drawn from R.E. Pubayev, 'P. A. Badmayev' pp. 90–93 in the anthology *Natsional'no-Osvoboditenel'noe Dvizhenie Buryatskogo Naroda*, Ulan-Udé, 1989. Pubayev draws upon V. P. Semeninkov's biography of Badmayev: *Za Kulisamk Tzarisma (Arkhiv Tibetskogo Vracha Badmayev)*, Leningrad, 1925.
17. René Fülöp Miller, *Rasputin, the Holy Devil*, p. 99.
18. In fact it is difficult to work out some of the exact details of Badmayev's Mongolian machinations. Some sources say that both Alexander III and Witte were unenthusiastic, others say quite the opposite.
19. Robert Rupen, 'The Buryat Intelligentsia', pp. 392–3.
20. Parliamentary Papers, 1904, vol. 67, Cmd. 1920, Enclosure in Item No. 34, 'Summaries of Articles in the Russian Press'.
21. Ibid., Items No. 35 and 36, Sir C. Scott to the Marquess of Lansdowne, St Petersburg, 4 July and 19 July 1901.

9. AMONG THE KALMYKS AND THE BURYATS 1901–1903

1. Tib. chos. rva.
2. A. Dorzhiev, op. cit., p. 31.
3. A doramba could be said to be the holder of a second-class geshé degree; a lharampa is the holder of a first class one.
4. A. Andreev, op. cit. p. 384, and G. Dorzhiev, op. cit., p. 129.
5. Unkrig, op. cit., p. 142.
6. Tib. mThsan.nyid.
7. G. Dorzhiev, op. cit., p. 129.
8. Unkrig, op. cit., p. 143, writes of Kalmyk religious scholarship:

The author of this article has, for example, found in the library of the Religious

Academy at Kazan on the River Volga far more than one hundred large and small books, mostly newly lithographed works in the Kalmyk language, and all of them of Buddhistic or Lamaistic content. But already in the 17th century, Zaya Pandita, a scholarly lama and creator of the Kalmyk alphabet (1648) – which of course is modelled on the Mongolian but, contrary to the latter, has for each sound a separate sign – has written approximately a hundred and fifty theses, the first literature in his own idiom though leaning mainly on Tibetan models. Lately the Kalmyk lamas Cimid Baldanov, the Bakshi Dalai Lama Bogdan, Ochir Dzungrujev, [the Kalmyk bakshi of the Baga Derbet clan who travelled to Lhasa with Norzunov in 1898; see Norzunov, 'Trois Voyages à Lhasa, 1898–1901', p. 218, where he is named as 'Boudache Johngruef'], the bakshis M. Bormandjinov, Sarab Tepkin [who later moved to the Petrograd temple] and Dorji Setenov have occupied themselves scientifically and literally with lexicology in particular. Dorji Setenov, the General Bakshi of the Xurul'e [monastery] of the district of Yeke Derbet in the guberniia of Stavropol has translated from the Tibetan into the language of his people a manual for the three classes of men who want to take refuge in religion. He also published a work of Lamaist dogmatics of which, during the Bolshevist unrest and in spite of strict censorship, one copy was brought across the border.

9. Most of the information concerning this monastic college is derived from Unkrig, op. cit., pp. 141–4 and from the articles of Aleksandr Andreyev. Incidentally, Friedrich V. Lustig, op. cit., p. 210, states that this 'Buddhist Ecclesiastical Academy' was 'at Tsere, in the Tundu Khurul district of Astrakhan Gubernia'; also that there were 'excellent professors and lecturers, not only from Russia, but from Tibet, Mongolia, China, India and Nepal' on the faculty.

10. G. Dorzhiev, op. cit., p. 129.

11. Tib. tshe.bum

12. See Panchen Ötrul Rinpoché, 'The Long Life Ceremony', *Chö Yang: The Voice of Tibetan Religion and Culture*, No. 3, undated, pp. 78–87. Also L. A. Waddell, *Lamaism*, reprint Cambridge, 1959, pp. 444 ff.

13. Report compiled by the Ministry of Internal Affairs on the arrival in St Petersburg of a Tibetan representative, Agvan Dorzhiev, with a view to petitioning the Russian Government to recognize the sovereignty of Tibet. St Petersburg: TsGIA, f. 821, op. 150, d. 476, I. 2–4. I am grateful to A. Andreyev for kindly providing me with a translation of this document.

14. These official rejections came in the years 1910 and 1911.

15. Ibid.

16. Robert Rupen, *Mongols of the Twentieth Century*, p. 105.

17. Fortunately in 1905, having suffered a grave reversal in the Far East and facing profound unrest at home, the Emperor published an Edict of Toleration which took much of the pressure out of the situation.

18. TsGIA, f. 821, d. 476, I. 2–7. I am indebted to Aleksandr Andreyev for providing me with a translation of this document.

19. Ibid.

20. Ibid.

21. TsGIA, f. 821, op. 150, d. 476, I. 2–4.

22. Ibid.

23. B. Bazarov and U. Shagdurov, op. cit., p. 122.
24. B. D. Tsybikov, 'Uchenby i Prosvetitel' Tsyben Zhamtsarano', in *Natsional'no-Osvoboditel'noe Dvizhenie Buryatskogo Naroda*, Ulan-Udé, 1989, pp. 64 ff.
25. Leonov, op. cit., p. 114.
26. N. Poppe, 'The Destruction of Buddhism in the USSR', p. 16. Today such a devazhin may be seen in the small collection of Buddhist art at the Museum of the History of Religion and Atheism in Kazan Cathedral, St Petersburg.
27. PRO: FO 17 1755, Sir C. Scott to Lord Lansdowne, St Petersburg, January 1902.
28. J. Deniker, 'The Dalai-Lama's New 'Tse-Boum' from Paris', p. 582.
29. According to the *Handbook of Russian Literature*, ed. V. Terras, Yale, 1985, p. 512, Voloshin was a 'poet, translator and artist associated with the Symbolist movement but never a member of its inner circles and unlike the Symbolists in some aspects of his work ... He acknowledged the Parnassians, especially José Maria Hérédia, as his predecessors ... [His] poems typically consist of intimate meditations ... He called himself a "neo-realist", which may be the best label for him ...'
30. B. L. Kupchenko, op. cit., p. 143.
31. Ibid., p. 143. Dorzhiev frequently went shopping in Europe for the Dalai Lama. In 1906 he placed an order for brocade with the Moscow business concern of Sapozhnikov. According to A. Andreyev, there are in Russian archives records of his placing a number of such orders with Russian business houses on behalf of the Dalai Lama and other high Tibetan officials.
32. Ibid., p. 143.
33. Ibid., p. 144. *The Handbook of Russian Literature* records that Voloshin subsequently travelled widely in the Mediterranean region and returned often to Russia. He eventually settled at Koktebel in the Crimea 'where his house became a refuge for writers and artists of any political persuasion'. During World War I, the Revolution and the Civil War, he wrote pacifist poems: 'He depicted the sufferings of Russia as a nation, invoked its dismal history, and expressed his belief in its Christian essence and mission.' See I T. Kuprianov, *Sud'ba poeta: lichnost'i poeziia M. Voloshina*, Kiev, 1978.
34. A. Dorzhiev, op. cit., p. 37.

10. THE YOUNGHUSBAND MISSION TO LHASA 1903–1904

1. Letters from India, vol. 139, No. 1376: Minute by Lord Curzon on Russian Ambitions in East Persia, 28 October 1901.
2. IOR: MSS Eur D 510/8, vol. XX, Curzon to Hamilton, 10 July 1901.
3. Private Correspondence, India, Pt. 11, Curzon to Hamilton, 11 September 1901.

4. IOR: L/P & S/11/19S: Col. F. E. Younghusband to L. W. Dane, Secretary to the Government of India, Foreign Dept, 7 October 1903, p. 5.

5. IOR: MSS EUR F. 111 344 (Curzon Collection) No. 6: Lansdowne to Satow, 17 November 1902.

6. There is an interesting file (IOR: MSS Eur F 111/342) in British records on the gold mines of Tibet. One item, 'Notes on the Gold Mines of Tibet' (23 Mar. 1899), records that the gold field was said to be adjacent to the Lhasa-Leh trade route, north of 'Dokthol province, which borders Nepal', and stretched for 300 miles between 81° and 87° E longitude and approximately in the parallel of 32° N latitude, and included the famous Thok Jalung mines north of the Mount Kailas region. 'The Russians can make a base at Kivia and though they have four or five hundred miles of rough travelling to reach the mines they can apparently utilize camels all the way. This is of course an enormous advantage.' Concessions would have to be obtained from Peking but, once obtained, the writer of the 'Notes' did not think that the local Tibetans ('in spite of their independence') could be long obstructive. A memorandum of 8 April 1899, meanwhile, from the Secretary of State for India in London to the Viceroy bears out British interest in the mines. A 'certain influential promoter' is concerned about Russian interest in the Tibetan gold mines and is concerned that his company may be pre-empted by the Russians if it is delayed. Alastair Lamb maintains that Rothschilds were interested in the Tibetan gold mines.

7. PRO: FO 17 1745, Curzon to Hamilton, 13 November 1902.

8. Messengers.

9. George Seaver, *Francis Younghusband*, London, 1952, pp. 201–3.

10. IOR: L/P & S/11/195: Col. F. E. Younghusband to L. W. Dane, Secretary to the Government of India, Foreign Dept, 7 October 1903, p. 6.

11. IOR: Range 1920, vol. 67, Item No. 158: Viceroy to Secretary of State for India, 13 December 1903.

12. E. Kawaguchi, op. cit., pp. 505–6, claims to have been told by an indiscreet official that a caravan of about three hundred camels had arrived in Tibet with a load consisting of Russian 'fire-arms, bullets and other interesting objects'.

13. Private Correspondence India, Pt. 11, Vol. XXVI, Curzon to Hamilton, 5 August 1903.

14. Parliamentary Papers, 1904, vol. 67, Cmd. 2054, Item No. 37, Younghusband to Secretary to the Government of India, 11 January 1904.

15. Edmund Candler, *The Unveiling of Lhasa*, p. 111.

16. Kawaguchi, op. cit., pp. 500–1. Kawaguchi is not exactly clear about the date when the episcopal robes were presented. He was in Lhasa from March 1901 but merely says that the gift took place 'two years ago' – presumably from the time of writing.

17. Gl. Ts. Tsybikov, *Buddhist-palomnik in Swiatyn Tibeta*, Petrograd, 1918. This English quotation by N. Rhodes based on p. 166 of the German translation of K. Gabrisch (publication details unavailable). I am greatly

indebted to Nicholas Rhodes, an expert on Tibetan numismatics, for much ancillary information as well.

18. bDog.bde.
19. W. J. Ottley, *With Mounted Infantry in Tibet*, London, 1906, p. 230.
20. C. Bell and R. Kennedy, diary entries for 9 Jan 1921, London, The British Library.
21. Later, around 1914, the arsenal was moved to the yamen of the Chinese Amban and copper coins were also struck there until 1932, when both mint and arsenal were combined in a single building at Trapchi; this was powered by hydro-electricity generated at Dodé.
22. K. Dondhup, op. cit., p. 22; and P. Fleming, op. cit., pp. 266–7. Fleming here quotes a communiqué from Ampthill to Brodrick of May 1904 and another from Ampthill to King Edward VII of 30 June; the reference for the second is simply 'Royal Archives'.
23. This may have been Gonsar, where the Dalai Lama used to go on retreat.
24. G. H. Mullin (tr.), op. cit., p. 67.
25. A. Dorzhiev, op. cit., p. 40.
26. Shakabpa, op. cit., p. 215.

11. THE DALAI LAMA IN EXILE 1904–1908

1. E. Candler, op. cit. pp. 207–8.
2. A. Dorzhiev, op. cit., p. 42.
3. A. Lamb, op. cit., p. 243.
4. E. E. Ukhtomsky, 'The English in Tibet: A Russian View', *American Review & Miscellaneous Journal*, No. 179, 1904, pp. 28–9. This article seems to be an extract of material included in Ukhtomsky's book *Iz Oblasti Lamaizma* (St Petersburg, 1904).
5. F. Younghusband, *India and Tibet*, London, 1910, p. 326.
6. C. Bell, *Portrait of the Dalai Lama*, p. 65, and N. Roerich, *Altai Himalaya*, p. 358.
7. Younghusband, op. cit., p. 325.
8. G. N. (Yuri) Roerich, op. cit., pp. 188ff.
9. Quoted in G. H. Mullin (tr), op. cit., p. 67.
10. S. Markov, op. cit., p. 94.
11. Berlin, op. cit., p. 146.
12. Dmitri Pokotilov (?–1908): 1887 attached to the Asiatic Department of the Ministry of Foreign Affairs in St Petersburg; later sent to join the Russian Legation at Peking; 1893 recalled to the Asiatic Department and, during the same year, nominated as Chief of the Chancery of General Affairs in the Ministry of Finance; 1898 appointed Director of the Russo-Chinese Bank at Peking (Beijing). Later became a member of the directory council of the bank in St Petersburg and, finally, was appointed Russian Minister

to China. In this position he died on 7 March 1908 at Peking. Pokotilov's narrative of his trip to Wu T'ai Shan (1889) was published in St Petersburg in 1893 and translated into German by W. A. Unkrig as 'Der Wu Tai Schan und Seine Klöster' in *Sinica-Sonderausgabe*, 1935, pp. 38–39. His intention to devote himself entirely to scientific studies did not materialize. (Based on a brief biography in the preliminaries to D. Pokotilov, in *History of the Eastern Mongols During the Ming Dynasty, 1368–1634*, tr. R. Loewenthal, vol. 1, *Studia Serica*, Chengtu, 1947.)

13. Berlin, op. cit., p. 147.
14. A. Dorzhiev, op. cit., pp. 43–4.
15. IOR: L/P&S/10/147, vol. 21: Mr Spring-Rice to Sir Edward Grey, St Petersburg, 14 March 1906.
16. IOR: L/P&S/19/147, vol. 21: Mr Spring-Rice to Sir Edward Grey, St Petersburg, 7 April 1906.
17. IOR: L/P&S/10/147, vol. 21: Draft telegram to Viceroy: Foreign Secret, Tibet, Satow.
18. A. Andreev, op. cit., p. 383.
19. Robert Rupen, in 'The Buryat Intelligentsia', p. 386, writes that a congress of Buryats was held at Irkutsk in 1905. It was led by Mikhail Bogdanov (1878–1919), a Buryat intellectual and politician educated at Kazan, Tomsk and St Petersburg University. A Social Revolutionary (SR) he went to Berlin but was forced to leave there for Zürich before returning to Russia in 1905.
20. B. D. Tsybikov, op. cit., p. 65.
21. F. I. Stcherbatsky, 'Kratky Otchet O Poezdke V Urgu', ('A Short Account of My Journey to Urga'), originally published 1906 in *Proceedings of the Russian Committee for the Study of Central and East Asia*, No. 6, s. 19–22, reproduced in *Vostok-Zapad*, Moscow, 1989.
22. A. Piatigorsky, 'The Departure of Dandaron', p. 173n.
23. This oral information from Dr Yaroslav Vasil'kov of the Oriental Insitute of the USSR Academy of Sciences in Leningrad.
24. Stcherbatsky, op. cit.
25. R. Rupen, *Mongols of the Twentieth Century*, pp. 109–10. Rupen gives as his reference: Bulletin, No. 7 (1907), 'Voyage à Ourga'.
26. S. Markov, op. cit., p. 102. Markov maintains that Tsybikov took the portrait from Urga. Certainly a portrait is presently lodged in the State Hermitage Museum in St Petersburg. I was shown a photograph of it by the former Curator of Tibetan and Mongolian Art, Gennady A. Leonov, but was unable to see the actual portrait when I was later in the museum.
27. S. Markov, op. cit., p. 102.
28. A. Dorzhiev, op. cit., p. 43.
29. IOR: L/P&S/10/92 2826/09: Report by Major W. F. T. O'Connor on his tour of North America and Asia with the Maharaja Kumar of Sikkim.
30. IOR: L/P&S/10/147, vol. 21: Sir Arthur Nicolson to Sir Edward Grey, St Petersburg, 13 July 1906.

31. Ibid.
32. IOR: L/P&S/10/147, vol. 21: Sir Arthur Nicolson to Sir Edward Grey, St Petersburg, 19 November 1906.
33. AGO (Archive of the Geographical Society), r. 97, op. 1, d. 11, 1. 1–3. I am indebted to Aleksandr Andreev for supplying a translation.
34. A. Dorzhiev, op. cit., p. 46.
35. PRO: FO 371 619 738: Mr Bryce to Sir Edward Grey, Washington, 17 December 1908, Enclosure: Mr Rockhill to the President, Peking, 8 November 1908.

12. A HEATHEN TEMPLE IN CHRISTIAN PETERSBURG 1908–1910

1. The following is based on 'A Brief Sketch of H. E. the Late Buddhist Archbishop of Latvia the Most Revd. Karlis A. M. Tennisons', by A. Disciple (almost certainly Friedrich Lustig), *The Maha Bodhi*, June (?), 1962; also Lustig's biography.
2. See C. Humphrey, *Karl Marx Collective*, Cambridge, 1983, p. 65: the first Barguzin temple was constructed in the early nineteenth century under the patronage of the Barguzin prince (taisha). The first wooden monastery was built in 1854. Tsarist legislation of 1854 cut the number of lamas from seventy to eight, but subsequently there were many 'unofficial lamas'. The monastery was rebuilt in 1861, and again by Agvan Dorzhiev after the Revolution, close to Barkhan Öndür, a mountain venerated by the local shamans. It was closed (destroyed?) in the early 1930s.
3. Letters to the author, 30 October 1989 and 22 February 1991.
4. Lustig, op. cit., p. 265, also mentions the following as having attended Princess Tundutova's salons: Baron Serge Korff, Prince Urusoff, Baron von Benckendorff, Prince Golytsin, Princess Volkonskaya, Princess Obolenskaya, Mr Manassavitch-Maniulov, Mr Stirrmer, Mr Trepov (later Premier), General Shvedov, Mr Shcheglovitov and officers of the Lancers of the Guard [all sic].
5. Lustig, op. cit., p. 275: Dorzhiev told Nicholas 'inter alia that the construction of the Buddhist cathedral Church would cost the Buddhists of Russia not less than 5,000,000 gold rubles, that three celebrated architects and several foremost artists of the time would be employed and that some of the materials for the construction would have to be ordered from Finland, Belgium, Germany, France and Italy. The eminent Lama also explained that Italian sculptors would be employed to carve the huge statue of Lord Buddha Gautama Shakyamuni in the central Prayer Hall.'
6. Tchaikovsky died in this apartment block in 1893 and Turgenev lived there for a time.
7. Orally reported to the author by Aleksandr Andreev, quoting notes of

documents found in the Archive of the Ministry of Finance in the Central State Historical Archive, St Petersburg (TsGAOR).

8. TsGIA (Central State Foreign Archive), feuilleton 821, op. 133, document 448 (1908), p.1; quoted in A. Andreev, op. cit. p. 385.

9. PRO: FO 371 619 738: Mr Rockhill to President Roosevelt, Peking, 8 November 1908, Enclosure 1 in Mr Bryce to Sir Edward Grey, Washington, 17 December 1908.

10. IOR: L/P&S/10/92 2826/09: Private Letter: Major O'Connor to R. Ritchie, Peking, 1 December 1908.

11. W. F. T O'Connor, *On the Frontier and Beyond*, London, 1931, pp. 125–6.

12. PRO: FO 371 619 738: Mr Rockhill to President Roosevelt, Peking, 8 November 1908, Enclosure 2: Imperial Edict issued 3 November 1908, by Her Imperial Majesty the Empress-Dowager.

13. PRO: FO 371 619 738: Mr Rockhill to President Roosevelt, Peking, 8 November 1908, Enclosure 1 in Mr. Bryce to Sir Edward Grey, Washington, 17 December 1908.

14. C. Bell, *Portrait of the Dalai Lama*, p. 76.

15. A. Dorzhiev, op. cit., pp. 46–7, also says that 'On two occasions I was able to meet His Holiness as part of a group of four abbots'; and adds that although these 'offered a great deal of praise to the precious Dalai Lama, this was not done with good intentions but out of fear of losing face before others'.

16. PRO: FO 371 619 490: Sir John Jordan to Sir Edward Grey, Peking, 23 December 1908.

17. Sanskrit, vihara; Tibetan, gompa – literally, 'lonely place'.

18. Andreev. op. cit., p. 386.

19. K. A. Tennisons, in a letter dated 19 January 1962 to the Editor of a Buddhist journal (photocopy extant, details lost), wrote: 'The father of Mr Yuri Roerich (namely, the late Mr N. K. Roerich) did not design nor ornament the Buddhist Temple in St Petersburg at all. In fact, the Roerich family had absolutely nothing to do with the erection of the famed Buddhist Cathedral in the former Russian capital.' He also, in the May 1961 issue of *The Maha Bodhi*, states that 'Prof. Stcherbatsky did not contribute even one kopeck to the building of the Buddhist Temple.' At the same time Revd Tennisons was calling himself the former 'Lord Abbot' of the temple. Is this perhaps a case of rivalry: of seeking to boost one's own status by diminishing the achievements and importance of others?

20. One of those unverifiable rumours that circulates in St Petersburg Orientalist and Buddhist circles is that Varvara Schneider was at one time Stcherbatsky's mistress.

21. N. K. Roerich, *Himalayas, Abode of Light*, Bombay and London, 1947, p. 110.

22. J. T. Fuhrmann, *Rasputin, A Life*, New York, 1990, p 250.

23. Andreev, op. cit., p. 387.

24. The meaning of 'khuvarak' is unclear, or at least its usage varies. Sometimes a khuvarak is said to be a novice or member of the lower clergy; but sometimes the term is applied to lay members of the Sangha (upasakas).
25. Andreev, op. cit., p. 388.
26. A. Dorzhiev, op. cit., pp. 47–9.

13. THE TURNING POINT 1909–1913

1. C. Bell, *Portrait of the Dalai Lama*, p. 106.
2. Andreev, op. cit., p. 391.
3. C. Bell, op. cit., p. 106.
4. This refers to attempts by Afanasius, Bishop of the Don and Novocherkassk regions, to convert the Kalmyks.
5. *Russkoe Znamya* ('Russian Banner'), Bulletin of the Union of the Russian People, Sunday 3 November 1910 (OS), No. 222; in 'Dokumenta, Stat'i, Materiala O Buddiyskom Khrame V Leningradye' ('Documents, Articles and Materials About the Buddhist Temple in Leningrad'), typewritten anthology, undated.
6. *Pech* ('Speech'), 30 December 1910 (OS) – 'Little Feuilleton'; in 'Dokumenta, Stat'i, Materiala O Buddiyskom Khrame V Leningradye'.
7. It has not been possible to trace this man or find out anything about him. He was probably an English member of St Petersburg society at around the turn of the century, and had deep but unconventional religious interests.
8. Andreev, op. cit., p. 381.
9. Unkrig, op. cit., p. 149.
10. Bell, op. cit., p. 132.
11. D. Macdonald, *Twenty Years in Tibet*, pp. 97–8.
12. PRO: FO 371 1327 30220: India Office to Foreign Office: Enclosure in No. 1: Government of India to the Marquess of Crewe, 15 July 1912.
13. PRO: FO 371 1327 30553: Enclosure in No. 1: Government of India to the Marquess of Crewe, 16 July 1912.
14. Macdonald, op. cit., p. 99.
15. A. Dorzhiev, op. cit., p. 53.
16. PRO: FO 371 1328 36999: Government of India to the Marquess of Crewe, 31 August 1912.
17. PRO: FO 371 1328 39709: Government of India to the Marquess of Crewe, 20 September 1912. There is no evidence that Dorzhiev had any command of English.
18. Korostovets, op. cit., p. 209.
19. PRO: FO 371 1609 7144: Sir George Buchanan to Sir Edward Grey, St Petersburg, 11 February 1913, Enclosure. See also H. E. Richardson, *Tibet and Its History*, Revised and updated edition, Boulder, 1984, pp. 280–2.

Dorzhiev merely says, 'I offered official gifts on account of the binding accords which had been and were to be ratified henceforth with Tibet and other lands' (A. Dorzhiev, op. cit., p. 54).

20. PRO: FO 371 1609 7570: Sir George Buchanan to Sir Edward Grey, St Petersburg, 13 February 1913.

21. Andreev, op. cit., p. 394.

22. Sazonov is generally reckoned to have been an able Foreign Minister. He entered the Imperial Russian Diplomatic Service in 1883, served in London and Rome, and in 1906 became Minister in Residence to the Vatican. He was made Izvolsky's assistant in 1909 and succeeded him the following year, serving until his dismissal in 1916. After the Revolution, he was a member of the Russian Political Conference in Paris and Foreign Minister in Admiral Kolchak's government during the Civil War. He died an émigré.

23. PRO: FO 371 1609 7144: Sir George Buchanan to Sir Edward Grey, St Petersburg, 11 February 1913, Enclosure.

24. PRO: FO 371 1609 7222: Sir George Buchanan to Sir Edward Grey, St Petersburg, 14 February 1913.

25. Private letter, George Deniker to Jeffrey Somers, Paris, 5 February 1981. Collection, Jeffrey Somers.

26. C. Bell, *Tibet Past and Present*, pp. 228–30.

27. Berlin, op. cit., p. 153.

28. W. D. Shakabpa, op. cit., p. 253.

14. THE FALL OF THE HOUSE OF ROMANOV 1914–1917

1. A. Andreev, op. cit. p. 394.

2. G. D. R. Phillips, op. cit., p. 108.

3. B. Bazarov and U. Shagdurov, op. cit., p. 122.

4. Andreev, op. cit., p. 394.

5. A. Andreev, op. cit., p. 392.

6. Quoted in ibid., p. 393, reference given as TsGIA, f. 821, op. 133, d. 448 ob.

7. Ibid., p. 393.

8. W. A. Unkrig, op. cit., p. 146.

9. Lustig calls these 'members of the construction committee', whereas in fact Rosenberg and Vladimirtsov are omitted from Andreev's more reliable listing.

10. Friedrich V. Lustig, op. cit., p. 428.

11. A. Andreev, letter to the author, 22 February 1991.

12. W. A. Unkrig, op. cit., p. 145.

13. Andreev, op. cit., p. 395.

14. A. Andreev, 'The Rape of the Buddhist Temple in Petrograd, 1919–20', unpublished typescript in English, p. 1.

15. W. A. Unkrig, op. cit., p. 145.

16. The Eight Auspicious Symbols (Skt ashta-mangala) include the conch shell (victory in battle), the endless knot (eternity), the parasol (royal dignity; that which shields from harm), the lotus (purity), the two fishes (the emblem of the chakravartin or universal monarch), the banner of victory (i.e. of spirituality), the vase (that contains the nectar of immortality), and the Wheel of the Dharma (Skt dharma-chakra).

17. Andreev, op. cit, note 1, says, 'There is undocumented evidence that the plaster Budadha [rupa] was replaced by a gilded statue 1.5 metres higher than the previous one, brought from Poland. V. A. Kaverin, in the novel *The Fulfilling of a Wish* [*Ispolneniye Zhelanii*, 1934–36, Collected Works, Vol. 2, Moscow 1981, pp. 240–1], says that the statue was in another place.'

18. Andreev, op. cit., p. 393.

19. When I was shown over the temple in 1991, I was told that the main room on this storey had served as Agvan Dorzhiev's own private office.

20. W. A. Unkrig, op. cit., p. 148.

21. A. Andreev, 'Iz Istorii Peterburgskogo Buddiystkogo Khrama', p. 392. In general, the foregoing description of the Leningrad Buddhist Temple is based on the following sources: 'Buddiyskii Khram V Staroi Derevnya, Primoskii Prospekt 91' ('The Buddhist Temple in Staraya Derevnya, etc.'), in A. N. Petrov et al., *Pamyatniki Arkitekturi Leningrada*, 4th revised edition, Leningrad, 1975; W. A. Unkrig, op. cit., and A. Andreev, op. cit.; also archival photographs, etc.

22. A. Dorzhiev, op. cit., p. 54.

23. Ibid. pp. 55–6. In Leningrad, Aleksandr Breslavetz told me about this controversy in the Tunka region, suggesting that the monastery that stayed put was the Khoimor or Khoimorai, while the new monastery was built at or near Kyren on the other side of the Irkut river. This does not seem quite consistent, however, for according to other sources the Khoimorai was not put up until later.

24. Fülöp Miller, op. cit., p. 100; in Richard Pipes, *The Russian Revolution, 1899–1919*, London, 1990, the original reference is given as M. Paléologue, *La Russie des Tsars pendant La Grande Guerre*, III, Paris 1922, pp. 92–3.

25. IOR&L:I/P&S/11/117: 'Retired Staff Captain Michael Yakuvitch Orloff', B. T. A. Gyantsé, Major W. L. Campbell, to Foreign Secretary, Government of India, 24 November 1916.

    The translation of Orlov's letter seems to have been very roughly done by Campbell or one of his staff; Campbell admits 'a portion of it I could not understand.' Orlov was evidently a native of Pyatigorsk, had been educated at military school and Russian Staff College, had seen service at Port Arthur and Tientsin, sailed around the world and was presently residing at '4th Rodjhestwenskaya Street, House No. 8, Room 69'. The Government of India rather unsportingly decided not to forward his letter.

26. Andreev, op. cit., p. 395.

27. F. Lustig, op. cit., p. 458.
28. Ibid. p. 459.
29. R. E. Bruce Lockhart, op. cit., p. 175.
30. A. Dorzhiev, op. cit., p. 57.
31. King Mahasammata, according to the Buddhist sutras the first king to rule the ancient north Indian city of Rajagrha (Rajgir).
32. A. Dorzhiev, op. cit., pp. 56–7.
33. It seems to have become Dorzhiev's habit when dealing with Russian officials to do so through the Foreign Ministry rather than any other government department. This may be the result of contacts made from 1889 onwards, or because, invested with plenipotentiary powers by the Dalai Lama, he felt he could make more headway by that route.
34. Friedrich V. Lustig, op. cit., p. 488.
35. A. Dorzhiev, op. cit., p. 57.

15. THE WORLD TURNED ON ITS HEAD 1917–1918

1. A. Andreev, 'The Rape of the Buddhist Temple in Petrograd, 1919–20', p. 5; and 'Iz Istorii Peterburgskogo Buddiystkogo Khrama' p. 395.
2. R. Rupen, *Mongols of the Twentieth Century*, p. 130.
3. Lustig, op. cit., p. 492.
4. K. M. Gerasimova, *Obnovlencheskoye Dvizheniye Buryatskogo Lamaistskogo Dukhovenstva* ('The Reform Movement of the Buryat Lamaist Clergy'), Ulan-Udé, 1983, p. 22.
5. According to Andreev, the proceedings of this conference are lodged in the Central State Archive of the Buryat ASSR, f. 483, d. 7.
6. G. D. R. Phillips, op. cit., p. 119.
7. Dorzhiev, op. cit., p. 58.
8. Robert Rupen, op. cit., p. 131.
9. Andreev, 'The Rape of the Buddhist Temple in Petrograd, 1919–20', p. 5.
10. A. Dorzhiev, op. cit., p. 59.
11. Gerasimova, op. cit., pp. 22 ff.
12. A. Dorzhiev, op. cit., p. 59.
13. Rupen, op. cit., p. 131.
14. John Reed, *Ten Days that Shook the World*, reprint Harmondsworth, 1977, pp. 107–8.
15. A. Dorzhiev, op. cit., p. 59.
16. Declared March 1918, replaced by the USSR in 1924.
17. Robert Rupen, op. cit., p. 131.
18. Yanson started out as a member of the Riga committee of the Russian Social Democratic Labour Party (B). He was active in the revolutionary movement between 1905 and 1907, then was arrested and sentenced to six months' imprisonment; in 1914 he was exiled to Siberia. He was Foreign Minister

of the Far Eastern Republic between 1920 and 1922, and in 1923 became a member of the collegium of the People's Commissariat of Foreign Trade. He was subsequently a member of various Soviet trade delegations to Italy, Great Britain and Germany, and later became Soviet trade representative in Japan. In the early thirties, he was chairman of Arcos, the Russian trade corporation in London, and subsequently chairman of the Soviet Board of Trade and member of the USSR Council of the Institute of Pacific Relations.

19. Grigorii Mikhailovich Semenov (1891–1946).

20. These names are given by Khensur Ngawang Nima in his commentarial notes to Dorzhiev's autobiography. The 'Kalota' monastery does not appear to be a Buryat foundation; perhaps it was in Kalmykia.

21. Paula Rubel, *The Kalmyk Mongols*, Bloomington, 1967, p. 18. Hostilities drove many Kalmyks into foreign exile, some of whom found their way to Belgrade, where they established a Buddhist temple. This was still functioning with three lamas in attendance when Dr Helmutt Klar, a medical officer with the Wehrmacht, arrived there during World War II, but it was destroyed during fighting in 1944. See F. Fenzl article on Buddhism in Russia.

22. This is oral information from Aleksandr Breslavetz in St Petersburg.

23. Marked Urbakh on old maps, Pushkino on newer ones, though the two places are probably not exactly coincident. According to the 1973 edition of the *Great Soviet Encyclopedia*, Pushkino is 'an urban-type settlement in Sovietskii raion, Saratov oblast, RSFSR. It is railway junction of lines (from Urbakh) to Saratov, Itesh and Astrakhan'.

24. A. Andreev, 'The Rape of the Buddhist Temple in Petrograd, 1919–20', p. 6; and A. Dorzhiev, op. cit., p. 61.

25. A. Solzhenitsyn, *The First Circle*, paperback edition London, 1978, pp. 398ff.

26. Information from the *Great Soviet Encyclopedia*, 3rd edition, Moscow, 1970.

27. According to A. Shifrin (*First Guidebook to the USSR* . . ., pp. 42ff) Khruschev announced that it was to be closed in 1957 but all that in fact happened was that a new apartment block was erected in front of the entrance; KGB and Interior Ministry employees lived there afterwards. Shifrin writes: 'The prison block consists of no fewer than 25 large buildings with rather spacious cells for 25 or even 50 people. Seventy to 100 inmates, however, are in fact often locked up at a time in a single cell.'

28. Anarchism is a much misunderstood political persuasion, for while it does have bomb throwers and hooligans on its extreme wing – it is not alone in this: many political parties have had these too – its moderate, pacifist proponents, like Prince Kropotkin, advocate mutual aid and personal self-regulation as gentle alternatives to authoritarian and coercive control by the state and its agencies, which is always open to exploitation and

abuse. In this century, authoritarian dictators like Hitler and Stalin have killed millions, whereas the most bloody private killer usually accounts for, at most, the lives of a handful of people (though this is of course not to be condoned). While Anarchists themselves, because they reject the whole concept of political power, could never form governments and impose their ideas in the usual way, their presence is vital to any healthy society as a foil to the perennial tendency of politicians to extend their power and be corrupted by it. Even in democratic Britain we had of late seen a long-standing female prime minister begin to assume an autocratic manner, to talk with the imperial 'we' and to practise that extreme secrecy in government that is the hall-mark of the totalitarian mind.

29. A. Dorzhiev, op. cit., pp. 62–3. He adds that, though he resolved to practise his Buddhism harder so as to gain liberation from samsara, he later, after his release, forgot about that – 'So who could possibly be more of a fool than myself?'

16. FELLOW TRAVELLER 1918–1920

1. A. Dorzhiev, op. cit., p. 65.
2. Ibid., p. 66.
3. Ibid., p. 66–7.
4. Lustig, op. cit., pp. 542–3. Lustig's is the only known reference to a massacre of Buddhist monks by Bolsheviks in this region.
5. Ibid., pp. 543–6.
6. Quoted in I. Lomakhina, *The Head of Ja-Lama*, Typescript of English translation by A. Andreyev, p. 38. Lomakhina's reference is: A. V. Burdukov, *V Staroi I Novoi Mongolii* . . . c. 353.
7. Much of the information here was contributed by Inessa Lomakhina, a Soviet journalist who worked for many years in Mongolia and has compiled the first biography of Ja-Lama/Danbi-Dzhaltsan. The best English-language accounts of Ja-Lama are in F. Ossendowski's *Men, Beasts and Gods* and G. N. Roerich's *Trails to Inmost Asia*; there is also useful material in C. R. Bawden's *The Modern History of Mongolia*.
8. *Great Soviet Encyclopedia*, New York and London, 1973. Dates given: birth, 14 September 1880 (OS); death, 17 April 1939. Biography: E. T. Kavachenko, *Anton Amur-Sanan*, Elista, 1967.
9. Amur Sanai, 'Kliuchi k Vostoku', *Zhizn Natsionalnostei*, No. 19 (27), 26 May 1919, p. 2. English translation in X. J. Eudin and R. C. North, *Soviet Russia and the East*, Stanford, 1957.
10. Ibid.
11. A. Andreev, 'The Rape of the Buddhist Temple in Petrograd, 1919–20', p. 5. Edited at the author's request.
12. According to V. Serge, *Memoirs of a Revolutionary*, P. Sedgwick (tr. and ed.), London, 1963, p. 235, Karakhan 'was always splendidly elegant

however carelessly he dressed on account of the extraordinary nobility of his features and bearing'. At first a Menshevik, later a Bolshevik, he was with G. V. Chicherin in the final negotiating team at Brest-Litovsk and afterwards served as Chicherin's assistant at the Narkomindel. As well as being posted to China in 1924–7, he served in Poland and Turkey. Having opposed Stalin's Chinese policy, he was shot in 1937.

13. For this information I am indebted to Dr Yaroslav Vasil'kov, who kindly provided the reference material for the talk between Karakhan and Stcherbatsky about sending an expedition with radio transmitter to Tibet: Archive of the Academy of Sciences, Moscow, f. 208 (Ol'denburg Collection), op. 3, d. 685, I. 162–7. There are two letters, presumably from Karakhan or Stcherbatsky to Ol'denburg, in which this conversation is mentioned; both are undated. According to other sources known to me, this conversation could have taken place in the summer of 1921, as I have a letter from Agvan Dozhiev to Narkomindel with similar proposals dated June or July 1921.

14. Lustig, op. cit., p. 547.

15. Ibid., pp. 549–50. This description of Tennisons' meeting with Stcherbatsky is probably unfairly to the academician's detriment. Lustig, on behalf of his mentor, was probably trying to make out that Tennisons was the only person in Petrograd seriously concerned about the fate of the temple at this time. Lustig's motive, then, was probably to exalt Tennisons by diminishing Stcherbatsky.

16. Ibid., op. cit., pp. 555–6.

17. Robert Rupen, op. cit. (1), n 47, p. 153.

18. For Dorzhiev's own complete listing see Appendix 2.

19. He has the date wrong; it should be [7–15] June 1917.

20. A. Andreev notes that there were eventually three brick buildings in the temple precincts. One, the surviving four-storey building, the facade of which looks out onto the Little Neva, has eight flats and thirty-three rooms (it has been extensively remodelled); a two-storey wing with four flats and eight rooms (this was demolished at the turns of the 1980s); and a two-storey house behind the temple (taken down in 1988).

21. Andreev notes that this – its name in fact originally was Petrograd Institute of Living Oriental Languages; later it was changed to Eastern Institute – was founded by a decree of the People's Congress of Commissars of 7 December 1920. It was situated at 7 Pirogov Periolok (formerly Maksimilianov Allee), and was closed in 1938. The scheme to have Buryat, Kalmyk, Mongol, Tuvinian and Tibetan students to pursue a two-year course in elementary Russian, had Narkomindel support. Dorzhiev himself considered it of great importance for bringing these peoples closer to the Russians.

22. TsGAOR (Central State Archive of the October Revolution, Leningrad), f. 8, op. 1, d. 2567a, p. 13.

23. Andreev, 'The History of the St Petersburg Buddhist Temple', p. 396.

24. V. Serge, *Conquered City*, tr. Richard Greeman, reprint, London, 1978.

25. Otto Ottonovich Rosenberg (1888–1919), Russian Buddhologist, pupil of Stcherbatsky, was a privat dozhent (lecturer) and later a professor at Petrograd University. His master's dissertation consisted of an introduction to the study of Buddhism in Japanese and Chinese sources, and in the second part he dealt with the problems of Buddhist philosophy. He was the first Buddhologist in the West to attempt to define a methodology for the study of Buddhist philosophy, to do research into basic categories and to disclose the full range of meaning of the key term 'dharma'.
26. G. Bongard-Levin and A. Vigasin, op. cit., p. 145.
27. Hans Bräker, 'Buddhism in the Soviet Union: Annihilation or Survival?', p. 38. The titles under which the lectures were published are given as: 'Prevaya Buddistskaya v Vystavka Peterburge', (Oldenburg); 'O Mirosozertsanii Sovremennogo Buddizma na Dalchnem Vostok', (Rosenberg); 'Filosofskoye Ucheniye Buddizma', (Stcherbatsky); all Petrograd, 1919.
28. Lustig, op. cit., p. 559.
29. N. Poppe maintains ('The Buddhists of the USSR', p. 176) that the Dalai Lama sent an envoy to Moscow in 1921. Otherwise there are no references either to confirm or deny that a Tibetan Mission of May 1922 arrived in Russia.
30. A transcript of this document was in the typewritten anthology 'Documenti, Stati, Materiali O Buddiyskom Khrame V Leningrade'.
31. N. Poppe, 'The Buddhists of Russia', p. 176.
32. Burobkom Party Archive, f. 1, op. 1, d. 657, II. 14–17. An English translation of this document was kindly provided by A. Andreyev, with the note, 'I received this document from a friend who is also a scholar, who asked me not to publish it in full.'
33. A. Dorzhiev, op. cit., p. 69.

17. REFORM AND RENAISSANCE 1920–1924

1. Berlin, op. cit., p. 155.
2. The former collection remains intact; the latter has since been broken up and spread about.
3. Leonov, op. cit., pp. 114–5.
4. F. M. Bailey, *Mission to Tashkent*, reprint London, 1946, p. 54.
5. N. Poppe, 'The Buddhists of the USSR', p. 172. Poppe adds that the department of Tibetan medicine that he mentions was 'under Feodorov'.
6. E. H. Carr, *The Bolshevik Revolution*, vol. 1, London, 1950, p. 355.
7. C. Humphrey, op. cit., p. 410.
8. A. Dorzhiev, op. cit., p. 71.
9. E. Benz, *Buddhism or Communism?*, London, 1966, p. 156; and W. Kolarz, *Religion in the Soviet Union*, London, 1961, p. 455.
10. A. Dorzhiev, op. cit., p. 73.
11. Gerasimova, op. cit., note 98, p. 65.

12. A. Dorzhiev, op. cit., p. 71.

13. In 1991, original newsreel footage of the anti-religious pogrom that befell the Orthodox Church was shown on British television. The people were shown looking on in dazed fascination, some of them smiling faintly – as though they were finding so much destruction terrifying but at the same time great fun.

14. *Bodhisattvacharyavatara*, by the Indian pandit, Shantideva. Translation by Stephen Batchelor, Dharamsala (India), 1987. I have been unable to trace this passage [SB].

15. Gerasimova, op. cit., pp. 65–6.

16. Ibid., p. 68.

17. Ibid., p. 73.

18. What Stalin told the Twelfth Party Congress in 1922 apropos the Kalmyks applied equally to the Buryats: 'All we have to do is to make one small mistake in relation to the small territory of the Kalmyks, who have ties with Tibet and China, and that will effect our work in a far worse way than mistakes in relation to the Ukraine.' Quoted in R. Rupen, 'Mongolia, Tibet and Buddhism, a Tale of Two Roerichs', p. 7 n.

19. This is mostly oral information from Aleksandr Andreev in St Petersburg. He has exhaustively researched in Russian archives, so I don't doubt the authenticity of his information.

20. IOR&L: L/P&S/11/19S: C. A. Bell Esq., Political Officer on Special Duty in Tibet to Secretary, Government of India, Lhasa-Gyantsé P.O., 6 February 1921. One wonders whether this was in fact the agent whose messages Stcherbatsky helped Narkomindel to translate.

21. N. Poppe, 'The Buddhists in the USSR', p. 176.

22. H. Richardson, *Tibetan Précis*, Calcutta, 1945, p. 32.

23. G. Bongard-Levin and A. Vigasin, op. cit., p. 148.

24. Berlin, op. cit., p. 156.

25. A. Dorzhiev, op. cit., p. 60.

26. Lustig, op. cit., p. 561.

27. This information is from Dr Yaroslav Vasil'kov of the Oriental Institute of the USSR Academy of Sciences (May 1991).

28. G. Bongard-Levin and A. Vigasin, op. cit., p. 121.

29. Ibid., p. 146.

30. I am indebted for the names of these British contacts of Stcherbatsky to A. Andreev, who obtained them as the result of research in Soviet archives. Mr Andreev hopes to do further research on the matter in Britain.

31. Based on oral information from Dr Yaroslav Vasil'kov.

32. Robert Rupen, op. cit., p. 187, says that Dorzhiev, Baradin and Rinchino were at the First Great Khural; Aleksandr Breslavetz maintains that Dorzhiev, Baradin and Kozlov attended – see plate 11.

33. Bulletin of the Soviet Plenipotentiary Mission in Mongolia, No. 26, Ulan-Bator, 1925: Protocol of the First Great Khural of the Mongolian People, pp. 25–6. English translation kindly provided by Aleksandr Breslavetz.

34. Ibid., p. 31.

18. GATHERING CLOUDS 1925–1929

1. Burobkom Party Archive, f. 1., op. 1, d. 657, II. 14–17.
2. Ibid.
3. Archive of the Foreign Policy of the USSR (AVP SSSR), Moscow, f. 100, op. 1, p. 1, d. 11, p. 2.
4. H. E. Richardson, *Tibetan Précis*, Calcutta, 1945, pp. 35–6.
5. W. D. Shakabpa, op. cit., p. 266.
6. H. E. Richardson, *Tibetan Précis*, pp. 35–6.
7. G. H. Mullin (tr.), op. cit., pp. 111–2.
8. Gerasiomova, op. cit., p. 109.
9. Gerasimova, op. cit., p. 110.
10. Bazarov and Shagdurov, op. cit., p. 125.
11. Ibid., p. 124.
12. Ibid., p. 125.
13. A Russian-language copy of the agreement was included in the typewritten anthology, 'Dokumenti, Stat'i, Materiali O Buddiiyskom Khrame V Leningrade'.
14. A. Andreev, 'Iz Istorii . . .', p. 398.
15. Ibid., p. 398.
16. 'Report of Tsanyid-Khambo Agvan Dorzhiev, to be delivered at the 1st International Buddhist Exhibition in Leningrad, 1926 'Buddhism as an oriental Culture,' Main Theses': TSGA of the Buryat Republic, f. 643, d. 11, pp. 14–5. English translation kindly provided by A. Andreev.
17. R. Craft, *Conversations with Igor Stravinsky*, 1959, pp. 105–6. Quoted in R. Rupen, 'Mongolia, Tibet and Buddhism, a Tale of Two Roerichs', p. 3.
18. J. Decter, *Nicholas Roerich, the Life and Art of a Russian Master*, p. 165.
19. I obtained this information from Ian Heron, who is writing a biography of Roerich, who had it from Alexander Piatigorsky, whose ultimate source was the lady who typed the secret reports: she apparently made the disclosures to one of Yuri Roerich's co-workers at the USSR Academy of Sciences in Moscow during Yuri's sojourn there in the period 1957–60.
20. P. Belikov and V. Knyazeva, *Rerikh*, Moscow, 1972, p. 91. Quoted in J. Decter, o. cit., p. 165.
21. Oral information obtained in Leningrad in 1991. It is partially corroborated in Rupen, 'Mongolia, Tibet and Buddhism, a Tale of Two Roerichs', pp. 7–8.
22. Translation given by A. Andreev from the notes of his researches in Soviet archives.
23. H. Bräker, op. cit., p. 40.

24. W. Kolarz, op. cit., p. 455.
25. Oral information.
26. Quoted in A. Andreev, *The Buddhist Shrine in Petrograd*, Ulan-Udé, 1991, pre-publication typescript p. 31.
27. Most of the information here was communicated in a letter from Aleksandr Breslavetz, dated 21 Dec. 1989.
28. Gerasimova, op. cit., p. 72.
29. E. Benz, *Buddhism in the Soviet Union*, p. 159.
30. I am indebted for this information to A. Andreev, who has consulted the relevant issues of *Buryat-Mongolskaya Pravda*.

19. THE DESTRUCTION OF BUDDHISM IN THE USSR AND THE DEATH OF AGVAN DORZHIEV 1930–1938

1. Actually in 1932, according to Phillips (op. cit., pp. 154–5), there were 4,690 Buryats in Ulan-Udé : 8.4% of the total population.
2. Ibid., p. 162.
3. Ibid., p. 150.
4. Phillips, ibid., p. 153.
5. H. Bräker, op. cit., p. 40.
6. S. Markov, op. cit., p. 104.
7. B. Dandaron, article on the Aga Monastery in G. P. Malalsekera (ed.), *The Encyclopedia of Buddhism*, Colombo.
8. A. Andreev, letter of 3 December 1991.
9. Letter from Aleksandr Breslavetz, 21 December 1989.
10. Letter from KGB (Leningrad branch) to A. Breslavetz (exact date not available).
11. Oral information provided by A. Andreev.
12. B. Bazarov and U. Shagdurov, op. cit., p. 123.
13. V. A. Kaverin, op. cit., English translation quoted here by A. Andreev, to whom I am indebted for drawing my attention to the piece.
14. A. Dorzhiev, op. cit., p. 70.
15. Dava-Sambu Dugarov, born 1898 in Urdo-Aga; Dodi Sodnompilov, born 1899 in Khara-Sibir; Odstor (Osor) Zham'yanovich Zham'yanov, born 1892 in Chelutai; Tsyren-Dorzhi Donbukovich Garmayev, born 1902 in Gubai ulus, Birnursty rayon; Batuna-Tsyren Sambuevich Sambuev, born 1914 in Ukurit village, Khiloksky rayon (in 1962 he was living in the spa of Darasun); Togmit Batuevich Batuev, born 1902 in Uronoisky soman, Aginsky okrug. Dava-Sam bu Dugarov . . . Listing provided by the Leningrad branch of the KGB to Aleksandr Breslavetz.
16. Ibid.
17. N. Poppe, 'The Destruction of Buddhism in the USSR', pp. 19–20.
18. N. Poppe, 'The Buddhists in the USSR', p. 179.
19. Ibid., p. 175.

20. G. D. R. Phillips, op. cit., p. 167.
21. An English transcript of Dorzhiev's will was kindly provided by A. Andreev, who appended the following note:

> I discovered the typescript text of Dorzhiev's last will by sheer chance in the Archives of the Foreign Policy of the USSR (AVP USSR, f. 100, op. 19, d. 26, II. 9 and 10), among other official Narkomindel papers relating to the affairs of the Tibet-Mongolian Mission in Leningrad. It is one of two original copies that were submitted to the Leningrad branch of the Narkomindel in 1936. It was delivered in person to the head of this department, Weinstein, by Sandzhe Dylykov ... On 11 September 1936, Weinstein sent it to the head office of the Narkomindel in Moscow, asking for advice, as he strongly doubted its validity on account of its lacking proper notarization.
>
> The original copy in Moscow, to which I also had access, was signed by Agvan Dorzhiev in Tibetan and sealed with the red seal [given to him by] the Dalai Lama. A brief covering letter was attached, also signed by Dorzhiev, in which he again stated that he had appointed Dylykov as his successor in the affairs of the Tibet-Mongolian Mission and heir to all his private property. It was also emphasized that Dylykov was assigned the task of looking after the Buddhist Temple in Leningrad together with its ancillary houses until a representative arrived from Tibet to replace him.
>
> It took some time before the top Narkomindel officials recognized the validity of the will, which effectively made Dylykov head of the Tibet-Mongolian Mission.

Andreev adds: 'There can be no doubt that the NKVD was involved in close surveillance of the activities of the Mission.'

22. A typed copy of this list was given to me by Aleksandr Breslavetz, who is a lay devotee at Kuntsechoinei Datsan, Leningrad, and who obtained it directly from the Leningrad branch of the KGB.
23. Aleksandr Solzhenitsyn writes in *The Gulag Archipelago* (London, 1974, p. 5), 'From our greatest expert on Tibet, Vostrikov, they confiscated ancient Tibetan manuscripts of great value; and it took the pupils of the deceased scholar thirty years to wrest them from the KGB!'
24. Much of this information on Stcherbatsky was obtained during an interview with Dr Yaroslav Vasil'kov at the Oriental Institute of the Academy of Sciences in May 1991.
25. This information was supplied by letter to Aleksandr Breslavetz by the Leningrad branch of the KGB and made available by him to the author.
26. B. Bazarov and U. Shagdurov, op. cit., p. 123.
27. N. N. Poppe in *Reminiscences*, p. 131, maintains that Dorzhiev 'was sent to the Aleksandrovskaya jail near Ilan-Udé'. Poppe's facts are not always correct, however; he writes in the same place, for instance, that Dorzhiev died in 1940.
28. Many high Buryat officials were involved in these travesties of justice. V. A. Tkachev, the Commissar for Internal Affairs, and L. E. Gaikovsky, the head of the local NKVD, were themselves later prosecuted – see Bazarov and Shagdurov, op. cit. p. 127.
29. Bazarov and Shagdurov, op. cit., p. 124.
30. Ibid., p. 124.

31. Ibid., p. 124.
32. Ibid., p. 125.
33. Ibid., p. 126.
34. Ibid., p. 126.
35. Bazarov and Shagdurov, op. cit., pp. 127–8.
36. Letter from A. Breslavetz, 21 December 1989.
37. Lustig, op. cit., p. 832.
38. Letter to the author from A. Breslavetz, 21 December 1989.
39. The details of the case are preserved by the KGB of the Buryat ASSR.
40. Bazarov and Shagdurov, op. cit., p. 128.
41. Unkrig, op. cit., p. 149.

20. AFTER DORZHIEV 1938–1991

1. D. Dallin, op. cit. pp. 137–43 and 191.
2. A. Piatigorsky, 'A Little About Buddhism in Tuva', unpublished type-script, p. 6.
3. Quoted in Ibid., p. 1; the reference is given as Ostrobskikh, P. E. Kratkiy otchet a poezdke v Todjinsky Khoshun Uriankhaiskogo Kraia, *Izvestiya Imperatorskogo Russkogo Geograficheskogo Otshestva*, 1898, v. XXXIV, N. 4, p. 20.
4. F. Fenzl, 'Der Buddhismus in Russland in Vergangenheit und Gegenwart', pp. 96–7.
5. V. Galkina, 'Around the Temple', *Teachers' Gazette*, 12. December 1972.
6. A. Andreev, 'Iz Istorii . . .', p. 400.
7. One oral source talks of thirty works, which would have included his two-volume *Description of Tibetan Manuscripts* (1960 and 1963).
8. This is mostly oral information from Aleksandr Breslavetz.
9. R. Rupen, op. cit., p. 134.
10. Information given in a talk by Dr A. M. Piatigorsky at Sharpham House in 1990.
11. Document in the archives of Keston College, Bromley, Kent, entitled 'Arrest of Buddhism [sic] Scholars in the Soviet Union', The bulk of the text comprises a letter from Vladimir Kreidenkov 'received by a Western scholar in mid-December 1972, through indirect channels'.
12. Document in the archives of Keston College, Bromley, Kent, with the note that two letters and Dylykov's reply were published in the *World Fellowship of Buddhists' Review*, November/December 1973.
13. Vadim Kreidenkov's letter, see note 11.
14. According to A. Shifrin, op. cit., p. 21, Vydrino was a camp in the Buryat ASSR for women and children.
15. 'Bidya Dandaron – Persecuted Buddhist', *Soviet Analyst*, vol. 3, No. 23, November 1974, p. 6.
16. See *The Guardian*, 12.1.91: members of this Zurich-based organization

include Tibet, Latvia, Estonia, Georgia, Armenia, the Volga region, the Crimea, West Papua, the American Indians, the Cordillera of the Philippines, the Greek minority of Albania, the non-Chinese of Taiwan and the Aborigines of Australia.

17. Astrakhan was the original administrative centre of the Kalmyk Autonomous Oblast (KAO); it was succeeded by Elista in 1927. In 1935 the autonomous oblast was transformed into an autonomous socialist republic (KASSR).

18. The question of ownership rests on the legality of the seizure of the building by the Soviet State in 1938. Up until then it was the property of the Tibet–Mongolian Mission, so both Mongolia and, if it was independent of China, Tibet could jointly claim it. The Buryats also feel they have a claim on the basis of the Dorzhiev connection and the local St Petersburg Buddhists do not want to be excluded either.

19. According to Aleksandr Breslavetz, Ven. Samayev was born in the village of Orlik, which lies on one of the main tributaries of the Oka river. A wooden house that once belonged to Agvan Dorzhiev still stands there. Ven. Samayev wants to transform this into a temple in memory of Dorzhiev and to this end has instructed that columns be added to the facade.

20. According to Aleksandr Breslavetz, at one point Tolstoy found himself in the same Kazan hospital ward as a Buryat lama named Dawa Zhaltsan Zhigmitov and they discussed Buddhist philosophy, after which positive references to Buddhism began to appear in the great man's writings.

APPENDIX 2 DORZHIEV'S INVENTORY OF ITEMS LOOTED FROM THE PETROGRAD BUDDHIST TEMPLE IN 1919

1. Andreev notes that 1 lan = 31.2 gm.
2. Andreev notes that this would amount to 627 metres.

GLOSSARY

BM = Buryat-Mongol; Ch = Chinese; KM = Kalmyk-Mongol; M = Mongol; R = Russian; Skt = Sanskrit; T = Tibetan

Abhidharma (Skt) 'Higher dharma': the early Indian philosophical systematization of the Buddha's teachings
abhisheka (Skt) Tantric initiation
agvan (BM) Variant of the Tibetan *'ngawang'*
apparatchik (R) Opportunistic bureaucrat; usually Communist
arhat (Skt) Fully enlightened practitioner
ataman (R) Cossack general

bakshi (M) Spiritual teacher
bandi (M) Novice monks
Bandido Khambo Lama (BM) Lit. 'Wise-Teacher Abbot Guru', title of the supreme head of the Buddhists of Russia. Originally just ' Khambo Lama' when created in 1741 by the Empress Elizabeth; changed to this form c1766 by Catherine the Great. *See also* khenpo, lama
bardo (T) The intermediate state between one life and another
beise (M) Mongolian corruption of the Chinese rank of *pei-tzu*
bhikshu (Skt) Buddhist monk
Black Hundreds (R) Gangs of ultra Right-wing urban thugs active in pre-revolutionary Russia
bodhi (Skt) Wisdom
bodhisattva (Skt) One striving for enlightenment, not for personal fulfilment, but in order to help other sentient beings escape the sufferings of *samsara*
Bogdo Gegen (M) Alternative title of the *Jebtsundamba Khutukhtu*
Bolshevik (R) Lit. 'Marjorityist': a faction of the Social-Democrats, led by Lenin, claiming its name from a temporary electoral supremacy over its rivals, the *Mencheviks*, at one party congress; later a separate political party
Bön (T) The pre-Buddhist shamanistic religion of Tibet
buddha (Skt) Lit. 'awakened one': one who by his own efforts rediscovers the dharma after it has been lost for many millennia
Buddha-dharma (Skt) The teachings of the Buddha
Buddha-rupa (Skt) The 'form' of the Buddha – usually a sculptural or painted image
Buddha Siddhartha Gautama (Skt) Also known as Shakyamuni; north Indian aristocrat who first taught the spiritual way known to the West as Buddhism

Chang-Shambhala North Shambhala
Cheka (R) Lit. 'Extraordinary Commission for Repression against Counter-revolution': the Bolshevik security police (1917–21)

Chikyab Khenpo (T) Lord Chamberlain
chinovnik (R) Bureaucrat
chögyal (T) Lit. 'Dharma King'
choira (T, M) College of *tsenyi*
chörten (T) Stupa

Dalai Lama (M, T) Full title, 'Dalai Lama Vajradhara', ('Lama, Ocean [of Wisdom], Holder of the Thunderbolt'), first conferred in 1587 by Altan Khan on Sonam Gyatso and subsequently on the two previous and eleven succeeding heads of the *Gelug* school. The Dalai Lamas, if they lived to their majority, combined the secular and spiritual leadership of Tibet in a single office.
datsan (BM) Buddhist temple or monastery; Buryat variant of the Tibet 'dratsang'
devazhin (BM) Model of Sukhavati, the Western Paradise of Amitabha Buddha
dharmapala (Skt) Occult protector deity, e.g. Pelden Lhamo
dorampa (T) Lower grade of geshe degree
dorji (T) Skt vajra: ritual object used in Tantric ritual based on the thunderbolt of the Hindu god Indra
dratsang (T) Monastic college
dugan (BM) Dukhang
dukhang (T) Monastic assembly hall; in Russia the term denotes a monastic building that also contains accommodation for monks and novices as well as other facilities
Duma (R) National Assembly, elected on a restricted mandate, summoned by Nicholas II to St Petersburg in 1905. Due to several dissolutions and recalls, there were in all four Dumas.
duma (R) Council
dzasak (M) Prince
dzong (T) Fort

gabzhi (BM) *Geshe*
gañjira (T) Gilded pinnacle of a temple
gelong (T) Fully ordained Buddhist monk
Gelug (T) Lit. 'Pure': the school of Tibetan Buddhism founded by Gendun-drup the disciple of Tsongkhapa
ger (BM) Felt tent; yurt
geshe (T) Holder of a scholarly degree in higher Buddhist studies
getsül (T) Novice monk
gompa (T, Skt vihara) Lit. 'lonely place'; a Buddist temple or monastery
gonkhang (T) Chapel in which *dharmapala* dwell
GPU (R) or OGPU: Unified State Political Directorate – i.e. security police
gubernia (R) Region overseen by a provincial governor
Gulag (R) The Soviet authority in charge of the prison camp system
gyeltsen (T) Gilded barrel-shaped decorations on the roof of Tibetan temples

hetman (R) Cossack leader

inoredsky (R) Outsiders

jabtru (T) A purification ritual

Jebtsundamba Khutukhtu (M) Chief Mongolian incarnate lama in the line stemming from Öndör Gegen (1635–1723); headquarters at Urga; the last, eighth, incumbent died in 1924

Jowo Rinpoché (T) Statue of the Buddha in the Jokhang temple in Lhasa reputed to have been brought to Tibet in the 7th century CE from China; the most venerated image in Tibet

kadet (R) Member of Constitutional Democrat Party

kalon (T) Member of the Tibetan *Kashag*

Kangyur (T) The part of the Tibetan Buddhist canon in which the sutras are collected

karma (Skt) Volitional action, which will inexorably produce a 'fruit' (vipaka)

Kashag (T) The Tibetan Cabinet

khada (T) White ceremonial offering scarf

khambo (BM) *khenpo*

khenpo (T) Abbot; high-ranking lama

khid (M) *datsan*

khubilgan (M) Tib. 'tulku'; 'living buddha'

khural (M) See *khuree*

khuree (M) Lit. 'great assembly'; a Buddhist monastery; an assembly of any sort; a Buddhist puja or ceremony

khutukhtu (M) Skt. 'arya', Tib. 'pagpa': 'holy one' or 'noble one'; title given by the Manchus to the great *tulkus* of Tibet and Mongolia, who were duly recorded in a special book kept in an office of the Manchu Government

khuvarak (M) Monastic term subject to various usages, most often to signify novices

kibitka (KM) Tent; yurt

kolkhoz (R) Agricultural commune

Komsomol (R) Communist youth league

kontora (R) Office; headquarters

kulak (R) Enterprising peasant, hence in Bolshevik eyes an exploitative and counterrevolutionary one fair game to persecution

Kurluks (M) Mongolian clan inhibiting the Tsaidam region

kurul (KM) See *khuree*

la (T) Pass (through mountains, etc.)

lama (T) Skt. 'guru'; spiritual teacher

lamyig (T) Travel pass or guide-book

lan (Ch) Measure of weight = 31.2 grams

lharampa (T) Highest grade of the *geshe* degree

ling (T) Buddhist temple

Losar (T) Tibetan new year festival

lun-dun (M) Mystical prophecy

Maidari (M) *Miatreya*

Maitreya The Coming Buddha
manba (M) School of Tibetan Medicine
manramba (M) Doctoral degree in Tibetan medicine
Menshevik (R) Lit. 'Minorityist'; Social Democrat faction
Monlam Chenmo (T) The Great Prayer Festival
muzhik (R) Peasant

Narkomindel (R) People's Commissariat of Foreign Affairs
narodnik (R) Composite name for a succession of Russian revolutionary groups
who believed in the theory of peasant revolution and in the practice of terror
against the autocracy
ngawang (T) Lit. 'skilled in speech'
NKVD (R) People's Commissariat of the Army and Navy – i.e. Soviet
security police
noyon (M) Nobleman
nyen-chen (T) Long retreat

oblast (R) Administrative region
Obnovlencheskoye (R) Religious reform movement
obo (M) Votive cairn
Okhrana (R) The 'Third Section': the imperial security police, precursor to the
Cheka, GPU, etc
omzé (T) Chant leader
ongon (M) Spirit dolls

Panchen Lama (T) Lama second in Gelugpa hierarchy of Tibet to the Dalai
Lama; seat at Tashilhunpo
pandit (Skt) Wise teacher
pei-tzu (Ch) Chinese rank, conferred, e.g. on the *dzasak* of the *Kurluk
Mongols*
polozhenie (R) Regulations
Potala The winter palace of the Dalai Lama just outside Lhasa

rabzhi (RM) Doctor of Tibetan medicine
rinpoché (T) Lit. 'precious jewel'; honorific bestowed on high lamas
rupa (Skt) Lit. 'form'; a metal, wood, clay, stone, etc. figure, e.g. of
the Buddha

sadhana (Skt) Tantric practice
samsara (Skt) The world of cyclic existence and suffering
sangar (T?) Defensive wall
sangha (Skt) The community of Buddhist monks and nuns; sometimes expanded
to include the laity
sazheny (R) Unit of measurement equivalent to seven English feet
selo (R) Large village
shapé (T) Member of the *Kashag*
shiretui (BM) Abbot
shloka (Skt) Stanza of verse

solpon (T) Fund-raising lama
sovkhoz (R) State farm
Sovnarkon (R) Council of People's Commissars
SRs (R) Members of the Socialist Revolutionary party
stupa (Skt) Buddhist reliquary or monument symbolic of the cosmic order
suburgan (M) *Stupa*
sutra (Skt) Scripture

tarantass (R) Unsprung four-wheeled carriage
Tengyur (T) The part of the Tibetan Buddhist canon in which the commentaries on the main *sutras* are collected
thangka (T) Tibetan Buddhist scroll painting
tovarich (R) Comrade
troika (R) Vehicle drawn by three horses; group of three persons
Tsagaansar (BM) The New Year celebrations (according to the Tibetan calendar, i.e. mid-February)
Tsaidam Basin (M) At the northerly edge of the Tibetan plateau; formerly inhabited by Mongolian clans
tse-boum (T) thse.bum. Ritual vase used in Tibetan Buddhist long-life ceremonies
tsenyi (T) tshan nyid, sometimes also transcribed as tsanit or tsanid: the classical dialectical programme of Buddhist doctrinal studies based on the systematic logic and epistemology of the Sautrantika philosophers Dharmakirti and Dignaga
tsenzab (T) mtshan zhabs: assistant tutor to the Dalai Lama
TsIK (R) Central Executive Committee of the Soviets
tso (T) Lake
Tsongdu (T) The Tibetan National Assembly
Tsongkhapa The 14th century Tibetan monastic reformer whose followers established the *Gelug* school
tulku (T) One in whom the spirit of a great spiritual luminary has reincarnated

uezd (R) District
ukaz (R) Imperial dictat
ulus (R) Number of households constituting an administrative district
upasaka (Skt) Lay Buddhist
Urga Capital of Outer Mongolia; seat of the *Jebtsundamba Khutukhtu*

volost (R) Smallest rural administrative unit

yidam (T) Tantric deity
yunker (R) Military cadet

zaisan (M) Nobleman; tribal or clan boss
zemstvo (R) Council; zemstva existed in Imperial Russia on both the district and provincial levels
zhud-khural (M) Buddhist ceremonies performed to promote success in battle

BIBLIOGRAPHY

Books and Texts

Amur-Sanan, A.M., *Mudreshkin Syn: Izbrannoe*, Moscow, 1966.

Avrich, P., *Anarchists in the Russian Revolution*, London, 1973.

Badmayev, P.A., (1) *Glavnoe Rukovodstvo Po Vrachebnoi Nauke Tibeta 'Uzhud-Shu'*, St. Petersburg, 1903. (2) *O Systeme Vrachebmoi Nauke Tibeta*, St. Petersburg, 1898.

Barborka, G., *H.P.B., Tibet and Tulku*, Adyar, 1966.

Batchelor, S., *Tibet Guide*, London, 1987.

Bates, L., *The Russian Road to China*, New York and London, 1910.

Bawden, C.R., (1) *The Modern History of Mongolia*, London, 1969. (2) *Shamans, Lamas and Evangelicals*, London, 1985. (3) *The Jebtsundampa Khutukhtus of Urga*, Wiesbaden, 1961.

Bell, C., (1) *Portrait of the Dalai Lama*, London, 1946. (2) *Tibet Past and Present*, Oxford, 1924. (3) *The Religion of Tibet*, Oxford, 1931.

Benz, E., *Buddhism or Communism?*, London, 1966.

Bergmann, B., *Nomadische Streiferein unter den Kalmücken in der Jahren 1802 und 1803*, Riga, 1804.

Bernbaum, E., *The Road to Shambhala*, New York, 1980.

Berry, S., *Stranger in Tibet*, London, 1989.

Bongard-Levin, G. (with Vigasin, A.), *The Image of India*, Moscow, 1984.

Bonvalot, G., *Across Tibet*, London, 1891.

Brown, A. (ed.), *The Soviet Union: A Biographical Dictionary*, London, 1990.

Bruce Lockhart, R.H., *Memoirs of a British Agent*, London, 1932.

Bumyantsev, G.N., *K Voprosu O Preiskozhdenii Khori-Buryat*, Ulan-Udé, 1948.

Butt, G.S., *Madame Blavatsky*, London, 1926.

Candler, E., *The Unveiling of Lhasa*, London, 1905.

Carr, E.H., *The Bolshevik Revolution, 1917–23*, Vol. 1, London, 1950.

Carruthers, D., *Unknown Mongolia*, London, 1913.

Dallin, D., *The Rise of Russia in Asia*, London, 1927.

Decter, J., *Nicholas Roerich: The Life of a Russian Master*, London, 1989.

Dhondup, K., *The Water-Bird and Other Years*, New Delhi, 1986.

Doroshinskaya, Y., (with Kruchina-Bogdanov, V.), *Leningrad and its Environs: A Guide*, Moscow, 1979.

Dorzhiev, A., *Chos. brgyad. gdon. gyis. zin. byas. te/rgyal. khams. don. med. nyul. ba. yi/dam. chos. nor. gyis. dbul. sprang. btsun, gzugs. shig. gi. bgyi. brjod. gtam* (Autobiography), commentary by Khensur Ngawang Nima, probably Mundgod, S., India, undated (1985 or 1986 likely). A Mongolian version or variant of this text also exists.

Dowman, K., *The Power-Places of Central Tibet*, London, 1988.

Eudin, J. X., and North, R. C., *Soviet Russia and the East, 1920–1927*, Stanford, 1957.

Fields, R., *How the Swans Came to the Lake*, Boston, 1986.

Filchner, W., *Sturm über Asien*, Berlin, 1926.

Fleming, P., (1) *Bayonets to Lhasa*, London, 1961. (2) *The Fate of Admiral Kolchak*, London, 1963. (3) *The Siege at Peking*, London, 1959.

Friters, Gerard M., *Outer Mongolia and its International Position*, Baltimore, 1949.

Frye, Stanley (tr.), *Sutra of the Wise and the Foolish or The Ocean of Narratives*, Dharamsala, 1981.

Fülöp Miller, R., *Rasputin, the Holy Devil*, paperback edition, London, 1967 (original edition London and New York, 1928).

Fuhrmann, J.T., *Rasputin, A Life*, New York, 1990.

Gerasimova, K.M., *Obnovlenschekoye Dvizheniye Buryatskogo Lamistskogo Dukhoventsva* ('The Reform/Revival Movement of the Buryat Lamaist Clergy'), Ulan-Udé, 1964.

Gilmour, J., *Among the Mongols*, London, undated.

Goldstein, M.C., *History of Modern Tibet, 1913–50*, 1990.

Grünwedel, A., (1) *Mythologie der Buddhismus in Tibet und der Mongolei*, Leipzig, 1900. (2) (ed.) *Der Weg nach Shambhala*, München, 1915.

Heissig, W., *The Religions of Mongolia*, London, 1980.

Hopkirk, P., (1) *Trespassers on the Roof of the World*, London, 1982. (2) *Setting the East Ablaze*, London, 1984. (3) *The Great Game*, London, 1990.

Huc, Abbé, *Travels in Tartary and Tibet*, tr. W. Hazlitt, London, 1852, edited reprint, London, 1970.

Humphrey, C., *Karl Marx Collective. Economy, Society and Religion in a Siberian Collective Farm*, Cambridge, 1983.

Kabachenko, E.T., *Anton Amur-Sanan*, Elitsa, 1967.

Karmay, Samten, *Secret Visions of the Fifth Dalai Lama*, London, 1988

Kaverin, V.A., *Ispolneniye Zhlenaii*, Collected Works, Vol. 2., Moscow, 1981.

Kawaguchi, E., *Three Years in Tibet*, Adyar (Madras), 1909.

Kipling, R., *Kim*, reprint London, 1958.

Kochetov, A.K., *Lamaizma*, ('Lamaism'), Moscow, 1973.

Kolarz, W., (1) *Religion in the Soviet Union*, London, 1961. (2) *The Peoples of the Soviet Far East*, London, 1954.

Korostovets, I.Y., *Von Cinggis Khan zur Sowjetrepublik*, Leipzig and Berlin, 1926.

Kozlov, P.K., *Mongolei, Amdo und die Tote Stadt Chara-Choto*, Berlin, 1925.

Labin, S., *Stalin's Russia*, London, 1949.

Lamb, A., (1) *The McMahon Line*, London, 1966. (2) *British India and Tibet, 1766–1910*, London and New York, 1986 (a second revised edition of *Britain and Chinese Central Asia*, London, 1960). (3) *Tibet, China and India, 1914–50*, Hertingfordbury, 1989.

Lobanov-Rostovsky, A., *Russia in Asia*, New York, 1933.

Lomakina, I., *Golova Dzha-Lama*, ('Ja-Lama's Head'), unpublished typescript.

Longworth, P., *The Cossacks*, London, 1969.

Lustig, F., *Biography of K.A.M. Tennisons*, unpublished typescript.

MacDonald, D., *Twenty Years in Tibet*, London, 1932.

McNeal, R.H., *Stalin: Man and Ruler*, Basingstoke and Oxford, 1988.

Minert, L.K., *Pamyatniki Architekturi Buryatii*, ('Buryat Architectural Monuments'), Novosibirsk, 1983.

Mullin, G. (ed. and tr.), *Path of the Bodhisattva Warrior. The Life and Teachings of the Thirteenth Dalai Lama*, Ithaca, N.Y., 1988.

Norton, H., *The Eastern Republic of Siberia*, London, 1923.

O'Connor, W.F.T., *On the Frontier and Beyond*, London, 1931.

Olcott, H.S., *Old Diary Leaves*, Series iv and vii, Madras, 1895–1935.

Ossendowsky, F., *Men, Beasts and Gods*, New York, 1922.

Paelian, G., *Nicholas Roerich. A Biography*, Sedona, Arizona, 1974.

Pares, B., *A History of Russia*, reprint London, 1962.

Paslovsky, L., *Russia in the Far East*, New York, 1922.

Petrov, A.N. et al., *Pamiatniki Arkitekturi Leningrada*, 4th revised edition, Leningrad, 1975.

Phillips, G.D.R., *Dawn in Siberia. The Mongols of Lake Baikal*, London, 1942.

Pipes, R., *The Russian Revolution, 1899–1919*, London, 1990.

Poppe, N.N., *Reminiscences*, Bellingham, Washington, 1983.

Pozdneev, A.M., (1) *Mongolia and the Mongols*, ed. John R. Krueger, Vol. 1. (1982) tr. J.R. Shaw and D. Plank, Bloomington, Indiana 1971; Vol. 2 (1983) tr. W.H. Dogherty, Bloomington, Indiana, 1977. (2) *Religion and Ritual in Mongolia*, English tr., Bloomington, Indiana, 1978.

Rayfield D., *The Dream of Lhasa: The Life of Nicholai Przhevalsky (1839–1888)* London, 1976.

Reed, J., *Ten Days that Shook the World*, reprint Harmondsworth, 1977.

Richardson, H., (1) *Tibet and Its History*, London, 1962. (2) *Tibetan Précis*, Calcutta, 1945.

Rinchen, (ed. and tr.) *Four Mongolian Historical Records*, New Delhi, 1959.

Roerich, G.N., (1) *Trails to Inmost Asia*, Newhaven, 1931. (2) *The Blue Annals*, (tr.) Pts. 1 and 2, reprint, Delhi, 1988.

Roerich, N., (1) *Altai Himalaya*, Brookfield, Conn., 1983. (2) *The Heart of Asia*, New York, 1929. (3) *Himalayas – Abode of Light*, Bombay and London, 1947.

Rubel, P.G., *The Kalmyk Mongols*, Bloomington, Indiana, 1967.

Rumyantsev, G.N., *K Voprosy o Proiskhozhdenii Khori-Buryat*, ('On the Question of the Khori Buryats'), Ulan-Udé, 1948.

Rupen, R., *Mongols of the Twentieth Century*, Bloomington, Indiana, 1964.

Sarkysianz, E., *Geschichte der Orientalischen Völker Russlands bis 1917*, Munich, 1961.

Seaver, G., *Francis Younghusband*, London, 1952.

Semmenikov, V.P., *Za Kulisamk Tsaisma (Archiv Tibetskogo Vracha Badmaeva)*, Leningrad, 1925.

Serge, V., (1) *Memoirs of a Revolutionary, 1901–41*, tr. and ed. Peter Sedgwick, London, 1962. (2) *Conquered City*, tr. Richard Greeman, London, 1978.

Seton-Watson, H., *The Decline of Imperial Russia*, paperback edition, London, 1952.

Shakabpa, W.D., *Tibet: A Political History*, reprint New York, 1984.

Sifrin, A., *The First Guidebook to the USSR (to prisons, concentration camps of the Soviet Union)*, Seewis (Switzerland), 1980.

Sholokov, M., (1) *And Quiet Flows the Don*, tr. S. Garry, reprint, London, 1988. (2) *The Don Flows Home to the Sea*, tr. S. Garry, London, 1940.

Singh, A.K.J., *Himalayan Triangle*, London, 1988.

Smith, G. (ed.), *The Nationalities Question in the Soviet Union*, London, 1990.

Solzhenitsyn, A., (1) *August 1914*, London, 1972. (2) *The First Circle*, London, 1978. (3) *The Gulag Archipelago*, London, 1974. (4) *Lenin in Zürich*, London, 1976.

Sopa, Geshè (with Jackson, Roger and Newman, John), *The Wheel of Time: The Kalachakra in Context*, Madison, Wisconsin, 1985.

Stcherbatsky, Th., (1) *Buddhist Logic*, 2 vols., reprint, New Delhi, 1984. (2) *The Conception of Buddhist Nirvana*, reprint, New Delhi, 1989. (3) *The Central Conception of Buddhism & the Meaning of the Word 'Dharma'*, reprint Delhi, 1974.

Sumner, B.H., (1) *Survey of Russian History*, London, 1944. (2) *Tsarist Imperialism in the Middle and Far East*, London, 1940.

Tharchin, Geshè L., *The Logic and Debate Tradition of India, Tibet and Mongolia*, Howell, N.J., 1979.

Tsybikov, G. Ts., *Buddhist Palomnik u Svyatih ('A Buddhist Pilgrim in the Holy Places of Tibet')*, St. Petersburg, 1919.

Ukhtomsky, E.E., (1) *Travels in the East of Nicholas 11*, 2 vols., London, 1896 and 1900. (2) *Iz Oblasti Lamaizma ('On Lamaism')*, St. Petersburg, 1904.

Ulyanov, D., *Predskazaniya Buddha o Dome Romanovih i Kratkii Otcherk Moih Puteschestvii v Tibet v 1904–7*, (' Predictions of the Buddha about the House of Romanov and a Brief Account of my Travels to Tibet in 1904–1907'), St. Petersburg, 1913.

Wang Furen (with Suo Wenging), *Highlights of Tibetan History*, Beijing, 1984.

Wangyal, Geshè, *The Jewelled Staircase*, Ithaca, N.Y., 1986.

Webb, J., (1) *Harmonious Circle*, London, 1979. (2) *The Occult Establishment*, LaSalle, Michigan, 1976.

Witte, S., *Memoirs*, London, 1921.

Yermoshin, N., *Buddhism and Buddhists in the USSR*, Moscow, undated, (probably early 1960s).

Younghusband, F., *India and Tibet*, London, 1910.

Russian Anthologies

Lamaizem V Buryatii, XVIII – Nachalya XX Veka ('Lamaism in Buryatia, 18th – beginning of the 20th Century'), Novosibirsk, 1983.

Lamaizm V Kalmykii, I Voprosi Nauchnogo Ateizma ('Lamaism in Kalmykia, and the Question of Scientific Atheism'), Elista, 1980.

National'no-Osvobiten'noye Dvikhenie Buryatskogo Naroda ('The National Liberation Movement of the Buryat Clergy'), Ulan-Udé, 1989.

Vostok-Zapad, Moscow, 1989.

Credited Articles

Andreev, A., (1) 'The Rape of the Buddhist Temple in Petrograd, 1919–20,' unpublished typescript in English. (2) 'Iz Istorii Peterburgskogo Buddiistkogo Khrama' ('On the Buddhist Temple in St. Petersburg'), *Minuvsheye Istorichesky Almanach* (Paris). No. 9, 1990, pp. 380–405. (3) 'Buddiisskie Lama iz Staroi Derevnyi' ('The Buddhist Lamas of Staraya Derevnya'), due for publication in 1991. (4) 'The Buddhist Sanctuary in Petrograd,' due for publication 1991. (5) 'N. Roerich i Stroitelstvo Buddiiskogo Khrama v Peterburge,' ('N. Roerich and the Construction of the Buddhist Temple in Petersburg'). (6) 'Agwan Dorjiev and the Buddhist Temple in Petrograd', *Chö-Yun* (Dharamsala), No. 4, 1991.

Bazarov, B. (with Shagdurov, U.), 'Agvan Dorzhiev: Poslednie Stranitsy Zhizny' (Agvan Dorzhiev: The Last Pages of his Life Story'), *Baikal*, No. 3, 1991, pp. 121–128.

Berlin, L., 'Khambo Agvan Dorzhiev (i borbe Tibeta za Nezavicimost)', ('Khambo Agvan Dorzhiev (in relation to Tibet's Struggle for Independence)', *Novy Vostok* (Moscow), No. 3, 1923.

Bongard-Levin, G., 'Fyodor I. Stcherbatsky and Indian Culture,' *Soviet Land*, No. 5/5, 1967.

Bräker, H., (1) 'Buddhism in the Soviet Union: Annihilation or Survival?', *Religion in Communist Lands*, Vol. 11, No. 1, 1983. (2) 'Kommunismus und Buddhismus: Zur Religions und Asienpoliitik der Sowjetunions und Chinas', *Moderne Welt*, No. 1, 1967, pp. 50–64.

Chan Htoon, U, 'Buddhism Mission from Burma', *World Buddhism*, No. 2, 1961.

David-Neel, A., 'Gurdjieff et Dordjieff', *Nouvelles Littéraraires*, April 22e, 1954.

Deniker, J., (1) 'The Dalai Lama's New "Tse-Boum" from Paris', *The Century*, Vol. LXVII, No. 4, Feb 1904. (2) 'A Leader of the Tibetans', *The Century*, Vol. LXIX, 1904/5. (3) 'New Light on Lhasa, The Forbidden City', *The Century*, August, 1903. (4) 'La Première Photographie de Lhassa,' La Géographie, Vol. IV, No. 10, October 15 1901(?). (5) (Other articles in *La Géographie:* July 15 1901, November 15 1903, February 15 1906.)

Disciple, A., 'Brief Sketch of H. E. the Late Buddhist Archbishop of Latvia, the Most Rev Karlis A Tennisons', *Maha Bodhi*, (Calcutta), 1962.

Dorzhiev, A., 'Lo-gun-ge-bo', Proceedings of the Imperial Russian Geographical Society, Vol. XXXIV, pp. 289–292, St. Petersburg, 1909.

Dorzhiev, G., 'Svyaz Narodov' ('Communication between Peoples') *Baikal*, No. 3, 1991, pp. 128–129.

Fenzl, F., 'Der Buddhismus in Russland in Vergangenheit und Gegenwart', *Bodhi Baum* (Vienna), 1985.

Galkina, V., 'Around the Temple', *Teacher's Gazette*, 12.12.72.

Heissig, W., 'W.A. Unkrig' (obiturary), *Central Asian Journal, 1957.*

Hyer, P., 'Japaner und Lamapriester', in *Zeitschrift für Geopolitik*, Vol. XXV, Aug. 1954, pp. 474–479.

Kupchenko, V., (with Demin, E.), 'V Zabaykalye – Cherez Parizh' ('To Trans-Baikalia via Paris'), *Baikal*, No. 2, 1989, pp. 143–144.

Lamb, A., 'Some Notes on Russian Intrigue in Tibet', *Journal of the Royal Central Asian Society*, 1959.

Lange, K., 'Maidari – Fest im Ivolginsker Kloster', in *Jahrbuch der Museums für Völkerkunde* (Leipzig), Vol. 27, pp. 90–98.

Leonov, G.A., 'E.E. Ukhtomskii: K Istorii Lamaistskogo Sobraniya Gosudar-stvennogo Ermitazha' ('E.E. Ukhtomskii: On the History of the Lamaist Collection in the State Hermitage Museum'), in *Buddizi limeramurno – chudomestvenie tvorzemvo narogov tschengravioi Azii* ('Buddhism and the Literary-Artistic of the Peoples of Central Asia'), Novosibirsk, 1985, pp. 101–115.

Markov, S., 'Tibetskie Chetki' ('Tibetan Rosary'), *Prostor* (Alma-Ata), No. 1, 1976.

Mehra, P., 'Tibet and Russian Intrigue', *Journal of the Royal Central Asian Society*, 1958.

Norzunov*, O. 'Trois Voyages à Lhasa (1898–1901)', *Le Tour du Monde*, Vol. 10, new series, 1904.

* Often mis-spelt 'Narzunov'

Piatigorsky, A., (1) 'Dandaron', *Kontinent*, No. 2, London (Hodder), 1978, pp.169–179. (2) 'A Little About Buddhism in Tuva', unpublished typescript.

Popov, A., 'Rossiya i Tibet' ('Russia and Tibet'), *Novy-Vostok* (Moscow), No. 18, 1927.

Poppe, N.N., (1) 'The Destruction of Buddhism in the USSR', Bulletin, Institute for the Study of the USSR (Munich), July 1956, p. 19ff. (2) 'The Buddhists of the USSR', *Religion in the USSR*, ed. B. Ivanov, Series 1, No. 59, Institute for the Study of the USSR (Munich), 1960. (3) B.J. Vladimirtsov (obituary), *Asia Major* (Leipzig), 5, 1933, pp. 565–570.

Pubayev, R.E., 'Agvan Dorzhiev', in *Natsionalno-osvoboditelnoye Dvizheniye Buryatskogo Naroda*, Ulan-Udé, 1989, pp. 94–98.

Rees, J.D., 'The Czar's Friend', *The Fortnightly Review*, April 1901.

Rupen, R. (1) 'The Buryat Intelligentsia', *Far Eastern Quarterly*, Vol. 15, No. 3, May 1956, pp. 383–398. (2) 'Mongolian Nationalism', *Journal of the Royal Central Asian Society*, Vol. XIV, pp. 157–178. (3) 'A Soviet Historical Novel about Mongolia', *Far Eastern Quarterly*, XIV, August 1955, pp. 553–557. (4) 'Mongolia, Tibet and Buddhism: A Tale of Two Roerichs', *Canada-Mongolia Review*, Vol. 5, No. 1, April 1979. (5) 'Zhamtsarano' (Bibliography), HJAS, XIX, 1956. (6) 'The City of Urga in the Manchu Period', *Ural-Altaische Bibliothek, Studia Altaica* (Festschrift für Nikolaus Poppe), Wiesbaden, 1957, pp. 165–167.

Sachse, F., 'Alexandra David-Néel, 1868–1969', *The Middle Way*, Vol. 59, No. 1, May 1984.

Schneider, A., 'Prof. J.P. Minaev', *Indian Historical Quarterly*, Vol. X, No. 4, 1934.

Shastri, D.N., 'The Contribution of Th. Stcherbatsky to Indian Philosophy', *The Modern Review*, Vol. 93, No. 2, 1953.

Snelling, J., (1) 'Agvan Dorjiev: Eminence Grise of Central Asian Politics', *Asian Affairs*, Vol. XXI (Old Series Vol. 77), February 1990. (2) 'Buddhism in Russia', *The Middle Way*, Vol. 65, No. 2, August 1990. (3) 'Kuntsechoinei Datsan, Leningrad–St. Petersburg', *The Middle Way*, Vol. 99, No. 3, November 1991, pp. 161ff.

Stanton, T., Report on the Buddhist Ceremony celebrated in the Musée Guimet on June 27 1898, *The Open Court*, No. 510, November 1898, pp. 671–672.

Stcherbatsky, F.I., 'Kratky Otchet O Poezdke V Urgu', ('A Short Account of My Journey to Urga'), originally published 1906 in *Proceedings of the Russian Committee for the Study of East Asia*, No. 6, pp. 19–22, reproduced in *Vostok-Zapad*, Moscow, 1989.

Tsybikov, G.Ts., (1) 'Journeys to Lhasa,' *Geographical Journal*, 23, 1904. (2) 'Lhasa and Central Tibet', Smithsonian Institute Annual Report, etc., 1902–03 (Washington), 1904.

Ukhtomsky, E.E., 'The English in Tibet: A Russian View', *North American Review and Miscellaneous Journal*, No. 179, 1904.

Ular, A., 'The Policy of the Dalai Lama', *Contemporary Review*, No. 87, January–June 1905.

Unkrig, W.A., 'Aus den letzten Jahrzehnten des Lamismus in Russland', *Zeitschrift für Buddhismus und verwandte Gebeite* (München-Neuberg), Vol VII, 1926, pp. 135–151.

Zhukovskaia, N.L., (1) 'Research on Lamaism in the USSR: 1917–1976', *Canada-Mongolia Review*, Vol. 5, No. 1, April 1979. (2) 'Sovremenny lamaizm (na materialakh Buryatskoi ASSR', *Voprosy Nauchnogo Ateizma*, Akademiya obschestvennykh nauk pri TsK KPSS, Institut nauchnogo ateizma, Moscow, 1969.

Uncredited Articles

'Bidya Dandaron – Persecuted Buddhist', *Soviet Analyst*, Vol. 3, No. 23, Nov. 1974, pp. 4–6.

'Buddhizm', *Bolshaya Sovetskaya Entsiklopediya*, 1st ed., Vol. VII, Moscow, 1927, pp. 772–797.

'Buddists', *Report on Restriction of Religion in the USSR*, prepared by the CSRC for the International Committee. Brussels: revised chapter, 1975 (typescript).

'Dordzhiev, Agvan', *Novy Entsikopedichesky Slovar*, St. Petersburg, 1911–16, col. 675.

'Dordzhiev', *Bolshaya Sovetskaya Entsiklopediya*, Vol. XXIII, Moscow, 1931, p. 290.

'Fyodor Ippolitovitch Stcherbatsky' (Obituary), *Journal of the Royal Central Asian Society*, Pt. 1, 1943.

Interview with K.A. Tennisons, *International Buddhist News Forum*, July 1961.

Report on the Buddhist Temple in St. Petersburg, *SOAS Bulletin*, Vol. 11, Pt. IV, 1925.

'A Story of Struggle and Intrigue in Central Asia', *Journal of the Royal Central Asian Society*, Vols. 14 and 15, 1927–28.

'The Soviet Role in World Buddhist Affairs', Munich, Radio Liberty Research, July 14 1972 (ref. CRD 172/72 – mimeographed).

INDEX